NON-LEAGUE FOOTBALL TABLES 1889-2002

EDITOR
Michael Robinson

British Library Cataloguing in Publication Data
A catalogue record for this book is available from the British Library

ISBN 1-86223-060-9

Printed by Bookcraft

FOREWORD

In selecting the Leagues to be included in this first edition of Non-League Football Tables we have initially chosen those forming the pinnacle of the Non-League Football Pyramid, i.e. The Football Conference and it's three direct feeders.

In addition we have included the briefly-lived Football Alliance which became, effectively, the 2nd Division of the Football League in 1892 together with three of the earliest major leagues to be formed. We realise that a number of other leagues were of similar importance and, subject to sales of this book being adequate, hope to bring out a further edition with the other leagues next year.

Furthermore, as league sponsors change frequently, we have not used sponsored names (eg. Rymans League) other than in an indicative way on the cover.

CONTENTS

FOOTBALL ALLIANCE

1889-90

Sheffield Wednesday	22	15	2	5	70	39	32
Bootle	22	13	2	7	66	39	28
Sunderland Albion	21	12	2	7	64	39	28
Grimsby Town	22	12	2	8	58	47	26
Crewe Alexandra	22	11	2	9	68	59	24
Darwen	22	10	2	10	70	75	22
Birmingham St George	21	9	3	9	62	49	21
Newton Heath	22	9	2	11	40	44	20
Walsall Town Swifts	22	8	3	11	44	59	19
Small Heath	22	6	5	11	44	67	17
Nottingham Forest	22	6	5	11	31	62	17
Long Eaton Rangers	22	4	2	16	35	73	10

Sunderland Albion record includes 2 points awarded when Birmingham St George refused to fulfil a fixture which the Alliance committee had ordered to be replayed.

1890-91

Stoke	22	13	7	2	57	39	33
Sunderland Albion	22	12	6	4	69	28	30
Grimsby Town	22	11	5	6	43	27	27
Birmingham St George	22	12	2	8	64	62	26
Nottingham Forest	22	9	7	6	66	39	25
Darwen	22	10	3	9	64	59	23
Walsall Town Swifts	22	9	3	10	34	61	21
Crewe Alexandra	22	8	4	10	59	67	20
Newton Heath	22	7	3	12	37	55	17
Small Heath	22	7	2	13	58	66	16
Bootle	22	3	7	12	40	61	13
Sheffield Wednesday	22	4	5	13	39	66	13

1891-92

Nottingham Forest	22	14	5	3	59	22	33
Newton Heath	22	12	7	3	69	33	31
Small Heath	22	12	5	5	53	36	29
Sheffield Wednesday	22	12	4	6	65	35	28
Burton Swifts	22	12	2	8	54	52	26
Grimsby Town	22	6	6	10	40	39	18
Crewe Alexandra	22	7	4	11	44	49	18
Ardwick	22	6	6	10	39	51	18
Bootle	22	8	2	12	42	64	18
Lincoln City	22	6	5	11	37	65	17
Walsall Town Swifts	22	6	3	13	33	59	15
Birmingham St George	22	5	3	14	34	64	13

SOUTHERN LEAGUE

1894-95

First Division

Millwall Athletic	16	12	4	0	68	19	28
Luton Town	16	9	4	3	36	22	22
Southampton St Mary's	16	9	2	5	34	25	20
Ilford	16	6	3	7	26	40	15
Reading	16	6	2	8	33	38	14
Chatham	16	4	5	7	22	25	13
Royal Ordnance Factories	16	3	6	7	20	30	12
Clapton	16	5	1	10	22	38	11
Swindon Town	16	4	1	11	24	48	9

Second Division

New Brompton	12	11	0	1	57	10	22
Sheppey United	12	6	1	5	25	23	13
Old St Stephen's	12	6	0	6	26	26	12
Uxbridge	12	4	3	5	14	20	11
Bromley	12	4	1	7	23	30	9
Chesham	12	3	3	6	20	42	9
Maidenhead	12	2	4	6	19	33	8

1895-96

First Division

Millwall Athletic	18	16	1	1	75	16	33
Luton Town	18	13	1	4	68	14	27
Southampton St Mary's	18	12	0	6	44	23	24
Reading	18	11	1	6	45	38	23
Chatham	18	9	2	7	43	45	20
New Brompton	18	7	4	7	30	37	18
Swindon Town	18	6	4	8	38	41	16
Clapton	18	4	2	12	30	67	10
Royal Ordnance Factories	18	3	3	12	23	44	9
Ilford	18	0	0	18	10	81	0

Second Division

Wolverton L & NW Railway	16	13	1	2	43	10	27
Sheppey United	16	11	3	2	60	19	25
1st Scots Guards	16	8	5	3	37	22	21
Uxbridge	16	9	1	6	28	23	19
Old St Stephen's	16	6	3	7	34	21	15
Guildford	16	7	1	8	29	41	15
Maidenhead	16	4	1	11	20	49	9
Chesham	16	2	3	11	15	48	7
Bromley	16	2	2	12	16	49	6

1896-97

First Division

Southampton St Mary's	20	15	5	0	63	18	35
Millwall Athletic	20	13	5	2	63	24	31
Chatham	20	13	1	6	54	29	27
Tottenham Hotspur	20	9	4	7	43	29	22
Gravesend United	20	9	4	7	35	34	22
Swindon Town	20	8	3	9	33	37	19
Reading	20	8	3	9	31	49	19
New Brompton	20	7	2	11	32	42	16
Northfleet	20	5	4	11	24	46	14
Sheppey United	20	5	1	14	34	47	11
Wolverton L & NW Railway	20	2	0	18	17	74	4

Second Division

Dartford	24	16	4	4	83	19	36
Royal Engineers Training Battalion	24	11	9	4	49	37	31
Freemantle	24	12	4	8	58	40	28
Uxbridge	24	11	5	8	62	37	27
Wycombe Wanderers	24	10	6	8	37	54	26
Chesham	24	11	3	10	41	55	25
Southall	24	9	6	9	55	52	24
1st Scot Guards	24	9	6	9	49	50	24
West Herts	24	11	1	12	41	49	23
Warmley (Bristol)	24	10	2	12	44	43	22
Old St Stephen's	24	5	7	12	36	52	17
Maidenhead	24	4	8	12	33	64	16
1st Coldstream Guards	24	3	6	15	30	66	12

1897-98

First Division

Southampton	22	18	1	3	53	18	37
Bristol City	22	13	7	2	67	33	33
Tottenham Hotspur	22	12	4	6	52	31	28
Chatham	22	12	4	6	50	34	28
Reading	22	8	7	7	39	31	23
New Brompton	22	9	4	9	37	37	22
Sheppey United	22	10	1	11	40	49	21
Gravesend United	22	7	6	9	28	39	20
Millwall Athletic	22	8	2	12	48	45	18
Swindon Town	22	7	2	13	36	48	16
Northfleet	22	4	3	15	29	60	11
Wolverton L & NW Railway	22	3	1	18	28	82	7

Second Division

Royal Artillery (Portsmouth)	22	19	1	2	75	22	39
Warmley (Bristol)	22	19	0	3	108	15	38
West Herts	22	11	6	5	50	48	28
Uxbridge	22	11	2	9	39	57	24
St Albans	22	9	5	8	47	41	23
Dartford	22	11	0	11	68	55	22
Southall	22	8	2	12	49	61	18
Chesham	22	8	2	12	38	48	18
Olsd St Stephen's	22	7	2	13	47	66	16
Wycombe Wanderers	22	7	2	13	37	55	16
Maidenhead	22	4	4	14	27	81	12
Royal Engineers Training Battalion	22	4	2	16	26	62	10

1898-99

First Division

Southampton	24	15	5	4	54	24	35
Bristol City	24	15	3	6	55	12	33
Millwall Athletic	24	12	6	6	59	35	30
Chatham	24	10	8	6	32	23	28
Reading	24	9	8	7	31	24	26
New Brompton	24	10	5	9	38	30	25
Tottenham Hotspur	24	10	4	10	40	36	24
Bedminster	24	10	4	10	35	39	24
Swindon Town	24	9	5	10	43	49	23
Brighton United	24	9	2	13	37	48	20
Gravesend United	24	7	5	12	42	52	19
Sheppey United	24	5	3	16	23	53	13
Royal Artillery (Portsmouth)	24	4	4	16	17	60	12

Second Division (London Section)

Thames Ironworks	22	19	1	2	64	16	39
Wolverton L & NW Railway	22	13	4	5	88	43	30
Watford	22	14	2	6	62	35	30
Brentford	22	11	3	8	59	39	25
Wycombe Wanderers	22	10	2	10	55	57	22
Southall	22	11	0	11	44	55	22
Chesham	22	9	2	11	45	62	20
St Albans	22	8	3	11	45	59	19
Shepherds Bush	22	7	3	12	37	53	17
Fulham	22	6	4	12	36	44	16
Uxbridge	22	7	2	13	29	48	16
Maidenhead	22	3	2	17	33	86	8

Second Division (South West Section)

Cowes	10	10	0	0	58	8	20
Ryde	10	7	0	3	30	11	14
Freemantle	10	4	1	5	18	31	9
Sandown	10	4	0	6	20	29	8
Eastleigh	10	2	1	7	17	37	5
Andover	10	2	0	8	14	41	4

1899-1900

First Division

Tottenham Hotspur	28	20	4	4	67	26	44
Portsmouth	28	20	1	7	58	27	41
Southampton	28	17	1	10	70	33	35
Reading	28	15	2	11	41	28	32
Swindon Town	28	15	2	11	50	42	32
Bedminster	28	13	2	13	44	45	28
Millwall Athletic	28	12	3	13	36	37	27
Queens Park Rangers	28	12	2	14	49	57	26
Bristol City	28	9	7	12	43	47	25
Bristol Rovers	28	11	3	14	46	55	25
New Brompton	28	9	6	13	39	49	24
Gravesend United	28	10	4	14	38	58	24
Chatham	28	10	3	15	38	58	23
Thames Ironworks	28	8	5	15	30	45	21
Sheppey United	28	3	7	18	24	66	13

Second Division

Watford	20	14	2	4	57	25	30
Fulham	20	10	4	6	44	23	24
Chesham Town	20	11	2	7	43	37	24
Wolverton L & NW Railway	20	9	6	5	46	36	24
Grays United	20	8	6	6	63	29	22
Shepherds Bush	20	9	4	7	45	37	22
Dartford	20	8	3	9	36	44	19
Wycombe Wanderers	20	8	3	9	35	50	19
Brentford	20	5	7	8	31	48	17
Southall	20	6	3	11	21	44	15
Maidenhead	20	1	2	17	16	64	4

1900-01

First Division

Southampton	28	18	5	5	58	26	41
Bristol City	28	17	5	6	54	27	39
Portsmouth	28	17	4	7	56	32	38
Millwall Athletic	28	17	2	9	55	32	36
Tottenham Hotspur	28	16	4	8	55	33	36
West Ham United	28	14	5	9	40	28	33
Bristol Rovers	28	14	4	10	46	35	32
Queens Park Rangers	28	11	4	13	43	48	26
Reading	28	8	8	12	24	25	24
Luton Town	28	11	2	15	43	49	24
Kettering	28	7	9	12	33	46	23
New Brompton	28	7	5	16	34	51	19
Gravesend United	28	6	7	15	32	85	19
Watford	28	6	4	18	24	52	16
Swindon Town	28	3	8	17	19	47	14

Second Division

Brentford	16	14	2	0	63	11	30
Grays United	16	12	2	2	62	12	26
Sheppey United	16	8	1	7	44	26	17
Shepherds Bush	16	8	1	7	30	30	17
Fulham	16	8	0	8	38	26	16
Chesham Town	16	5	1	10	26	39	11
Maidenhead	16	4	1	11	21	49	9
Wycombe Wanderers	16	4	1	11	23	68	9
Southall	16	4	1	11	22	68	9

1901-02

First Division

Portsmouth	30	20	7	3	67	24	47
Tottenham Hotspur	30	18	6	6	61	22	42
Southampton	30	18	6	6	71	28	42
West Ham United	30	17	6	7	45	28	40
Reading	30	16	7	7	57	24	39
Millwall Athletic	30	13	6	11	48	31	32
Luton Town	30	11	10	9	31	35	32
Kettering	30	12	5	13	44	39	29
Bristol Rovers	30	12	5	13	43	39	29
New Brompton	30	10	7	13	39	38	27
Northampton	30	11	5	14	53	64	27
Queens Park Rangers	30	8	7	15	34	56	23
Watford	30	9	4	17	36	60	22
Wellingborough	30	9	4	17	34	75	22
Brentford	30	7	6	17	34	61	20
Swindon Town	30	2	3	25	17	93	7

Second Division

Fulham	16	13	0	3	51	19	26
Grays United	16	12	1	3	49	14	25
Brighton & Hove Albion	16	11	0	5	34	17	22
Wycombe Wanderers	16	7	3	6	36	30	17
West Hampstead	16	6	4	6	39	29	16
Shepherds Bush	16	6	1	9	31	31	13
Southall	16	5	2	9	28	52	12
Maidenhead	16	3	1	12	23	59	7
Chesham Town	16	2	2	12	24	64	6

1902-03

First Division

Southampton	30	20	8	2	83	20	48
Reading	30	19	7	4	72	30	45
Portsmouth	30	17	7	6	69	32	41
Tottenham Hotspur	30	14	7	9	47	31	35
Bristol Rovers	30	13	8	9	46	34	34
New Brompton	30	11	11	8	37	35	33
Millwall Athletic	30	14	3	13	52	37	31
Northampton Town	30	12	6	12	39	48	30
Queens Park Rangers	30	11	6	13	34	42	28
West Ham United	30	9	10	11	35	49	28
Luton Town	30	10	7	13	43	44	27
Swindon Town	30	10	7	13	38	46	27
Kettering	30	8	11	11	33	40	27
Wellingborough	30	11	3	16	36	56	25
Watford	30	6	4	20	35	87	16
Brentford	30	2	1	27	16	84	5

Second Division

Fulham	10	7	1	2	27	7	15
Brighton & Hove Albion	10	7	1	2	34	11	15
Grays United	10	7	0	3	28	12	14
Wycombe Wanderers	10	3	3	4	13	19	9
Chesham Town	10	2	1	7	9	37	5
Southall	10	1	0	9	10	35	2

1903-04

First Division

Southampton	34	22	6	6	75	30	50
Tottenham Hotspur	34	16	11	7	54	37	43
Bristol Rovers	34	17	8	9	66	42	42
Portsmouth	34	17	8	9	41	38	42
Queens Park Rangers	34	15	11	8	53	37	41
Reading	34	14	13	7	48	35	41
Millwall	34	16	8	10	64	42	40
Luton Town	34	14	12	8	38	33	40
Plymouth Argyle	34	13	10	11	44	34	36
Swindon Town	34	10	11	13	30	42	31
Fulham	34	9	12	13	33	34	30
West Ham United	34	10	7	17	38	43	27
Brentford	34	9	9	16	34	48	27
Wellingborough	34	11	5	18	44	63	27
Northampton Town	34	10	7	17	36	69	27
New Brompton	34	6	13	15	26	43	25
Brighton & Hove Albion	34	6	12	16	45	79	24
Kettering	34	6	7	21	30	78	19

Second Division

Watford	20	18	2	0	70	15	38
Portsmouth Reserves	20	15	2	3	85	25	32
Millwall Reserves	20	9	4	7	35	39	22
Southampton Reserves	20	9	3	8	59	35	21
Grays United	20	9	3	8	25	55	21
Fulham Reserves	20	8	4	8	40	34	20
Swindon Town Reserves	20	8	3	9	50	44	19
Reading Reserves	20	8	2	10	43	42	18
Wycombe Wanderers	20	5	5	10	29	64	15
Southall	20	4	2	14	25	62	10
Chesham Town	20	1	2	17	19	65	4

1904-05

First Division

Bristol Rovers	34	20	8	6	74	36	48
Reading	34	18	7	9	57	38	43
Southampton	34	18	7	9	54	40	43
Plymouth Argyle	34	18	5	11	57	39	41
Tottenham Hotspur	34	15	8	11	53	34	38
Fulham	34	14	10	10	46	34	38
Queens Park Rangers	34	14	8	12	51	46	36
Portsmouth	34	16	4	14	61	56	36
New Brompton	34	11	11	12	40	41	33
West Ham United	34	12	8	14	48	42	32
Brighton & Hove Albion	34	13	6	15	44	45	32
Northampton Town	34	12	8	14	43	54	32
Watford	34	14	3	17	41	44	31
Brentford	34	10	9	15	33	38	29
Millwall	34	11	7	16	38	47	29
Swindon Town	34	12	5	17	41	59	29
Luton Town	34	12	3	19	45	54	27
Wellingborough	34	5	3	26	25	104	13

Second Division

Fulham Reserves	22	16	4	2	78	25	36
Portsmouth Reserves	22	14	2	6	75	28	30
Swindon Town Reserves	22	12	3	7	54	47	27
Grays United	22	11	3	8	61	40	25
Southampton Reserves	22	10	5	7	52	35	25
Brighton & Hove Albion	22	9	3	10	48	49	21
West Ham United Reserves	22	8	5	9	45	47	21
Clapton Orient	22	7	7	8	47	56	21
Watford Reserves	22	5	6	11	30	62	16
Southall	22	7	2	13	31	66	16
Wycombe Wanderers	22	6	2	14	37	70	14
Reading Reserves	22	4	4	14	24	57	12

1905-06

First Division

Fulham	34	19	12	3	44	15	50
Southampton	34	19	7	8	58	39	45
Portsmouth	34	17	9	8	61	35	43
Luton Town	34	17	7	10	64	40	41
Tottenham Hotspur	34	16	7	11	46	29	39
Plymouth Argyle	34	16	7	11	52	33	39
Norwich City	34	13	10	11	46	38	36
Bristol Rovers	34	15	5	14	56	56	35
Brentford	34	14	7	13	43	52	35
Reading	34	12	9	13	53	46	33
West Ham United	34	14	5	15	42	39	33
Millwall	34	11	11	12	38	41	33
Queens Park Rangers	34	12	7	15	58	44	31
Watford	34	8	10	16	38	57	26
Swindon Town	34	8	9	17	31	52	25
Brighton & Hove Albion	34	9	7	18	30	55	25
New Brompton	34	7	8	19	20	62	22
Northampton Town	34	8	5	21	32	79	21

Second Division

Crystal Palace	24	19	4	1	66	14	42
Leyton	24	16	6	2	61	18	38
Portsmouth Reserves	24	12	8	4	52	24	32
Fulham Reserves	24	11	6	7	52	39	28
Southampton Reserves	24	7	9	8	39	41	23
Southern United	24	8	7	9	45	49	23
St Leonard's United	24	9	4	11	54	50	22
Watford Reserves	24	8	5	11	43	47	21
West Ham United Reserves	24	7	5	12	46	48	19
Grays United	24	8	3	13	24	77	19
Reading Reserves	24	6	5	13	36	49	15
Swindon Town Reserves	24	5	5	14	36	51	15
Wycombe Wanderers	24	5	3	16	36	83	13

1906-07

First Division

Fulham	38	20	13	5	58	32	53
Portsmouth	38	22	7	9	64	36	51
Brighton & Hove Albion	38	18	9	11	53	43	45
Luton Town	38	18	9	11	52	52	45
West Ham United	38	15	14	9	60	41	44
Tottenham Hotspur	38	17	9	12	63	45	43
Millwall	38	18	6	14	71	50	42
Norwich City	38	15	12	11	57	48	42
Watford	38	13	16	9	46	43	42
Brentford	38	17	8	13	57	56	42
Southampton	38	13	9	16	49	56	35
Reading	38	14	6	18	57	47	34
Leyton	38	11	12	15	38	60	34
Bristol Rovers	38	12	9	17	55	54	33
Plymouth Argyle	38	10	13	15	43	50	33
New Brompton	38	12	9	17	47	59	33
Swindon Town	38	11	11	16	43	54	33
Queens Park Rangers	38	11	10	17	47	55	32
Crystal Palace	38	8	9	21	46	66	25
Northampton Town	38	5	9	24	29	88	19

Second Division

Southend United	22	14	5	3	58	23	33
West Ham United Reserves	22	14	3	5	64	30	31
Portsmouth Reserves	22	11	6	5	53	24	28
Fulham Reserves	22	11	4	7	47	32	26
Hastings & St Leonards	21	10	4	7	46	31	24
Tunbridge Wells Rangers	22	10	1	11	46	36	21
Salisbury City	22	9	2	11	40	42	20
Southampton Reserves	22	8	2	12	37	56	18
Swindon Town Reserves	22	7	3	12	35	43	17
Reading Reserves	22	6	4	12	32	47	16
Royal Engineers (Aldershot)	21	5	4	12	27	58	14
Wycombe Wanderers	22	4	6	12	28	68	14

The match between Tunbridge Wells Rangers and Royal Engineers (Aldershot) was not completed.

1907-08

First Division

Queens Park Rangers	38	21	9	8	82	57	51
Plymouth Argyle	38	19	11	8	50	31	49
Millwall	38	19	8	11	49	32	46
Crystal Palace	38	17	10	11	54	51	44
Swindon Town	38	16	10	12	55	40	42
Bristol Rovers	38	16	10	12	59	56	42
Tottenham Hotspur	38	17	7	14	59	48	41
Northampton Town	38	15	11	12	50	41	41
Portsmouth	38	17	6	15	63	52	40
West Ham United	38	15	10	13	47	48	40
Southampton	38	16	6	16	51	60	38
Reading	38	15	6	17	55	50	36
Bradford Park Avenue	38	12	12	14	53	54	36
Watford	38	12	10	16	47	49	34
Brentford	38	14	5	19	49	52	33
Norwich City	38	12	9	17	46	49	33
Brighton & Hove Albion	38	12	8	18	46	59	32
Luton Town	38	12	6	20	33	56	30
Leyton	38	8	11	19	51	73	27
New Brompton	38	9	7	22	44	75	25

Second Division

Southend	18	13	3	2	47	16	29
Portsmouth Reserves	18	10	5	3	39	22	25
Croydon Common	18	10	3	5	35	25	23
Hastings & St Leonard's	18	10	2	6	43	29	22
Southampton Reserves	18	7	4	7	54	46	18
Tunbridge Wells Rangers	18	7	3	8	42	38	17
Salisbury City	18	6	4	8	35	46	16
Swindon Town Reserves	18	5	5	8	36	40	15
Brighton & Hove Albion Reserves	18	4	4	10	34	47	12
Wycombe Wanderers	18	1	1	16	16	72	3

1908-09

First Division

Northampton Town	40	25	5	10	90	45	55
Swindon Town	40	22	5	13	96	55	49
Southampton	40	19	10	11	67	58	48
Portsmouth	40	18	10	12	68	60	46
Bristol Rovers	40	17	9	14	60	63	43
Exeter City	40	18	6	16	56	65	42
New Brompton	40	17	7	16	48	59	41
Reading	40	11	18	11	60	57	40
Luton Town	40	17	6	17	59	60	40
Plymouth Argyle	40	15	10	15	46	47	40
Millwall	40	16	6	18	59	61	38
Southend United	40	14	10	16	52	54	38
Leyton	40	15	8	17	52	55	38
Watford	40	14	9	17	51	64	37
Queens Park Rangers	40	12	12	16	52	50	36
Crystal Palace	40	12	12	16	62	62	36
West Ham United	40	16	4	20	56	60	36
Brighton & Hove Albion	40	14	7	19	60	61	35
Norwich City	40	12	11	17	59	75	35
Coventry City	40	15	4	21	64	91	34
Brentford	40	13	7	20	59	74	33

Second Division

Croydon Common	12	10	0	2	67	14	20
Hastings & St Leonard's	12	8	1	3	42	18	17
Depot Battalion Royal Engineers	12	8	1	3	23	22	17
2nd Grenadier Guards	12	5	0	7	21	33	10
South Farnborough Athletic	12	2	4	6	20	39	8
Salisbury City	12	3	1	8	24	36	7
Chesham Town	12	2	1	9	17	52	5

1909-10

First Division

Brighton & Hove Albion	42	23	13	6	69	28	59
Swindon Town	42	22	10	10	92	46	54
Queens Park Rangers	42	19	13	10	56	47	51
Northampton Town	42	22	4	16	90	44	48
Southampton	42	16	16	10	64	55	48
Portsmouth	42	20	7	15	70	63	47
Crystal Palace	42	20	6	16	69	50	46
Coventry City	42	19	8	15	71	60	46
West Ham United	42	15	15	12	69	56	45
Leyton	42	16	11	15	60	46	43
Plymouth Argyle	42	16	11	15	61	54	43
New Brompton	42	19	5	18	76	74	43
Bristol Rovers	42	16	10	16	37	48	42
Brentford	42	16	9	17	50	58	41
Luton Town	42	15	11	16	72	92	41
Millwall	42	15	7	20	45	59	37
Norwich City	42	13	9	20	59	78	35
Exeter City	42	14	6	22	60	69	34
Watford	42	10	13	19	51	76	33
Southend United	42	12	9	21	51	90	33
Croydon Common	42	13	5	24	52	96	31
Reading	42	7	10	25	38	73	24

Second Division - Section A

Stoke	10	10	0	0	48	9	20
Ton Pentre	10	4	2	4	17	21	10
Merthyr Town	9	4	1	4	16	21	9
Salisbury City	8	2	1	5	7	18	5
Burton United	6	2	0	4	8	21	4
Aberdare	7	1	0	6	6	11	2

Second Division - Section B

Hastings & St Leonard's	9	6	3	0	26	11	15
Kettering	10	6	0	4	34	19	12
Chesham Town	10	5	2	3	25	25	12
Peterborough City	10	4	2	4	16	23	10
South Farnborough Athletic	10	4	1	5	23	19	9
Romford	9	0	0	9	7	33	0

1910-11

First Divison

Swindon Town	38	24	5	9	80	31	53
Northampton Town	38	18	12	8	54	27	48
Brighton & Hove Albion	38	20	8	10	58	35	48
Crystal Palace	38	17	13	8	55	48	47
West Ham United	38	17	11	10	63	46	45
Queens Park Rangers	38	13	14	11	52	41	40
Leyton	38	16	8	14	57	52	40
Plymouth Argyle	38	15	9	14	54	55	39
Luton Town	38	15	8	15	67	63	38
Norwich City	38	15	8	15	46	48	38
Coventry City	38	16	6	16	65	68	38
Brentford	38	14	9	15	41	42	37
Exeter City	38	14	9	15	51	53	37
Watford	38	13	9	16	49	65	35
Millwall	38	11	9	18	42	54	31
Bristol Rovers	38	10	10	18	42	55	30
Southampton	38	11	8	19	42	67	30
New Brompton	38	11	8	19	34	65	30
Southend United	38	10	9	19	47	64	29
Portsmouth	38	8	11	19	34	53	27

Second Division

Reading	22	16	3	3	55	11	35
Stoke	22	17	1	4	72	21	35
Merthyr Town	22	15	3	4	52	22	33
Cardiff City	22	12	4	6	48	29	28
Croydon Common	22	11	3	8	61	26	25
Treharris	22	10	3	9	38	31	23
Aberdare	22	9	5	8	38	33	23
Ton Pentre	22	10	3	9	44	40	23
Walsall	22	7	4	11	37	41	18
Kettering	22	6	1	15	34	68	13
Chesham Town	22	1	3	18	16	93	5
Salisbury City	22	0	3	19	16	92	3

1911-12

First Division

Queens Park Rangers	38	21	11	6	59	35	53
Plymouth Argyle	38	23	6	9	63	31	52
Northampton Town	38	22	7	9	82	41	51
Swindon Town	38	21	6	11	82	50	48
Brighton & Hove Albion	38	19	9	10	73	35	47
Coventry City	38	17	8	13	66	54	42
Crystal Palace	38	15	10	13	70	46	40
Millwall	38	15	10	13	60	57	40
Watford	38	13	10	15	56	68	36
Stoke	38	13	10	15	51	63	36
Reading	38	11	14	13	43	69	36
Norwich City	38	10	14	14	40	60	34
West Ham United	38	13	7	18	64	69	33
Brentford	38	12	9	17	60	65	33
Exeter City	38	11	11	16	48	62	33
Southampton	38	10	11	17	46	63	31
Bristol Rovers	38	9	13	16	41	62	31
New Brompton	38	11	9	18	35	72	31
Luton Town	38	9	10	19	49	61	28
Leyton	38	7	11	20	27	62	25

Second Division

Merthyr Town	26	19	3	4	60	14	41
Portsmouth	26	19	3	4	73	20	41
Cardiff City	26	15	4	7	55	26	34
Southend United	26	16	1	9	73	24	33
Pontypridd	26	13	6	7	39	24	32
Ton Pentre	26	12	3	11	56	45	27
Walsall	26	13	1	11	44	41	27
Treharris	26	11	5	10	44	47	27
Aberdare	26	10	3	13	39	44	23
Kettering	26	11	0	15	37	62	22
Croydon Common	26	8	2	15	43	45	18
Mardy	26	6	6	12	37	51	18
Cwm Albion	26	5	1	16	27	70	11
Chesham Town	26	1	0	25	18	131	2

1912-13

First Division

Plymouth Argyle	38	27	6	10	77	36	50
Swindon Town	38	20	8	10	66	41	48
West Ham United	38	18	12	8	66	43	48
Queens Park Rangers	38	18	10	10	46	35	43
Crystal Palace	38	17	11	10	55	36	45
Millwall	38	19	7	12	62	43	45
Exeter City	38	18	8	12	48	44	44
Reading	38	17	8	13	59	55	42
Brighton & Hove Albion	38	13	12	13	48	47	38
Northampton Town	38	12	12	14	61	48	36
Portsmouth	38	14	8	16	41	49	36
Merthyr Town	38	12	12	14	42	60	36
Coventry City	38	13	8	17	53	59	34
Watford	38	12	10	16	43	50	34
Gillingham	38	12	10	16	36	53	34
Bristol Rovers	38	12	9	17	55	64	33
Southampton	38	10	11	17	40	72	31
Norwich City	38	10	9	19	39	50	29
Brentford	38	11	5	22	42	55	27
Stoke	38	10	4	24	39	75	24

Second Division

Cardiff City	24	18	5	1	54	15	41
Southend United	24	14	6	4	43	23	34
Swansea Town	24	12	7	5	29	23	31
Croydon Common	24	13	4	7	51	29	30
Luton Town	24	13	4	7	52	39	30
Llanelly	24	9	6	9	33	39	24
Pontypridd	24	6	11	7	30	28	23
Mid Rhondda	24	9	4	11	33	31	22
Aberdare	24	8	6	10	38	40	22
Newport County	24	7	5	12	29	36	19
Mardy	24	6	3	15	38	38	15
Treharris	24	5	2	17	18	60	12
Ton Pentre	24	3	3	18	22	69	9

1913-14

First Division

Swindon Town	38	21	8	9	81	41	50
Crystal Palace	38	17	16	5	60	32	50
Northampton Town	38	14	19	5	50	37	47
Reading	38	17	10	11	43	36	44
Plymouth Argyle	38	15	13	10	46	42	43
West Ham United	38	15	12	11	61	60	42
Brighton & Hove Albion	38	15	12	11	43	45	42
Queens Park Rangers	38	16	9	13	45	43	41
Portsmouth	38	14	12	12	57	48	40
Cardiff City	38	13	12	13	46	42	38
Southampton	38	15	7	16	55	54	37
Exeter City	38	10	16	12	39	38	36
Gillingham	38	13	9	16	48	49	35
Norwich City	38	9	17	12	49	51	35
Millwall	38	11	12	15	51	56	34
Southend Unied	38	10	12	16	41	66	32
Bristol Rovers	38	10	11	17	46	67	31
Watford	38	10	9	19	50	56	29
Merthyr Town	38	9	10	19	38	61	28
Coventry City	38	6	14	18	43	68	26

Second Division

Croydon Common	30	23	5	2	76	14	51
Luton Town	30	24	3	3	92	22	51
Brentford	30	20	4	6	80	18	44
Swansea Town	30	20	4	6	66	23	44
Stoke	30	19	2	9	71	34	40
Newport County	30	14	8	8	49	38	36
Mid Rhondda	30	13	7	10	55	37	33
Pontypridd	30	14	5	11	43	38	33
Llanelly	30	12	4	14	45	39	28
Barry	30	9	8	13	44	70	26
Abertillery	30	8	4	18	44	57	20
Ton Pentre	30	8	4	18	33	61	20
Mardy	30	6	6	18	30	60	18
Caerphilly	30	4	7	19	21	103	15
Aberdare	30	4	5	21	33	87	13
Treharris	30	2	4	24	19	106	8

1914-15

First Division

Watford	38	22	8	8	68	46	52
Reading	38	21	7	10	68	43	49
Cardiff City	38	22	4	12	72	38	48
West Ham United	38	18	9	11	58	47	45
Northampton Town	38	16	11	11	56	51	43
Southampton	38	19	5	14	78	74	43
Portsmouth	38	16	10	12	54	42	42
Millwall	38	16	10	12	50	51	42
Swindon Town	38	15	11	12	77	59	41
Brighton & Hove Albion	38	16	7	15	46	47	39
Exeter City	38	15	8	15	50	41	38
Queens Park Rangers	38	13	12	13	55	56	38
Norwich City	38	11	14	13	53	56	36
Luton Town	38	13	8	17	61	73	34
Crystal Palace	38	13	8	17	47	61	34
Bristol Rovers	38	14	3	21	53	75	31
Plymouth Argyle	38	8	14	16	51	61	30
Southend United	38	10	8	20	44	64	28
Croydon Common	38	9	9	20	47	63	27
Gillingham	38	6	8	24	43	82	20

Second Division

Stoke	24	17	4	3	62	15	38
Stalybridge Celtic	24	17	3	4	47	22	37
Merthyr Town	24	15	5	4	46	20	35
Swansea Town	24	16	1	7	48	21	33
Coventry City	24	13	2	9	56	33	28
Ton Pentre	24	11	6	7	42	43	28
Brentford	24	8	7	9	35	45	23
Llanelly	24	10	1	13	39	32	21
Barry	24	6	5	13	30	35	17
Newport County	24	7	3	14	27	42	17
Pontypridd	24	5	6	13	31	58	16
Mid Rhondda	24	3	6	15	17	40	12
Ebbw Vale	24	3	1	20	23	88	7

1919-20

First Division

Portsmouth	42	23	12	7	73	27	58
Watford	42	26	6	10	69	42	58
Crystal Palace	42	22	12	8	69	43	56
Cardiff City	42	18	17	7	70	43	53
Plymouth Argyle	42	20	10	12	57	29	50
Queens Park Rangers	42	18	10	14	62	50	46
Reading	42	16	13	13	51	43	45
Southampton	42	18	8	16	72	63	44
Swansea Town	42	16	11	15	53	45	43
Exeter City	42	17	9	16	57	51	43
Southend United	42	13	17	12	46	48	43
Norwich City	42	15	11	16	64	57	41
Swindon Town	42	17	7	18	65	68	41
Millwall	42	14	12	16	52	55	40
Brentford	42	15	10	17	52	59	40
Brighton & Hove Albion	42	14	8	20	60	72	36
Bristol Rovers	42	11	13	18	61	78	35
Newport County	42	13	7	22	45	70	33
Northampton Town	42	12	9	21	64	103	33
Luton Town	42	10	10	22	51	76	30
Merthyr Town	42	9	11	22	47	78	29
Gillingham	42	10	7	25	34	74	27

Second Division

Mid Rhondda	20	17	3	0	79	10	37
Ton Pentre	20	12	7	1	50	14	31
Llanelly	20	10	5	5	47	30	25
Pontypridd	20	10	3	7	33	29	23
Ebbw Vale	20	7	7	6	38	40	21
Barry	20	7	5	8	32	27	19
Mardy	20	7	5	8	29	30	19
Abertillery	20	6	5	9	29	40	17
Porth Athletic	20	4	4	12	30	74	12
Aberaman Athletic	20	4	3	13	28	48	11
Caerphilly	20	1	3	16	20	74	5

1920-21

English Section

Brighton & Hove Albion Reserves	24	16	3	5	65	29	35
Portsmouth Reserves	24	13	7	4	44	20	33
Millwall Reserves	24	12	4	8	46	24	28
Southampton Reserves	24	10	7	7	53	35	27
Boscombe	24	10	6	8	25	40	26
Reading Reserves	24	11	3	10	41	34	25
Luton Town Reserves	24	8	8	8	38	35	24
Charlton Athletic	24	8	8	8	41	41	24
Watford Reserves	24	9	4	11	43	45	22
Norwich City Reserves	24	7	7	10	31	39	21
Gillingham Reserves	24	6	5	13	32	47	17
Chatham	24	5	6	13	24	47	16
Thornycrofts	24	4	6	14	29	74	14

Welsh Section

Barry	20	13	4	3	35	12	30
Aberdare Athletic	20	12	3	5	29	23	27
Ebbw Vale	20	10	5	5	34	23	25
Pontypridd	20	10	3	7	34	23	23
Mid Rhondda	20	10	3	7	26	18	23
Abertillery Town	20	8	5	7	35	24	21
Ton Pentre	20	7	5	8	32	34	19
Aberaman Athletic	20	5	7	8	30	33	17
Llanelly	20	7	2	11	28	46	16
Mardy	20	2	6	12	18	39	10
Porth Athletic	20	3	3	14	28	54	9

1921-22

English Section

Plymouth Argyle Reserves	36	22	5	9	91	38	49
Bristol City Reserves	36	18	8	10	73	50	44
Portsmouth Reserves	36	17	10	9	63	41	44
Southampton Reserves	36	19	5	12	70	47	43
Gillingham Reserves	36	17	9	10	65	47	43
Charlton Athletic Reserves	36	18	6	12	69	54	42
Boscombe	36	17	5	14	38	55	39
Luton Town Reserves	36	17	4	15	50	54	38
Watford Reserves	36	15	7	14	65	53	37
Brighton & Hove Albion Reserves	36	12	13	11	60	52	37
Bath City	36	16	5	15	55	53	37
Swindon Town Reserves	36	14	7	15	59	46	35
Bristol Rovers Reserves	36	13	7	16	50	82	33
Millwall Reserves	36	13	4	19	49	53	30
Reading Reserves	36	11	7	18	46	59	29
Exeter City Reserves	36	10	9	17	42	63	29
Guildford United	36	11	6	19	44	56	28
Norwich City Reserves	36	10	6	20	47	86	26
Southend United Reserves	36	9	3	24	47	92	21

Welsh Section

Ebbw Vale	16	11	3	2	33	11	25
Ton Pentre	16	9	4	3	35	14	22
Aberaman Athletic	16	7	5	4	25	19	19
Porth Athletic	16	6	6	4	31	20	18
Pontypridd	16	7	4	5	28	19	18
Swansea Town Reserves	16	7	4	5	24	17	18
Barry	16	3	3	10	14	35	9
Abertillery Town	16	3	2	11	21	45	8
Mardy	16	2	3	11	14	43	7

1922-23

English Section

Bristol City Reserves	38	24	5	9	84	39	53
Boscombe	38	22	7	9	67	34	51
Portsmouth Reserves	38	23	3	12	93	51	49
Bristol Rovers Reserves	38	20	8	10	59	41	48
Plymouth Argyle Reserves	38	20	7	11	74	41	47
Torquay United	38	18	8	12	63	38	44
Brighton & Hove Albion Reserves	38	20	3	15	95	60	43
Luton Town Reserves	38	16	11	11	67	56	43
Southend United Reserves	38	18	6	14	69	68	42
Southampton Reserves	38	18	5	15	65	54	41
Millwall Reserves	38	15	10	13	61	55	40
Coventry City Reserves	38	15	8	15	56	61	38
Guildford Town Reserves	38	15	7	16	65	59	37
Swindon Town Reserves	38	13	6	19	54	73	32
Bath City	38	10	8	20	44	71	28
Watford Reserves	38	11	6	21	34	79	28
Yeovil & Petters United	38	10	6	22	56	104	26
Norwich City Reserves	38	9	7	22	42	68	25
Exeter City Reserves	38	10	5	23	43	81	25
Reading Reserves	38	7	6	25	43	95	20

Welsh Section

Ebbw Vale	12	6	5	1	22	15	17
Aberaman Athletic	12	7	2	3	30	19	16
Swansea Town Reserves	12	6	2	4	25	14	14
Pontypridd	12	6	2	4	18	18	14
Barry	12	4	3	5	15	11	11
Bridgend Town	12	4	2	6	15	21	10
Porth Athletic	12	0	2	10	18	24	2

1923-24

Eastern Section

Peterborough & Fletton United	30	20	2	8	54	31	42
Leicester City Reserves	30	19	3	8	72	30	41
Southampton Reserves	30	18	5	7	60	36	41
Millwall Reserves	30	18	3	9	56	38	39
Portsmouth Reserves	30	16	2	12	66	37	34
Brighton & Hove Albion Reserves	30	13	7	10	55	42	33
Norwich City Reserves	30	13	6	11	46	34	32
Folkestone	30	12	5	13	61	51	29
Coventry City Reserves	30	10	8	12	39	4	28
Watford Reserves	30	11	6	13	36	48	28
Reading Reserves	30	11	6	13	32	43	28
Northampton Town Reserves	30	9	10	11	32	47	28
Luton Town Reserves	30	10	7	13	40	49	27
Guildford United	30	7	5	18	38	72	19
Kettering	30	5	8	17	30	67	18
Bournemouth Reserves	30	4	5	21	40	85	13

Western Section

Yeovil & Petters United	34	25	3	6	71	30	53
Plymouth Argyle Reserves	34	21	5	8	74	37	47
Pontypridd	34	19	8	7	81	44	46
Torquay United	34	19	7	8	59	25	45
Bristol City Reserves	34	17	9	8	63	39	43
Swansea Town Reserves	34	19	5	10	62	38	43
Bristol Rovers Reserves	34	17	6	11	69	43	40
Cardiff City Reserves	34	15	4	15	55	31	34
Exeter City Reserves	34	11	11	12	48	47	33
Weymouth	34	15	3	16	48	60	33
Llanelly	34	14	5	15	47	62	33
Swindon Town Reserves	34	11	6	17	36	60	28
Bridgend Town	34	11	5	18	57	72	27
Newport County Reserves	34	10	7	17	57	79	27
Ebbw Vale	34	8	8	18	38	62	24
Bath City	34	6	9	19	32	71	21
Barry	34	6	7	21	36	74	19
Aberaman Athletic	34	6	4	24	41	87	16

1924-25

Eastern Section

Southampton Reserves	32	17	10	5	65	30	44
Kettering Town	32	17	6	9	67	39	40
Brighton & Hove Albion Reserves	32	15	10	7	68	42	40
Millwall Reserves	32	15	10	7	65	48	40
Peterborough & Fletton United	32	15	9	8	56	29	39
Bournemouth Reserves	32	15	9	8	66	48	39
Leicester City Reserves	32	15	7	10	61	45	37
Portsmouth Reserves	32	15	7	10	51	40	37
Folkestone	32	13	11	8	55	46	37
Norwich City Reserves	32	13	8	11	65	58	34
Coventry City Reserves	32	12	9	11	51	41	33
Luton Town Reserves	32	15	2	15	48	63	32
Northampton Town Reserves	32	10	5	17	38	59	25
Watford Reserves	32	7	7	18	44	71	21
Nuneaton Town	32	8	2	22	37	62	18
Reading Reserves	32	8	1	23	38	87	17
Guildford United	32	4	3	25	40	107	11

Western Section

Swansea Town Reserves	38	25	4	9	73	26	54
Plymouth Argyle Reserves	38	22	10	6	97	35	54
Pontypridd	38	24	4	10	81	39	52
Bridgend Town	38	20	11	7	74	52	51
Mid Rhondda United	38	21	6	11	79	48	48
Weymouth	38	21	4	13	77	50	46
Cardiff City Reserves	38	18	6	14	56	44	42
Newport County Reserves	38	17	8	13	71	60	42
Swindon Town Reserves	38	17	8	13	48	46	42
Bristol City Reserves	38	18	5	15	51	43	41
Yeovil & Petters United	38	15	10	13	49	50	40
Exeter City Reserves	38	16	6	16	78	55	38
Taunton Unied	38	15	6	17	55	51	36
Bristol Rovers Reserves	38	13	6	19	45	50	32
Torquay United	38	9	11	18	41	73	29
Llanelly	38	6	12	20	49	94	24
Ebbw Vale	38	9	6	23	40	91	24
Bath City	38	8	8	22	28	85	24
Barry	38	8	6	24	38	82	22
Aberaman Athletic	38	6	7	25	39	95	19

1925-26

Eastern Section

Millwall Reserves	34	24	6	4	106	37	54
Leicester City Reserves	34	23	2	9	105	60	48
Brighton & Hove Albion Reserves	34	21	4	9	105	69	46
Kettering Town	34	19	5	10	98	68	43
Peterborough & Fletton United	34	19	3	12	76	62	41
Portsmouth Reserves	34	17	5	12	76	67	39
Norwich City Reserves	34	17	4	13	85	90	38
Bournemouth Reserves	34	15	7	12	76	67	37
Southampton Reserves	34	14	7	13	65	72	35
Fulham Reserves	34	13	6	15	86	77	32
Grays Thurrock United	34	13	5	16	63	77	31
Guildford United	34	11	8	15	71	87	30
Watford Reserves	34	12	2	20	62	94	26
Luton Town Reserves	34	11	3	20	70	78	25
Folkestone	34	9	6	19	67	93	24
Reading Reserves	34	10	3	21	58	84	23
Coventry City Reserves	34	9	5	20	54	93	23
Nuneaton Town	34	7	3	24	61	113	17

Western Section

Plymouth Argyle Reserves	26	20	1	5	67	31	41
Bristol City Reserves	26	16	4	6	48	28	36
Bristol Rovers Reserves	26	13	4	9	51	35	30
Swindon Town Reserves	26	13	4	9	57	40	30
Ebbw Vale	26	13	3	10	60	46	29
Torquay United	26	12	5	9	59	46	29
Yeovil & Petters United	26	9	8	9	43	48	26
Mid Rhondda	26	12	1	13	47	49	25
Weymouth	26	10	3	13	64	60	23
Exeter City Reserves	26	8	5	13	40	49	21
Barry	26	8	4	14	47	55	20
Taunton United	26	9	2	15	44	60	20
Pontypridd	26	7	5	14	44	77	19
Bath City	26	7	1	18	38	86	15

1926-27

Eastern Section

Brighton & Hove Albion Reserves	32	21	6	5	86	47	48
Peterborough & Fletton United	32	18	9	5	80	39	45
Portsmouth Reserves	32	19	6	7	95	65	44
Kettering Town	32	15	10	7	66	41	40
Millwall Reserves	32	16	5	11	67	56	37
Bournemouth Reserves	32	14	6	12	69	64	34
Norwich City Reserves	32	14	5	13	79	74	33
Dartford	32	13	7	12	60	71	33
Reading Reserves	32	12	8	12	75	79	32
Luton Town Reserves	32	10	11	11	75	70	1
Leicester City Reserves	32	12	5	15	94	72	29
Watford Reserves	32	10	8	14	74	84	28
Southampton Reserves	32	10	6	16	57	77	26
Poole	32	9	6	17	55	86	24
Grays Thurrock United	32	10	3	19	49	66	23
Guildford United	32	6	7	19	57	106	19
Folkestone	32	7	4	21	57	98	18

Western Section

Torquay United	26	17	4	5	63	30	38
Bristol City Reserves	26	14	10	2	77	37	38
Plymouth Argyle Reserves	26	15	4	7	56	38	34
Ebbw Vale	26	14	2	10	67	45	30
Bristol Rovers Reserves	26	12	4	10	51	43	28
Swindon Town Reserves	26	11	5	10	60	57	27
Barry	26	11	4	11	65	50	26
Essex City Reserves	26	10	6	10	62	49	26
Weymouth	26	12	2	12	48	65	26
Newport County Reserves	26	9	6	11	57	53	24
Bath City	26	7	9	10	44	52	23
Yeovil & Petters United	26	9	5	12	49	66	23
Taunton United	26	4	4	18	36	83	12
Mid Rhondda United	26	2	5	19	22	89	9

1927-28

Easter Section

Kettering Town	34	23	6	5	90	39	52
Peterborough & Fletton United	34	21	3	10	73	43	45
Northfleet United	34	17	7	10	83	54	41
Brighton & Hove Albion Reserves	34	20	0	14	90	63	40
Norwich City Reserves	34	17	6	11	69	69	40
Southampton Reserves	34	16	7	11	92	70	39
Aldershot Town	34	17	5	12	85	66	39
Sittingbourne	34	16	5	13	64	70	37
Millwall Reserves	34	15	6	13	66	59	36
Poole	34	15	5	14	69	84	35
Folkestone	34	12	6	16	71	91	30
Guildford City	34	12	5	17	65	89	29
Dartford	34	12	4	18	46	49	28
Gillingham Reserves	34	10	7	17	72	84	27
Sheppey United	34	11	3	20	57	87	25
Chatham	34	10	4	20	49	70	24
Grays Thurrock United	34	10	3	21	48	88	23
Bournemouth Reserves	34	9	4	21	48	62	22

Western Section

Bristol City Reserves	30	20	3	7	95	51	43
Exeter City Reserves	30	18	4	8	104	56	40
Bristol Rovers Reserves	30	16	3	11	80	64	35
Plymouth Argyle Reserves	30	16	2	12	88	53	34
Newport County Reserves	30	13	8	9	99	70	34
Ebbw Vale	30	15	3	12	67	74	33
Swindon Town Reserves	30	13	4	13	80	74	30
Aberdare & Aberaman	30	12	6	12	62	68	30
Yeovil & Petters United	30	11	7	12	64	57	29
Torquay United Reserves	30	11	6	13	51	67	28
Bath City	30	12	3	15	64	68	27
Taunton Town	30	11	5	14	60	65	27
Weymouth	30	10	6	14	50	83	26
Merthyr Town Reserves	30	9	4	17	50	77	22
Barry	30	8	6	16	45	87	22
Mid Rhondda United	30	7	6	17	36	81	20

1928-29

Eastern Section

Kettering Town	36	24	4	8	96	46	52
Peterborough & Fletton United	36	21	5	10	86	44	47
Brighton & Hove Albion Reserves	36	19	9	8	91	56	47
Millwall Reserves	36	21	4	11	90	67	46
Bournemouth Reserves	36	20	5	11	82	58	45
Aldershot Town	36	18	5	13	68	52	41
Sheppey United	36	17	7	12	58	58	41
Folkestone	36	17	6	13	83	80	40
Northfleet United	36	17	4	15	87	65	38
Gillingham Reserves	36	15	8	13	68	70	38
Guildford City	36	13	11	12	85	78	37
Southampton Reserves	36	14	6	16	86	79	34
Poole	36	13	8	15	62	66	34
Thames Association	36	13	5	18	67	74	31
Dartford	36	10	6	20	55	106	26
Chatham	36	8	8	20	47	81	24
Sittingbourne	36	11	1	24	59	98	23
Norwich City Reserves	36	8	6	22	48	96	22
Grays Thurrock United	36	6	6	24	47	91	18

Western Section

Plymouth Argyle Reserves	26	15	6	5	69	27	36
Newport County Reserves	26	15	2	9	64	58	32
Bristol Rovers Reserves	26	14	3	9	54	45	31
Bristol City Reserves	26	14	2	10	70	46	30
Torquay United Reserves	26	13	4	9	52	42	30
Bath City	26	13	4	9	43	59	30
Exeter City Reserves	26	11	6	9	69	53	28
Lovells Athletic	26	11	6	9	54	48	28
Swindon Town Reserves	26	11	5	10	68	74	27
Yeovil & Petters United	26	11	2	13	49	57	24
Taunton Town	26	9	5	12	58	66	23
Ebbw Vale	26	9	5	12	56	66	23
Barry	26	6	3	17	38	66	15
Merthyr Town Reserves	26	3	1	22	37	92	7

1929-30

Eastern Section

Aldershot Town	32	21	6	5	84	39	48
Millwall Reserves	32	21	3	8	75	56	45
Thames Association	32	17	6	9	80	60	40
Peterborough & Fletton United	32	18	3	11	66	39	39
Northampton Town Reserves	32	17	4	11	86	60	38
Southampton Reserves	32	14	7	11	73	62	35
Sheppey United	32	15	5	12	76	69	35
Kettering Town	32	13	7	12	70	69	33
Dartford	32	14	5	13	57	59	33
Norwich City Reserves	32	14	3	15	69	69	31
Guildford City	32	13	2	17	65	97	28
Bournemouth Reserves	32	10	7	15	59	63	27
Brighton & Hove Albion Reserves	32	12	2	18	56	79	26
Folkestone	32	13	0	19	56	82	26
Sittingbourne	32	10	5	17	55	59	25
Northfleet United	32	6	7	19	53	77	19
Grays Thurrock United	32	7	2	23	54	101	16

Western Section

Bath City	28	16	6	6	85	52	38
Bristol Rovers Reserves	28	16	4	8	66	50	36
Taunton Town	28	14	7	7	50	40	35
Barry	28	15	3	10	65	55	33
Yeovil & Petters United	28	12	7	9	63	47	31
Plymouth Argyle Reserves	28	14	3	11	68	52	31
Newport County Reserves	28	13	4	11	68	76	30
Lovells Athletic	28	13	2	13	59	57	28
Exeter City Reserves	28	11	6	11	49	54	28
Bristol City Reserves	28	11	5	12	59	63	27
Swindon Town Reserves	28	10	6	12	69	67	26
Torquay United Reserves	28	10	6	12	76	77	26
Llanelly	28	10	4	14	55	52	24
Ebbw Vale	28	5	6	17	52	97	16
Merthyr Town Reserves	28	5	1	22	48	93	11

1930-31

Eastern Section

Dartford	16	9	5	2	39	18	23
Aldershot Town	16	10	3	3	50	28	23
Norwich City Reserves	16	9	1	6	47	38	19
Peterborough & Fletton United	16	6	5	5	35	29	17
Thames Association Reserves	16	7	2	7	38	31	16
Millwall Reserves	16	7	0	9	47	40	14
Folkestone	16	4	3	9	31	46	11
Guildford City	16	5	1	10	28	53	11
Sheppey United	16	4	2	10	31	63	10

Western Section

Exeter City Reserves	22	15	2	5	59	28	32
Llanelly	22	10	8	4	72	39	28
Merthyr Town	22	12	3	7	62	49	27
Plymouth Argyle Reserves	22	12	2	8	55	34	26
Bath City	22	10	6	6	47	39	26
Torquay United Reserves	22	9	5	8	66	49	23
Swindon Town Reserves	22	7	7	8	48	52	21
Bristol Rovers Reserves	22	7	6	9	58	64	20
Barry	22	7	5	10	29	39	19
Taunton Town	22	5	7	10	36	62	17
Newport County Reserves	22	6	2	14	36	66	14
Ebbw Vale	22	5	1	16	32	79	11

1931-32

Eastern Section

Dartford	18	12	3	3	53	18	27
Folkestone	18	12	2	4	58	27	26
Guildford City	18	11	1	6	33	24	23
Norwich City Reserves	18	9	2	7	46	33	20
Millwall Reserves	18	9	2	7	41	39	20
Tunbridge Wells Rangers	18	7	5	6	23	25	19
Bournemouth Reserves	18	6	4	8	43	61	16
Peterborough & Fletton United	18	4	5	9	28	29	13
Aldershot Town	18	3	5	10	17	30	11
Sheppey United	18	2	1	15	16	72	5

Western Section

Yeovil & Petters United	24	16	4	4	65	31	36
Plymouth Argyle Reserves	24	15	5	4	81	31	35
Bath City	24	12	7	5	50	33	31
Llanelly	24	12	4	8	65	46	28
Taunton Town	24	13	2	9	53	58	28
Newport County Reserves	24	10	6	8	70	51	26
Exeter City Reserves	24	9	7	8	59	43	25
Merthyr Town	24	9	4	11	66	73	22
Bristol Rovers Reserves	24	8	4	12	54	47	20
Swindon Town Reserves	24	8	4	12	54	95	20
Barry	24	7	3	14	58	76	17
Torquay United Reserves	24	5	6	13	43	66	16
Ebbw Vale	24	3	2	19	34	102	8

1932-33

Eastern Section

Norwich City Reserves	14	9	2	3	34	22	20
Dartford	14	8	2	4	26	23	18
Folkestone	14	7	1	6	35	32	15
Bournemouth Reserves	14	5	4	5	36	33	14
Tunbridge Wells Rangers	14	5	2	7	23	24	12
Guildford City	14	5	2	7	22	28	12
Millwall Reserves	14	5	1	8	27	31	11
Aldershot Reserves	14	3	4	7	24	34	10

Western Section

Bath City	20	13	4	3	62	34	30
Exeter City Reserves	20	12	3	5	62	46	27
Torquay United Reserves	20	12	1	7	56	37	25
Plymouth Argyle Reserves	20	11	2	7	68	38	24
Yeovil & Petters United	20	11	2	7	59	44	24
Llanelly	20	10	2	8	53	33	22
Bristol Rovers Reserves	20	7	3	10	53	65	17
Newport County Reserves	20	6	4	10	42	55	16
Merthyr Tydfil	20	7	1	12	39	58	15
Barry	20	3	4	13	30	72	10
Taunton Town	20	4	2	14	21	63	10

1933-34

Eastern Section

Norwich City Reserves	16	9	4	3	41	15	22
Margate	16	8	3	5	23	20	19
Millwall Reserves	16	7	4	5	28	28	18
Clapton Orient Reserves	16	8	1	7	33	34	17
Bournemouth Reserves	16	6	3	7	28	30	15
Tunbridge Wells Rangers	16	6	2	8	25	36	14
Folkestone	16	5	3	8	26	26	13
Guildford City	16	5	3	8	27	33	13
Dartford	16	4	5	7	15	24	13

Western Section

Plymouth Argyle Reserves	20	13	6	1	62	22	32
Bristol Rovers Reserves	20	14	3	3	56	27	31
Bath City	20	11	3	6	43	25	25
Torquay United Reserves	20	9	4	7	54	36	22
Yeovil & Petters United	20	10	1	9	35	39	21
Exeter City Reserves	20	8	3	9	54	47	19
Merthyr Town	20	8	2	10	39	50	18
Llanelly	20	8	1	11	25	39	17
Barry	20	4	5	11	37	64	13
Newport County Reserves	20	4	3	13	36	54	11
Taunton Town	20	5	1	14	27	65	11

Central Section

Plymouth Argyle Reserves	18	16	1	1	47	14	33
Clapton Orient Reserves	18	9	3	6	35	25	21
Norwich City Reserves	18	8	4	6	41	27	20
Yeovil & Petters United	18	7	4	7	34	38	18
Bath City	18	7	3	8	31	36	17
Dartford	18	6	4	8	28	26	16
Tunbridge Wells Rangers	18	7	1	10	26	37	15
Llanelly	18	6	2	10	28	39	14
Folkestone	18	6	1	11	30	41	13
Guildford City	18	6	1	11	28	45	13

1934-35

Eastern Section

Norwich City Reserves	18	12	1	5	52	21	25
Dartford	18	8	6	4	36	22	22
Margate	18	7	6	7	38	30	20
Bournemouth Reserves	18	8	3	8	34	26	19
Guildford City	18	7	5	6	41	34	19
Aldershot Reserves	18	7	3	8	29	43	17
Folkestone	18	5	6	7	30	39	16
Tunbridge Wells Rangers	18	6	4	8	32	56	16
Clapton Orient Reserves	18	5	4	9	33	35	14
Millwall Reserves	18	3	6	9	26	45	12

Western Section

Yeovil & Petters United	16	11	2	3	49	18	24
Newport County Reserves	16	8	5	3	45	29	21
Plymouth Argyle Reserves	16	7	5	4	40	24	19
Exeter City Reserves	16	7	2	7	38	32	16
Bath City	16	6	4	6	35	32	16
Bristol Rovers Reserves	16	5	5	6	33	37	15
Barry	16	6	3	7	30	40	15
Torquay United Reserves	16	5	3	8	24	29	13
Taunton Town	16	1	3	12	13	66	5

Central Section

Folkestone	20	11	4	5	43	31	26
Guildford City	20	11	4	5	43	39	26
Plymouth Argyle Reserves	20	6	9	5	40	28	21
Torquay United Reserves	20	7	6	7	34	35	20
Bristol Rovers Reserves	20	8	4	8	38	46	20
Margate	20	8	3	9	40	34	19
Dartford	20	8	3	9	43	38	19
Aldershot Reserves	20	8	3	9	33	44	19
Tunbridge Wells Rangers	20	8	2	10	33	37	18
Yeovil & Petters United	20	8	1	11	45	51	17
Bath City	20	6	3	11	34	43	15

1935-36

Eastern Section

Margate	18	13	2	3	49	16	28
Folkestone	18	11	3	4	46	23	25
Dartford	18	9	3	6	47	25	21
Tunbridge Wells Rangers	18	9	1	8	26	41	19
Clapton Orient Reserves	18	7	4	7	39	31	18
Millwall Reserves	18	7	3	8	42	39	17
Norwich City Reserves	18	8	0	10	39	38	16
Guildford City	18	6	3	9	32	52	15
Aldershot Reserves	18	6	1	11	24	45	13
Bournemouth Reserves	18	3	2	13	25	59	8

Western Section

Plymouth Argyle Reserves	16	12	3	1	51	18	27
Bristol Rovers Reserves	16	8	3	5	35	30	19
Newport County Reserves	16	8	3	5	29	30	19
Torquay United Reserves	16	7	1	8	25	28	15
Bath City	16	5	5	6	18	26	15
Cheltenham Town	16	6	2	8	32	28	14
Yeovil & Petters United	16	5	3	8	31	35	13
Barry	16	5	2	9	29	41	12
Exeter City Reserves	16	4	2	10	24	38	10

Central Section

Margate	20	14	3	3	57	18	31
Bristol Rovers Reserves	20	13	1	6	51	37	27
Plymouth Argyle Reserves	20	12	2	6	53	32	26
Aldershot Reserves	20	9	4	7	37	37	22
Folkestone	20	9	3	8	51	36	21
Tunbridge Wells Rangers	20	7	4	9	40	41	18
Dartford	20	7	3	10	34	42	17
Guildford City	20	7	3	10	33	47	17
Cheltenham Town	20	5	5	10	32	45	15
Bath City	20	5	5	10	34	52	15
Yeovil & Petters United	20	3	5	12	40	75	11

1936-37

Ipswich Town	30	19	8	3	68	35	46
Norwich City Reserves	30	18	5	7	70	35	41
Folkestone	30	17	4	9	71	62	38
Margate	30	15	4	11	64	49	34
Guildford City	30	15	4	11	54	60	34
Bath City	30	14	5	11	65	55	33
Yeovil & Petters United	30	15	3	12	77	69	33
Plymouth Argyle Reserves	30	11	8	11	64	58	30
Newport County Reserves	30	11	8	11	72	68	30
Barry	30	12	4	14	58	72	28
Cheltenham Town	30	10	4	16	61	70	24
Dartford	30	9	5	16	41	55	23
Exeter City Reserves	30	8	7	15	57	78	23
Tunbridge Wells Rangers	30	8	6	16	62	64	22
Torquay United Reserves	30	8	5	17	46	76	21
Aldershot Reserves	30	7	6	17	47	74	20

Midweek Section

Margate	18	12	1	5	48	24	25
Bath City	18	10	5	3	38	28	25
Norwich City Reserves	18	9	5	4	44	27	23
Folkestone	18	7	6	5	32	36	20
Millwall Reserves	18	8	3	7	44	47	19
Portsmouth Reserves	18	6	5	7	40	27	17
Tunbridge Wells Rangers	18	5	4	9	30	41	14
Aldershot Reserves	18	6	2	10	20	30	14
Guildford City	18	3	6	9	24	36	12
Dartford	18	4	3	11	19	43	11

1937-38

Guildford City	34	22	5	7	94	60	49
Plymouth Argyle Reserves	34	18	9	7	98	58	45
Ipswich Town	34	19	6	9	89	54	44
Yeovil & Petters United	34	14	14	6	72	45	42
Norwich City Reserves	34	15	11	8	77	55	41
Colchester United	34	15	8	11	90	58	38
Bristol Rovers Reserves	34	14	8	12	63	62	36
Swindon Town Reserves	34	14	7	13	70	76	35
Tunbridge Wells Rangers	34	14	6	14	68	74	34
Aldershot Reserves	34	10	12	12	42	55	32
Cheltenham Town	34	13	5	16	72	68	31
Exeter City Reserves	34	13	5	16	71	75	31
Dartford	34	9	11	14	51	70	29
Bath City	34	9	9	16	45	65	27
Folkestone	34	10	6	18	58	82	26
Newport County Reserves	34	10	6	18	56	86	26
Barry	34	8	7	19	50	88	23
Torquay United Reserves	34	8	7	19	46	81	23

Midweek Section

Millwall Reserves	18	13	3	2	59	21	29
Colchester United	18	13	1	4	42	23	27
Aldershot Reserves	18	11	3	4	38	29	25
Norwich City Reserves	18	9	1	8	45	39	19
Portsmouth Reserves	18	5	5	8	31	30	15
Dartford	18	6	3	9	32	35	15
Folkestone	18	6	3	9	34	38	15
Tunbridge Wells Rangers	18	5	4	9	28	36	14
Bath City	18	5	3	10	27	45	13
Guildford City	18	4	0	14	21	61	8

1938-39

Colchester United	44	31	5	8	110	37	67
Guildford City	44	30	6	8	126	52	66
Gillingham	44	29	6	9	104	57	64
Plymouth Argyle Reserves	44	26	5	13	128	63	57
Yeovil & Petters United	44	22	10	12	85	70	54
Arsenal Reserves	44	21	9	14	92	57	51
Cardiff City Reserves	44	24	3	17	105	72	51
Tunbridge Wells Rangers	44	22	6	16	93	76	50
Norwich City Reserves	44	23	4	17	86	76	50
Chelmsford City	44	18	8	18	74	73	44
Bath City	44	16	12	16	58	74	44
Barry	44	18	7	19	76	90	43
Cheltenham Town	44	16	9	19	76	105	41
Ipswich Town Reserves	44	14	12	18	64	76	40
Worcester City	44	13	14	17	72	90	40
Folkestone	44	16	6	22	74	85	38
Newport County Reserves	44	13	10	21	74	108	36
Exeter City Reserves	44	12	9	23	51	107	33
Torquay United Reserves	44	12	8	24	53	89	32
Swindon Town Reserves	44	11	9	24	66	101	31
Aldershot Reserves	44	12	6	26	69	92	30
Bristol Rovers Reserves	44	9	11	24	66	85	29
Dartford	44	8	5	31	53	119	21

Midweek Section

Tunbridge Wells Rangers	16	8	7	1	37	18	23
Colchester United	16	9	2	5	36	21	20
Norwich City Reserves	16	7	4	5	40	26	18
Millwall Reserves	16	7	4	5	33	23	18
Portsmouth Reserves	16	5	4	7	21	29	14
Guildford City	16	4	6	6	24	39	14
Aldershot Reserves	16	4	5	7	22	25	13
Folkestone	16	4	5	7	24	35	13
Dartford	16	4	3	9	24	45	11

1939-40

Eastern Section

Chelmsford City	7	5	0	2	29	9	10
Guildford City	8	4	1	3	26	13	9
Tunbridge Wells Rangers	7	2	3	2	21	16	7
Dartford	7	2	1	4	17	30	5
Norwich City Reserves	7	2	1	4	9	34	5

Western Section

Lovells Athletic	14	11	1	2	53	22	23
Worcester City	14	9	2	3	55	30	20
Hereford United	14	8	0	6	45	31	16
Yeovil & Petters United	14	7	2	5	30	24	16
Gloucester City	14	5	0	9	35	49	10
Barry	14	4	1	9	31	56	9
Cheltenham Town	13	3	2	8	21	38	8
Bath City	13	3	2	8	21	41	8

1945-46

Chelmsford City	18	15	1	2	66	23	34
Hereford United	20	13	3	4	59	31	29
Bath City	20	12	2	6	62	32	26
Cheltenham Town	18	9	1	8	35	54	22
Barry Town	20	8	4	8	42	42	20
Yeovil & Petters United	18	7	1	10	57	52	18
Worcester City	20	8	2	10	60	58	18
Colchester United	20	7	3	10	29	47	17
Bedford Town	16	4	1	11	30	49	15
Swindon Town Reserves	18	4	3	11	36	65	14
Cardiff City Reserves	20	4	5	11	39	60	13

1946-47

Gillingham	31	20	6	5	103	45	47
Guildford City	32	21	4	7	86	39	46
Merthyr Tydfil	31	21	2	8	104	37	45
Yeovil Town	32	19	6	7	100	49	44
Chelmsford City	31	17	3	11	90	60	38
Gravesend & Northfleet	32	17	4	11	82	58	38
Barry Town	30	14	6	10	89	61	36
Colchester United	31	15	4	12	65	60	35
Cheltenham Town	31	14	3	14	68	75	32
Millwall	24	8	5	11	59	57	29
Dartford	32	10	5	17	71	100	25
Bedford Town	32	8	8	16	63	98	24
Hereford United	32	8	7	17	37	85	23
Worcester City	31	8	5	18	55	90	22
Exeter City Reserves	32	10	2	20	69	126	22
Bath City	32	7	7	18	52	93	21
Gloucester City	32	8	1	23	57	120	17

1947-48

Merthyr Tydfil	34	23	7	4	84	38	53
Gillingham	34	21	5	8	81	43	47
Worcester City	34	21	3	10	74	45	45
Colchester United	34	17	10	7	88	41	44
Hereford United	34	16	10	8	77	53	42
Lovells Athletic	34	17	6	11	74	50	40
Exeter City Reserves	34	15	7	12	65	57	37
Yeovil Town	34	12	11	11	56	50	35
Chelmsford City	34	14	7	13	62	58	35
Cheltenham Town	34	13	9	12	71	71	35
Bath City	34	12	8	14	55	62	32
Barry Town	34	10	9	15	60	70	29
Gravesend & Northfleet	34	11	6	17	52	81	28
Guildford City	34	11	4	19	69	74	26
Dartford	34	10	6	18	35	62	26
Gloucester City	34	8	6	20	45	78	22
Torquay United Reserves	34	6	9	19	43	95	21
Bedford Town	34	6	3	25	41	104	15

1948-49

Gillingham	42	26	10	6	104	48	62
Chelmsford City	42	27	7	8	115	64	61
Merthyr Tydfil	42	26	8	8	133	54	60
Colchester United	42	21	10	11	94	61	52
Worcester City	42	22	7	13	87	56	51
Dartford	42	21	9	12	73	53	51
Gravesend & Northfleet	42	20	9	13	60	46	49
Yeovil Town	42	19	9	14	90	53	47
Cheltenham Town	42	19	9	14	71	64	47
Kidderminster Harriers	42	19	6	17	77	96	44
Exeter City Reserves	42	18	7	17	83	73	43
Hereford United	42	17	6	19	83	84	40
Bath City	42	15	8	19	72	87	38
Hastings United	42	14	10	18	69	93	38
Torquay United Reserves	42	15	7	20	73	93	37
Lovells Athletic	42	14	8	20	73	74	36
Guildford City	42	12	12	18	58	85	36
Gloucester City	42	12	10	20	78	100	34
Barry Town	42	12	10	20	55	95	34
Tonbridge	42	9	7	26	54	105	25
Chingford Town	42	6	9	27	43	94	21
Bedford Town	42	5	8	29	32	101	18

1949-50

Merthyr Tydfil	46	34	3	9	143	62	71
Colchester United	46	31	9	6	109	51	71
Yeovil Town	46	29	7	10	104	45	65
Chelmsford City	46	26	9	11	121	64	61
Gillingham	46	23	9	14	92	61	55
Dartford	46	20	9	17	70	65	49
Worcester City	46	21	7	18	85	80	49
Guildford City	46	18	11	17	79	73	47
Weymouth	46	19	9	18	80	81	47
Barry Town	46	18	10	18	78	72	46
Exeter City Reserves	46	16	14	16	73	83	46
Lovells Athletic	46	17	10	19	86	78	44
Tonbridge	46	16	12	18	65	76	44
Hastings United	46	17	8	21	92	450	42
Gravesend & Northfleet	46	16	9	21	88	81	41
Torquay United Reserves	46	14	12	20	80	89	40
Bath City	46	16	7	23	61	78	39
Gloucester City	46	14	11	21	72	101	39
Hereford United	46	15	8	23	74	76	38
Cheltenham Town	46	13	11	22	75	96	37
Headington United	46	15	7	24	72	97	37
Bedford Town	46	12	11	23	63	79	35
Kidderminster Harriers	46	12	11	23	64	108	35
Chingford Town	46	10	6	30	63	151	26

1950-51

Merthyr Tydfil	44	29	8	7	156	66	66
Hereford United	44	27	7	10	110	69	61
Guildford City	44	23	8	13	88	60	54
Chelmsford City	44	21	12	11	84	58	54
Llanelly	44	19	13	12	89	73	51
Cheltenham Town	44	21	8	15	91	61	50
Headington United	44	18	11	15	84	83	47
Torquay United Reserves	44	20	6	18	93	79	46
Exeter City Reserves	44	16	12	16	90	94	44
Weymouth	44	16	12	16	82	88	44
Tonbridge	44	16	12	16	79	87	44
Gloucester City	44	16	11	17	81	76	43
Yeovil Town	44	13	15	16	72	72	41
Worcester City	44	15	11	18	69	78	41
Bath City	44	15	10	19	66	73	40
Dartford	44	14	11	19	61	70	39
Bedford Town	44	15	9	20	64	94	39
Gravesend & Northfleet	44	12	14	18	65	83	38
Kettering Town	44	13	11	20	87	87	37
Lovells Athletic	44	12	13	19	81	93	37
Kidderminster Harriers	44	13	9	22	58	103	35
Barry Town	44	13	7	24	54	104	33
Hastings United	44	11	6	27	91	143	28

1951-52

Merthyr Tydfil	42	27	6	9	128	60	60
Weymouth	42	22	13	7	81	42	57
Kidderminster Harriers	42	22	10	10	70	40	54
Guildford City	42	18	16	8	66	47	52
Hereford United	42	21	9	12	80	59	51
Worcester City	42	23	4	15	86	73	50
Kettering Town	42	18	10	14	83	56	46
Lovells Athletic	42	18	10	14	87	68	46
Gloucester City	42	19	8	15	68	55	46
Bath City	42	19	6	17	75	67	44
Headington United	42	16	11	15	55	53	43
Bedford Town	42	16	10	16	75	64	42
Barry Town	42	18	6	18	84	89	42
Chelmsford City	42	15	10	17	67	80	40
Dartford	42	15	9	18	63	65	39
Tonbridge	42	15	6	21	63	84	36
Yeovil Town	42	12	11	19	56	76	35
Cheltenham Town	42	15	4	23	59	85	34
Exeter City Reserves	42	13	7	22	76	106	33
Llanelly	42	13	6	23	70	111	32
Gravesend & Northfleet	42	12	7	23	68	88	31
Hastings United	42	3	5	34	41	131	11

1952-53

Headington United	42	23	12	7	93	50	58
Merthyr Tydfil	42	25	8	9	117	66	58
Bedford Town	42	24	8	10	91	61	56
Kettering Town	42	23	8	11	88	50	54
Bath City	42	22	10	10	71	46	54
Worcester City	42	20	11	11	100	66	51
Llanelly	42	21	9	12	95	72	51
Barry Town	42	22	3	17	89	69	47
Gravesend & Northfleet	42	19	7	16	83	76	45
Gloucester City	42	17	9	16	50	78	43
Guildford City	42	17	8	17	64	60	42
Hastings United	42	18	5	19	75	66	41
Cheltenham Town	42	15	11	16	70	89	41
Weymouth	42	15	10	17	70	75	40
Hereford United	42	17	5	20	76	73	39
Tonbridge	42	12	9	21	62	88	33
Lovells Athletic	42	12	8	22	68	81	32
Yeovil Town	42	11	10	21	75	99	32
Chelmsford City	42	12	7	23	58	92	31
Exeter City Reserves	42	13	4	25	71	94	30
Kidderminster Harriers	42	12	5	25	54	85	29
Dartford	42	6	5	31	40	121	17

1953-54

Merthyr Tydfil	42	27	8	7	97	55	62
Headington United	42	22	9	11	68	43	53
Yeovil Town	42	20	8	14	87	76	48
Bath City	42	17	12	13	73	67	46
Kidderminster Harriers	42	18	9	15	62	59	45
Weymouth	42	18	8	16	83	72	44
Barry Town	42	17	9	16	108	91	43
Bedford Town	42	19	5	18	80	84	43
Gloucester City	42	16	11	15	69	77	43
Hastings United	42	16	10	16	73	67	42
Kettering Town	42	15	12	15	65	63	42
Hereford United	42	16	9	17	66	62	41
Llanelly	42	16	9	17	80	85	41
Guildford City	42	15	11	16	56	60	41
Gravesend & Northfleet	42	16	8	18	76	77	40
Worcester City	42	17	6	19	66	71	40
Lovells Athletic	42	14	11	17	62	60	39
Tonbridge	42	15	9	18	85	91	39
Chelmsford City	42	14	10	18	67	71	38
Exeter City Reserves	42	11	13	18	61	72	35
Cheltenham Town	42	11	12	19	56	83	34
Dartford	42	6	13	23	42	89	25

1954-55

Yeovil Town	42	23	9	10	105	66	55
Weymouth	42	24	7	11	105	84	55
Hastings United	42	21	9	12	94	60	51
Cheltenham Town	42	21	8	13	85	72	50
Guildford City	42	20	8	14	72	59	48
Worcester City	42	19	10	13	80	73	48
Barry Town	42	16	15	11	82	87	47
Gloucester City	42	16	13	13	66	54	45
Bath City	42	18	9	15	73	80	45
Headington Town	42	18	7	17	82	62	43
Kidderminster Harriers	42	18	7	17	84	86	43
Merthyr Tydfil	42	17	8	17	97	94	42
Exeter City Reserves	42	19	4	19	67	78	42
Lovells Athletic	42	15	11	16	71	68	41
Kettering Town	42	15	11	16	70	69	41
Hereford United	42	17	5	20	91	72	39
Llanelly	42	16	7	19	78	81	39
Bedford Town	42	16	3	23	75	103	35
Tonbridge	42	11	8	23	68	91	30
Dartford	42	9	12	21	55	76	30
Chelmsford City	42	11	6	25	73	111	28
Gravesend & Northfleet	42	9	9	24	62	97	27

1955-56

Guildford City	42	26	8	8	74	34	60
Cheltenham Town	42	25	6	11	82	53	56
Yeovil Town	42	23	9	10	98	55	55
Bedford Town	42	21	9	12	99	69	51
Dartford	42	20	9	13	78	62	49
Weymouth	42	19	10	13	83	63	48
Gloucester City	42	19	9	14	72	60	47
Lovells Athletic	42	19	9	14	91	78	47
Chelmsford City	42	18	10	14	67	55	46
Kettering Town	42	16	11	15	105	86	43
Exeter City Reserves	42	17	9	16	75	76	43
Gravesend & Northfleet	42	17	8	17	79	75	42
Hereford United	42	17	7	18	90	90	41
Hastings United	42	15	10	17	90	76	40
Headington United	42	17	6	19	82	86	40
Kidderminster Harriers	42	14	7	21	86	108	35
Llanelly	42	14	6	22	64	98	34
Barry Town	42	11	11	20	91	108	33
Worcester City	42	12	9	21	66	83	33
Tonbridge	42	11	11	20	53	74	33
Merthyr Tydfil	42	7	10	25	52	127	24
Bath City	42	7	10	25	43	107	24

1956-57

Kettering Town	42	28	10	4	106	47	66
Bedford Town	42	25	8	9	89	52	58
Weymouth	42	22	10	10	92	71	54
Cheltenham Town	42	19	15	8	73	46	53
Gravesend & Northfleet	42	21	11	10	74	58	53
Lovells Athletic	42	21	7	14	99	84	49
Guildford City	42	18	11	13	68	49	47
Hereford United	42	19	8	15	96	60	46
Headington United	42	19	7	16	64	61	45
Gloucester City	42	18	8	16	74	72	44
Hastings United	42	17	9	16	70	58	43
Worcester City	42	16	10	16	81	80	42
Dartford	42	16	10	16	79	88	42
Chelmsford City	42	16	9	17	73	85	41
Tonbridge	42	14	12	16	74	65	40
Yeovil Town	42	14	11	17	83	85	39
Bath City	42	15	8	19	56	78	38
Exeter City Reserves	42	10	10	22	52	89	30
Merthyr Tydfil	42	9	11	22	72	95	29
Barry Town	42	6	11	25	39	84	23
Kidderminster Harriers	42	7	10	25	60	83	20
Llanelly	42	5	8	29	39	123	18

1957-58

Gravesend & Northfleet	42	27	5	10	109	71	59
Bedford Town	42	25	7	10	112	64	57
Chelmsford City	42	24	9	9	93	57	57
Weymouth	42	25	5	12	90	61	55
Worcester City	42	23	7	12	95	59	53
Cheltenham Town	42	21	10	11	115	66	52
Hereford United	42	21	6	15	79	56	48
Kettering Town	42	18	9	15	99	76	45
Headington Town	42	18	7	17	90	83	43
Poole Town	42	17	9	16	82	81	43
Hasting United	42	13	15	14	78	77	41
Gloucester City	42	17	7	18	70	70	41
Yeovil Town	42	16	9	17	70	84	41
Dartford	42	14	9	19	66	92	37
Lovells Athletic	42	15	6	21	60	83	36
Bath City	42	13	9	20	65	64	35
Guildford City	42	12	10	20	58	92	34
Tonbridge	42	16	7	22	77	100	33
Exeter City Reserves	42	12	8	22	60	94	32
Barry Town	42	11	9	22	72	101	31
Kidderminster Harriers	42	10	10	22	60	101	30
Merthyr Tydfil	42	9	3	30	69	137	21

1958-59

North-Western Zone

Hereford United	34	22	5	7	80	37	49
Kettering Town	34	20	7	7	83	63	47
Boston United	34	18	8	8	73	47	44
Cheltenham Town	34	20	4	10	65	47	44
Worcester City	34	19	4	11	74	47	42
Bath City	34	17	5	12	89	62	39
Wellington Town	34	15	9	10	74	58	39
Nuneaton Borough	34	17	5	12	76	66	39
Wisbech Town	34	16	5	13	77	54	37
Headington United	34	16	3	15	76	61	35
Barry Town	34	15	5	14	64	67	35
Merthyr Tydfil	34	16	3	15	54	59	35
Gloucester City	34	12	6	16	50	65	30
Corby Town	34	10	8	16	59	79	28
Lovells Athletic	34	10	3	21	51	70	23
Rugby Town	34	7	6	21	45	93	20
Kidderminster Harriers	34	7	3	24	42	94	17
Burton Albion	34	3	3	28	41	104	9

South-Eastern Zone

Bedford Town	32	21	6	5	90	41	48
Gravesend & Northfleet	32	21	2	9	79	54	44
Dartford	32	20	3	9	77	41	43
Yeovil Town	32	17	8	7	60	41	42
Weymouth	32	13	11	8	61	43	37
Chelmsford City	32	12	12	8	74	53	36
King's Lynn	32	14	5	13	70	63	33
Poole Town	32	12	8	12	60	65	32
Cambridge City	32	12	7	13	61	54	31
Hastings United	32	13	5	14	60	59	31
Tonbridge	32	14	3	15	51	59	31
Cambridge United	32	11	8	13	55	77	30
Trowbridge Town	32	12	4	16	53	75	28
Exeter City Reserves	32	7	12	13	47	71	26
Guildford City	11	7	6	19	45	67	20
Clacton Town	32	6	7	19	44	81	19
Yiewsley	32	3	7	22	36	78	13

1959-60

Premier Division

Bath City	42	32	3	7	116	50	67
Headington United	42	23	8	11	78	61	54
Weymouth	42	22	9	11	93	69	53
Cheltenham Town	42	21	6	15	82	68	48
Cambridge City	42	18	11	13	81	72	47
Chelmsford Town	42	19	7	16	90	70	45
Bedford Town	42	21	3	18	97	85	45
King's Lynn	42	17	11	14	89	78	45
Boston United	42	17	10	15	83	80	44
Wisbech Town	42	17	10	15	81	84	44
Yeovil Town	42	17	8	17	81	73	42
Hereford United	42	15	12	15	70	74	42
Tonbridge	42	16	8	18	79	73	40
Hastings United	42	16	8	18	63	77	40
Wellington Town	42	13	11	18	63	78	37
Dartford	42	15	7	20	64	82	37
Gravesend & Northfleet	42	14	8	20	69	84	36
Worcester City	42	13	10	19	72	89	36
Nuneaton Borough	42	11	11	20	64	78	33
Barry Town	42	14	5	23	78	103	33
Poole Town	42	10	8	24	69	96	28
Kettering Town	42	9	10	23	60	90	28

First Division

Clacton Town	42	27	5	10	106	69	59
Romford	42	21	11	10	65	40	53
Folkestone Town	42	23	5	14	93	71	51
Exeter City Reserves	42	23	3	16	85	62	49
Guildford City	42	19	9	14	79	56	47
Sittingbourne	42	20	7	15	66	55	47
Margate	42	20	6	16	88	77	46
Trowbridge Town	42	18	9	15	90	78	45
Cambridge United	42	18	9	15	71	72	45
Yiewsley	42	17	10	15	83	69	44
Bexleyheath & Welling	42	16	11	15	85	77	43
Merthyr Tydfil	42	16	10	16	63	65	42
Ramsgate Athletic	42	16	8	18	83	84	40
Ashford Town	42	14	12	16	61	70	40
Tunbridge Wells United	42	17	5	20	77	73	39
Hinckley Athletic	42	14	8	20	62	75	36
Gloucester City	42	13	9	20	56	84	35
Dover	42	14	6	22	59	85	34
Kidderminster Harriers	42	14	6	22	59	97	34
Corby Town	42	15	3	24	75	91	33
Burton Albion	42	11	10	21	52	79	32
Rugby Town	42	10	11	21	67	91	31

1960-61

Premier Division

Oxford United	42	28	5	9	118	46	61
Bath City	42	25	7	10	102	70	57
Guildford City	42	24	8	10	79	49	56
Yeovil Town	42	23	8	11	97	59	54
Chelmsford City	42	19	12	11	74	60	50
Weymouth	42	20	7	15	80	64	47
Kettering Town	42	21	5	16	90	84	47
Hereford United	42	21	2	19	81	68	44
Cambridge City	42	18	8	16	70	71	44
Bexleyheath & Welling	42	19	5	18	69	75	43
Romford	42	15	9	18	63	70	39
Cambridge United	42	13	12	17	76	78	38
Wellington Town	42	14	10	18	75	78	38
Gravesend & Northfleet	42	17	4	21	59	92	38
Bedford Town	42	16	5	21	73	79	37
Worcester City	42	15	7	20	51	64	37
Merthyr Tydfil	42	13	11	18	62	80	37
Clacton Town	42	13	10	19	74	91	36
Tonbridge	42	10	14	18	71	92	34
King's Lynn	42	12	8	22	59	74	32
Folkestone Town	42	12	6	24	64	103	30
Cheltenham Town	42	9	7	26	48	86	25

First Division

Wisbech Town	38	21	11	6	76	42	53
Poole Town	38	23	6	9	81	47	52
Dartford	38	21	8	9	89	50	50
Rugby Town	38	20	9	9	82	49	49
Margate	38	20	6	12	73	55	46
Corby Town	38	19	6	13	82	60	44
Sittingbourne	38	16	12	10	69	51	44
Dover	38	19	6	13	66	55	44
Yiewsley	38	18	6	14	64	51	42
Barry Town	38	14	11	13	55	51	39
Ashford Town	38	14	11	13	66	70	39
Hinckley Athletic	38	15	8	15	75	65	38
Burton Albion	38	16	5	17	70	79	37
Nuneaton Borough	38	12	12	14	63	69	36
Tunbridge Wells United	38	12	7	19	60	85	31
Canterbury City	38	11	8	19	60	82	30
Ramsgate Athletic	38	10	9	19	48	70	29
Trowbridge Town	38	9	9	20	45	69	27
Gloucester City	38	6	4	28	46	104	16
Hastings United	38	5	4	29	45	115	14

1961-62

Premier Division

Oxford United	42	28	5	9	118	46	61
Bath City	42	25	7	10	102	70	57
Guildford City	42	24	8	10	79	49	56
Yeovil Town	42	23	8	11	97	59	54
Chelmsford City	42	19	12	11	74	60	50
Weymouth	42	20	7	15	80	64	47
Kettering Town	42	21	5	16	90	84	47
Hereford United	42	21	2	19	81	68	44
Cambridge City	42	18	8	16	70	71	44
Bexleyheath & Welling	42	19	5	18	69	75	43
Romford	42	15	9	18	63	70	39
Cambridge United	42	13	12	17	76	78	38
Wellington United	42	14	10	18	75	78	38
Gravesend & Northfleet	42	17	4	21	59	92	38
Bedford Town	42	16	5	21	73	79	37
Worcester City	42	15	7	20	51	64	37
Merthyr Tydfil	42	13	11	18	62	80	37
Clacton Town	42	13	10	19	74	91	36
Tonbridge	42	10	14	18	71	92	34
King's Lynn	42	12	8	22	59	74	32
Folkestone Town	42	12	6	24	64	103	30
Cheltenham	42	9	7	26	48	86	25

First Division

Wisbech Town	38	21	11	6	76	42	53
Poole Town	38	23	6	9	81	47	52
Dartford	38	21	8	9	89	50	50
Rugby Town	38	20	9	9	82	49	49
Margate	38	20	6	12	73	55	46
Corby Town	38	19	6	13	82	60	44
Sittingbourne	38	16	12	10	69	51	44
Dover	38	19	6	13	66	55	44
Yiewsley	38	18	6	14	64	51	42
Barry Town	38	14	11	13	55	51	39
Ashford Town	38	14	11	13	66	70	39
Hinckley Athletic	38	15	8	15	75	65	38
Burton Albion	38	16	5	17	70	79	37
Nuneaton Borough	38	12	12	14	63	69	36
Tunbridge Wells United	38	12	7	19	60	85	31
Canterbury City	38	11	8	19	60	82	30
Ramsgate Athletic	38	10	9	19	48	70	29
Trowbridge Town	38	9	9	20	45	69	27
Gloucester City	38	6	4	28	46	104	16
Hastings United	38	5	4	29	45	115	14

1962-63

Premier Division

Cambridge City	40	25	6	9	99	64	56
Cambridge United	40	23	7	10	74	50	53
Weymouth	40	20	11	9	82	43	51
Guildford City	40	20	11	9	70	50	51
Kettering Town	40	22	7	11	66	49	51
Wellington Town	40	19	9	12	71	49	47
Dartford	40	19	9	12	61	54	47
Chelmsford City	40	18	10	12	63	50	46
Bedford Town	40	18	8	14	61	45	44
Bath City	40	18	6	16	58	56	42
Yeovil Town	40	15	10	15	64	54	40
Romford	40	14	11	15	73	68	39
Bexleyheath & Welling	40	13	11	16	55	63	37
Hereford United	40	14	7	19	56	66	35
Merthyr Tydfil	40	15	4	21	54	71	34
Rugby Town	40	14	5	21	65	76	33
Wisbech Town	40	15	3	22	64	84	33
Worcester City	40	12	9	19	47	65	33
Poole Town	40	10	12	18	54	66	32
Gravesend & Northfleet	40	10	3	27	62	91	23
Clacton Town	40	3	7	30	50	135	13

First Division

Margate	38	21	13	4	86	47	55
Hinckley Athletic	38	22	9	7	66	38	53
Hastings United	38	22	8	8	86	36	52
Nuneaton Borough	38	21	10	7	82	41	52
Tonbridge	38	22	8	8	81	51	52
Dover	38	22	7	9	78	56	51
Corby Town	38	19	8	11	79	50	46
King's Lynn	38	19	7	15	76	66	45
Cheltenham Town	38	18	7	13	83	52	43
Folkestone Town	38	15	10	13	79	57	40
Canterbury City	38	14	8	16	42	56	36
Yiewsley	38	11	10	17	63	71	32
Ramsgate Athletic	38	12	7	19	58	82	31
Trowbridge Town	38	11	9	18	50	81	31
Burton Albion	38	10	10	18	48	76	30
Gloucester City	38	9	11	18	42	78	29
Sittingbourne	38	12	3	23	56	75	27
Ashford Town	38	9	6	23	58	76	24
Barry Town	38	6	5	27	35	75	17
Tunbridge Wells United	38	6	2	30	43	118	14

1963-64

Premier Division

Yeovil Town	42	29	5	8	93	36	63
Chelmsford City	42	26	7	9	99	55	59
Bath City	42	24	9	9	88	51	57
Guildford City	42	21	9	12	90	55	51
Romford	42	20	9	13	71	58	49
Hastings United	42	20	8	14	75	61	48
Weymouth	42	20	7	15	65	53	47
Bedford Town	42	19	9	14	71	68	47
Cambridge United	42	17	9	16	92	77	43
Cambridge City	42	17	9	16	76	70	43
Wisbech Town	42	17	8	17	64	68	42
Bexley United	42	16	10	16	70	77	42
Dartford	42	16	8	18	56	71	40
Worcester City	42	12	15	15	70	74	39
Nuneaton Borough	42	15	8	19	58	61	38
Rugby Town	42	15	8	19	68	86	38
Margate	42	12	13	17	68	81	37
Wellington Town	42	12	9	21	73	85	33
Merthyr Tydfil	42	12	8	22	69	108	32
Hereford United	42	12	7	23	58	86	31
Kettering Town	42	10	5	27	49	89	25
Hinckley Athletic	42	7	6	29	51	104	20

First Division

Folkstone Town	42	28	7	7	82	38	63
King's Lynn	42	28	5	9	94	44	61
Cheltenham Town	42	25	10	7	92	49	60
Tonbridge	42	24	11	7	98	54	59
Corby town	42	24	7	11	114	56	55
Stevenage Town	42	21	6	15	70	59	48
Ashford Town	42	19	9	14	73	57	47
Burton Albion	42	19	8	15	76	70	46
Poole Town	42	17	11	14	75	61	45
Dover	42	18	9	15	86	75	45
Canterbury City	42	16	12	14	66	66	44
Crawley Town	42	20	2	20	81	71	42
Trowbridge Town	42	16	9	17	71	78	41
Clacton Town	42	19	1	22	76	88	39
Gloucester City	42	17	4	21	88	89	38
Yiewsley	42	15	8	19	63	77	38
Sittingbourne	42	15	8	19	52	70	38
Ramsgate Athletic	42	13	9	20	57	55	35
Tunbridge Wells Rangers	42	10	8	24	47	89	28
Gravesend & Northfleet	42	7	9	26	43	96	23
Deal Town	42	5	7	30	48	106	17
Barry Town	42	3	6	33	33	137	12

1964-65 Premier Division

Weymouth	42	24	8	10	99	50	56
Guildford City	42	21	12	9	73	49	54
Worcester City	42	22	6	14	100	62	50
Yeovil Town	42	18	14	10	76	55	50
Chelmsford City	42	21	8	13	86	77	50
Margate	42	20	9	13	88	79	49
Dartford	42	17	11	14	74	64	45
Nuneaton Borough	42	19	7	16	57	55	45
Cambridge United	42	16	11	15	78	66	43
Bedford Town	42	17	9	16	66	70	43
Cambridge City	42	16	9	17	72	69	41
Cheltenham Town	42	15	11	16	72	78	41
Folkestone Town	42	17	7	18	72	79	41
Romford	42	17	7	18	61	70	41
King's Lynn	42	13	13	16	56	79	39
Tonbridge	42	10	16	16	66	75	36
Wellington Town	42	13	10	19	63	78	36
Rugby Town	42	15	6	21	71	98	36
Wisbech Town	42	14	6	22	75	91	34
Bexley United	42	14	5	23	67	74	33
Hastings United	42	9	14	19	58	86	32
Bath City	42	13	3	26	60	86	29

First Division

Hereford United	42	34	4	4	124	39	72
Wimbledon	42	24	13	5	108	52	61
Poole Town	42	26	6	10	92	56	58
Corby Town	42	24	7	11	88	55	55
Stevenage Town	42	19	13	10	83	43	51
Hillingdon Borough	42	21	7	14	105	63	49
Crawley Town	42	22	5	15	83	52	49
Merthyr Tydfil	42	20	9	13	75	59	49
Gloucester City	42	19	10	13	68	65	48
Burton Albion	42	20	7	15	83	75	47
Canterbury City	42	13	16	13	73	53	42
Kettering Town	42	14	13	15	74	64	41
Ramsgate Athletic	42	16	8	18	51	59	40
Dover	42	14	10	18	54	59	38
Hinckley Athletic	42	13	9	20	56	81	35
Trowbridge Town	42	13	5	24	68	106	31
Ashford Town	42	11	8	23	60	98	30
Barry Town	42	11	7	24	47	103	29
Deal Town	42	7	13	22	61	127	27
Tunbridge Wells Rangers	42	10	6	26	51	107	26
Gravesend & Northfleet	42	9	7	26	57	101	25
Sittingbourne	42	8	5	29	58	103	21

1965-66

Premier Division

Weymouth	42	22	13	7	70	35	57
Chelmsford City	42	21	12	9	74	50	54
Hereford United	42	21	10	11	81	49	52
Bedford Town	42	23	6	13	80	57	52
Wimbledon	42	20	10	12	80	47	50
Cambridge City	42	19	11	12	67	52	49
Romford	42	21	7	14	87	72	49
Worcester City	42	20	8	14	69	54	48
Yeovil Town	42	17	11	14	91	70	45
Cambridge United	42	18	9	15	72	64	45
King's Lynn	42	18	7	17	75	72	43
Corby Town	42	16	9	17	66	73	41
Wellington Town	42	13	13	16	65	70	39
Nuneaton Borough	42	15	8	19	60	74	38
Folkestone Town	42	14	9	19	53	75	37
Guildford City	42	14	8	20	70	84	36
Poole Town	42	14	7	21	61	75	35
Cheltenham Town	42	13	9	20	69	99	35
Dartford	42	13	7	22	62	69	33
Rugby Town	42	11	10	21	67	95	32
Tonbridge	42	11	6	25	63	101	28
Margate	42	8	10	24	66	111	26

First Division

Barnet	46	30	9	7	114	49	69
Hillingdon Borough	46	27	10	9	101	46	64
Burton Albion	46	28	8	10	121	60	64
Bath City	46	25	13	8	88	50	63
Hastings United	46	25	10	11	104	59	60
Wisbech Town	46	25	9	12	98	54	59
Canterbury City	46	25	8	13	89	66	58
Stevenage Town	46	23	9	14	86	49	55
Kettering Town	46	22	9	15	77	74	53
Merthyr Tydfil	46	22	6	18	95	68	50
Dunstable Town	46	15	14	17	76	72	44
Crawley Town	46	17	10	19	72	71	44
Bexley United	46	20	4	22	65	71	44
Trowbridge Town	46	16	11	19	79	81	43
Dover	46	17	8	21	59	62	42
Barry Town	46	16	10	20	72	94	42
Gravesend & Northfleet	46	16	9	21	84	86	41
Gloucester City	46	14	12	20	75	98	40
Sittingbourne	46	11	12	23	77	121	34
Ramsgate Athletic	46	9	15	22	35	76	33
Hinckley Athletic	46	10	12	24	59	93	32
Tunbridge Wells Rangers	46	12	8	26	47	88	32
Ashford Town	46	9	10	27	44	92	28
Deal Town	46	3	4	39	29	165	10

1966-67 Premier Division

Romford	42	22	8	12	80	60	52
Nuneaton Borough	42	21	9	12	82	54	51
Weymouth	42	18	14	10	64	40	50
Wimbledon	42	19	11	12	88	60	49
Barnet	42	18	13	11	86	66	49
Guildford City	42	19	10	13	65	51	48
Wellington Town	42	20	7	15	70	67	47
Cambridge United	42	16	13	13	75	67	45
Chelmsford City	42	15	15	12	66	59	45
Hereford United	42	16	12	14	79	61	44
King's Lynn	42	15	14	13	78	72	44
Cambridge City	42	15	13	14	66	70	43
Cheltenham Town	42	16	11	15	60	71	43
Yeovil Town	42	14	14	14	66	72	42
Burton Albion	42	17	5	20	63	71	39
Corby Town	42	15	9	18	60	75	39
Poole Town	42	14	11	17	52	65	39
Hillingdon Borough	42	11	13	18	49	70	35
Bath City	42	11	12	19	51	74	34
Worcester City	42	11	8	23	59	79	30
Bedford Town	42	8	13	21	54	72	29
Folkestone Town	42	6	15	21	44	81	27

First Division

Dover	46	29	12	5	92	35	70
Margate	46	31	7	8	127	54	69
Stevenage Town	46	29	8	9	90	32	66
Hastings United	46	25	16	5	89	45	66
Kettering Town	46	27	9	10	105	62	63
Canterbury City	46	26	8	12	81	48	60
Ramsgate Athletic	46	23	8	15	79	62	54
Dartford	46	19	15	12	92	67	53
Tonbridge	46	21	10	15	91	69	52
Trowbridge Town	46	20	12	14	73	60	52
Ashford Town	46	18	8	20	74	68	44
Merthyr Tydfil	46	17	9	20	81	71	43
Gloucester City	46	18	6	22	69	83	42
Canterbury City	46	17	8	21	57	75	42
Wisbech Town	46	16	9	21	87	93	41
Bexley United	46	13	15	18	53	69	41
Banbury United	46	13	14	19	88	100	40
Rugby Town	46	15	7	24	57	77	37
Dunstable Town	46	14	6	26	55	87	34
Barry Town	46	11	11	24	62	89	33
Gravesend & Northfleet	46	11	9	26	63	106	31
Hinckley Athletic	46	10	8	28	44	100	28
Tunbridge Wells Rangers	46	4	15	27	31	96	23
Sittingbourne	46	5	10	31	44	136	20

1967-68

Premier Division

Chelmsford City	42	25	7	10	85	50	57
Wimbledon	42	24	7	11	85	47	55
Cambridge United	42	20	13	9	73	42	53
Cheltenham Town	42	23	7	12	97	67	53
Guildford City	42	18	13	11	56	43	49
Romford	42	20	8	14	72	60	48
Barnet	42	20	8	14	81	71	48
Margate	42	19	8	15	80	71	46
Wellington Town	42	16	13	13	70	66	45
Hillingdon Borough	42	18	9	155	53	54	45
King's Lynn	42	18	8	16	66	57	44
Yeovil Town	42	16	12	14	45	43	44
Weymouth	42	17	8	17	65	62	42
Hereford United	42	17	7	18	58	62	41
Nuneaton Borough	42	13	14	15	62	64	40
Dover	42	17	6	19	54	56	40
Poole Town	42	13	10	19	55	74	36
Stevenage Town	42	13	9	20	57	75	35
Burton Albion	42	14	6	22	51	73	34
Corby Town	42	7	13	22	40	77	27
Cambridge City	42	10	6	26	51	81	26
Hastings United	42	4	8	30	33	94	16

First Division

Worcester City	42	23	14	5	92	35	60
Kettering Town	42	24	10	8	88	40	58
Bedford Town	42	24	7	11	101	40	55
Rugby Town	42	20	15	7	72	44	55
Dartford	42	23	9	10	70	48	55
Bath City	42	21	12	9	78	51	54
Banbury United	42	22	9	11	79	59	53
Ramsgate Athletic	42	17	7	8	70	37	51
Merthyr Tydfil	42	18	13	11	80	66	49
Tonbridge	42	18	9	15	76	71	45
Canterbury City	42	16	11	15	66	63	43
Ashford Town	42	18	6	18	73	78	42
Brentwood Town	42	16	9	17	63	73	41
Bexley United	42	12	13	17	56	64	37
Trowbridge Town	42	12	11	19	64	70	35
Gloucester City	42	12	9	21	54	68	33
Wisbech Town	42	11	10	21	43	78	32
Crawley Town	42	10	8	24	54	85	28
Folkestone Town	42	10	7	25	49	80	27
Dunstable Town	42	8	10	24	44	94	26
Barry Town	42	7	12	23	36	81	26
Gravesend & Northfleet	42	6	7	29	28	112	19

1968-69

Premier Division

Cambridge United	42	27	5	10	72	39	59
Hillingdon Borough	42	24	10	8	68	47	58
Wimbledon	42	21	12	9	66	48	54
King's Lynn	42	20	9	13	68	60	49
Worcester City	42	19	11	12	53	47	49
Romford	42	18	12	12	58	52	48
Weymouth	42	16	15	11	52	41	47
Yeovil Town	42	16	13	13	52	50	45
Kettering Town	42	18	8	16	51	55	44
Dover	42	17	9	16	66	61	43
Nuneaton Borough	42	17	7	18	74	58	41
Barnet	42	15	10	17	72	66	40
Chelmsford City	42	17	6	19	56	58	40
Hereford United	42	15	9	18	66	62	39
Telford United	42	14	10	18	62	61	38
Poole Town	42	16	6	20	75	76	38
Burton Albion	42	16	5	21	55	71	37
Margate	42	14	7	21	79	90	35
Cheltenham Town	42	15	5	22	55	64	35
Bedford Town	42	11	12	19	46	63	34
Rugby Town	42	10	6	26	38	83	26
Guildford City	42	7	11	24	41	73	25

First Division

Brentwood Town	42	26	12	4	44	37	64
Bath City	42	26	10	6	96	40	62
Gloucester City	42	25	9	8	100	53	59
Crawley Town	42	21	13	8	65	32	55
Corby Town	42	22	6	14	81	65	50
Dartford	42	20	8	14	79	51	48
Ramsgate Athletic	42	19	9	14	72	57	47
Salisbury	42	20	6	16	69	52	46
Cambridge City	42	18	10	14	73	63	46
Banbury United	42	16	12	14	67	72	44
Trowbridge Town	42	15	8	19	70	60	44
Folkestone Town	42	19	5	18	53	59	43
Canterbury City	42	17	7	18	67	63	41
Ashford Town	42	16	8	18	72	73	40
Bexley United	42	15	9	18	62	75	39
Hastings United	42	15	9	18	58	69	39
Wisbech Town	42	11	13	18	57	70	35
Dunstable Town	42	14	6	22	73	99	34
Merthyr Tydfil	42	10	7	25	49	101	27
Barry Town	42	8	10	24	39	78	26
Gravesend & Northfleet	42	8	9	25	51	79	25
Tonbridge	42	2	6	34	36	137	10

1969-70

Premier Division

Cambridge United	42	26	6	10	86	49	58
Yeovil Town	42	25	7	10	78	48	57
Chelmsford City	42	20	11	11	76	58	51
Weymouth	42	18	14	10	59	37	50
Wimbledon	42	19	12	11	64	52	50
Hillingdon Borough	42	19	12	11	56	50	50
Barnet	42	16	15	11	71	54	47
Telford United	42	18	10	14	61	62	46
Brentwood Town	42	16	13	13	61	38	45
Hereford United	42	18	9	15	74	65	45
Bath City	42	18	8	16	63	55	44
King's Lynn	42	16	11	15	72	68	43
Margate	42	17	8	17	70	64	42
Dover	42	15	10	17	51	50	40
Kettering Town	42	18	3	21	64	75	39
Worcester City	42	14	10	18	35	44	38
Romford	42	13	11	18	50	62	37
Poole Town	42	8	19	15	48	57	35
Gloucester City	42	12	9	21	53	73	33
Nuneaton Borough	42	11	10	21	52	74	32
Crawley Town	42	6	15	21	53	101	27
Burton Albion	42	3	9	30	24	82	15

First Division

Bedford Town	42	26	9	7	93	37	61
Cambridge City	42	26	8	8	104	43	60
Dartford	42	24	11	7	33	46	58
Ashford Town	42	19	15	8	71	43	53
Rugby Town	42	20	10	12	82	66	50
Trowbridge Town	42	20	8	14	72	65	48
Hastings United	42	18	11	13	67	51	47
Guildford City	42	19	9	14	68	58	54
Cheltenham Town	42	20	5	17	78	81	45
Canterbury City	42	15	13	14	61	57	43
Corby Town	42	14	15	13	58	53	43
Folkestone Town	42	19	5	18	57	55	43
Ramsgate Athletic	42	14	13	15	53	57	41
Salisbury	42	13	13	16	48	53	39
Gravesend & Northfleet	42	13	11	18	62	71	37
Bexley United	42	10	11	21	58	76	31
Dunstable Town	42	11	9	22	52	82	31
Merthyr Tydfil	42	9	11	22	40	80	29
Barry Town	42	11	6	25	39	76	28
Wisbech Town	42	8	9	25	58	116	25
Tonbridge	42	4	10	28	46	101	18

1970-71

Premier Division

Yeovil Town	42	25	7	10	66	31	57
Cambridge City	42	22	11	9	67	38	55
Romford	42	23	9	10	63	42	55
Hereford United	42	23	8	11	71	53	54
Chelmsford City	42	20	11	11	61	32	51
Barnet	42	18	14	10	69	49	50
Bedford Town	42	20	10	12	62	46	50
Wimbledon	42	20	8	14	72	54	48
Worcester City	42	20	8	14	61	46	48
Weymouth	42	14	16	12	64	48	44
Dartford	42	15	12	15	53	51	42
Dover	42	16	9	17	64	63	41
Margate	42	15	10	17	64	70	40
Hillingdon Borough	42	17	6	19	61	68	40
Bath City	42	13	12	17	48	68	38
Nuneaton Borough	42	12	12	18	43	66	36
Telford United	42	13	8	21	64	70	34
Poole Town	42	14	6	22	57	75	34
King's Lynn	42	11	7	24	44	67	29
Ashford Town	42	8	13	21	52	86	29
Kettering Town	42	8	11	23	48	84	27
Gloucester City	42	6	10	26	34	81	21

First Division

Guildford City	38	22	10	6	76	36	54
Merthyr Tydfil	38	19	12	7	52	33	50
Gravesend & Northfleet	38	19	10	9	74	42	48
Folkestone	38	20	8	10	83	53	48
Burton Albion	38	19	10	9	56	37	48
Rugby Town	38	17	14	7	58	40	48
Ramsgate Athletic	38	20	5	13	83	54	45
Trowbridge Town	38	19	7	12	78	55	45
Bexley United	38	17	11	10	57	45	45
Crawley Town	38	15	11	12	84	68	41
Hastings United	38	13	12	13	51	50	38
Banbury United	38	13	11	14	58	53	37
Corby Town	38	14	8	16	57	60	36
Salisbury	38	13	7	18	56	60	33
Cheltenham Town	38	8	15	15	44	58	31
Stevenage Athletic	38	12	7	19	55	79	21
Tonbridge	38	8	8	22	48	83	24
Barry Town	38	9	6	23	35	82	24
Dunstable Town	38	8	4	26	32	81	20
Canterbury City	38	5	4	29	37	105	14

1971-72

Premier Division

Chelmsford City	42	28	6	8	109	46	62
Hereford United	42	24	12	6	68	30	60
Dover	42	20	11	11	67	45	51
Barnet	42	21	7	14	80	57	49
Dartford	42	20	8	14	75	68	48
Weymouth	42	21	5	16	69	43	47
Yeovil Town	42	18	11	13	67	51	47
Hillingdon Borough	42	20	6	16	64	58	46
Margate	42	19	8	15	74	68	46
Wimbledon	42	19	7	16	75	64	45
Romford	42	16	13	13	54	49	45
Guildford City	42	20	5	17	71	65	45
Telford United	42	18	7	17	83	68	43
Nuneaton Borough	42	16	10	16	46	47	42
Bedford Town	42	16	9	17	59	66	41
Worcester City	42	17	7	18	46	57	41
Cambridge City	42	12	14	16	68	71	38
Folkestone	42	14	7	21	58	64	35
Poole Town	42	9	11	22	43	72	29
Bath City	42	11	4	27	45	86	26
Merthyr Tydfil	42	7	8	27	29	93	22
Gravesend & Northfleet	42	5	6	31	30	110	16

First Division (North)

Kettering Town	34	23	6	5	70	27	52
Burton Albion	34	18	13	3	58	27	49
Cheltenham Town	34	20	4	10	72	51	44
Rugby Town	34	18	7	9	52	36	43
Wellingborough Town	34	15	10	9	73	44	40
Stourbridge	34	13	14	7	59	42	40
King's Lynn	34	14	11	9	62	45	39
Corby Town	34	15	9	10	47	35	39
Ilkeston Town	34	14	11	9	44	38	39
Banbury United	34	14	5	15	54	46	33
Bury Town	34	14	5	15	47	44	33
Wealdstone	34	14	5	15	51	58	33
Lockheed Leamington	34	15	3	16	41	52	33
Gloucester City	34	8	8	18	46	61	24
Stevenage Athletic	34	8	8	18	41	69	24
Bletchley	34	7	7	20	36	70	21
Dunstable Town	34	5	7	22	29	75	17
Barry Town	34	1	7	26	22	84	9

First Division (South)

Waterlooville	30	15	9	6	40	22	39
Ramsgate Athletic	30	14	11	5	42	27	39
Maidstone United	30	14	10	6	48	28	38
Crawley Town	30	15	5	10	67	55	35
Metropolitan Police	30	15	3	12	48	41	33
Tonbridge	30	12	9	9	37	34	33
Bexley United	30	14	4	12	52	46	32
Basingstoke Town	30	14	4	12	37	36	32
Andover	30	11	9	10	32	34	31
Ashford Town	30	12	4	14	43	48	28
Salisbury	30	10	7	13	45	44	27
Winchester City	30	10	7	13	40	47	27
Hastings United	30	10	7	13	28	42	27
Trowbridge Town	30	8	7	15	41	49	23
Canterbury City	30	7	8	15	39	56	22
Woodford Town	30	4	6	20	22	52	14

1972-73

Premier Division

Kettering Town	42	20	17	5	74	44	57
Yeovil Town	42	21	14	7	67	61	56
Dover	42	23	9	10	61	68	55
Chelmsford City	42	23	7	12	75	43	53
Worcester City	42	20	13	9	68	47	53
Weymouth	42	20	12	10	72	51	52
Margate	42	17	15	10	80	60	49
Bedford Town	42	16	15	11	43	36	47
Nuneaton Borough	42	16	14	12	51	41	46
Telford United	42	12	20	10	57	47	44
Cambridge City	42	14	15	13	64	53	43
Wimbledon	42	14	14	14	50	50	42
Barnet	42	15	11	16	60	59	41
Romford	42	17	5	20	51	65	39
Hillingdon Borough	42	16	6	20	52	58	38
Dartford	42	12	11	19	49	63	35
Folkestone	42	11	11	20	41	72	33
Guildford City	42	10	11	21	59	84	31
Ramsgate	42	9	13	20	35	61	31
Poole Town	42	10	10	22	50	88	30
Burton Albion	42	9	7	26	43	81	25
Waterlooville	42	4	16	22	33	63	24

First Division (North)

Grantham	42	29	8	5	113	41	66
Atherstone Town	42	23	11	8	82	48	57
Cheltenham Town	42	24	8	10	87	47	56
Rugby Town	42	20	10	12	60	47	50
Kidderminster Harriers	42	19	12	11	67	56	50
Merthyr Tydfil	42	17	12	13	51	40	46
Corby Town	42	14	16	12	62	56	44
Stourbridge	42	16	11	15	70	64	43
Gloucester City	42	18	7	17	55	64	43
Bromsgrove Rovers	42	17	8	17	63	54	42
Redditch United	42	18	6	18	58	59	42
Banbury United	42	18	5	19	60	53	41
Wellingborough Town	42	17	7	18	58	71	41
King's Lynn	42	14	12	16	45	49	40
Lockheed Leamington	42	13	12	17	51	58	38
Enderby Town	42	12	14	16	50	61	38
Stevenage Athletic	42	12	13	17	50	63	37
Tamworth	42	14	8	20	45	65	36
Bury Town	42	13	9	20	52	69	35
Barry Town	42	11	10	21	45	71	32
Ilkeston Town	42	9	6	27	35	68	24
Bedworth United	42	10	3	29	42	94	23

First Division (South)

Maidstone United	42	25	12	5	90	38	62
Tonbridge	42	26	7	9	70	44	59
Ashford Town	42	24	7	11	90	40	55
Bideford	42	19	14	9	70	43	52
Minehead	42	20	12	10	65	47	52
Gravesend & Northfleet	42	22	7	13	81	55	51
Bath City	42	18	11	13	56	54	47
Wealdstone	42	16	12	14	81	61	44
Bletchley Town	42	14	13	15	54	51	41
Hastings United	42	14	13	15	53	53	41
Andover	42	15	11	16	62	70	41
Canterbury City	42	14	12	16	51	59	40
Basingstoke Town	42	14	12	16	48	57	40
Crawley Town	42	14	11	17	59	76	39
Metropolitan Police	42	15	8	19	82	75	38
Trowbridge Town	42	15	8	19	65	77	38
Bexley United	42	12	14	16	54	64	38
Salisbury	42	14	10	18	49	60	38
Bognor Regis Town	42	12	9	21	41	66	33
Dorchester Town	42	10	12	20	47	73	32
Winchester City	42	7	11	24	41	79	25
Dunstable Town	42	4	10	28	38	105	18

1973-74

Dartford	42	22	13	7	67	37	57
Grantham	42	18	13	11	70	49	49
Chelmsford City	42	19	10	13	62	49	48
Kettering Town	42	16	16	10	62	51	48
Maidstone United	42	16	14	12	54	43	46
Yeovil Town	42	13	20	9	45	39	46
Weymouth	42	19	7	16	60	41	45
Barnet	42	18	9	15	55	46	45
Nuneaton Borough	42	13	19	10	54	47	45
Cambridge City	42	15	12	15	45	54	42
Atherstone Town	42	16	9	17	61	59	41
Wimbledon	42	15	11	16	50	56	41
Telford United	42	12	16	14	51	57	40
Dover	42	11	17	14	41	46	39
Tonbridge	42	12	15	15	38	45	39
Romford	42	11	17	14	39	52	39
Margate	42	15	8	19	56	63	38
Guildford City	42	13	11	18	48	67	37
Worcester City	42	11	14	17	53	67	36
Bedford Town	42	11	14	17	38	51	36
Folkestone	42	11	12	19	56	65	34
Hillingdon Borough	42	9	15	18	44	65	33

First Division (North)

Stourbridge	42	29	11	2	103	36	69
Burton Albion	42	27	9	6	88	32	63
Cheltenham Town	42	24	9	10	75	51	56
AP Leamington	42	21	12	9	82	45	54
Enderby Town	42	19	14	9	60	36	52
Witney Town	42	20	10	12	69	55	50
Stevenage Athletic	42	19	11	12	65	46	49
Banbury United	42	19	11	12	69	57	49
King's Lynn	42	19	10	13	65	50	48
Kidderminster Harriers	42	15	14	13	67	53	44
Merthyr Tydfil	42	16	12	14	70	61	44
Redditch United	42	14	11	17	56	73	39
Bromsgrove Rovers	42	14	10	18	54	61	38
Bedworth United	42	14	10	18	50	77	38
Tamworth	42	13	11	18	42	51	37
Corby Town	42	12	11	19	40	57	35
Bletchley Town	42	10	15	17	47	71	35
Barry Town	42	10	8	24	53	85	29
Bury Town	42	10	6	26	57	84	26
Gloucester City	42	10	6	26	52	81	26
Wellingborough Town	42	7	9	26	42	87	23
Dunstable Town	42	5	11	26	26	83	21

First Division (South)

Wealdstone	38	26	7	5	75	35	59
Bath City	38	20	8	10	55	34	48
Waterlooville	38	16	15	7	55	38	47
Minehead	38	16	15	7	69	52	47
Bideford	38	17	12	9	61	51	46
Poole Town	38	18	9	11	67	47	45
Bexley United	38	18	7	13	50	42	43
Hastings United	38	16	9	13	45	36	41
Basingstoke Town	38	14	11	13	55	44	39
Gravesend & Northfleet	38	13	13	12	58	52	39
Bognor Regis Town	38	13	12	13	48	54	38
Ashford Town	38	14	8	16	41	42	36
Ramsgate	38	13	9	16	46	44	35
Dorchester Town	38	10	13	15	40	48	33
Canterbury City	38	9	12	17	37	46	30
Trowbridge Town	38	8	14	16	44	61	30
Salisbury	38	10	9	19	40	60	29
Metropolitan Police	38	9	11	18	37	61	29
Andover	38	11	3	24	38	70	25
Crawley Town	38	6	9	23	35	79	21

1974-75

Premier Division

Wimbledon	42	25	7	10	63	33	57
Nuneaton Borough	42	23	8	11	56	37	54
Yeovil Town	42	21	9	12	64	34	51
Kettering Town	42	20	10	12	73	41	50
Burton Albion	42	18	13	11	54	48	49
Bath City	42	20	8	14	63	50	48
Margate	42	17	12	13	64	64	46
Wealdstone	42	17	11	14	62	61	45
Telford United	42	16	13	13	55	56	45
Chelmsford City	42	16	12	14	62	51	44
Grantham	42	16	11	15	70	62	43
Dover	42	15	13	14	43	53	43
Maidstone United	42	15	12	15	52	50	42
Atherstone Town	42	14	14	14	48	53	42
Weymouth	42	13	13	16	66	58	39
Stourbridge	42	13	12	17	56	70	38
Cambridge	42	11	14	17	51	56	36
Tonbridge	42	11	12	19	44	66	34
Romford	42	10	13	19	46	62	33
Dartford	42	9	13	20	52	70	31
Barnet	42	10	9	23	44	76	29
Guildford & Dorking United	42	10	5	27	45	82	25

First Division (North)

Bedford Town	42	28	9	5	85	33	65
Dunstable Town	42	25	8	9	105	61	58
AP Leamington	42	25	7	10	68	48	57
Redditch United	42	22	12	8	76	40	56
Worcester City	42	24	8	10	84	50	56
Cheltenham Town	42	21	9	12	72	53	51
Tamworth	42	21	8	13	74	53	50
King's Lynn	42	19	10	13	71	64	48
Enderby Town	42	17	12	13	61	48	46
Banbury United	42	18	10	14	52	51	46
Stevenage Athletic	42	16	13	13	62	48	45
Bromsgrove Rovers	42	18	9	15	63	52	45
Merthyr Tydfil	42	11	15	16	53	64	37
Witney Town	42	16	4	22	57	76	36
Corby Town	42	11	13	18	60	57	35
Kidderminster Harriers	42	12	11	19	50	66	35
Gloucester City	42	13	8	21	55	75	34
Wellingborough Town	42	9	13	20	42	61	31
Barry Town	42	10	10	22	49	73	30
Bedworth United	42	9	9	24	60	91	27
Milton Keynes City	42	7	5	30	48	100	19
Bury Town	42	5	7	30	36	119	17

First Division (South)

Gravesend & Northfleet	38	24	12	2	70	30	60
Hillingdon Borough	38	22	8	8	87	45	52
Minehead	38	21	9	8	74	33	51
Ramsgate	38	19	11	8	70	37	49
Bexley United	38	19	7	12	61	44	45
Waterlooville	38	17	11	10	67	49	45
Ashford Town	38	16	12	10	64	55	44
Basingstoke Town	38	16	11	11	64	50	43
Canterbury City	38	16	9	13	54	43	41
Hastings United	38	13	14	11	54	45	40
Poole Town	38	11	13	14	50	60	35
Metropolitan Police	38	11	13	14	54	66	35
Folkestone & Shepway	38	10	14	14	53	57	34
Andover	38	12	8	18	52	71	32
Bognor Regis Town	38	10	11	17	49	64	31
Salisbury	38	9	11	18	45	66	29
Trowbridge Town	38	10	9	19	48	76	29
Bideford	38	10	8	20	40	71	28
Dorchester Town	38	8	10	20	40	63	26
Crawley Town	38	3	5	30	31	102	11

1975-76

Premier Division

Wimbledon	42	26	10	6	74	29	62
Yeovil Town	42	21	12	9	68	35	54
Atherstone Town	42	18	15	9	56	55	51
Maidstone United	42	17	16	9	52	39	50
Nuneaton Borough	42	16	18	8	41	33	50
Gravesend & Northfleet	42	16	18	8	49	47	50
Grantham	42	15	14	13	56	47	44
Dunstable Town	42	17	9	16	52	43	43
Bedford Town	42	13	17	12	55	51	43
Burton Albion	42	17	9	16	52	53	43
Margate	42	15	12	15	62	60	42
Hillingdon Borough	42	13	14	15	61	54	40
Telford United	42	14	12	16	54	51	40
Chelmsford City	42	13	14	15	52	57	40
Kettering Town	42	11	17	14	48	52	39
Bath City	42	11	16	15	62	57	38
Weymouth	42	13	9	20	51	67	35
Dover	42	8	18	16	51	60	34
Wealdstone	42	12	9	21	61	82	33
Tonbridge AFC	42	11	11	20	45	70	33
Cambridge City	42	8	15	19	41	67	31
Stourbridge	42	10	9	23	38	72	29

First Division (North)

Redditch United	42	29	11	2	101	39	69
AP Leamington	42	27	10	5	85	31	64
Witney Town	42	24	9	9	66	40	57
Worcester City	42	24	8	10	90	49	56
Cheltenham Town	42	20	10	12	87	55	50
Barry Town	42	19	10	13	52	47	48
King's Lynn	42	17	14	11	52	48	48
Tamworth	42	18	11	13	65	43	47
Barnet	42	15	12	15	56	56	42
Oswestry Town	42	16	8	18	63	71	40
Enderby Town	42	16	6	20	48	51	38
Banbury United	42	15	8	19	58	67	38
Merthyr Tydfil	42	11	15	16	59	67	37
Bromsgrove Rovers	42	13	11	18	49	65	37
Milton Keynes City	42	15	6	21	51	63	36
Bury Town	42	12	11	19	52	72	35
Gloucester City	42	13	9	20	49	78	35
Kidderminster Harriers	42	13	8	21	54	70	34
Bedworth United	42	8	18	16	41	66	34
Corby Town	42	11	10	21	50	65	32
Wellingborough Town	42	9	11	22	42	68	29
Stevenage Athletic	42	6	6	30	46	105	18

First Division (South)

Minehead	38	27	8	3	102	35	62
Dartford	38	26	4	8	84	46	56
Romford	38	21	9	8	66	37	51
Salisbury	38	17	11	10	73	53	45
Hastings United	38	15	15	8	67	51	45
Poole United	38	20	2	16	57	57	42
Bexley United	38	14	13	11	62	53	41
Waterlooville	38	13	13	12	62	54	39
Basingstoke Town	38	13	12	13	69	71	38
Ashford Town	38	14	8	16	67	73	36
Canterbury City	38	11	13	14	53	60	35
Folkestone & Shepway	38	10	14	14	36	51	34
Metropolitan Police	38	9	14	15	46	58	32
Trowbridge Town	38	11	10	17	48	75	32
Guildford & Dorking United	38	9	13	16	43	50	31
Bognor Regis Town	38	6	17	15	44	72	29
Ramsgate	38	9	10	19	57	76	28
Crawley Town	38	9	10	19	46	66	28
Andover	38	9	10	19	42	62	28
Dorchester Town	38	11	6	21	45	69	28

1976-77

Premier Division

Wimbledon	42	28	7	7	64	22	63
Minehead	42	23	12	7	73	39	58
Kettering Town	42	20	16	6	66	46	56
Bath City	42	20	15	7	51	30	55
Nuneaton Borough	42	20	11	11	52	35	51
Bedford Town	42	17	14	11	54	47	48
Yeovil Town	42	15	16	11	54	42	46
Dover	42	13	16	13	46	43	42
Grantham	42	14	12	16	55	50	40
Maidstone United	42	13	14	15	46	50	40
Gravesend & Northfleet	42	13	13	16	38	43	39
AP Leamington	42	12	15	15	44	53	39
Redditch United	42	12	14	16	45	54	38
Wealdstone	42	13	12	17	54	66	38
Hillingdon Borough	42	14	10	18	45	59	38
Atherstone Town	42	14	9	19	41	49	37
Weymouth	42	16	5	21	53	73	37
Dartford	42	13	10	19	52	57	36
Telford United	42	11	12	19	36	50	34
Chelmsford City	42	9	13	20	56	68	31
Burton Albion	42	10	10	22	41	52	30
Margate	42	9	10	23	47	85	28

First Division (North)

Worcester City	38	32	5	1	97	22	69
Cheltenham Town	38	23	8	7	85	35	54
Witney Town	38	21	8	9	48	31	50
Bromsgrove Rovers	38	20	8	10	61	37	48
Barry Town	38	19	8	11	62	45	46
Cambridge City	38	17	10	11	68	43	44
Stourbridge	38	17	9	12	48	35	43
Kidderminster Harriers	38	17	6	15	74	65	40
Banbury United	38	15	10	13	51	47	40
Gloucester City	38	18	4	16	70	81	40
Enderby Town	38	15	9	14	50	44	39
King's Lynn	38	13	11	14	47	53	37
Corby Town	38	11	13	14	56	64	35
Tamworth	38	11	13	14	49	58	35
Merthyr Tydfil	38	12	6	20	60	69	30
Oswestry Town	38	8	10	20	30	60	26
Wellingborough Town	38	8	7	23	37	73	23
Dunstable	38	7	7	24	38	84	21
Bedworth United	38	5	10	23	28	68	20
Milton Keynes City	38	7	6	25	31	76	20

First Division (South)

Barnet	34	23	8	3	65	25	54
Hastings United	34	18	11	5	47	18	47
Waterlooville	34	19	6	9	50	25	44
Dorchester Town	34	16	11	7	48	30	43
Salisbury	34	15	11	8	57	39	41
Romford	34	18	5	11	47	32	41
Poole Town	34	17	7	10	40	35	41
Trowbridge Town	34	15	8	11	47	39	38
Crawley Town	34	14	9	11	53	42	37
Folkestone & Shepway	34	12	11	11	39	42	35
Basingstoke Town	34	12	10	12	51	43	34
Canterbury City	34	6	16	12	36	46	28
Bognor Regis Town	34	9	9	16	33	50	27
Tonbridge AFC	34	9	9	16	33	50	27
Metropolitan Police	34	5	12	17	37	61	22
Andover	34	4	11	19	17	49	19
Ashford Town	34	5	8	21	32	65	18
Aylesbury United	34	5	6	23	27	68	16

1977-78

Premier Division

Bath City	42	22	18	2	83	32	62
Weymouth	42	21	16	5	64	36	58
Maidstone United	42	20	11	11	59	41	51
Worcester City	42	20	11	11	67	50	51
Gravesend & Northfleet	42	19	11	12	57	42	49
Kettering Town	42	18	11	13	58	48	47
Barnet	42	18	11	13	63	58	47
Wealdstone	42	16	14	12	54	48	46
Telford United	42	17	11	14	52	45	45
Nuneaton Borough	42	15	14	13	38	36	44
Dartford	42	14	15	13	57	65	43
Yeovil Town	42	14	14	14	57	49	42
Hastings United	42	15	9	18	49	60	39
Cheltenham Town	42	12	14	16	43	52	38
Hillingdon Borough	42	13	9	20	45	54	35
Atherstone Town	42	10	15	17	41	56	35
Redditch United	42	15	5	22	40	55	35
AP Leamington	42	11	13	18	34	57	35
Minehead	42	11	12	19	43	48	34
Dover	42	9	13	20	41	63	31
Bedford Town	42	8	13	21	51	75	29
Grantham	42	11	6	25	40	66	28

First Division (North)

Witney Town	38	20	15	3	54	27	55
Bridgend Town	38	20	9	9	59	45	49
Burton Albion	38	17	11	10	48	32	45
Enderby Town	38	17	10	11	59	44	44
Bromsgrove Rovers	38	16	12	10	56	41	44
Banbury United	38	17	10	11	52	47	44
Kidderminster Harriers	38	16	11	11	58	41	43
Merthyr Tydfil	38	18	6	14	85	62	42
Cambridge City	38	14	12	12	56	45	40
Barry Town	38	14	11	13	58	48	39
Wellingborough Town	38	11	15	12	47	43	37
King's Lynn	38	12	13	13	55	55	37
Gloucester City	38	14	8	16	68	75	36
Corby Town	38	9	17	12	46	48	35
Dunstable Town	38	11	13	14	49	59	35
Stourbridge	38	9	15	14	52	53	33
Tamworth	38	10	11	17	37	48	31
Bedworth United	38	8	14	16	36	58	30
Milton Keynes City	38	5	11	22	26	74	21
Oswestry Town	38	6	8	24	29	85	20

First Division (South)

Margate	38	24	10	4	92	32	58
Dorchester Town	38	23	10	5	67	31	56
Salisbury	38	21	10	7	60	27	52
Waterlooville	38	19	13	6	66	36	51
Romford	38	17	15	6	58	37	49
Aylesbury United	38	20	7	11	56	42	47
Trowbridge Town	38	16	11	11	65	59	43
Chelmsford City	38	15	11	12	58	46	41
Folkestone & Shepway	38	16	9	13	64	56	41
Taunton Town	38	15	10	13	57	54	40
Addlestone	38	14	10	14	57	60	38
Crawley Town	38	14	9	15	61	60	37
Basingstoke Town	38	11	11	16	44	50	33
Tonbridge AFC	38	13	5	20	64	77	31
Ashford Town	38	9	13	16	39	60	31
Hounslow	38	10	10	18	43	62	30
Bognor Regis Town	38	9	8	21	52	69	26
Poole Town	38	8	10	20	43	68	26
Andover	38	4	12	22	30	68	20
Canterbury City	38	2	6	30	31	113	10

1978-79

Premier Division

Worcester City	42	27	11	4	92	33	65
Kettering Town	42	27	7	8	109	43	61
Telford United	42	22	10	10	60	39	54
Maidstone United	42	18	18	6	55	35	54
Bath City	42	17	19	6	59	41	53
Weymouth	42	18	15	9	71	51	51
AP Leamington	42	19	11	12	65	53	49
Redditch United	42	19	10	13	70	57	48
Yeovil Town	42	15	16	11	59	49	46
Witney Town	42	17	10	15	53	52	44
Nuneaton Borough	42	13	17	12	59	50	43
Gravesend & Northfleet	42	15	12	15	56	55	42
Barnet	42	16	10	16	52	64	42
Hillingdon Borough	42	12	16	14	50	41	40
Wealdstone	42	12	12	18	51	59	36
Atherstone Town	42	9	17	16	46	65	35
Dartford	42	10	14	18	40	56	34
Cheltenham Town	42	11	10	21	38	72	32
Margate	42	10	9	23	44	75	29
Dorchester Town	42	7	11	24	46	86	25
Hastings United	42	5	13	24	37	85	23
Bridgend Town	42	6	6	30	39	90	18

First Division (North)

Grantham	38	21	10	7	70	45	52
Merthyr Tydfil	38	22	7	9	90	53	51
Alvechurch	38	20	10	8	70	42	50
Bedford Town	38	19	9	10	74	49	47
King's Lynn	38	17	11	10	57	46	45
Oswestry Town	38	18	8	12	63	43	44
Gloucester City	38	18	8	12	76	59	44
Burton Albion	38	16	10	12	51	40	42
Kidderminster Harriers	38	13	14	11	70	60	40
Bedworth United	38	13	14	11	41	34	40
Tamworth	38	15	8	15	47	45	38
Stourbridge	38	15	7	16	64	61	37
Barry Town	38	14	9	15	51	53	37
Enderby Town	38	14	8	16	46	55	36
Banbury United	38	10	13	15	42	58	33
Wellingborough Town	38	13	6	19	50	71	32
Cambridge City	38	9	9	20	37	62	27
Bromsgrove Rovers	38	6	14	18	33	61	26
Milton Keynes City	38	7	9	22	37	87	23
Corby Town	38	5	6	27	40	85	16

First Division (South)

Dover	40	28	9	3	88	20	65
Folkestone & Shepway	40	22	6	12	84	50	50
Gosport Borough	40	19	11	10	62	47	49
Chelmsfor d City	40	20	7	13	65	61	47
Minehead	40	16	13	11	58	39	45
Poole Town	40	15	15	10	48	44	45
Hounslow	40	16	12	12	56	45	44
Waterlooville	40	17	10	13	52	43	44
Trowbridge Town	40	15	12	13	65	61	42
Aylesbury United	40	16	9	15	54	52	41
Taunton Town	40	16	9	15	53	51	41
Bognor Regis Town	40	17	7	16	58	58	41
Dunstable	40	18	4	18	57	55	40
Tonbridge AFC	40	15	10	15	43	47	40
Salisbury	40	13	10	17	47	51	36
Basingstoke Town	40	12	11	17	49	62	35
Addlestone	40	12	9	19	56	64	33
Andover	40	12	6	22	47	69	30
Ashford Town	40	10	10	20	28	53	30
Crawley Town	40	9	9	22	44	75	27
Canterbury City	40	6	3	31	31	98	15

1979-80

Midland Division

Bridgend Town	42	28	6	8	85	39	62
Minehead	42	22	15	5	70	42	59
Bedford Town	42	20	12	10	71	42	52
Kidderminster Harriers	42	23	6	13	81	59	52
Merthyr Tydfil	42	20	11	11	70	47	51
Enderby Town	42	21	8	13	62	50	50
Stourbridge	42	19	11	12	67	49	49
Alvechurch	42	17	14	11	78	60	48
Trowbridge Town	42	19	9	14	62	61	47
Bromsgrove Rovers	42	18	10	14	67	56	46
Barry Town	42	15	12	15	64	58	42
King's Lynn	42	15	11	16	48	55	41
Banbury United	42	13	14	15	56	56	40
Taunton Town	42	16	8	18	55	62	40
Witney Town	42	10	19	13	43	45	39
Bedworth United	42	12	15	15	40	42	39
Milton Keynes City	42	15	7	20	46	59	37
Gloucester City	42	10	14	18	55	68	32
Cheltenham Town	42	13	5	24	49	70	31
Wellingborough Town	42	9	7	26	54	106	25
Cambridge City	42	6	9	27	30	73	21
Corby Town	42	5	9	28	40	94	19

Southern Division

Dorchester Town	46	25	12	9	81	53	62
Aylesbury United	46	25	11	10	73	40	61
Dover	46	22	13	11	78	47	57
Gosport Borough	46	21	15	10	70	50	57
Dartford	46	21	14	11	66	45	56
Bognor Regis Town	46	20	15	11	66	38	55
Hillingdon Borough	46	19	16	11	64	41	54
Dunstable	46	17	19	10	93	64	53
Addlestone	46	20	13	13	72	57	53
Hastings United	46	19	15	12	74	65	53
Fareham Town	46	16	16	14	61	53	48
Waterlooville	46	17	12	17	67	64	46
Andover	46	16	13	17	65	65	45
Poole Town	46	16	13	17	49	64	45
Canterbury City	46	15	15	17	56	60	44
Hounslow	46	14	14	17	44	57	43
Margate	46	17	8	21	51	62	42
Folkestone & Shepway	46	14	11	21	54	63	39
Ashford Town	46	12	14	20	54	71	38
Crawley Town	46	13	11	22	55	72	37
Chelmsford City	46	9	18	19	47	69	36
Basingstoke Town	46	9	15	22	48	79	33
Salisbury	46	10	12	24	47	59	32
Tonbridge AFC	46	3	9	34	30	128	15

1980-81 Midland Division

Alvechurch	42	26	9	7	76	40	61
Bedford Town	42	25	11	6	63	32	61
Trowbridge Town	42	24	9	9	69	39	57
Kidderminster Harriers	42	23	9	10	67	41	55
Barry Town	42	21	9	12	60	40	51
Stourbridge	42	17	16	9	75	49	50
Enderby Town	42	21	8	13	71	47	50
Cheltenham Town	42	18	12	12	70	59	48
Bromsgrove Rovers	42	19	9	14	65	50	47
Corby Town	42	19	7	16	69	58	45
Bridgend Town	42	19	7	16	74	64	45
Minehead	42	19	7	16	54	60	45
Gloucester City	42	19	6	17	82	72	44
Merthyr Tydfil	42	15	12	15	60	50	42
Bedworth United	42	14	12	16	49	46	40
Banbury United	42	11	11	20	51	65	33
Taunton Town	42	10	9	23	48	68	29
Cambridge City	42	8	12	22	46	87	28
Witney Town	42	9	9	24	44	65	27
Wellingborough Town	42	10	7	25	43	91	27
Redditch United	42	11	4	27	54	92	26
Milton Keynes City	42	3	7	32	28	103	13

Southern Division

Dartford	46	26	14	6	76	39	66
Bognor Regis Town	46	25	13	8	95	43	63
Hastings United	46	24	14	8	87	43	62
Gosport Borough	46	24	12	10	84	52	60
Waterlooville	46	19	21	6	67	50	59
Dorchester Town	46	21	13	12	84	56	55
Dover	46	22	10	14	70	50	54
Poole Town	46	19	14	13	70	56	52
Addlestone & Weybridge	46	21	9	16	66	57	51
Dunstable	46	19	13	14	73	68	51
Aylesbury United	46	20	10	16	66	60	50
Hounslow	46	17	13	16	65	55	47
Hillingdon Borough	46	16	15	15	50	49	47
Basingstoke Town	46	16	14	16	69	58	46
Crawley Town	46	18	4	24	64	78	40
Ashford Town	46	12	15	19	55	76	39
Tonbridge AFC	46	12	15	19	44	68	39
Chelmsford City	46	13	12	21	54	78	38
Canterbury City	46	12	13	21	40	59	37
Salisbury	46	14	8	24	57	76	36
Folkestone	46	11	11	24	47	65	33
Margate	46	11	7	28	65	117	29
Fareham Town	46	5	18	23	31	73	28
Andover	46	6	10	30	41	94	22

1981-82

Midland Division

Nuneaton Borough	42	27	11	4	88	32	65
Alvechurch	42	26	10	6	79	34	62
Kidderminster Harriers	42	22	12	8	71	40	56
Stourbridge	42	21	10	11	69	47	52
Gloucester City	42	21	9	12	64	48	51
Bedworth United	42	20	10	12	59	40	50
Enderby Town	42	20	10	12	79	66	50
Witney Town	42	19	8	15	71	49	46
Barry Town	42	16	14	12	59	46	46
Corby Town	42	19	8	15	70	59	46
Merthyr Tydfil	42	16	12	14	63	54	44
Wellingborough Town	42	15	12	15	50	45	42
Bridgend Town	42	13	13	16	50	62	39
Bromsgrove Rovers	42	15	8	19	57	63	38
Bedford Town	42	12	13	17	45	54	37
Cheltenham Town	42	11	14	17	65	68	36
Taunton Town	42	12	8	22	46	76	32
Banbury United	42	11	8	23	63	91	30
Minehead	42	12	6	24	38	69	30
Cambridge City	42	10	8	24	38	80	28
Milton Keynes City	42	6	11	25	34	70	23
Redditch United	42	8	5	29	37	103	21

Southern Division

Wealdstone	46	32	8	6	100	32	72
Hastings United	46	31	9	6	79	34	71
Dorchester Town	46	21	18	7	76	41	60
Gosport Borough	46	26	8	12	76	45	60
Fareham Town	46	20	14	12	58	48	54
Poole Town	46	19	15	12	92	63	53
Waterlooville	46	22	9	15	75	53	53
Welling United	46	19	13	14	70	48	51
Addlestone & Weybridge	46	17	17	12	71	53	51
Chelmsford City	46	20	11	15	64	53	51
Aylesbury United	46	19	12	15	79	61	50
Basingstoke Town	46	18	12	16	75	61	48
Dover	46	19	8	19	61	63	46
Ashford Town	46	16	14	16	52	56	46
Tonbridge AFC	46	19	7	20	62	70	45
Dunstable	46	18	8	20	63	68	44
Salisbury	46	16	10	20	64	81	42
Hounslow	46	15	11	20	59	83	41
Hillingdon Borough	46	14	10	22	46	58	38
Canterbury City	46	10	16	20	49	78	36
Crawley Town	46	9	12	25	46	81	30
Folkestone	46	10	6	30	49	101	26
Andover	46	4	11	31	39	100	19
Thanet United	46	5	7	34	37	110	17

1982-83

Premier Division

AP Leamington	38	25	4	9	78	50	79
Kidderminster Harriers	38	23	7	8	69	40	76
Welling United	38	21	6	11	63	40	69
Chelmsford City	38	16	11	11	57	40	59
Bedworth United	38	16	11	11	47	39	59
Dartford	38	16	8	14	48	38	56
Gosport Borough	38	14	13	11	47	43	55
Fareham Town	38	16	7	15	73	82	55
Dorchester Town	38	14	12	12	52	50	54
Gravesend & Northfleet	38	14	12	12	49	50	54
Gloucester City	38	13	12	13	61	57	51
Witney Town	38	12	13	13	60	48	47
Alvechurch	38	13	8	17	60	66	47
Stourbridge	38	12	11	15	48	54	47
Corby Town	38	12	11	15	58	67	47
Hastings United	38	11	11	16	48	61	44
Enderby Town	38	11	9	18	44	62	42
Waterlooville	38	10	9	19	62	83	39
Poole Town	38	9	9	20	57	73	36
Addlestone & Weybridge	38	5	10	23	24	62	25

Midland Division

Cheltenham Town	32	22	5	5	65	29	71
Sutton Coldfield Town	32	21	7	4	62	24	70
Forest Green Rovers	32	21	3	8	68	32	66
Merthyr Tydfil	32	17	7	8	64	45	58
Willenhall Town	32	17	6	9	74	49	57
Oldbury United	32	16	6	10	52	49	54
Banbury United	32	15	3	14	59	55	48
Bridgend Town	32	12	11	9	46	37	47
Wellingborough Town	32	13	7	12	49	37	46
Bromsgrove Rovers	32	13	5	14	47	47	44
Dudley Town	32	12	7	13	40	45	43
Bridgwater Town	32	12	6	14	42	43	42
Aylesbury United	32	12	5	15	37	51	41
Redditch United	32	8	6	18	51	73	30
Taunton Town	32	5	7	20	30	64	22
Minehead	32	5	7	20	24	62	22
Milton Keynes City	32	0	4	28	22	90	4

Southern Division

Fisher Athletic	34	23	5	6	79	34	74
Folkestone	34	22	6	6	79	41	72
RS Southampton	34	21	7	6	66	30	70
Dunstable	34	19	5	10	57	39	62
Hillingdon Borough	34	14	11	9	41	30	53
Salisbury	34	14	10	10	59	49	52
Crawley Town	34	14	9	11	51	43	51
Ashford Town	34	13	10	11	51	41	49
Tonbridge AFC	34	14	5	15	57	57	47
Hounslow	34	11	12	11	46	47	45
Canterbury City	34	12	9	13	52	63	45
Cambridge City	34	12	5	17	56	63	41
Dover	34	11	7	16	35	52	40
Thanet United	34	10	5	19	30	61	35
Basingstoke Town	34	8	10	16	37	56	34
Woodford Town	34	6	9	19	29	57	27
Andover	34	6	8	20	28	53	26
Erith & Belvedere	34	5	9	20	26	62	24

1983-84

Premier Division

Dartford	38	23	9	6	67	32	78
Fisher Athletic	38	22	9	7	80	42	75
Chelmsford City	38	19	9	10	67	45	66
Gravesend & Northfleet	38	18	9	11	50	38	63
Witney Town	38	18	6	14	75	50	60
King's Lynn	38	18	6	14	42	45	60
Folkestone	38	16	9	13	60	56	57
Cheltenham Town	38	16	7	15	63	56	55
Gloucester City	38	13	15	10	55	50	54
Hastings United	38	15	9	14	55	57	54
Bedworth United	38	15	9	14	51	55	54
Welling United	38	15	7	16	61	61	52
AP Leamington	38	14	9	15	73	83	51
Corby Town	38	12	14	12	55	54	50
Fareham Town	38	13	11	14	65	70	50
Alvechurch	38	12	12	14	56	62	48
Sutton Coldfield Town	38	10	14	14	49	53	44
Gosport Borough	38	6	15	17	31	64	33
Dorchester Town	38	4	8	26	40	69	20
Stourbridge	38	4	7	27	30	82	19

Midland Division

Willenhall Town	38	27	4	7	100	44	85
Shepshed Charterhouse	38	25	5	8	88	37	80
Bromsgrove Rovers	38	20	8	10	73	43	68
Dudley Town	38	18	13	7	71	43	67
Aylesbury United	38	17	15	6	62	35	66
Moor Green	38	18	12	8	63	44	66
Rushden Town	38	17	12	9	68	42	63
Merthyr Tydfil	38	18	8	12	63	44	62
Redditch United	38	17	9	12	67	67	60
VS Rugby	38	15	12	11	68	51	57
Forest Green Rovers	38	15	12	11	67	51	57
Bridgnorth Town	38	16	9	13	64	52	57
Leicester United	38	12	9	17	58	58	45
Oldbury United	38	10	13	15	53	51	43
Coventry Sporting	38	11	7	20	40	67	40
Bridgwater Town	38	10	8	20	39	65	38
Wellingborough Town	38	7	9	22	43	80	30
Banbury United	38	6	11	21	37	78	29
Milton Keynes City	38	3	9	26	31	110	18
Tamworth	38	2	7	29	25	118	13

Southern Division

RS Southampton	38	26	6	6	83	35	84
Crawley Town	38	22	9	7	68	28	75
Basingstoke Town	38	20	9	9	54	36	69
Tonbridge AFC	38	20	9	9	61	44	69
Addlestone & Weybridge	38	19	11	8	58	34	68
Poole Town	38	20	7	11	68	42	67
Hillingdon Borough	38	18	11	9	43	20	65
Ashford Town	38	19	5	14	65	47	62
Salisbury	38	17	8	13	61	48	59
Cambridge City	38	13	9	16	43	53	48
Canterbury City	38	12	9	17	44	52	45
Waterlooville	38	12	9	17	56	69	45
Dover Athletic	38	12	9	17	51	74	45
Chatham Town	38	11	10	17	46	56	43
Andover	38	12	6	20	35	54	42
Erith & Belvedere	38	11	9	18	43	68	42
Dunstable	38	10	8	20	38	65	38
Thanet United	38	9	8	21	40	65	35
Woodford Town	38	7	8	23	30	69	29
Hounslow	38	4	12	22	30	58	24

1984-85

Premier Division

Cheltenham Town	38	24	5	9	83	41	77
King's Lynn	38	23	6	9	73	48	75
Crawley Town	38	22	8	8	76	52	74
Willenhall Town	38	20	8	10	57	38	68
RS Southampton	38	21	4	13	76	52	67
Welling United	38	18	11	9	55	38	65
Folkestone	38	19	6	13	70	54	63
Fisher Athletic	38	19	5	14	67	57	62
Chelmsford City	38	17	10	11	52	50	61
Shepshed Charterhouse	38	18	5	15	67	50	59
Corby Town	38	15	6	17	56	54	51
Bedworth United	38	14	8	16	48	52	50
Gravesend & Northfleet	38	12	12	14	46	46	48
Fareham Town	38	13	8	17	52	55	47
Alvechurch	38	11	7	20	53	59	40
Hastings United	38	11	7	20	46	71	40
Witney Town	38	9	12	17	51	58	39
Gloucester City	38	10	6	22	49	74	36
Trowbridge	38	10	5	23	45	83	35
AP Leamington	38	2	5	31	22	112	11

Midland Division

Dudley Town	34	21	8	5	70	36	71
Aylesbury United	34	[illegible]	7	7	62	30	67
Hednesford Town	34	18	7	9	58	42	61
Moor Green	34	17	9	8	63	43	60
VS Rugby	34	17	9	8	59	41	60
Bromsgrove Rovers	34	16	10	8	53	42	58
Stourbridge	34	15	11	8	52	45	56
Redditch United	34	12	11	11	68	57	47
Sutton Coldfield Town	34	13	6	15	50	56	45
Bridgnorth Town	34	13	5	16	67	65	44
Coventry Sporting	34	11	9	14	45	52	42
Merthyr Tydfil	34	10	11	13	43	46	41
Rushden Town	34	10	7	17	42	52	37
Forest Green Rovers	34	9	10	15	49	65	37
Wellingborough Town	34	10	7	17	39	63	37
Oldbury United	34	10	6	18	52	66	36
Banbury United	34	9	5	20	33	59	32
Leicester United	34	3	6	25	17	62	15

Southern Division

Basingstoke Town	38	24	9	5	61	22	81
Gosport Borough	38	22	6	10	78	41	72
Poole Town	38	20	12	6	69	38	72
Hillingdon	38	19	10	9	51	23	67
Thanet United	38	19	9	10	63	47	66
Salisbury	38	19	5	14	55	54	62
Sheppey United	38	18	6	14	49	45	60
Addlestone & Weybridge	38	16	9	13	68	54	57
Waterlooville	38	15	10	13	71	63	55
Canterbury City	38	15	7	16	61	64	52
Woodford Town	38	13	13	12	46	53	52
Tonbridge AFC	38	16	3	19	59	62	51
Andover	38	15	5	18	42	54	50
Dorchester Town	38	13	7	18	45	60	46
Cambridge City	38	11	11	16	59	71	44
Chatham Town	38	12	8	18	44	66	44
Ashford Town	38	10	9	19	54	69	69
Dunstable	38	8	10	20	35	56	64
Dover Athletic	38	7	7	24	39	78	28
Erith & Belvedere	38	6	8	24	36	65	26

1985-86

Premier Division

Welling United	38	29	6	3	95	31	93
Chelmsford City	38	20	10	8	68	41	70
Fisher Athletic	38	20	7	11	67	45	67
Alvechurch	38	19	9	10	71	56	66
Worcester City	38	19	9	10	64	50	66
Crawley Town	38	18	5	15	76	59	59
Shepshed Charterhouse	38	19	1	18	51	52	58
Aylesbury United	38	14	10	14	52	49	52
Folkestone	38	14	10	14	56	56	52
Bedworth United	38	14	8	16	44	49	50
Willenhall Town	38	12	13	13	51	44	49
Dudley Town	38	15	4	19	58	62	49
Corby Town	38	14	7	17	61	67	49
King's Lynn	38	12	10	16	39	42	46
Basingstoke Town	38	13	4	21	36	67	43
RS Southampton	38	11	9	18	44	61	42
Witney Town	38	11	6	21	44	74	39
Gosport Borough	38	10	8	20	42	66	38
Fareham Town	38	8	13	17	40	62	37
Gravesend & Northfleet	38	9	9	20	29	55	36

Midland Division

Bromsgrove Rovers	40	29	5	6	95	44	92
Redditch United	40	23	6	11	70	42	75
Merthyr Tydfil	40	21	10	9	60	40	73
VS Rugby	40	17	14	9	41	31	65
Stourbridge	40	15	14	11	62	49	59
Rusden Town	40	17	7	16	69	74	58
Bilston Town	40	15	12	13	60	48	57
Bridgnorth Town	40	13	18	9	56	45	57
Gloucester City	40	15	12	13	61	57	57
Grantham	40	16	7	17	46	59	55
Wellingborough Town	40	15	9	16	56	56	54
Sutton Coldfield Town	40	13	14	13	60	45	53
Hednesford Town	40	14	9	17	67	70	51
Forest Green Rovers	40	14	9	17	52	56	51
Mile Oak Rovers	40	14	8	18	56	73	50
Leicester United	40	13	10	17	41	48	49
Banbury United	40	13	8	19	38	55	47
Coventry Sporting	40	10	15	15	42	48	45
Moor Green	40	12	6	22	63	91	42
Leamington	40	10	6	24	40	77	36
Oldbury United	40	8	7	25	50	87	31

Southern Division

Cambridge City	40	23	11	6	87	41	80
Salisbury	40	24	8	8	84	51	80
Hastings Town	40	23	9	8	83	51	78
Dover Athletic	40	23	6	11	89	53	75
Corinthian	40	20	9	11	79	45	69
Tonbridge AFC	40	17	13	10	65	51	64
Dunstable	40	17	11	12	70	61	62
Ruislip	40	17	6	17	67	66	57
Erith & Belvedere	40	14	12	14	35	40	54
Waterlooville	40	16	6	18	52	58	54
Burnham & Hillingdon	40	16	6	18	44	59	54
Canterbury City	40	13	13	14	58	58	52
Trowbridge Town	40	13	13	14	57	63	52
Sheppey United	40	14	10	16	43	53	52
Thanet United	40	13	7	20	58	63	46
Woodford Town	40	12	10	18	49	62	46
Poole Town	40	12	7	21	55	63	43
Ashford Town	40	10	12	18	45	65	42
Chatham Town	40	8	15	17	53	70	39
Andover	40	10	8	22	52	92	38
Dorchester Town	40	5	8	27	35	94	23

1986-87

Premier Division

Fisher Athletic	42	25	11	6	72	29	86
Bromsgrove Rovers	42	24	11	7	82	41	83
Aylesbury United	42	24	11	7	72	40	83
Dartford	42	19	12	11	76	43	69
Chelmsford City	42	17	13	12	48	45	64
Cambridge City	42	14	20	8	68	52	62
Redditch United	42	16	14	12	59	54	62
Alvechurch	42	18	8	16	66	62	62
Corby Town	42	14	17	11	65	51	59
Worcester City	42	16	11	15	62	55	59
Shepshed Charterhouse	42	16	10	16	59	59	58
Bedworth United	42	15	12	15	55	51	57
Crawley Town	42	14	11	17	59	60	53
Fareham Town	42	11	17	14	58	49	50
Willenhall Town	42	13	11	18	48	57	50
Basingstoke Town	42	12	12	18	53	78	48
Witney Town	42	12	12	18	29	56	48
Gosport Borough	42	11	13	18	42	57	46
Salisbury	42	12	7	23	52	82	43
King's Lynn	42	9	13	20	48	72	40
Dudley Town	42	9	9	24	39	76	36
Folkestone	42	8	11	23	36	79	35

Midland Division

VS Rugby	38	25	5	8	81	43	80
Leicester United	38	26	1	11	89	49	79
Merthyr Tydfil	38	23	6	9	95	54	75
Moor Green	38	22	6	10	73	55	72
Halesowen Town	38	19	12	7	72	50	69
Hednesford Town	38	21	5	12	84	56	68
Gloucester City	38	19	5	14	77	59	62
Coventry Sporting	38	17	8	13	55	54	59
Forest Green Rovers	38	16	9	13	65	53	57
Stourbridge	38	16	7	15	56	56	55
Grantham	38	15	9	14	74	54	54
Banbury United	38	14	7	17	55	65	49
Buckingham Town	38	13	9	16	55	59	48
Bridgnorth Town	38	12	9	17	59	63	45
Wellingborough Town	38	13	6	19	55	76	45
Mile Oak Rovers	38	11	10	17	50	63	43
Sutton Coldfield Town	38	8	10	20	56	78	34
Bilston Town	38	8	7	23	37	76	31
Leamington	38	4	13	21	37	80	25
Rushden Town	38	1	10	27	42	124	13

Southern Division

Dorchester Town	38	23	8	7	83	42	77
Ashford Town	38	23	7	8	63	32	76
Woodford Town	38	22	6	10	72	44	72
Hastings Town	38	20	10	8	74	54	70
Dover Athletic	38	20	6	12	66	43	66
Gravesend & Northfleet	38	18	7	13	67	46	61
Tonbridge AFC	38	16	10	12	73	67	58
Erith & Belvedere	38	15	12	11	57	50	57
Chatham Town	38	16	9	13	53	46	57
Thanet United	38	14	14	10	56	50	56
Waterlooville	38	16	8	14	66	65	56
Trowbridge Town	38	15	9	14	77	65	54
Dunstable	38	13	9	16	60	57	48
Corinthian	38	11	12	15	56	65	45
Sheppey United	38	9	12	17	43	65	39
Andover	38	9	9	20	51	80	36
Burnham & Hillingdon	38	7	11	20	32	62	32
Poole Town	38	8	6	24	50	90	30
Ruislip	38	6	12	20	35	75	30*
Canterbury City	38	8	5	25	46	82	29

1987-88

Premier Division

Aylesbury United	42	27	8	7	79	35	89
Dartford	42	27	8	7	79	39	89
Cambridge City	42	24	8	10	84	43	80
Bromsgrove Rovers	42	22	11	9	65	39	77
Worcester City	42	22	6	14	58	48	72
Crawley Town	42	17	14	11	73	63	65
Alvechurch	42	17	13	12	54	52	64
Leicester United	42	15	14	13	68	59	59
Fareham Town	42	16	11	15	51	59	59
Corby Town	42	16	8	18	61	64	56
Dorchester Town	42	14	14	14	51	57	56
Ashford Town	42	12	16	14	45	54	52
Shepshed Charterhouse	42	13	11	18	53	62	50
Bedworth United	42	12	14	16	49	64	50
Gosport Borough	42	10	17	15	39	49	47
Burton Albion	42	11	14	17	62	74	47
VS Rugby	42	10	16	16	52	57	46
Redditch United	42	10	13	19	55	63	43
Chelmsford City	42	11	10	21	60	75	43
Willenhall Town	42	9	12	21	39	76	39
Nuneaton Borough	42	8	13	21	58	77	37
Witney Town	42	8	11	23	45	71	35

Midland Division

Merthyr Tydfil	42	30	4	8	102	40	94
Moor Green	42	26	8	8	91	49	86
Grantham Town	42	27	4	11	97	53	85
Atherstone United	42	22	10	10	93	56	76
Sutton Coldfield Town	42	22	6	14	71	47	72
Halesowen Town	42	18	15	9	75	59	69
Gloucester City	42	18	14	10	86	62	68
Dudley Town	42	20	5	17	64	55	65
Forest Green Rovers	42	14	16	12	67	54	58
Banbury United	42	17	7	18	48	46	58
Bridgnorth Town	42	16	7	19	59	75	55
Buckingham Town	42	15	9	18	74	75	54
King's Lynn	42	16	6	20	53	63	54
Wellingborough Town	42	14	10	18	67	70	52
Rushden Town	42	14	9	19	69	85	51
Trowbridge Town	42	14	3	25	53	82	45
Bilston Town	42	12	8	22	52	87	44
Hednesford Town	42	11	10	21	50	81	43
Mile Oak Rovers	42	9	14	19	43	65	41
Coventry Sporting	42	11	8	23	46	83	41
Stourbridge	42	10	10	22	46	79	40
Paget Rangers	42	10	9	23	49	89	39

Southern Division

Dover Athletic	40	28	10	2	81	28	94
Waterlooville	40	27	10	3	88	33	91
Salisbury	40	24	11	5	71	33	83
Gravesend & Northfleet	40	20	12	8	60	32	72
Thanet United	40	17	13	10	60	38	64
Andover	40	17	13	10	64	58	64
Dunstable	40	17	12	11	78	56	63
Burnham	40	17	10	13	61	45	61
Bury Town	40	17	7	16	80	67	58
Erith & Belvedere	40	16	9	15	52	56	57
Sheppey United	40	14	10	16	58	52	52
Hastings Town	40	14	10	16	62	70	52
Tonbridge AFC	40	14	8	18	51	56	50
Poole Town	40	13	10	17	69	70	49
Baldock Town	40	12	12	16	44	53	48
Hounslow	40	11	8	21	41	76	41
Folkestone	40	9	11	20	47	76	38
Corinthian	40	9	10	21	49	67	37
Ruislip	40	5	13	22	33	80	28
Canterbury City	40	7	6	27	33	87	27
Chatham Town	40	7	5	28	39	88	26

1988-89

Premier Division

Merthyr Tydfil	42	26	7	9	104	58	85
Dartford	42	25	7	10	79	33	82
VS Rugby	42	24	7	11	64	43	79
Worcester City	42	20	13	9	72	49	73
Cambridge City	42	20	10	12	72	51	70
Dover Athletic	42	19	12	11	65	47	69
Gosport Borough	42	18	12	12	73	57	66
Burton Albion	42	18	10	14	79	68	64
Bath City	42	15	13	14	66	51	59
Bromsgrove Rovers	42	14	16	12	68	56	59
Wealdstone	42	16	10	16	60	53	59
Crawley Town	42	14	16	12	61	56	59
Dorchester Town	42	14	16	12	56	61	59
Alvechurch	42	16	8	18	56	59	56
Moor Green	42	14	13	15	58	70	55
Corby Town	42	14	11	17	55	59	53
Waterlooville	42	13	13	16	61	63	52
Ashford Town	42	13	13	16	59	76	52
Fareham Town	42	15	6	21	43	68	51
Leicester United	42	6	11	25	46	84	29
Redditch United	42	5	7	30	36	105	22
Bedworth United	42	4	7	31	36	102	19

Midland Division

Gloucester City	42	28	8	6	95	37	92
Atherstone United	42	26	9	7	85	38	87
Tamworth	42	26	9	7	85	45	87
Halesowen Town	42	25	10	7	85	42	85
Grantham Town	42	23	11	8	66	37	80
Nuneaton Borough	42	19	9	14	71	58	66
Rushden Town	42	19	8	15	71	50	65
Spalding United	42	17	13	12	72	64	64
Dudley Town	42	16	13	13	73	62	61
Sutton Coldfield Town	42	18	7	17	56	56	61
Willenhall Town	42	16	12	14	65	71	60
Forest Green Rovers	42	12	16	14	64	67	52
Bilston Town	42	15	7	20	63	71	52
Ashtree Highfield	42	12	15	15	57	62	51
Hednesford Town	42	12	15	15	49	57	51
Banbury United	42	10	14	18	53	74	44
Bridgnorth Town	42	12	7	23	59	77	43
Stourbridge	42	11	10	21	37	65	43
King's Lynn	42	7	13	22	31	67	34
Coventry Sporting	42	6	13	23	39	91	31
Wellingborough Town	42	5	15	22	39	72	30
Mile Oak Rovers	42	5	10	27	46	98	25

Southern Division

Chelmsford City	42	30	5	7	106	38	95
Gravesend & Northfleet	42	27	6	9	70	40	87
Poole Town	42	24	11	7	98	48	83
Bury Town	42	25	7	10	75	34	82
Burnham	42	22	13	7	78	47	79
Baldock Town	42	23	5	14	69	40	74
Hastings Town	42	21	11	10	75	48	74
Hounslow	42	21	6	15	75	60	69
Salisbury	42	20	5	17	79	58	65
Trowbridge Town	42	19	7	16	59	52	64
Folkestone	42	17	8	17	62	65	59
Corinthian	42	13	13	16	59	69	52
Canterbury City	42	14	8	20	52	60	50
Witney Town	42	13	11	18	61	71	50
Dunstable	42	11	14	17	42	57	47
Buckingham Town	42	12	10	20	56	79	46
Erith & Belvedere	42	11	10	21	48	63	43
Andover	42	11	9	22	56	90	42
Sheppey United	42	10	8	24	50	90	38
Thanet United	42	7	15	20	47	95	36
Tonbridge AFC	42	7	6	29	50	98	27
Ruislip	42	6	8	28	47	112	26

1989-90

Premier Division

Dover Athletic	42	32	6	4	87	27	102
Bath City	42	30	8	4	81	28	98
Dartford	42	26	9	7	80	35	87
Burton Albion	42	20	12	10	64	40	72
VS Rugby	42	19	12	11	51	35	69
Atherstone United	42	19	10	13	60	52	67
Gravesend & Northfleet	42	18	12	12	44	50	66
Cambridge City	42	17	11	14	76	56	62
Gloucester City	42	17	11	14	80	68	62
Bromsgrove Rovers	42	17	10	15	56	48	61
Moor Green	42	18	7	17	62	59	61
Wealdstone	42	16	9	17	55	54	57
Dorchester Town	42	16	7	19	52	67	55
Worcester City	42	15	10	17	62	63	54
Crawley Town	42	13	12	17	53	57	51
Waterlooville	42	13	10	19	63	81	49
Weymouth	42	11	13	18	50	70	46
Chelmsford City	42	11	10	21	52	72	43
Ashford Town	42	10	7	25	43	75	37
Corby Town	42	10	6	26	57	77	36
Alvechurch	42	7	5	30	46	95	26
Gosport Borough	42	6	5	31	28	93	23

Midland Division

Halesowen Town	42	28	8	6	100	49	92
Rushden Town	42	28	5	9	82	39	89
Nuneaton Borough	42	26	7	9	81	47	85
Tamworth	42	22	8	12	82	70	74
Barry Town	42	21	8	13	67	53	71
Spalding United	42	20	7	15	73	63	67
Sutton Coldfield Town	42	18	10	14	72	69	64
Stourbridge	42	17	12	13	73	61	63
Dudley Town	42	18	9	15	69	64	63
Stroud	42	16	13	13	75	62	61
Leicester United	42	17	5	20	66	77	56
Bridgnorth Town	42	13	14	15	68	73	53
King's Lynn	42	16	5	21	57	69	53
Grantham Town	42	14	10	18	57	63	52
Bedworth United	42	14	9	19	50	60	51
Hednesford Town	42	11	14	17	50	62	47
Bilston Town	42	11	14	17	40	54	47
Redditch United	42	11	13	18	57	64	46
Racing Club Warwick	42	11	11	20	45	66	44
Willenhall Town	42	9	9	24	37	66	36
Banbury United	42	9	9	24	46	83	34
Sandwell Borough	42	6	12	24	46	79	30

Southern Division

Bashley	42	25	7	10	80	47	82
Poole Town	42	23	8	11	85	60	77
Buckingham Town	42	22	10	10	67	46	76
Dunstable	42	20	14	8	56	38	74
Salisbury	42	21	9	12	72	50	72
Hythe Town	42	20	12	10	69	48	72
Trowbridge Town	42	20	9	13	79	64	69
Hastings Town	42	20	9	13	64	54	69
Bury Town	42	18	12	12	76	62	66
Baldock Town	42	18	11	13	69	52	65
Burnham	42	17	11	14	77	52	62
Fareham Town	42	14	14	14	49	53	56
Yate Town	42	16	6	20	53	52	54
Witney Town	42	16	6	20	54	56	54
Canterbury City	42	14	10	18	52	52	52
Margate	42	12	15	15	46	45	51
Folkestone	42	14	9	19	61	83	51
Andover	42	13	11	18	54	70	50
Hounslow	42	11	5	26	39	82	38
Erith & Belvedere	42	8	11	23	34	73	35
Corinthian	42	6	10	26	44	93	28
Sheppey United	42	6	7	29	35	83	25

1990-91

Premier Division

Farnborough Town	42	26	7	9	79	43	85
Gloucester City	42	23	14	5	86	49	83
Cambridge City	42	21	14	7	63	43	77
Dover Athletic	42	21	11	10	56	37	74
Bromsgrove Rovers	42	20	11	11	68	49	71
Worcester City	42	18	12	12	55	42	66
Burton Albion	42	15	15	12	59	48	60
Halesowen Town	42	17	9	16	73	67	60
VS Rugby	42	16	11	15	56	46	59
Bashley	42	15	12	15	56	52	57
Dorchester Town	42	15	12	15	47	54	57
Wealdstone	42	16	8	18	57	58	56
Dartford	42	15	9	18	61	64	54
Rushden Town	42	14	11	17	64	66	53
Atherstone United	42	14	10	18	55	58	52
Moor Green	42	15	6	21	64	75	51
Poole Town	42	12	13	17	56	69	49
Chelmsford City	42	11	15	16	37	68	48
Crawley Town	42	12	12	18	45	67	48
Waterlooville	42	11	13	18	51	70	46
Gravesend & Northfleet	42	9	7	26	46	91	34
Weymouth	42	4	12	26	50	88	24

Midland Division

Stourbridge	42	28	6	8	80	48	90
Corby Town	42	27	4	11	99	48	85
Hednesford Town	42	25	7	10	79	47	82
Tamworth	42	25	5	12	84	45	80
Nuneaton Borough	42	21	11	10	74	51	70
Barry Town	42	20	7	15	61	48	67
Newport AFC	42	19	6	17	54	46	63
King's Lynn	42	17	9	16	53	62	60
Grantham Town	42	17	7	18	62	56	56
Redditch United	42	16	10	16	66	75	58
Hinckley Town	42	16	9	17	72	68	57
Sutton Coldfield Town	42	15	11	16	56	65	56
Bedworth United	42	15	9	18	57	73	54
Bilston Town	42	14	9	19	69	79	51
Leicester United	42	14	10	18	65	77	51
Racing Club Warwick	42	12	13	17	56	65	49
Bridgnorth Town	42	13	9	20	62	74	48
Stroud	42	11	14	17	51	64	47
Dudley Town	42	11	13	18	48	73	46
Alvechurch	42	10	8	24	54	92	38
Willenhall Town	42	10	10	22	58	69	37
Spalding United	42	8	9	25	35	70	33

Southern Division

Buckingham Town	40	25	8	7	73	38	83
Trowbridge Town	40	22	12	6	67	31	78
Salisbury	40	22	11	7	63	39	77
Baldock Town	40	21	9	10	66	52	72
Ashford Town	40	22	5	13	82	52	71
Yate Town	40	21	8	11	76	48	71
Hastings Town	40	18	11	11	66	46	65
Hythe Town	40	17	9	14	55	44	59
Andover	40	16	6	18	69	76	54
Margate	40	14	11	15	52	55	53
Burnham	40	12	16	12	57	49	52
Bury Town	40	15	5	20	58	74	50
Sudbury Town	40	13	0	17	60	68	49
Newport IOW	40	13	9	18	56	62	48
Gosport Borough	40	12	11	17	47	58	47
Witney Town	40	12	11	17	57	75	47
Dunstable	40	9	15	16	48	63	42
Canterbury City	40	12	6	22	60	83	42
Erith & Belvedere	40	10	0	24	46	73	36
Fareham Town	40	9	9	22	46	74	36
Corinthian	40	5	12	23	34	78	27

1991-92

Premier Division

Bromsgrove Rovers	42	27	9	6	78	34	90
Dover Athletic	42	23	15	4	66	30	84
VS Rugby	42	23	11	8	70	44	80
Bashley	42	22	8	12	70	44	74
Cambridge City	42	18	14	10	71	53	68
Dartford	42	17	15	10	62	45	66
Trowbridge Town	42	17	10	15	69	51	61
Halesowen Town	42	15	15	12	61	49	60
Moor Green	42	15	11	16	61	59	56
Burton Albion	42	15	10	17	59	61	55
Dorchester Town	42	14	13	15	66	73	55
Gloucester City	42	15	9	18	67	70	54
Atherstone United	42	15	8	19	54	66	53
Corby Town	42	13	12	17	66	81	51
Waterlooville	42	13	11	18	43	56	50
Worcester City	42	12	13	17	56	59	49
Crawley Town	42	12	12	18	62	67	48
Chelmsford City	42	12	12	18	49	56	48
Wealdstone	42	13	7	22	52	69	46
Poole Town	42	10	13	19	46	77	43
Fisher Athletic	42	9	11	22	53	89	38
Gravesend & Northfleet	42	8	9	25	39	87	33

Midland Division

Solihull Borough	42	29	10	3	92	40	97
Hednesford Town	42	26	13	3	81	37	91
Sutton Coldfield Town	42	21	11	10	71	51	74
Barry Town	42	21	6	15	88	56	69
Bedworth United	42	16	15	11	67	63	63
Nuneaton Borough	42	17	11	14	68	53	62
Tamworth	42	16	12	14	66	52	60
Rushden Town	42	16	12	14	69	63	60
Stourbridge	42	17	8	17	85	62	59
Newport AFC	42	15	13	14	72	60	58
Yate Town	42	14	15	13	65	64	57
Bilston Town	42	15	10	17	56	67	55
Grantham Town	42	11	17	14	59	55	50
King's Lynn	42	13	11	18	61	68	50
Hinckley Town	42	14	8	20	61	87	50
Leicester United	42	12	13	17	56	63	49
Bridgnorth Town	42	12	12	18	61	74	48
Racing Club Warwick	42	11	14	17	45	61	47
Stroud	42	14	4	24	66	88	46
Redditch United	42	12	8	22	52	92	44
Alvechurch	42	11	10	21	54	88	43
Dudley Town	42	8	9	25	41	92	33

Southern Division

Hastings Town	42	28	7	7	80	37	91
Weymouth	42	22	12	8	64	35	78
Havant Town	42	21	12	9	67	46	75
Braintree Town	42	21	8	13	77	58	71
Buckingham Town	42	19	15	8	57	26	69
Andover	42	18	10	14	73	68	64
Ashford Town	42	17	12	13	66	57	63
Sudbury Town	42	18	9	15	70	66	63
Sittingbourne	42	19	10	13	63	41	61
Burnham	42	15	14	13	57	55	59
Baldock Town	42	16	10	16	62	67	58
Salisbury	42	13	16	13	67	51	55
Hythe Town	42	15	10	17	61	62	55
Margate	42	13	16	13	49	56	55
Newport IOW	42	13	10	19	58	63	49
Dunstable	42	12	12	18	55	67	48
Bury Town	42	14	4	24	52	94	46
Witney Town	42	11	12	19	55	76	45
Fareham Town	42	12	8	22	45	71	44
Erith & Belvedere	42	11	10	21	44	67	43
Canterbury City	42	8	14	20	43	69	38
Gosport Borough	42	6	9	27	32	65	27

1992-93

Premier Division

Dover Athletic	40	25	11	4	65	23	86
Cheltenham Town	40	21	10	9	76	40	73
Corby Town	40	20	12	8	68	43	72
Hednesford Town	40	21	7	12	72	52	70
Trowbridge Town	40	18	8	14	70	66	62
Crawley Town	40	16	12	12	68	59	60
Solihull Borough	40	17	9	14	68	59	60
Burton Albion	40	16	11	13	53	50	59
Bashley	40	18	8	14	60	60	59
Halesowen Town	40	15	11	14	67	54	56
Waterlooville	40	15	9	16	59	62	54
Chelmsford City	40	15	9	16	59	69	54
Gloucester City	40	14	11	15	66	68	53
Cambridge City	40	14	10	16	62	73	52
Atherstone United	40	13	14	13	56	60	50
Hastings Town	40	13	11	16	50	55	50
Worcester City	40	12	9	19	45	62	45
Dorchester Town	40	12	6	22	52	74	42
Moor Green	40	10	6	24	58	79	36
VS Rugby	40	10	6	24	40	63	36
Weymouth	40	5	10	25	39	82	23

Bashley had 3 points deducted

Midland Division

Nuneaton Borough	42	29	5	8	102	45	92
Gresley Rovers	42	27	6	9	94	55	87
Rushden & Diamonds	42	25	10	7	85	41	85
Barri	42	26	5	11	82	49	83
Newport AFC	42	23	8	11	73	58	77
Bedworth United	42	22	8	12	72	55	74
Stourbridge	42	17	9	16	93	79	60
Sutton Coldfield Town	42	17	9	16	82	78	60
Redditch United	42	18	6	18	75	79	60
Tamworth	42	16	11	15	65	51	59
Weston-super-Mare	42	17	7	18	79	86	58
Leicester United	42	16	9	17	67	67	57
Grantham Town	42	16	9	17	60	73	57
Bilston Town	42	15	10	17	74	69	55
Evesham United	42	15	8	19	67	83	53
Bridgnorth Town	42	15	7	20	61	68	52
Dudley Town	42	14	8	20	60	75	50
Yate Town	42	15	5	22	63	81	50
Forest Green Rovers	42	12	6	24	61	97	42
Hinckley Athletic	42	9	11	22	56	89	37
King's Lynn	42	10	6	26	45	90	36
Racing Club Warwick	42	3	7	32	40	88	16

Southern Division

Sittingbourne	42	26	12	4	102	43	90
Salisbury	42	27	7	8	87	50	88
Witney Town	42	25	9	8	77	37	84
Gravesend & Northfleet	42	25	4	13	99	63	79
Havant Town	42	23	6	13	78	55	75
Sudbury Town	42	20	11	11	89	54	71
Erith & Belvedere	42	22	5	15	73	66	71
Ashford Town	42	20	8	14	91	66	68
Braintree Town	42	20	6	16	95	65	66
Margate	42	19	7	16	65	58	64
Wealdstone	42	18	7	17	75	69	61
Buckingham Town	42	16	11	15	61	58	59
Baldock Town	42	15	9	18	59	63	54
Poole Town	42	15	7	20	61	69	52
Fareham Town	42	14	8	20	67	65	50
Burnham	42	14	8	20	53	77	50
Canterbury City	42	12	10	20	54	76	46
Newport IOW	42	9	16	17	44	56	43
Fisher Athletic	42	8	9	25	38	98	33
Andover	42	7	9	26	42	99	30
Dunstable	42	5	14	23	42	92	29
Bury Town	42	8	5	29	46	119	29

1993-94

Premier Division

Farnborough Town	42	25	7	10	74	44	82
Cheltenham Town	42	21	12	9	67	38	75
Halesowen Town	42	21	11	10	69	46	74
Atherstone United	42	22	7	13	57	43	73
Crawley Town	42	21	10	11	56	42	73
Chelmsford City	42	21	7	14	74	59	70
Trowbridge Town	42	16	17	9	52	41	65
Sittingbourne	42	17	13	12	65	48	64
Corby Town	42	17	8	17	52	56	59
Gloucester City	42	17	6	19	55	60	57
Burton Albion	42	15	11	10	57	49	56
Hastings Town	42	16	7	19	51	60	55
Hednesford Town	42	15	9	18	67	66	54
Gresley Rovers	42	14	11	17	61	72	53
Worcester City	42	14	9	19	61	70	51
Solihull Borough	42	13	11	18	52	57	50
Cambridge City	42	13	11	18	50	60	50
Dorchester Town	42	12	11	19	38	51	47
Moor Green	42	11	10	21	49	66	43
Waterlooville	42	11	10	21	47	69	43
Bashley	42	11	10	21	47	80	43
Nuneaton Borough	42	11	8	23	42	66	41

Midland Division

Rushden & Diamonds	42	29	11	2	109	37	98
VS Rugby	42	28	8	6	98	41	92
Weston-super-Mare	42	27	10	5	94	39	91
Newport AFC	42	26	9	7	84	37	87
Clevedon Town	42	24	10	8	75	46	82
Redditch United	42	19	11	12	79	62	68
Tamworth	42	19	7	16	82	68	64
Bilston Town	42	16	10	16	65	73	58
Stourbridge	42	17	6	19	71	75	57
Evesham United	42	16	8	18	50	60	56
Grantham Town	42	16	6	20	77	73	54
Bridgnorth Town	42	15	6	21	56	68	51
Racing Club Warwick	42	13	12	17	53	66	51
Dudley Town	42	13	10	19	64	61	49
Forest Green Rangers	42	12	12	18	61	84	48
Sutton Coldfield Town	42	12	8	22	53	75	44
Bedworth United	42	12	7	23	62	81	43
Hinckley Town	42	11	10	21	44	71	43
Leicester United	42	11	9	22	34	73	42
King's Lynn	42	9	11	22	47	72	38
Yate Town	42	10	6	26	48	86	36
Armitage	42	8	11	23	45	103	35

Southern Division

Gravesend & Northfleet	42	27	11	4	87	24	92
Sudbury Town	42	27	8	7	98	47	89
Witney Town	42	27	8	7	69	36	89
Salisbury City	42	26	10	6	90	39	88
Havant Town	42	27	4	11	101	41	85
Ashford Town	42	24	13	5	93	46	85
Baldock Town	42	26	7	9	76	40	85
Newport IOW	42	22	8	12	74	51	74
Margate	42	20	8	14	76	58	68
Weymouth	42	18	9	15	71	65	63
Tonbridge	42	19	5	18	59	62	62
Buckingham Town	42	14	14	14	43	42	56
Braintree Town	42	16	7	19	72	84	55
Fareham Town	42	12	12	18	54	75	48
Poole Town	42	13	6	23	54	86	45
Burnham	42	10	9	23	53	92	39
Fisher 93	42	9	10	23	52	81	37
Dunstable	42	9	7	26	50	91	34
Erith & Belvedere	42	9	5	28	40	72	32
Canterbury City	42	8	7	27	35	80	31
Wealdstone	42	6	7	29	45	95	25
Bury Town	42	3	5	34	36	121	14

1994-95

Premier Division

Hednesford Town	42	28	9	5	99	49	93
Cheltenham Town	42	25	11	6	87	39	86
Burton Albion	42	20	15	7	55	39	75
Gloucester City	42	22	8	12	76	48	74
Rushden & Diamonds	42	19	11	12	99	65	68
Dorchester Town	42	19	10	13	84	61	67
Leek Town	42	19	10	13	72	60	67
Gresley Rovers	42	17	12	13	70	63	63
Cambridge City	42	18	8	16	60	55	62
Worcester City	42	14	15	13	46	34	57
Crawley Town	42	15	10	17	64	71	55
Hastings Town	42	13	14	15	55	57	53
Halesowen Town	42	14	10	18	81	80	52
Gravesend & Northfleet	42	16	13	16	38	55	52
Chelmsford City	42	14	6	22	56	60	48
Atherstone United	42	12	12	18	51	67	48
VS Rugby	42	11	14	17	49	61	47
Sudbury Town	42	12	10	20	50	77	46
Solihull Borough	42	10	15	17	39	65	45
Sittingbourne	42	11	10	21	51	73	43
Trowbridge Town	42	9	13	20	43	69	40
Corby Town	42	4	10	28	36	113	21

Corby Town had 1 point deducted for fielding ineligible players

Midland Division

Newport AFC	42	29	8	5	106	39	95
Ilkeston Town	42	25	6	11	101	75	81
Tamworth	42	24	8	10	98	70	80
Moor Green	42	23	8	11	105	63	77
Bridgnorth Town	42	22	10	10	75	49	76
Buckingham Town	42	20	14	8	55	37	74
Nuneaton Borough	42	19	11	12	76	55	68
Rothwell Town	42	19	7	16	71	71	64
King's Lynn	42	18	8	16	76	64	62
Racing Club Warwick	42	17	11	14	68	63	62
Dudley Town	42	17	10	15	65	69	61
Bilston Town	42	17	8	17	73	64	59
Bedworth United	42	17	7	18	64	68	58
Evesham United	42	14	10	18	57	56	52
Hinckley Town	42	14	0	18	61	76	52
Stourbridge	42	15	7	20	59	77	52
Sutton Coldfield Town	42	12	10	20	62	72	46
Forest Green Rovers	42	11	13	18	56	76	46
Redditch United	42	8	14	20	47	64	38
Leicester United	42	10	8	24	51	99	38
Grantham Town	42	8	9	25	55	93	33
Armitage	42	2	5	35	35	116	11

Southern Division

Salisbury City	42	30	7	5	88	37	97
Baldock Town	42	28	10	4	92	44	94
Havant Town	42	25	10	7	81	34	85
Waterlooville	42	24	8	10	77	36	80
Ashford Town	42	21	12	9	106	72	75
Weston-super-Mare	42	18	13	11	82	54	67
Bashley	42	18	11	13	62	49	65
Weymouth	42	16	13	13	60	55	61
Newporth IOW	42	17	10	15	67	67	61
Witney Town	42	14	14	14	57	57	56
Clevedon Town	42	14	13	15	73	64	55
Tonbridge Angels	42	14	12	16	74	87	54
Margate	42	15	7	20	60	72	52
Braintree Town	42	12	13	17	64	71	49
Wealdstone	42	13	8	21	76	94	47
Yate Town	42	11	13	18	57	75	46
Fisher 93	42	9	16	17	54	70	43
Bury Town	42	11	8	23	59	86	41
Erith & Belvedere	42	10	9	23	49	94	39
Poole Town	42	10	8	24	53	79	38
Fareham Town	42	10	8	24	46	91	38
Burnham	42	7	7	28	40	89	28

1995-96

Premier Division

Rushden & Diamonds	42	29	7	6	99	41	94
Halesowen Town	42	27	11	4	70	36	92
Cheltenham Town	42	21	11	10	76	57	74
Gloucester City	42	21	8	13	65	47	71
Gresley Rovers	42	20	10	12	70	58	70
Worcester City	42	19	12	11	61	43	69
Merthyr Tydfil	42	19	6	17	67	59	63
Hastings Town	42	16	13	13	68	56	61
Crawley Town	42	15	13	14	57	56	58
Sudbury Town	42	15	10	17	69	71	55
Gravesend & Northfleet	42	15	10	17	60	62	55
Chelmsford City	42	13	16	13	46	53	55
Dorchester Town	42	15	8	19	62	57	53
Newport AFC	42	13	13	16	53	59	52
Salisbury City	42	14	10	18	57	69	52
Burton Albion	42	13	12	17	55	56	51
Atherstone United	42	12	12	18	58	75	48
Baldock Town	42	11	14	17	51	56	47
Cambridge City	42	12	10	20	56	68	46
Ilkeston Town	42	11	10	21	53	87	43
Stafford Rangers	42	11	4	27	58	90	37
VS Rugby	42	5	10	27	37	92	25

Midland Division

Nuneaton Borough	42	30	5	7	82	35	95
King's Lynn	42	27	5	10	85	43	84
Bedworth United	42	24	10	8	76	42	81
Moor Green	42	22	8	12	81	47	74
Paget Rangers	42	21	9	12	70	45	72
Tamworth	42	22	3	17	97	64	69
Solihull Borough	42	19	9	14	77	64	66
Rothwell Town	42	17	14	11	79	62	65
Buckingham Town	42	18	9	15	74	62	63
Dudley Town	42	15	16	11	83	66	61
Stourbridge	42	17	8	17	60	63	59
Bilston Town	42	16	9	17	61	62	57
Sutton Coldfield Town	42	16	9	17	62	67	57
Grantham Town	42	17	5	20	71	83	56
Redditch United	42	14	11	17	57	77	53
Leicester United	42	13	13	16	58	72	52
Hinckley Town	42	14	7	21	62	83	49
Racing Club Warwick	42	10	13	19	67	90	43
Evesham United	42	11	6	25	59	94	39
Corby Town	42	9	7	26	52	95	34
Bury Town	42	8	8	26	57	95	32
Bridgnorth Town	42	7	6	29	53	112	27

Bedworth United 1 point deducted, King's Lynn had 2 points deducted

Southern Division

Sittingbourne	42	28	4	10	102	44	88
Ashford Town	42	25	9	8	75	44	84
Waterlooville	42	24	8	10	87	44	80
Newport IOW	42	24	6	12	75	58	78
Braintree Town	42	24	8	10	93	70	77
Weymouth	42	24	4	14	75	55	76
Havant Town	42	23	11	8	73	42	74
Forest Green Rovers	42	22	8	12	85	55	74
Trowbridge Town	42	18	8	16	86	51	62
Yate Town	42	17	8	17	85	71	59
Margate	42	18	5	19	68	62	59
Witney Town	42	16	11	15	60	54	59
Weston-super-Mare	42	16	9	17	78	68	57
Cinderford Town	42	16	8	18	74	77	56
Fisher 93	42	14	13	15	58	59	55
Bashley	42	14	11	17	63	61	53
Clevedon Town	42	15	6	21	70	80	51
Tonbridge Angels	42	13	10	19	58	79	49
Fleet Town	42	14	5	23	58	79	47
Fareham Town	42	12	5	25	71	97	41
Erith & Belvedere	42	4	4	34	38	111	16
Poole Town	42	0	1	41	17	188	1

Braintree Town 3 points deducted, Havant Town had 6 points deducted

1996-97

Premier Division

Gresley Rovers	42	25	10	7	75	40	85
Cheltenham Town	42	21	11	10	76	44	74
Gloucester City	42	21	10	11	81	56	73
Halesowen Town	42	21	10	11	77	54	73
King's Lynn	42	20	8	14	65	61	68
Burton Albion	42	18	12	12	70	53	66
Nuneaton Borough	42	19	9	14	61	52	66
Sittingbourne	42	19	7	16	76	65	64
Merthyr Tydfil	42	17	9	16	69	61	60
Worcester City	42	15	14	13	52	50	59
Atherstone United	42	15	13	14	46	47	58
Salisbury City	42	15	13	14	57	66	58
Sudbury Town	42	16	7	19	72	72	55
Gravesend & Northfleet	42	16	7	19	63	73	55
Dorchester Town	42	14	9	19	62	66	51
Hastings Town	42	12	15	15	49	60	51
Crawley Town	42	13	8	21	49	67	47
Cambridge City	42	11	13	18	57	65	46
Ashford Town	42	9	18	15	53	79	45
Baldock Town	42	11	8	23	52	90	41
Newport AFC	42	9	13	20	40	60	40
Chelmsford City	42	6	14	22	49	70	32

Midland Division

Tamworth	40	30	7	3	90	28	97
Rothwell Town	40	20	11	9	82	54	71
Ilkeston Town	40	19	13	8	76	50	70
Grantham Town	40	22	4	14	65	46	70
Bedworth United	40	18	11	11	77	41	65
Solihull Borough	40	19	8	13	84	62	65
Bilston Town	40	18	10	12	74	57	64
Moor Green	40	18	7	15	88	68	61
Stafford Rangers	40	17	9	14	68	62	60
Raunds Town	40	16	11	13	61	66	59
Racing Club Warwick	40	16	10	14	70	72	58
Shepshed Dynamo	40	14	12	14	64	65	54
Redditch United	40	15	8	17	56	59	53
Paget Rangers	40	13	9	18	42	55	48
Dudley Town	40	12	10	18	70	89	46
Hinckley Town	40	11	11	18	39	63	44
Stourbridge	40	10	9	21	61	81	39
Evesham United	40	9	12	19	55	77	39
VS Rugby	40	9	9	22	49	81	36
Corby Town	40	8	8	24	49	88	32
Sutton Coldfield Town	40	7	9	24	29	85	30

Leicester United FC closed down and their record was expunged from the League table

Southern Division

Forest Green Rovers	42	27	10	5	87	40	91
St Leonards Stamcroft	42	26	9	7	95	48	87
Havant Town	42	23	10	9	81	49	79
Weston-super-Mare	42	21	13	8	82	43	76
Margate	42	21	9	12	70	47	72
Witney Town	42	20	11	11	71	42	71
Weymouth	42	20	10	12	82	51	70
Tonbridge Angels	42	17	15	10	56	44	66
Newport IOW	42	15	15	12	73	58	60
Fisher Athletic (London)	42	18	6	18	77	77	60
Clevedon Town	42	17	9	16	75	76	60
Fareham Town	42	14	12	16	53	70	54
Bashley	42	15	8	19	73	84	53
Dartford	42	14	10	18	59	64	52
Waterlooville	42	14	9	19	58	67	51
Cirencester Town	42	12	12	18	50	68	48
Cinderford Town	42	13	7	22	64	76	46
Trowbridge Town	42	11	11	20	50	61	44
Yate Town	42	12	8	22	55	87	44
Fleet Town	42	12	6	24	47	91	42
Erith & Belvedere	42	9	10	23	60	95	37
Buckingham Town	42	2	8	32	27	107	14

1997-98

Premier Division

Forest Green Rovers	42	27	8	7	93	55	89
Merthyr Tydfil	42	24	12	6	80	42	84
Burton Albion	42	21	8	13	64	43	71
Dorchester Town	42	19	13	10	63	38	70
Halesowen Town	42	18	15	9	70	38	69
Bath City	42	19	12	11	72	51	69
Worcester City	42	19	12	11	54	44	69
King's Lynn	42	18	11	13	64	65	65
Atherstone United	42	17	12	13	55	49	63
Crawley Town	42	17	8	17	63	60	59
Gloucester City	42	16	11	15	57	57	59
Nuneaton Borough	42	17	6	19	68	61	57
Cambridge City	42	16	8	18	62	70	56
Hastings Town	42	14	12	16	67	70	54
Tamworth	42	14	11	17	68	65	53
Rothwell Town	42	11	16	15	55	73	49
Gresley Rovers	42	14	6	22	59	77	48
Salisbury City	42	12	12	18	53	72	48
Bromsgrove Rovers	42	13	6	23	67	85	45
Sittingbourne	42	12	8	22	47	66	44
Ashford Town	42	8	5	29	34	85	29
St Leonards Stamcroft	42	5	10	27	48	97	25

Midland Division

Grantham Town	40	30	4	6	87	39	94
Ilkeston Town	40	29	6	5	123	39	93
Solihull Borough	40	22	9	9	81	48	75
Raunds Town	40	20	8	12	73	44	68
Wisbech Town	40	20	7	13	79	57	67
Moor Green	40	20	7	13	72	55	67
Bilston Town	40	20	5	15	69	57	65
Blakenall	40	17	13	10	66	55	64
Stafford Rangers	40	18	6	16	57	56	60
Redditch United	40	16	11	13	59	41	59
Stourbridge	40	16	9	15	57	55	57
Hinckley United	40	15	11	14	59	56	56
Brackley Town	40	15	7	18	45	57	52
Bedworth United	40	15	5	20	50	73	50
Racing Club Warwick	40	11	9	20	49	56	42
Shepshed Dynamo	40	9	14	17	55	74	41
Sutton Coldfield Town	40	9	12	19	42	68	39
Paget Rangers	40	9	12	19	40	75	39
VS Rugby	40	8	12	20	53	93	36
Evesham United	40	7	9	24	47	94	30
Corby Town	40	2	8	30	41	112	14

Southern Division

Weymouth	42	32	2	8	107	48	98
Chelmsford City	42	29	8	5	86	39	95
Bashley	42	29	4	9	101	59	91
Newport IOW	42	25	9	8	72	34	84
Fisher Athletic (London)	42	25	5	12	87	50	80
Margate	42	23	8	11	71	42	77
Newport AFC	42	21	6	15	83	65	69
Witney Town	42	20	9	13	74	58	69
Clevedon Town	42	20	7	15	57	55	67
Waterlooville	42	17	7	18	69	64	58
Dartford	42	17	7	18	60	60	58
Havant Town	42	13	14	16	65	70	53
Fleet Town	42	16	5	21	63	83	53
Tonbridge Angels	42	14	10	18	49	55	52
Trowbridge Town	42	14	6	22	55	69	48
Erith & Belvedere	42	11	13	18	47	68	46
Fareham Town	42	12	9	21	75	87	45
Cirencester Town	42	12	7	23	63	88	43
Weston-super-Mare	42	12	5	25	49	86	41
Baldock Town	42	10	5	27	53	81	35
Cinderford Town	42	6	5	31	40	112	23
Yate Town	42	5	7	30	44	97	22

1998-99

Premier Division

Nuneaton Borough	42	27	9	6	91	33	90
Boston United	42	17	16	9	69	51	67
Ilkeston Town	42	18	13	11	72	59	67
Bath City	42	18	11	13	70	44	65
Hastings Town	42	18	11	13	57	49	65
Gloucester City	42	18	11	13	57	52	65
Worcester City	42	18	9	15	58	54	63
Halesowen Town	42	17	11	14	72	60	62
Tamworth	42	19	5	18	62	67	62
King's Lynn	42	17	10	15	53	46	61
Crawley Town	42	17	10	15	57	58	61
Salisbury City	42	16	12	14	56	61	60
Burton Albion	42	17	7	18	58	52	58
Weymouth	42	14	14	14	56	55	56
Merthyr Tydfil	42	15	8	19	52	62	53
Atherstone United	42	12	14	16	47	52	50
Grantham Town	42	14	8	20	51	58	50
Dorchester Town	42	11	15	16	49	63	48
Rothwell Town	42	13	9	20	47	67	48
Cambridge City	42	11	12	19	47	68	45
Gresley Rovers	42	12	8	22	49	73	44
Bromsgrove Rovers	42	8	7	27	38	84	31

Hastings Town resigned from the League

Midland Division

Clevedon Town	42	28	8	6	83	35	92
Newport AFC	42	26	7	9	92	51	85
Redditch United	42	22	12	8	81	45	75
Hinckley United	42	20	12	10	58	40	72
Stafford Rangers	42	21	8	13	92	60	71
Bilston Town	42	20	11	11	79	69	71
Solihull Borough	42	19	12	11	76	53	69
Moor Green	42	20	7	15	71	61	67
Blakenall	42	17	14	11	65	54	65
Shepshed Dynamo	42	17	12	13	62	54	63
Sutton Coldfield Town	42	17	8	17	46	57	59
Stourbridge	42	16	10	16	60	55	58
Evesham United	42	16	9	17	63	63	57
Wisbech Town	42	16	9	17	59	66	57
Weston-super-Mare	42	15	10	17	59	56	55
Bedworth United	42	15	9	18	63	52	54
Cinderford Town	42	13	8	21	61	74	47
Stamford AFC	42	13	7	22	60	75	46
Paget Rangers	42	11	12	19	49	58	45
VS Rugby	42	12	9	21	53	74	45
Racing Club Warwick	42	5	8	29	38	93	23
Bloxwich Town	42	1	2	39	26	151	5

Southern Division

Havant & Waterlooville	42	29	7	6	86	32	94
Margate	42	27	8	7	84	33	89
Folkestone Invicta	42	26	8	8	92	47	86
Newport IOW	42	23	7	12	68	40	76
Chelmsford City	42	20	12	10	91	51	72
Raunds Town	42	19	13	10	87	50	70
Ashford Town	42	17	12	13	59	54	63
Baldock Town	42	17	9	16	60	59	60
Fisher Athletic (London)	42	16	11	15	58	54	59
Bashley	42	17	7	18	74	77	58
Witney Town	42	15	12	15	56	48	57
Cirencester Town	42	16	8	18	61	66	56
Sittingbourne	42	11	18	12	53	56	54
Dartford	42	14	10	18	48	53	52
Erith & Belvedere	42	15	7	20	48	64	52
Tonbridge Angels	42	12	15	15	48	59	51
St Leonards	42	14	8	20	57	72	50
Fleet Town	42	11	11	19	54	72	47
Corby Town	42	10	10	22	48	73	40
Yate Town	42	10	7	25	37	79	37
Andover	42	6	10	26	50	115	28
Brackley Town	42	6	8	28	41	105	26

1999-2000

Premier Division

Boston United	42	27	11	4	102	39	92
Burton Albion	42	23	9	10	73	43	78
Margate	42	23	8	11	64	43	77
Bath City	42	19	15	8	70	49	72
King's Lynn	42	19	14	9	59	43	71
Tamworth	42	20	10	12	80	51	70
Newport County	42	16	18	8	67	50	66
Clevedon Town	42	18	9	15	52	52	63
Ilkeston Town	42	16	12	14	77	69	60
Weymouth	42	14	16	12	60	51	58
Halesowen Town	42	14	14	14	52	54	56
Crawley Town	42	15	8	19	68	82	53
Havant & Waterlooville	42	13	13	16	63	68	52
Cambridge City	42	14	10	18	52	66	52
Worcester City	42	13	11	18	60	66	50
Salisbury City	42	14	8	20	70	84	50
Merthyr Tydfil	42	13	9	20	51	63	48
Dorchester Town	42	10	17	15	56	65	47
Grantham Town	42	14	5	23	63	76	47
Gloucester City	42	8	14	20	40	82	38
Rothwell Town	42	5	14	23	48	85	29
Atherstone United	42	5	13	24	30	76	28

Eastern Division

Fisher Athletic (London)	42	31	5	6	107	42	98
Folkestone Invicta	42	30	7	5	101	39	97
Newport IOW	42	25	7	10	74	40	82
Chelmsford City	42	24	8	10	74	38	80
Hastings Town	42	22	9	11	76	56	75
Ashford Town	42	21	9	12	70	49	72
Tonbridge Angels	42	20	10	12	82	60	70
Dartford	42	17	6	19	52	58	57
Burnham	42	15	9	18	55	64	54
Baldock Town	42	14	10	18	57	69	52
Erith & Belvedere	42	14	9	19	62	68	51
Witney Town	42	13	11	18	48	60	50
VS Rugby	42	13	11	18	58	79	50
Wisbech Town	42	14	7	21	58	66	49
Spalding United	42	14	6	22	52	71	48
Sittingbourne	42	13	7	22	48	75	46
Stamford	42	9	18	15	50	62	45
St Leonards	42	11	12	19	67	81	45
Raunds Town	42	11	12	19	44	63	45
Bashley	42	12	7	23	56	95	43
Corby Town	42	11	12	19	56	62	42
Fleet Town	42	8	8	26	54	104	32

Corby Town had 3 points deducted for fielding an ineligible player
Raunds Town gave notice to withdraw and take the place of the 2nd relegated Club. They then unsuccessfully sought re-election

Western Division

Stafford Rangers	42	29	6	7	107	47	93
Moor Green	42	26	12	4	85	33	90
Hinckley United	42	25	12	5	89	47	87
Tiverton Town	42	26	7	9	91	44	85
Solihull Borough	42	20	11	11	85	66	71
Blakenall	42	19	12	11	70	46	69
Cirencester Town	42	20	8	14	72	64	68
Bilston Town	42	16	18	8	66	52	66
Cinderford Town	42	17	11	14	62	64	62
Redditch United	42	17	10	15	73	65	61
Gresley Rovers	42	14	15	13	54	49	57
Weston-super-Mare	42	16	9	17	55	55	57
Sutton Coldfield Town	42	13	17	12	49	52	56
Evesham Town	42	13	12	17	69	61	51
Bedworth Town	42	13	10	19	52	71	49
Rocester	42	12	12	18	63	78	48
Bromsgrove Rovers	42	13	7	22	59	72	46
Shepshed Dynamo	42	12	7	23	46	66	43
Paget Rangers	42	11	4	27	44	82	37
Racing Club Warwick	42	7	14	21	41	82	35
Stourbridge	42	10	3	29	45	101	33
Yate Town	42	3	3	36	28	108	12

2000-2001 Premier Division

Margate	42	28	7	7	75	27	91
Burton Albion	42	25	13	4	76	36	88
King's Lynn	42	18	11	13	67	58	65
Welling United	42	17	13	12	59	55	64
Weymouth	42	17	12	13	69	51	63
Havant & Waterlooville	42	18	9	15	65	53	63
Stafford Rangers	42	18	9	15	70	59	63
Worcester City	42	18	8	16	52	53	62
Moor Green	42	18	8	16	49	53	62
Newport County	42	17	10	15	70	61	61
Crawley Town	42	17	10	15	61	54	61
Tamworth	42	17	8	17	58	55	59
Salisbury City	42	17	8	17	64	69	59
Ilkeston Town	42	16	11	15	51	61	59
Bath City	42	15	13	14	67	68	55
Cambridge City	42	13	11	18	56	59	50
Folkestone Invicta	42	14	6	22	49	74	48
Merthyr Tydfil	42	11	13	18	49	62	46
Clevedon Town	42	11	7	24	61	74	40
Fisher Athletic (London)	42	12	6	24	51	85	39
Dorchester Town	42	10	8	24	40	70	38
Halesowen Town	42	8	13	21	47	69	37

Bath City and Fisher Athletic (London) both had 3 points deducted

Eastern Division

Newport IOW	42	28	10	4	91	30	94
Chelmsford City	42	27	9	6	102	45	90
Grantham Town	42	25	11	6	100	47	86
Histon	42	23	11	8	84	53	80
Baldock Town	42	23	10	9	81	44	79
Hastings Town	42	22	10	10	72	50	76
Stamford	42	20	11	11	69	59	71
Tonbridge Angels	42	18	11	13	79	58	65
Langney Sports	42	19	8	15	75	55	65
Rothwell Town	42	20	5	17	86	74	62
Corby Town	42	14	10	18	64	92	52
Ashford Town	42	15	4	23	53	83	49
Banbury United	42	12	11	19	57	54	47
Witney Town	42	12	11	19	55	71	47
Bashley	42	10	14	18	57	71	44
Dartford	42	11	11	20	49	67	44
Burnham	42	10	14	18	39	65	43
Wisbech Town	42	10	9	23	45	89	39
St Leonards	42	9	10	23	55	87	37
Erith & Belvedere	42	10	7	25	49	92	37
Sittingbourne	42	8	9	25	41	79	33
Spalding United	42	7	12	23	35	73	33

Burnham had 1 point deducted, Rothwell Town had 3 points deducted

Western Division

Hinckley United	42	30	8	4	102	38	98
Tiverton Town	42	28	7	7	97	36	91
Bilston Town	42	27	9	6	88	48	90
Evesham United	42	27	5	10	86	46	86
Mangotsfield United	42	25	9	8	91	45	84
Solihull Borough	42	22	12	8	73	43	78
Redditch United	42	17	13	12	76	69	64
Weston-super-Mare	42	17	10	15	68	58	61
Atherstone United	42	16	11	15	64	58	59
Rochester	42	18	5	19	57	77	59
Cirencester Town	42	14	15	13	65	74	57
Rugby United	42	13	10	19	51	68	49
Gloucester City	42	12	11	19	76	86	47
Blakenall	42	13	10	19	54	64	46
Shepshed Dynamo	42	12	9	21	56	73	45
Bedworth United	42	12	9	21	38	60	45
Racing Club Warwick	42	13	6	23	46	77	45
Gresley Rovers	42	11	8	23	46	65	41
Cinderford Town	42	11	8	23	56	84	41
Sutton Coldfield Town	42	7	14	21	45	66	35
Paget Rovers	42	9	4	29	38	93	31
Bromsgrove Rovers	42	7	9	26	47	92	30

Blakenall had 3 points deducted

2001-2002

Premier Division

Kettering Town	42	27	6	9	80	41	87
Tamworth	42	24	13	5	81	41	85
Havant & Waterlooville	42	22	9	11	74	50	75
Crawley Town	42	21	10	11	67	48	73
Newport County	42	19	9	14	61	48	66
Tiverton Town	42	17	10	15	70	63	61
Moor Green	42	18	7	17	64	62	61
Worcester City	42	16	12	14	65	54	60
Stafford Rangers	42	17	9	16	70	62	60
Ilkeston Town	42	14	16	12	58	61	58
Weymouth United	42	15	11	16	59	67	56
Hinckley Town	42	14	13	15	64	62	55
Folkestone Invicta	42	14	12	16	51	61	54
Cambridge City	42	12	16	14	60	70	52
Welling United	42	13	12	17	69	66	51
Hednesford Town	42	15	6	21	59	70	51
Bath City	42	13	11	18	56	65	50
Chelmsford City	42	13	11	18	63	75	50
Newport IOW	42	12	12	18	38	61	48
King's Lynn	42	11	13	18	44	57	46
Merthyr Tydfil	42	12	8	22	53	71	44
Salisbury City	42	6	8	28	36	87	26

Eastern Division

Hastings Town	42	29	8	5	85	38	95
Grantham Town	42	29	6	7	99	43	93
Dorchester Town	42	26	10	6	81	36	88
Histon	42	23	8	11	83	49	77
Stamford	42	24	4	14	76	61	76
Fisher Athletic (London)	42	20	10	12	83	56	70
Eastbourne Borough	42	21	6	15	63	46	69
Dartford	42	18	5	19	62	66	59
Erith & Belvedere	42	18	3	21	75	79	57
Bashley	42	15	11	16	71	63	56
Burnham	42	15	10	17	52	54	55
Rugby United	42	16	6	20	55	67	54
Rothwell Town	42	14	8	20	46	66	50
Ashford Town	42	14	6	22	58	78	48
Banbury United	42	13	9	20	53	66	47
Chatham Town	42	13	8	21	56	87	47
Sittingbourne	42	14	4	24	46	69	46
Spalding	42	13	6	23	72	84	45
Tonbridge Angels	42	13	6	23	65	80	45
St Leonards	42	14	3	25	52	88	45
Corby Town	42	10	13	19	54	82	43
Wisbech Town	42	11	8	23	56	84	41

Western Division

Halesowen Town	40	27	9	4	85	24	90
Chippenham Town	40	26	9	5	81	28	87
Weston-super-Mare	40	22	10	8	70	38	76
Solihull Borough	40	20	11	9	75	42	71
Gresley Rovers	40	19	9	12	59	50	66
Sutton Coldfield Town	40	17	11	12	53	46	62
Mangotsfield United	40	17	10	13	74	54	61
Stourport Swifts	40	18	6	16	59	59	60
Atherstone United	40	16	8	16	61	59	56
Clevedon Town	40	15	11	14	57	58	56
Bedworth United	40	16	7	17	59	63	55
Evesham United	40	16	7	17	54	70	55
Cirencester Town	40	17	3	20	64	69	54
Gloucester City	40	14	10	16	48	63	52
Cinderford Town	40	14	9	17	54	67	51
Shepshed Dynamo	40	10	10	20	64	84	40
Bilston Town	40	11	7	22	50	72	40
Redditch United	40	11	6	23	47	77	39
Swindon Supermarine	40	11	4	25	52	76	37
Racing Club Warwick	40	8	11	21	38	63	35
Rocester	40	5	12	23	33	75	27

FOOTBALL CONFERENCE

1979-80

Altrincham	38	24	8	6	79	35	56
Weymouth	38	22	10	6	73	37	54
Worcester City	38	19	11	8	53	36	49
Boston United	38	16	13	9	52	43	45
Gravesend & Northfleet	38	17	10	11	49	44	44
Maidstone United	38	16	11	11	54	37	43
Kettering Town	38	15	13	10	55	50	43
Northwich Victoria	38	16	10	12	50	38	42
Bangor City	38	14	14	10	41	46	42
Nuneaton Borough	38	13	13	12	58	44	39
Scarborough	38	12	15	11	47	38	39
Yeovil Town	38	13	10	15	46	49	36
Telford United	38	13	8	17	52	60	34
Barrow	38	14	6	18	47	55	34
Wealdstone	38	9	15	14	42	54	33
Bath City	38	10	12	16	43	69	32
Barnet	38	10	10	18	32	48	30
AP Leamington	38	7	11	20	32	63	25
Stafford Rangers	38	6	10	22	41	57	22
Redditch United	38	5	8	25	26	69	18

1980-81

Altrincham	38	23	8	7	72	41	54
Kettering Town	38	21	9	8	66	37	51
Scarborough	38	17	13	8	49	29	47
Northwich Victoria	38	17	11	10	53	40	45
Weymouth	38	19	6	13	54	40	44
Bath City	38	16	10	12	51	32	42
Maidstone United	38	16	9	13	64	53	41
Boston United	38	16	9	13	63	58	41
Barrow	38	15	8	15	50	49	38
Frickley Athletic	38	15	8	15	61	62	38
Stafford Rangers	38	11	15	12	56	56	37
Worcester City	38	14	7	17	47	54	35
Telford United	38	13	9	16	47	59	35
Yeovil Town	38	14	6	18	60	64	34
Gravesend & Northfleet	38	13	8	17	48	55	34
AP Leamington	38	10	11	17	47	66	31
Barnet	38	12	7	19	39	64	31
Nuneaton Borough	38	10	9	19	49	65	29
Wealdstone	38	9	11	18	37	56	29
Bangor City	38	6	12	20	35	68	24

1981-82

Runcorn	42	28	9	5	75	37	93
Enfield	42	26	8	8	90	46	86
Telford United	42	23	8	11	70	51	77
Worcester City	42	21	8	13	70	60	71
Dagenham	42	19	12	11	69	51	69
Northwich Victoria	42	20	9	13	56	46	69
Scarborough	42	19	11	12	65	52	68
Barrow	42	18	11	13	59	50	65
Weymouth	42	18	9	15	56	47	63
Boston United	42	17	11	14	61	57	62
Altrincham	42	14	13	15	66	56	55
Bath City	42	15	10	17	50	57	55
Yeovil Town	42	14	11	17	56	68	53
Stafford Rangers	42	12	16	14	48	47	52
Frickley Athletic	42	14	10	18	47	60	52
Maidstone United	42	11	15	16	55	59	48
Trowbridge Town	42	12	11	19	38	54	47
Barnet	42	9	14	19	36	52	41
Kettering Town	42	9	13	20	64	76	40
Gravesend & Northfleet	42	10	10	22	51	69	40
Dartford	42	10	9	23	47	69	39
AP Leamington	42	4	10	28	40	105	22

1982-83

Enfield	42	25	9	8	95	48	84
Maidstone United	42	25	8	9	83	34	83
Wealdstone	42	22	13	7	80	41	79
Runcorn	42	22	8	12	73	53	74
Boston United	42	20	12	10	77	57	72
Telford United	42	20	11	11	69	48	71
Weymouth	42	20	10	12	63	48	70
Northwich Victoria	42	18	10	14	68	63	64
Scarborough	42	17	12	13	71	58	63
Bath City	42	17	9	16	58	55	60
Nuneaton Borough	42	15	13	14	57	60	58
Altrincham	42	15	10	17	62	56	55
Bangor City	42	14	13	15	71	77	55
Dagenham	42	12	15	15	60	65	51
Barnet	42	16	3	23	55	78	51
Frickley Athletic	42	12	13	17	66	77	49
Worcester City	42	12	10	20	58	87	46
Trowbridge Town	42	12	7	23	56	88	43
Kettering Town	42	11	7	24	69	99	40
Yeovil Town	42	11	7	24	63	99	40
Barrow	42	8	12	22	46	74	36
Stafford Rangers	42	5	14	23	40	75	29

1983-84

Maidstone United	42	23	13	6	71	34	70
Nuneaton Borough	42	24	11	7	70	40	69
Altrincham	42	23	9	10	64	39	65
Wealdstone	42	21	14	7	75	36	62
Runcorn	42	20	13	9	61	45	62
Bath City	42	17	12	13	60	48	53
Northwich Victoria	42	16	14	12	54	47	51
Worcester City	42	15	13	14	64	55	49
Barnet	42	16	10	16	55	58	49
Kidderminster Harriers	42	14	14	14	54	61	49
Telford United	42	17	11	14	50	58	49
Frickley Athletic	42	17	10	15	68	56	48
Scarborough	42	14	16	12	52	55	48
Enfield	42	14	9	19	61	58	43
Weymouth	42	13	8	21	54	65	42
Gateshead	42	12	13	17	59	73	42
Boston United	42	13	12	17	66	80	41
Dagenham	42	14	8	20	57	69	40
Kettering Town	42	12	9	21	53	67	37
Yeovil Town	42	12	8	22	55	77	35
Bangor City	42	10	6	26	54	82	29
Trowbridge Town	42	5	7	30	33	87	19

2 points awarded for a Home win; 3 points awarded for an Away win;
1 point awarded for any Draw

1984-85

Wealdstone	42	20	10	12	64	54	62
Nuneaton Borough	42	19	14	9	85	53	58
Dartford	42	17	13	12	57	48	57
Bath City	42	21	9	12	52	49	57
Altrincham	42	21	6	15	63	47	56
Scarborough	42	17	13	12	69	62	54
Enfield	42	17	13	12	84	61	53
Kidderminster Harriers	42	17	8	17	79	77	51
Northwich Victoria	42	16	11	15	50	46	50
Telford United	42	15	14	13	59	54	49
Frickley Athletic	42	18	7	17	65	71	49
Kettering Town	42	15	12	15	68	59	48
Maidstone United	42	15	13	14	58	51	48
Runcorn	42	13	15	14	48	47	48
Barnet	42	15	11	16	59	52	47
Weymouth	42	15	13	14	70	66	45
Boston United	42	15	10	17	69	69	45
Barrow	42	11	16	15	47	57	43
Dagenham	42	13	10	19	47	67	41
Worcester City	42	12	9	21	55	84	38
Gateshead	42	9	12	21	51	82	33
Yeovil Town	42	6	11	25	44	87	25

2 points awarded for a Home win; 3 points awarded for an Away win;
1 point awarded for any Draw
Gateshead had 1 point deducted

1985-86

Enfield	42	27	10	5	94	47	76
Frickley Athletic	42	25	10	7	78	50	69
Kidderminster Harriers	42	24	7	11	99	62	67
Altrincham	42	22	11	9	70	49	63
Weymouth	42	19	15	8	75	60	61
Runcorn	42	19	14	9	70	44	60
Stafford Rangers	42	19	13	10	61	54	60
Telford United	42	18	10	14	68	66	51
Kettering Town	42	15	15	12	55	53	49
Wealdstone	42	16	9	17	57	56	47
Cheltenham Town	42	16	11	15	69	69	46
Bath City	42	13	11	18	53	54	45
Boston United	42	16	7	19	66	76	44
Barnet	42	13	11	18	56	60	41
Scarborough	42	13	11	18	54	66	40
Northwich Victoria	42	10	12	20	42	54	37
Maidstone United	42	9	16	17	57	66	36
Nuneaton Borough	42	13	5	24	58	73	36
Dagenham	42	10	12	20	48	66	36
Wycombe Wanderers	42	10	13	19	55	84	36
Dartford	42	8	9	25	51	82	26
Barrow	42	7	8	27	41	86	24

2 points awarded for a Home win; 3 points awarded for an Away win;
1 point awarded for any Draw

1986-87

Scarborough	42	27	10	5	64	33	91
Barnet	42	25	10	7	86	39	85
Maidstone United	42	21	10	11	71	48	73
Enfield	42	21	7	14	66	47	70
Altrincham	42	18	15	9	66	53	69
Boston United	42	21	6	15	82	74	69
Sutton United	42	19	11	12	81	51	68
Runcorn	42	18	13	11	71	58	67
Telford United	42	18	10	14	69	59	64
Bath City	42	17	12	13	63	62	63
Cheltenham Town	42	16	13	13	64	50	61
Kidderminster Harriers	42	17	4	21	77	81	55
Stafford Rangers	42	14	11	17	58	60	53
Weymouth	42	13	12	17	68	77	51
Dagenham	42	14	7	21	56	72	49
Kettering Town	42	12	11	19	54	66	47
Northwich Victoria	42	10	14	18	53	69	44
Nuneaton Borough	42	10	14	18	48	73	44
Wealdstone	42	11	10	21	50	70	43
Welling United	42	10	10	22	61	84	40
Frickley Athletic	42	7	11	24	47	82	32
Gateshead	42	6	13	23	48	95	31

1987-88

Lincoln City	42	24	10	8	86	48	82
Barnet	42	23	11	8	93	45	80
Kettering Town	42	22	9	11	68	48	75
Runcorn	42	21	11	10	68	47	74
Telford United	42	20	10	12	65	50	70
Stafford Rangers	42	20	9	13	79	58	69
Kidderminster Harriers	42	18	15	9	75	66	69
Sutton United	42	16	18	8	77	54	66
Maidstone United	42	18	9	15	79	64	63
Weymouth	42	18	9	15	53	43	63
Macclesfield Town	42	18	9	15	64	62	63
Enfield	42	15	10	17	68	78	55
Cheltenham Town	42	11	20	11	64	67	53
Altrincham	42	14	10	18	59	59	52
Fisher Athletic	42	13	13	16	58	61	52
Boston United	42	14	7	21	60	75	49
Northwich Victoria	42	10	17	15	46	57	47
Wycombe Wanderers	42	11	13	18	50	76	46
Welling United	42	11	9	22	50	72	42
Bath City	42	9	10	23	48	76	37
Wealdstone	42	5	17	20	39	76	32
Dagenham	42	5	6	31	37	104	21

1988-89

Maidstone United	40	25	9	6	92	46	84
Kettering Town	40	23	7	10	56	39	76
Boston United	40	22	8	10	61	51	74
Wycombe Wanderers	40	20	11	9	68	52	71
Kidderminster Harriers	40	21	6	13	68	57	69
Runcorn	40	19	8	13	77	53	65
Macclesfield Town	40	17	10	13	63	57	61
Barnet	40	18	7	15	64	69	61
Yeovil Town	40	15	11	14	68	67	56
Northwich Victoria	40	14	11	15	64	65	53
Welling United	40	14	11	15	45	46	53
Sutton United	40	12	15	13	64	54	51
Enfield	40	14	8	18	62	67	50
Altrincham	40	13	10	17	51	61	49
Cheltenham Town	40	12	12	16	55	58	48
Telford United	40	13	9	18	37	43	48
Chorley	40	13	6	21	57	71	45
Fisher Athletic	40	10	11	19	55	65	41
Stafford Rangers	40	11	7	22	49	74	40
Aylesbury United	40	9	9	22	43	71	36
Weymouth	40	7	10	23	37	70	31
Newport County	29	4	7	18	31	62	19

Newport County expelled from League – their record was deleted.

1989-90

Darlington	42	26	9	7	76	25	87
Barnet	42	26	7	9	81	41	85
Runcorn	42	19	13	10	79	62	70
Macclesfield Town	42	17	15	10	56	41	66
Kettering Town	42	18	12	12	66	53	66
Welling United	42	18	10	14	62	50	64
Yeovil Town	42	17	12	13	62	54	63
Sutton United	42	19	6	17	68	64	63
Merthyr Tydfil	42	16	14	12	67	63	62
Wycombe Wanderers	42	17	10	15	64	56	61
Cheltenham Town	42	16	11	15	58	60	59
Telford United	42	15	13	14	56	63	58
Kidderminster Harriers	42	15	9	18	64	67	54
Barrow	42	12	16	14	51	67	52
Northwich Victoria	42	15	5	22	51	67	50
Altrincham	42	12	13	17	49	48	49
Stafford Rangers	42	12	12	18	50	62	48
Boston United	42	13	8	21	48	67	47
Fisher Athletic	42	13	7	22	55	78	46
Chorley	42	13	6	23	42	67	45
Farnborough Town	42	10	12	20	60	73	42
Enfield	42	10	6	26	52	89	36

1990-91

Barnet	42	26	9	7	103	52	87
Colchester United	42	25	10	7	68	35	85
Altrincham	42	23	13	6	87	46	82
Kettering Town	42	23	11	8	67	45	80
Wycombe Wanderers	42	21	11	10	75	46	74
Telford United	42	20	7	15	62	52	67
Macclesfield Town	42	17	12	13	63	52	63
Runcorn	42	16	10	16	69	67	58
Merthyr Tydfil	42	16	9	17	62	61	57
Barrow	42	15	12	15	59	65	57
Welling United	42	13	15	14	55	57	54
Northwich Victoria	42	13	13	16	65	75	52
Kidderminster Harrier	42	14	10	18	56	67	52
Yeovil Town	42	13	11	18	58	58	50
Stafford Rangers	42	12	14	16	48	51	50
Cheltenham Town	42	12	12	18	54	72	48
Gateshead	42	14	6	22	52	92	48
Boston United	42	12	11	19	55	69	47
Slough Town	42	13	6	23	51	80	45
Bath City	42	10	12	20	55	61	42
Sutton United	42	10	9	23	62	82	39
Fisher Athletic	42	5	15	22	38	79	30

1991-92

Colchester United	42	28	10	4	98	40	94
Wycombe Wanderers	42	30	4	8	84	35	94
Kettering Town	42	20	13	9	72	50	73
Merthyr Tydfil	42	18	14	10	59	56	68
Farnborough Town	42	18	13	12	68	53	66
Telford United	42	19	7	16	62	66	64
Redbridge Forest	42	18	9	15	69	56	63
Boston United	42	18	9	15	71	66	63
Bath City	42	16	12	14	54	51	60
Witton Albion	42	16	10	16	63	60	58
Northwich Victoria	42	16	6	20	63	58	54
Welling United	42	14	12	16	69	79	54
Macclesfield Town	42	13	13	16	50	50	52
Gateshead	42	12	13	18	49	57	48
Yeovil Town	42	11	14	17	40	49	47
Runcorn	42	11	13	18	50	63	46
Stafford Rangers	42	10	16	16	41	59	46
Altrincham	42	11	12	19	61	82	45
Kidderminster Harriers	42	12	9	21	56	77	45
Slough Town	42	13	6	23	56	82	45
Cheltenham Town	42	10	13	19	56	83	43
Barrow	42	8	14	20	52	72	38

1992-93

Wycombe Wanderers	42	24	11	7	84	37	83
Bromsgrove Rovers	42	18	14	10	67	49	68
Dagenham & Redbridge	42	19	11	12	75	47	67
Yeovil Town	42	18	12	12	59	49	66
Slough Town	42	18	11	13	60	55	65
Stafford Rangers	42	18	10	14	55	47	64
Bath City	42	15	14	13	53	46	59
Woking	42	17	8	17	58	62	59
Kidderminster Harriers	42	14	16	12	60	60	58
Altrincham	42	15	13	14	49	52	58
Northwich Victoria	42	16	8	18	68	55	56
Stalybridge Celtic	42	13	17	12	48	55	56
Kettering Town	42	14	13	15	61	63	55
Gateshead	42	14	10	18	53	56	52
Telford United	42	14	10	18	55	60	52
Merthyr Tydfil	42	14	10	18	51	79	52
Witton Albion	42	11	17	14	62	65	50
Macclesfield	42	12	13	17	40	50	49
Runcorn	42	13	10	19	58	76	49
Welling United	42	12	12	18	57	72	48
Farnborough Town	42	12	11	19	68	87	47
Boston United	42	9	13	20	50	69	40

Dagenham & Redbridge had 1 point deducted

1993-94

Kidderminster Harriers	42	22	9	11	63	35	75
Kettering Town	42	18	15	8	46	24	72
Woking	42	18	13	11	58	58	67
Southport	42	18	12	12	57	51	66
Runcorn	42	14	19	9	63	57	61
Dagenham & Redbridge	42	15	14	13	62	54	59
Macclesfield Town	42	16	11	15	48	49	59
Dover Athletic	42	17	7	18	48	49	58
Stafford Rangers	42	14	15	13	56	52	57
Altrincham	42	16	9	17	41	42	57
Gateshead	42	15	12	15	45	53	57
Bath City	42	13	17	12	47	38	56
Halifax Town	42	13	16	13	55	49	55
Stalybridge Celtic	42	14	12	16	54	55	54
Northwich Victoria	42	11	19	12	44	45	52
Welling United	42	13	12	17	47	49	51
Telford United	42	13	12	17	41	49	51
Bromsgrove Rovers	42	12	15	15	54	66	51
Yeovil Town	42	14	9	19	49	62	51
Merthyr Tydfil	42	12	15	15	60	61	49
Slough Town	42	11	14	17	44	58	47
Witton Albion	42	7	13	22	37	63	44

Merthyr Tydfil had 2 points deducted

1994-95

Macclesfield Town	42	24	8	10	70	40	80
Woking	42	21	12	9	76	54	75
Southport	42	21	9	12	68	50	72
Altrincham Town	42	20	8	14	77	60	68
Stevenage Borough	42	20	7	15	68	49	67
Kettering Town	42	19	10	13	73	56	67
Gateshead	42	19	10	13	61	53	67
Halifax Town	42	17	12	13	68	54	63
Runcorn	42	16	10	16	59	71	58
Northwich Victoria	42	14	15	13	77	66	57
Kidderminster Harriers	42	16	9	17	63	61	57
Bath City	42	15	12	15	55	56	57
Bromsgrove Rovers	42	14	3	15	66	69	55
Farnborough Town	42	15	10	17	45	64	55
Dagenham & Redbridge	42	13	13	16	56	69	52
Dover Athletic	42	11	16	15	48	55	49
Welling United	42	13	10	19	57	74	49
Stalybridge Celtic	42	11	14	17	52	72	47
Telford United	42	10	16	16	53	62	46
Merthyr Tydfil	42	11	11	20	53	63	44
Stafford Rangers	42	9	11	22	53	79	38
Yeovil Town	42	8	14	20	50	71	37

Yeovil Town had 1 point deducted for fielding an ineligible player

1995-96

Stevenage Borough	42	27	10	5	101	44	91
Woking	42	25	8	9	83	54	83
Hednesford Town	42	23	7	12	71	46	76
Macclesfield Town	42	22	9	11	66	49	75
Gateshead	42	18	13	11	58	46	67
Southport	42	18	12	12	77	64	66
Kidderminster Harriers	42	18	10	14	78	66	64
Northwich Victoria	42	16	12	14	72	64	60
Morecambe	42	17	8	17	78	72	59
Farnborough Town	42	15	14	13	63	58	59
Bromsgrove Rovers	42	15	14	13	59	57	59
Altrincham	42	15	13	14	59	64	58
Telford United	42	15	10	17	51	56	55
Stalybridge Celtic	42	16	7	19	59	68	55
Halifax Town	42	13	13	16	49	63	52
Kettering Town	42	13	9	20	68	84	48
Slough Town	42	13	8	21	63	76	47
Bath City	42	13	7	22	45	66	46
Welling United	42	10	15	17	42	53	45
Dover Athletic	42	11	7	24	51	74	40
Runcorn	42	9	8	25	48	87	35
Dagenham & Redbridge	42	7	12	23	43	73	33

1996-97

Macclesfield Town	42	27	9	6	80	30	90
Kidderminster Harriers	42	26	7	9	84	42	85
Stevenage Borough	42	24	10	8	87	53	82
Morecambe	42	19	9	14	69	56	66
Woking	42	18	10	14	71	63	64
Northwich Victoria	42	17	12	13	61	54	63
Farnborough Town	42	16	13	13	58	53	61
Hednesford Town	42	16	12	14	52	50	60
Telford United	42	16	10	16	46	56	58
Gateshead	42	15	11	16	59	63	56
Southport	42	15	10	17	51	61	55
Rushden & Diamonds	42	14	11	17	61	63	53
Stalybridge Celtic	42	14	10	18	53	58	52
Kettering Town	42	14	9	19	53	62	51
Hayes	42	12	14	16	54	55	50
Slough Town	42	12	14	16	62	65	50
Dover Athletic	42	12	14	16	57	68	50
Welling United	42	13	9	20	50	60	48
Halifax Town	42	12	12	18	55	74	48
Bath City	42	12	11	19	53	80	47
Bromsgrove Rovers	42	12	5	25	41	67	41
Altrincham	42	9	12	21	49	73	39

1997-98

Halifax Town	42	25	12	5	74	43	87
Cheltenham Town	42	23	9	10	63	43	78
Woking	42	22	8	12	72	46	74
Rushden & Diamonds	42	23	5	14	79	57	74
Morecambe	42	21	10	11	77	64	73
Hereford United	42	18	13	11	56	49	67
Hednesford Town	42	18	12	12	59	50	66
Slough Town	42	18	10	14	58	49	64
Northwich Victoria	42	15	15	12	63	59	60
Welling United	42	17	9	16	64	62	60
Yeovil Town	42	17	8	17	73	63	59
Hayes	42	16	10	16	62	52	58
Dover Athletic	42	15	10	17	60	70	55
Kettering Town	42	13	13	16	53	60	52
Stevenage Borough	42	13	12	17	59	63	51
Southport	42	13	11	18	56	58	50
Kidderminster Harriers	42	11	14	17	56	63	49
Farnborough Town	42	12	8	22	56	70	44
Leek Town	42	10	14	18	52	67	44
Telford United	42	10	12	20	53	76	42
Gateshead	42	8	11	23	51	87	35
Stalybridge Celtic	42	7	8	27	48	93	29

1998-99

Cheltenham Town	42	22	14	6	71	36	80
Kettering Town	42	22	10	10	58	37	76
Hayes	42	22	8	12	63	50	74
Rushden & Diamonds	42	20	12	10	71	42	72
Yeovil Town	42	20	11	11	68	54	71
Stevenage Borough	42	17	17	8	62	45	68
Northwich Victoria	42	19	9	14	60	51	66
Kingstonian	42	17	13	12	50	49	64
Woking	42	18	9	15	51	45	62
Hednesford Town	42	15	16	11	49	44	61
Dover Athletic	42	15	13	14	54	48	58
Forest Green Rovers	42	15	13	14	55	50	58
Hereford United	42	15	10	17	49	46	55
Morecambe	42	15	8	19	60	76	53
Kidderminster Harriers	42	14	9	19	56	52	51
Doncaster Rovers	42	12	12	18	51	55	48
Telford United	42	10	16	16	44	60	46
Southport	42	10	15	17	47	59	45
Barrow	42	11	10	21	40	63	43
Welling United	42	9	14	19	44	65	41
Leek Town	42	8	8	26	48	76	32
Farnborough United	42	7	11	24	41	89	32

1999-2000

Kidderminster Harriers	42	26	7	9	75	40	85
Rushden & Diamonds	42	21	13	8	71	42	76
Morecambe	42	18	16	8	70	48	70
Scarborough	42	19	12	11	60	35	69
Kingstonian	42	20	7	15	58	44	67
Dover Athletic	42	18	12	12	65	56	66
Yeovil Town	42	18	10	14	60	63	64
Hereford United	42	15	14	13	61	52	59
Southport	42	15	13	14	55	56	58
Stevenage Borough	42	16	9	17	60	54	57
Hayes	42	16	8	18	57	58	56
Doncaster Rovers	42	15	9	18	46	48	54
Kettering Town	42	12	16	14	44	50	52
Woking	42	13	13	16	45	53	52
Nuneaton Borough	42	12	15	15	49	53	51
Telford United	42	14	9	19	56	66	51
Hednesford Town	42	15	6	21	45	68	51
Northwich Victoria	42	13	12	17	53	78	51
Forest Green Rovers	42	13	8	21	54	63	47
Welling United	42	13	8	21	54	66	47
Altrincham	42	9	19	14	51	60	46
Sutton United	42	8	10	24	39	75	34

2000-2001

Rushden & Diamonds	42	25	11	6	78	36	86
Yeovil Town	42	24	8	10	73	50	80
Dagenham & Redbridge	42	23	8	11	71	54	77
Southport	42	20	9	13	58	46	69
Leigh RMI	42	19	11	12	63	57	68
Telford United	42	19	8	15	51	51	65
Stevenage Borough	42	15	18	9	71	61	63
Chester City	42	16	14	12	49	43	62
Doncaster Rovers	42	15	13	14	47	43	58
Scarborough	42	14	16	12	56	54	58
Hereford United	42	14	15	13	60	46	57
Boston United	42	13	17	12	74	63	56
Nuneaton Borough	42	13	15	14	60	60	54
Woking	42	13	15	14	52	57	54
Dover Athletic	42	14	11	17	54	56	53
Forest Green Rovers	42	11	15	16	43	54	48
Northwich Victoria	42	11	13	18	49	67	46
Hayes	42	12	10	20	44	71	46
Morecambe	42	11	12	19	64	66	45
Kettering Town	42	11	10	21	46	62	43
Kingstonian	42	8	10	24	47	73	34
Hednesford Town	42	5	13	24	46	86	28

2001-2002

Boston United	42	25	9	8	84	42	84
Dagenham & Redbridge	42	24	12	6	70	47	84
Yeovil Town	42	19	13	10	66	53	70
Doncaster Rovers	42	18	13	11	68	46	67
Barnet	42	19	10	13	64	48	67
Morecambe	42	17	11	14	63	67	62
Farnborough Town	42	18	7	17	66	54	61
Margate	42	14	16	12	59	53	58
Telford United	42	14	15	13	63	58	57
Nuneaton Borough	42	16	9	17	57	57	57
Stevenage Borough	42	15	10	17	57	60	55
Scarborough	42	14	14	14	55	63	55
Northwich Victoria	42	16	7	19	57	70	55
Chester City	42	15	9	18	54	51	54
Southport	42	13	14	15	53	49	53
Leigh RMI	42	15	8	19	56	58	53
Hereford United	42	14	10	18	50	53	52
Forest Green Rovers	42	12	15	15	54	76	51
Woking	42	13	9	20	59	70	48
Hayes	42	13	5	24	53	80	44
Stalybridge Celtic	42	11	10	21	40	69	43
Dover Athletic	42	11	6	25	41	65	39

ISTHMIAN LEAGUE

1905-06

London Caledonians	10	7	1	2	25	8	15
Clapton	10	6	1	3	11	13	13
Casuals	10	3	4	3	14	14	10
Civil Service	10	4	1	5	16	20	9
Ealing Association	10	3	2	5	15	19	8
Ilford	10	1	3	6	5	12	5

1906-07

Ilford	10	8	2	0	26	9	18
London Caledonians	10	6	0	4	19	14	12
Clapton	10	4	3	3	18	11	11
Civil Service	10	3	1	6	11	19	7
Ealing Association	10	3	1	6	12	22	7
Casuals	10	2	1	7	15	26	5

1907-08

London Caledonians	10	5	2	3	20	15	12
Clapton	10	4	3	3	24	14	11
Ilford	10	5	1	4	28	22	11
Oxford City	10	5	1	4	20	20	11
Dulwich Hamlet	10	3	2	5	15	18	8
West Norwood	10	3	1	6	13	31	7

1908-09

Bromley	18	11	1	6	42	29	23
Leytonstone	18	9	4	5	43	31	22
Ilford	18	9	4	5	37	36	22
Dulwich Hamlet	18	9	2	7	39	30	20
Clapton	18	8	4	6	34	32	20
Oxford City	18	6	4	8	29	32	16
Nunhead	18	7	2	9	31	35	16
Shepherd's Bush	18	6	3	9	26	44	15
London Caledonians	18	4	6	8	25	34	14
West Norwood	18	5	2	11	40	43	12

1909-10

Bromley	18	11	4	3	32	10	26
Clapton	18	10	4	4	56	19	24
Nunhead	18	10	4	4	49	26	24
Ilford	18	10	3	5	31	17	23
Dulwich Hamlet	18	8	4	6	26	26	20
Leytonstone	18	7	3	8	44	46	17
Oxford City	18	5	4	9	28	45	14
London Caledonians	18	5	3	10	19	40	13
West Norwood	18	5	2	11	28	54	12
Shepherd's Bush	18	2	3	13	23	55	7

1910-11

Clapton	18	11	4	3	39	19	26
Leytonstone	18	12	1	5	47	30	25
Dulwich Hamlet	18	8	5	5	28	22	21
Oxford City	18	7	4	7	32	43	18
Ilford	18	8	1	9	41	32	17
Shepherd's Bush	18	7	3	8	31	27	17
Bromley	18	8	4	6	32	27	16
Nunhead	18	5	4	9	32	36	14
West Norwood	18	4	5	9	24	43	13
London Caledonians	18	3	3	12	18	45	9

Bromley had 4 points deducted

1911-12

London Caledonians	20	11	7	2	39	25	29
Ilford	20	11	3	6	37	24	25
Nunhead	20	10	5	5	36	30	25
Dulwich Hamlet	20	8	5	7	33	23	21
West Norwood	20	9	3	8	38	38	21
Clapton	20	7	5	8	37	37	19
Woking	20	7	5	8	38	41	19
Shepherd's Bush	20	5	6	9	39	49	16
Leytonstone	20	5	6	9	28	38	16
Oxford City	20	5	5	10	33	36	15
Tunbridge Wells	20	5	4	11	23	40	14

1912-13

London Caledonians	20	14	5	1	38	12	33
Leytonstone	20	12	3	5	45	20	27
Nunhead	20	12	3	5	36	23	27
Clapton	20	7	7	6	23	20	21
Dulwich Hamlet	20	8	4	8	34	28	20
Woking	20	7	5	8	33	40	19
Oxford City	20	6	6	8	23	39	18
Ilford	20	6	5	9	27	37	17
Shepherd's Bush	20	5	5	10	26	38	15
Tunbridge Wells	20	5	4	11	22	36	14
West Norwood	20	3	3	14	23	37	9

1913-14

London Caledonians	20	12	6	2	55	23	30
Nunhead	20	11	6	3	49	27	28
Ilford	20	11	4	5	52	35	26
Dulwich Hamlet	20	10	4	6	34	22	24
New Crusaders	20	10	3	7	40	30	23
Oxford City	20	10	0	10	42	42	20
Leytonstone	20	8	4	8	29	32	20
Clapton	20	8	3	9	29	27	19
Shepherd's Bush	20	7	2	11	24	46	16
West Norwood	20	4	3	13	27	47	11
Woking	20	1	1	18	11	61	3

1919

Leytonstone	8	5	1	2	21	7	11
Ilford	8	4	2	2	22	16	10
Dulwich Hamlet	8	3	2	3	19	17	8
Nunhead	8	3	2	3	18	19	8
Clapton	8	0	3	5	14	35	3

1919-20

Dulwich Hamlet	22	15	3	4	58	16	33
Nunhead	22	14	5	3	48	26	33
Tufnell Park	22	12	4	6	45	32	28
Ilford	22	13	1	8	63	42	27
Oxford City	22	12	3	7	63	51	27
London Caledonians	22	10	3	9	32	30	23
Leytonstone	22	8	3	11	50	43	19
Clapton	22	8	3	11	38	44	19
Civil Service	22	7	4	11	35	40	18
Woking	22	6	3	13	36	42	15
West Norwood	22	5	4	13	19	53	14
Casuals	22	3	2	17	20	88	8

1920-21

Ilford	22	16	4	2	70	24	36
London Caledonians	22	13	5	4	45	17	31
Tufnell Park	22	14	3	5	43	24	31
Nunhead	22	12	5	5	53	33	29
Dulwich Hamlet	22	11	6	5	60	30	28
Oxford City	22	12	3	7	56	38	27
Leytonstone	22	8	6	8	36	29	22
Clapton	22	7	7	8	33	52	21
Civil Service	22	3	7	12	28	45	13
Woking	22	3	5	14	16	43	11
Casuals	22	3	3	16	31	87	9
West Norwood	22	2	2	18	18	67	6

1921-22

Ilford	26	17	4	5	66	34	38
Dulwich Hamlet	26	14	8	4	65	24	36
London Caledonians	26	16	4	6	41	21	36
Nunhead	26	12	5	9	65	41	29
Clapton	26	13	3	10	51	46	29
Tufnell Park	26	10	7	9	44	39	27
Oxford City	26	18	2	12	48	47	26
Wycombe Wanderers	26	18	2	12	61	64	26
Civil Service	26	9	8	9	60	48	26
Woking	26	10	6	10	39	49	26
Leytonstone	26	9	6	11	41	48	24
West Norwood	26	8	5	13	43	57	21
Wimbledon	26	7	4	15	52	56	18
Casuals	26	0	2	24	25	107	2

1922-23

Clapton	26	15	7	4	51	33	37
Nunhead	26	15	5	6	52	32	35
London Caledonians	26	13	7	6	43	26	33
Ilford	26	11	7	8	57	38	29
Casuals	26	12	5	9	68	51	29
Civil Service	26	9	10	7	39	36	28
Wycombe Wanderers	26	11	4	11	61	61	26
Dulwich Hamlet	26	9	7	10	60	44	25
Leytonstone	26	9	7	10	45	56	25
Tufnell Park	26	9	5	12	41	45	23
Wimbledon	26	10	2	14	49	50	22
Woking	26	7	6	13	42	67	20
Oxford City	26	6	5	15	45	68	17
West Norwood	26	5	5	16	25	71	15

1923-24

St Albans City	26	17	5	4	72	38	39
Dulwich Hamlet	26	15	6	5	49	28	36
Clapton	26	14	5	7	73	50	33
Wycombe Wanderers	26	14	5	7	88	65	33
London Caledonians	26	14	3	9	53	49	31
Civil Service	26	12	5	9	52	47	29
Casuals	26	13	1	12	65	54	27
Ilford	26	9	6	11	56	59	24
Nunhead	26	8	8	10	41	46	24
Wimbledon	26	8	4	14	43	62	20
Tufnell Park	26	8	2	16	38	53	18
Woking	26	5	8	13	31	62	18
Oxford City	26	7	2	17	53	74	16
Leytonstone	26	6	4	16	41	68	16

1924-25

London Caledonians	26	18	5	3	76	36	41
Clapton	26	19	1	6	64	34	39
St Albans City	26	16	2	8	69	39	34
Tufnell Park	26	11	4	11	47	41	26
Ilford	26	11	4	11	46	42	26
Leytonstone	26	12	2	12	55	63	26
The Casuals	26	12	1	13	55	58	25
Wycombe Wanderers	26	11	2	13	58	61	24
Civil Service	26	10	4	12	52	64	24
Nunhead	26	9	5	12	45	43	23
Wimbledon	26	10	2	14	50	54	22
Dulwich Hamlet	26	8	5	13	42	57	21
Oxford City	26	9	2	15	38	71	20
Woking	26	5	3	18	33	67	13

1925-26

Dulwich Hamlet	26	20	1	5	80	49	41
London Caledonians	26	18	1	7	81	44	37
Clapton	26	14	4	8	64	50	32
Wycombe Wanderers	26	14	3	9	97	83	31
St Albans City	26	12	6	8	76	54	30
Nunhead	26	13	4	9	49	43	30
Ilford	26	13	2	11	81	70	28
Leytonstone	26	12	1	13	75	63	25
Woking	26	8	6	12	56	73	22
Tufnell Park	26	8	5	13	36	53	21
The Casuals	26	8	4	14	48	61	20
Wimbledon	26	9	1	16	61	77	19
Oxford City	26	8	1	17	48	76	17
Civil Service	26	5	1	20	43	99	11

1926-27

St Albans City	26	20	1	5	96	34	41
Ilford	26	18	0	9	76	57	34
Wimbledon	26	15	3	8	72	45	33
Nunhead	26	11	8	7	51	33	30
Woking	26	12	6	8	68	60	30
London Caledonians	26	11	7	8	58	47	29
Clapton	26	11	4	11	58	60	26
Leytonstone	26	11	1	14	54	78	23
Dulwich Hamlet	26	9	4	13	60	58	22
Wycombe Wanderers	26	10	2	14	59	86	22
Tufnell Park	26	8	4	14	45	55	20
Oxford City	26	7	5	14	46	72	19
The Casuals	26	8	3	15	37	78	19
Civil Service	26	6	4	16	48	65	16

1927-28

St Albans City	26	15	5	6	86	50	35
London Caledonians	26	12	9	5	63	38	33
Ilford	26	14	4	8	72	54	32
Woking	26	13	5	8	72	56	31
Nunhead	26	13	2	11	57	54	28
Wimbledon	26	12	3	11	57	48	27
Leytonstone	26	13	1	12	53	56	27
Clapton	26	8	10	8	52	47	26
Dulwich Hamlet	26	8	9	9	56	49	25
The Casuals	26	8	8	10	54	58	24
Wycombe Wanderers	26	9	5	12	60	69	23
Oxford City	26	7	7	12	36	57	21
Civil Service	26	8	4	14	38	76	20
Tufnell Park	26	4	4	18	38	82	12

1928-29

Nunhead	26	15	6	5	47	35	36
London Caledonians	26	15	4	7	65	33	34
Dulwich Hamlet	26	14	6	6	65	34	34
Wimbledon	26	9	10	7	66	54	28
Ilford	26	12	3	11	67	52	27
Clapton	26	11	5	10	60	55	27
Tufnell Park	26	11	5	10	58	55	27
St Albans City	26	12	3	11	63	69	27
Leytonstone	26	11	3	12	56	79	25
Wycombe Wanderers	26	10	3	13	58	60	23
Oxford City	26	10	3	13	61	71	23
The Casuals	26	8	5	13	49	60	21
Woking	26	8	3	15	39	65	19
Civil Service	26	4	5	17	39	71	13

1929-30

Nunhead	26	19	3	4	69	36	41
Dulwich Hamlet	26	15	6	5	74	39	36
Kingstonian	26	15	4	7	57	37	34
Ilford	26	16	1	9	84	60	33
Woking	26	11	5	10	66	65	27
Wimbledon	26	11	2	13	64	66	24
Wycombe Wanderers	26	10	4	12	49	52	24
The Casuals	26	8	7	11	50	51	23
Oxford City	26	10	3	13	45	60	23
St Albans City	26	9	4	13	54	77	22
Clapton	26	8	4	14	47	57	20
London Caledonians	26	8	3	15	49	69	19
Leytonstone	26	8	3	15	48	68	19
Tufnell Park	26	6	7	13	35	54	19

1930-31

Wimbledon	26	18	6	2	69	37	42
Dulwich Hamlet	26	12	9	5	51	39	33
Wycombe Wanderers	26	12	6	8	67	45	30
The Casuals	26	12	6	8	71	56	30
St Albans City	26	11	7	8	67	66	29
Ilford	26	10	6	10	70	62	26
Oxford City	26	10	5	11	43	48	25
London Caledonians	26	8	8	10	43	53	24
Kingstonian	26	10	4	12	49	64	24
Tufnell Park	26	9	5	12	45	61	23
Nunhead	26	9	4	13	49	54	22
Woking	26	9	4	13	56	63	22
Clapton	26	7	4	15	62	75	18
Leytonstone	26	6	4	16	46	65	16

1931-32

Wimbledon	26	17	2	7	60	35	36
Ilford	26	13	9	4	71	45	35
Dulwich Hamlet	26	15	3	8	69	43	33
Wycombe Wanderers	26	14	5	7	72	50	33
Oxford City	26	15	2	9	63	49	32
Kingstonian	26	13	3	10	71	50	29
Tufnell Park	26	9	7	10	50	48	25
Nunhead	26	9	7	10	54	61	25
The Casuals	26	10	4	12	59	65	24
Clapton	26	9	5	12	50	57	23
Leytonstone	26	9	3	14	36	61	21
St Albans City	26	8	4	14	57	78	20
Woking	26	6	5	15	44	64	17
London Caledonians	26	2	7	17	24	74	11

1932-33

Dulwich Hamlet	26	15	6	5	71	45	36
Leytonstone	26	16	4	6	66	43	36
Kingstonian	26	15	2	9	77	49	32
Ilford	26	14	0	12	60	58	28
The Casuals	26	12	2	12	48	36	26
Tufnell Park	26	11	3	12	51	51	25
St Albans City	26	12	1	13	57	63	25
Clapton	26	10	5	11	51	65	25
Oxford City	26	9	6	11	49	54	24
Woking	26	10	4	12	53	61	24
Wycombe Wanderers	26	10	4	12	47	56	24
Nunhead	26	8	6	12	42	50	22
Wimbledon	26	8	5	13	55	67	21
London Caledonians	26	5	6	15	35	64	16

1933-34

Kingstonian	26	15	7	4	80	42	37
Dulwich Hamlet	26	15	5	6	68	36	35
Wimbledon	26	13	7	6	62	35	33
Tufnell Park	26	14	5	7	55	50	33
Ilford	26	15	2	9	60	56	32
The Casuals	26	13	5	8	47	32	31
Leytonstone	26	13	3	10	55	48	29
Nunhead	26	10	5	11	48	44	25
London Caledonians	26	7	8	11	29	51	22
Wycombe Wanderers	26	9	2	15	57	60	20
St Albans City	26	8	4	14	44	75	20
Oxford City	26	7	4	15	45	57	18
Clapton	26	5	6	15	35	62	16
Woking	26	6	1	19	43	81	13

1934-35

Wimbledon	26	14	7	5	63	30	35
Oxford City	26	14	4	8	69	50	32
Leytonstone	26	15	2	9	49	36	32
Dulwich Hamlet	26	11	7	8	66	45	29
Tufnell Park	26	11	7	8	53	44	29
Kingstonian	26	11	6	9	44	40	28
Nunhead	26	10	7	9	35	34	27
London Caledonians	26	9	7	10	40	41	25
St Albans City	26	9	6	11	61	80	24
Ilford	26	9	6	11	40	56	24
Clapton	26	7	7	12	46	48	21
Woking	26	9	3	14	44	68	21
Wycombe Wanderers	26	7	6	13	51	69	20
The Casuals	26	6	5	15	37	57	17

1935-36

Wimbledon	26	19	2	5	82	29	40
The Casuals	26	14	5	7	60	45	33
Ilford	26	13	3	10	67	47	29
Dulwich Hamlet	26	10	8	8	64	47	28
Nunhead	26	11	6	9	51	40	28
Wycombe Wanderers	26	13	2	11	60	68	28
Clapton	26	11	5	10	42	46	27
Oxford City	26	11	4	11	60	58	26
St Albans City	26	11	2	13	59	64	24
Woking	26	9	4	13	43	62	22
Tufnell Park	26	9	3	14	42	61	21
London Caledonians	26	9	3	14	35	52	21
Kingstonian	26	9	2	15	43	56	20
Leytonstone	26	7	3	16	34	67	17

1936-37

Kingstonian	26	18	3	5	63	43	39
Nunhead	26	17	3	6	77	32	37
Leytonstone	26	16	4	6	71	42	36
Ilford	26	14	5	7	86	39	33
Dulwich Hamlet	26	12	6	8	64	48	30
Wycombe Wanderers	26	10	5	11	55	52	25
Wimbledon	26	9	7	10	52	53	25
Clapton	26	10	5	11	42	51	25
The Casuals	26	10	3	13	46	58	23
Woking	26	9	4	13	53	69	22
Oxford City	26	8	5	13	56	89	21
St Albans City	26	7	5	14	44	62	19
Tufnell Park	26	4	7	15	43	74	15
London Caledonians	26	5	4	17	26	66	14

1937-38

Leytonstone	26	17	6	3	72	34	40
Ilford	26	17	3	6	70	39	37
Tufnell Park	26	15	2	9	62	47	32
Nunhead	26	14	3	9	52	44	31
Wycombe Wanderers	26	12	5	9	69	55	29
Dulwich Hamlet	26	13	3	10	57	46	29
Kingstonian	26	12	4	10	51	48	28
Clapton	26	9	6	11	49	53	24
Wimbledon	26	10	3	13	62	49	23
London Caledonians	26	9	4	13	44	55	22
Oxford City	26	7	7	12	35	71	21
The Casuals	26	8	3	15	51	74	19
Woking	26	7	2	17	41	72	16
St Albans City	26	4	5	17	31	60	13

1938-39

Leytonstone	26	18	4	4	68	32	40
Ilford	26	17	4	5	68	32	38
Kingstonian	26	17	3	6	62	39	37
Dulwich Hamlet	26	15	5	6	60	32	35
Wimbledon	26	14	3	9	88	56	31
Nunhead	26	11	6	9	54	44	28
The Casuals	26	11	6	9	54	51	28
Clapton	26	12	2	12	69	61	26
Wycombe Wanderers	26	10	6	10	62	62	26
St Albans City	26	8	5	13	44	50	21
Woking	26	9	2	15	35	56	20
Oxford City	26	4	4	18	44	84	12
Tufnell Park	26	4	4	18	33	87	12
London Caledonians	26	3	4	19	26	81	10

1945-46

Walthamstow Avenue	26	21	0	5	100	31	42
Oxford City	26	17	6	3	91	40	40
Romford	26	15	3	8	83	59	33
Dulwich Hamlet	26	14	2	10	63	59	30
Tufnell Park	26	12	4	10	70	55	28
Woking	26	10	7	9	56	54	27
Ilford	26	12	2	12	56	71	26
Leytonstone	26	11	3	12	61	75	25
Wycombe Wanderers	26	9	3	14	80	88	21
Wimbledon	26	7	6	13	52	72	20
Corinthian Casuals	26	8	4	14	58	83	20
Clapton	26	8	3	15	51	62	19
St Albans City	26	6	6	14	48	85	18
Kingstonian	26	6	3	17	48	86	15

1946-47

Leytonstone	26	19	2	5	92	36	40
Dulwich Hamlet	26	17	3	6	78	46	37
Romford	26	13	8	5	76	52	34
Walthamstow Avenue	26	13	4	9	64	37	30
Oxford City	26	12	6	8	70	51	30
Kingstonian	26	12	4	10	54	57	28
Wycombe Wanderers	26	9	8	9	62	62	26
Wimbledon	26	10	5	11	68	64	25
Ilford	26	7	7	12	66	78	21
Tufnell Park	26	8	5	13	45	69	21
Woking	26	7	7	12	34	62	21
Clapton	26	6	8	12	41	59	20
St Albans City	26	7	5	14	47	79	19
Corinthian Casuals	26	4	4	18	36	80	12

1947-48

Leytonstone	26	19	1	6	87	38	39
Kingstonian	26	16	6	4	74	39	38
Walthamstow Avenue	26	17	3	6	61	37	37
Dulwich Hamlet	26	17	2	7	71	39	36
Wimbledon	26	13	6	7	66	40	32
Romford	26	14	1	11	53	47	29
Oxford City	26	10	5	11	50	68	25
Woking	26	10	3	13	63	55	23
Ilford	26	7	8	11	51	59	22
St Albans City	26	9	2	15	43	56	20
Wycombe Wanderers	26	7	5	14	51	65	19
Tufnell Park	26	7	4	15	38	83	18
Clapton	26	5	4	17	35	69	14
Corinthian Casuals	26	5	2	19	33	81	12

1948-49

Dulwich Hamlet	26	15	6	5	60	31	36
Walthamstow Avenue	26	16	4	6	65	38	36
Wimbledon	26	15	4	7	64	41	34
Ilford	26	14	3	9	56	36	31
Oxford City	26	13	5	8	48	34	31
Leytonstone	26	12	6	8	49	41	30
Woking	26	14	1	11	64	59	29
Romford	26	11	3	12	47	54	25
Kingstonian	26	10	4	12	43	47	24
Corinthian Casuals	26	11	2	13	47	59	24
Wycombe Wanderers	26	11	2	13	49	61	24
St Albans City	26	6	6	14	40	60	16
Clapton	26	5	5	16	32	61	15
Tufnell Park	26	1	5	20	28	70	7

St Albans City had 2 points deducted

1949-50

Leytonstone	26	17	5	4	77	31	39
Wimbledon	26	18	2	6	72	51	38
Kingstonian	26	16	3	7	59	39	35
Walthamstow Avenue	26	14	6	6	73	42	34
Dulwich Hamlet	26	14	3	9	60	47	31
St Albans City	26	12	3	11	59	45	27
Woking	26	10	6	10	60	71	26
Wycombe Wanderers	26	9	7	10	51	52	25
Romford	26	10	4	12	45	49	24
Ilford	26	10	4	12	46	53	24
Clapton	26	8	6	12	51	59	22
Oxford City	26	6	6	14	35	54	18
Corinthian Casuals	26	4	5	17	41	69	13
Tufnell Park	26	3	2	21	24	91	8

1950-51

Leytonstone	26	20	3	3	72	26	43
Walthamstow Avenue	26	15	4	7	57	37	34
Romford	26	15	3	8	58	49	33
Wimbledon	26	13	5	8	58	39	31
Dulwich Hamlet	26	14	2	10	54	43	30
Woking	26	11	6	9	65	55	28
Ilford	26	12	4	10	44	45	28
Corinthian Casuals	26	13	0	13	62	60	26
St Albans City	26	11	4	11	32	36	26
Kingstonian	26	9	4	13	46	54	22
Wycombe Wanderers	26	8	3	15	46	64	19
Oxford City	26	7	4	15	47	65	18
Clapton	26	6	5	15	29	50	17
Tufnell Park Edmonton	26	4	1	21	24	73	9

1951-52

Leytonstone	26	13	9	4	63	36	35
Wimbledon	26	16	3	7	65	44	35
Walthamstow Avenue	26	15	4	7	71	43	34
Romford	26	14	4	8	64	42	32
Kingstonian	26	11	7	8	62	48	29
Wycombe Wanderers	26	12	5	9	64	59	29
Woking	26	11	5	10	60	71	27
Dulwich Hamlet	26	11	4	11	60	53	26
Corinthian Casuals	26	11	4	11	55	66	26
St Albans City	26	9	7	10	48	53	25
Ilford	26	8	5	13	32	47	21
Clapton	26	9	2	15	50	59	20
Oxford City	26	6	3	17	50	72	15
Tufnell Park Edmonton	26	2	6	18	25	73	10

1952-53

Walthamstow Avenue	28	19	6	3	53	25	44
Bromley	28	17	4	7	71	35	38
Leytonstone	28	14	6	8	60	38	34
Wimbledon	28	14	5	9	68	37	33
Kingstonian	28	13	6	9	62	50	32
Dulwich Hamlet	28	15	2	11	62	52	32
Romford	28	12	8	8	62	52	32
Wycombe Wanderers	28	14	2	12	54	62	30
St Albans City	28	11	6	11	43	57	28
Barking	28	9	7	12	42	51	25
Ilford	28	10	4	14	59	57	24
Woking	28	10	4	14	57	72	24
Corinthian Casuals	28	7	9	12	45	56	23
Oxford City	28	5	2	21	37	87	12
Clapton	28	2	5	21	27	71	9

1953-54

Bromley	28	18	3	7	76	45	39
Walthamstow Avenue	28	13	7	8	55	30	33
Wycombe Wanderers	28	15	3	10	65	44	33
Ilford	28	11	10	7	48	44	32
Corinthian Casuals	28	12	7	9	59	44	31
Woking	28	13	4	11	54	58	30
Leytonstone	28	12	5	11	58	48	29
St Albans City	28	11	6	11	54	55	28
Dulwich Hamlet	28	11	6	11	55	57	28
Romford	28	11	5	12	57	54	27
Clapton	28	11	5	12	42	56	27
Barking	28	11	2	15	59	84	24
Kingstonian	28	8	7	13	59	71	23
Wimbledon	28	7	8	13	43	59	22
Oxford City	28	4	6	18	49	84	14

1954-55

Walthamstow Avenue	28	21	1	6	80	38	43
St Albans City	28	18	3	7	61	41	39
Bromley	28	18	2	8	66	34	38
Wycombe Wanderers	28	16	3	9	68	43	35
Ilford	28	13	5	10	64	46	31
Barking	28	15	1	12	55	51	31
Woking	28	12	3	13	75	79	27
Kingstonian	28	10	7	11	47	57	27
Leytonstone	28	10	4	14	35	51	24
Oxford City	28	10	3	15	43	74	23
Clapton	28	9	4	15	41	50	22
Wimbledon	28	10	2	16	48	62	22
Corinthian Casuals	28	9	3	16	50	65	21
Dulwich Hamlet	28	7	5	16	48	60	19
Romford	28	4	10	14	43	73	18

1955-56

Wycombe Wanderers	28	19	5	4	82	36	43
Bromley	28	12	7	9	54	43	31
Leytonstone	28	12	7	9	50	44	31
Woking	28	14	3	11	62	60	31
Barking	28	12	7	9	41	45	31
Kingstonian	28	12	6	10	67	64	30
Walthamstow Avenue	28	13	3	12	61	45	29
Ilford	28	10	8	10	44	52	28
Oxford City	28	10	7	11	48	55	27
Clapton	28	9	8	11	45	48	26
Wimbledon	28	12	2	14	51	62	26
Corinthian Casuals	28	9	7	12	56	56	25
Dulwich Hamlet	28	9	6	13	55	67	24
Romford	28	9	6	13	42	55	24
St Albans City	28	2	10	16	36	62	14

1956-57

Wycombe Wanderers	30	18	6	6	86	53	42
Woking	30	20	1	9	104	47	41
Bromley	30	16	5	9	78	60	37
Oxford City	30	16	3	11	65	57	35
Ilford	30	12	8	10	59	65	32
Tooting & Mitcham United	30	10	11	9	53	48	31
Kingstonian	30	11	9	10	72	77	31
Walthamstow Avenue	30	11	8	11	48	46	30
Dulwich Hamlet	30	13	3	14	65	54	29
St Albans City	30	13	3	14	62	71	29
Leytonstone	30	11	6	13	50	50	28
Clapton	30	9	9	12	48	59	27
Wimbledon	30	10	5	15	47	66	25
Romford	30	10	5	15	53	81	25
Barking	30	7	6	17	48	72	20
Corinthian Casuals	30	7	4	19	46	78	18

1957-58

Tooting & Mitcham United	30	20	6	4	79	33	46
Wycombe Wanderers	30	19	4	7	78	42	42
Walthamstow Avenue	30	17	5	8	63	35	39
Bromley	30	13	9	8	66	51	35
Oxford City	30	13	6	11	59	48	32
Leytonstone	30	13	6	11	49	48	32
Wimbledon	30	15	2	13	64	66	32
Corinthian Casuals	30	12	8	10	62	68	32
Woking	30	12	7	11	70	58	31
Barking	30	10	6	14	49	61	26
St Albans City	30	11	3	16	56	76	25
Clapton	30	8	9	13	42	65	25
Kingstonian	30	7	8	15	45	66	22
Dulwich Hamlet	30	7	7	16	49	64	21
Ilford	30	8	4	18	46	70	20
Romford	30	6	8	16	45	71	20

1958-59

Wimbledon	30	22	3	5	91	38	47
Dulwich Hamlet	30	18	5	7	68	44	41
Wycombe Wanderers	30	18	4	8	93	50	40
Oxford City	30	17	4	9	87	58	38
Walthamstow Avenue	30	16	5	9	59	40	37
Tooting & Mitcham United	30	15	4	11	84	55	34
Barking	30	14	2	14	59	53	30
Woking	30	12	6	12	66	66	30
Bromley	30	11	7	12	56	55	29
Clapton	30	10	6	14	55	67	26
Ilford	30	10	6	14	46	67	26
Kingstonian	30	9	4	17	54	72	22
St Albans City	30	8	6	16	53	89	22
Leytonstone	30	7	6	17	40	87	20
Romford	30	7	5	18	54	76	19
Corinthian Casuals	30	7	5	18	44	92	19

1959-60

Tooting & Mitcham United	30	17	8	5	75	43	42
Wycombe Wanderers	30	19	3	8	84	46	41
Wimbledon	30	18	3	9	66	36	39
Kingstonian	30	18	3	9	76	51	39
Corinthian Casuals	30	18	1	11	69	61	37
Bromley	30	15	6	9	75	46	36
Dulwich Hamlet	30	14	6	10	65	47	34
Walthamstow Avenue	30	11	11	8	48	38	33
Oxford City	30	10	10	10	57	57	30
Leytonstone	30	10	8	12	43	46	28
Woking	30	10	6	14	54	61	26
St Albans City	30	10	6	14	50	65	26
Maidstone United	30	10	5	15	53	60	25
Barking	30	7	4	19	30	75	18
Ilford	30	5	6	19	34	86	16
Clapton	30	3	4	23	32	92	10

1960-61

Bromley	30	20	6	4	89	42	46
Walthamstow Avenue	30	20	5	5	87	38	45
Wimbledon	30	18	6	6	72	43	42
Dulwich Hamlet	30	17	4	9	71	59	35
Maidstone United	30	14	8	8	63	39	36
Leytonstone	30	15	6	9	46	34	36
Tooting & Mitcham United	30	14	3	13	69	51	31
Wycombe Wanderers	30	12	5	13	63	61	29
St Albans City	30	12	4	14	45	72	28
Oxford City	30	10	7	13	59	59	27
Corinthian Casuals	30	9	9	12	49	59	27
Kingstonian	30	10	6	14	55	61	26
Woking	30	10	6	14	58	71	26
Ilford	30	5	8	17	30	69	18
Barking	30	3	8	19	30	76	14
Clapton	30	3	5	22	25	77	11

1961-62

Wimbledon	30	19	6	5	68	24	44
Leytonstone	30	17	7	6	61	44	41
Walthamstow Avenue	30	14	8	8	51	31	36
Kingstonian	30	15	5	10	65	48	35
Tooting & Mitcham United	30	12	10	8	62	47	34
Oxford City	30	12	9	9	56	49	33
Wycombe Wanderers	30	12	7	11	57	51	31
Corinthian Casuals	30	12	7	11	45	51	31
St Albans City	30	10	9	11	55	55	29
Woking	30	9	9	12	51	60	27
Dulwich Hamlet	30	11	4	15	55	66	26
Barking	30	9	8	13	40	64	26
Ilford	30	7	10	13	50	59	24
Bromley	30	10	4	16	49	69	24
Clapton	30	6	8	16	45	67	20
Maidstone United	30	6	7	17	34	59	19

1962-63

Wimbledon	30	19	8	3	84	33	46
Kingstonian	30	18	8	4	79	37	44
Tooting & Mitcham United	30	17	8	5	65	37	42
Ilford	30	19	3	8	70	44	41
Walthamstow Avenue	30	14	7	9	51	44	35
Maidstone United	30	13	8	9	56	45	34
Bromley	30	12	10	8	57	51	34
Leytonstone	30	12	7	11	48	50	31
Wycombe Wanderers	30	10	10	10	56	61	30
St Albans City	30	11	5	14	54	49	27
Barking	30	8	10	12	39	50	26
Oxford City	30	8	9	13	55	64	25
Woking	30	8	6	16	42	66	22
Clapton	30	7	4	19	30	71	18
Dulwich Hamlet	30	4	5	21	30	71	13
Corinthian Casuals	30	4	4	22	28	71	12

1963-64

Wimbledon	38	27	6	5	87	44	60
Hendon	38	25	4	9	124	38	54
Kingstonian	38	24	4	10	100	62	52
Sutton United	38	23	5	10	99	64	51
Enfield	38	20	10	8	96	56	50
Oxford City	38	20	8	10	90	55	48
Tooting & Mitcham United	38	19	8	11	78	51	46
St Albans City	38	14	12	12	62	63	40
Ilford	38	16	8	14	75	79	40
Maidstone United	38	15	8	15	65	71	38
Walthamstow Avenue	38	15	6	17	70	66	36
Leytonstone	38	14	8	16	66	71	36
Wycombe Wanderers	38	13	6	19	74	80	32
Hitchin Town	38	14	4	20	67	100	32
Bromley	38	11	8	19	64	75	30
Barking	38	10	9	19	46	69	29
Woking	38	10	9	19	48	88	29
Corinthian Casuals	38	10	4	24	52	92	24
Dulwich Hamlet	38	6	12	20	47	97	24
Clapton	38	2	5	31	31	120	9

1964-65

Hendon	38	28	7	3	123	49	63
Enfield	38	29	5	4	98	35	63
Kingstonian	38	24	8	6	86	44	56
Leytonstone	38	24	5	9	115	62	53
Oxford City	38	20	7	11	76	51	47
St Albans City	38	18	9	11	63	43	45
Sutton United	38	17	11	10	74	57	45
Wealdstone	38	19	6	13	93	68	44
Bromley	38	14	11	13	71	80	39
Tooting & Mitcham United	38	15	7	16	71	66	37
Hitchin Town	38	13	9	16	61	66	35
Walthamstow Avenue	38	15	5	18	63	82	35
Wycombe Wanderers	38	13	7	18	70	85	33
Corinthian Casuals	38	13	7	18	56	77	33
Barking	38	10	8	20	58	80	28
Ilford	38	8	8	22	43	89	24
Maidstone United	38	8	6	24	49	86	22
Dulwich Hamlet	38	8	5	25	45	79	21
Clapton	38	8	3	27	43	91	19
Woking	38	7	4	27	45	113	18

Hendon beat Enfield in a play-off to decide the Championship

1965-66

Leytonstone	38	27	7	4	98	33	63
Hendon	38	27	5	6	111	55	59
Enfield	38	24	8	6	104	54	56
Wycombe Wanderers	38	25	6	7	100	65	56
Kingstonian	38	24	5	9	94	55	53
Wealdstone	38	20	6	12	90	64	46
Maidstone United	38	19	6	13	74	61	44
St Albans City	38	19	5	14	57	56	43
Sutton United	38	17	7	14	83	72	41
Tooting & Mitcham United	38	16	7	15	65	58	39
Corinthian Casuals	38	17	5	16	74	67	39
Woking	38	12	10	16	60	83	34
Walthamstow Avenue	38	12	9	17	81	75	33
Oxford City	38	10	9	19	49	72	29
Barking	38	10	7	21	51	72	27
Bromley	38	10	5	23	69	101	25
Ilford	38	7	10	21	50	84	24
Hitchin Town	38	6	8	24	57	118	20
Clapton	38	5	6	27	46	103	16
Dulwich Hamlet	38	5	5	28	30	95	15

1966-67

Sutton United	38	26	7	5	89	33	59
Walthamstow Avenue	38	22	12	4	89	47	56
Wycombe Wanderers	38	23	8	7	92	54	54
Enfield	38	25	2	11	87	33	52
Hendon	38	20	9	9	64	37	49
Tooting & Mitcham United	38	19	10	9	76	60	48
Leytonstone	38	19	9	10	67	38	47
St Albans City	38	16	12	10	59	45	44
Kingstonian	38	18	8	12	60	49	44
Oxford City	38	15	9	14	74	61	39
Woking	38	13	10	15	65	71	36
Wealdstone	38	13	8	17	72	73	34
Barking	38	11	12	15	56	61	34
Bromley	38	12	7	19	50	67	31
Clapton	38	10	8	20	49	92	28
Ilford	38	8	10	20	43	77	26
Corinthian Casuals	38	9	7	22	45	68	25
Maidstone United	38	6	10	22	43	90	22
Hitchin Town	38	8	6	24	39	89	22
Dulwich Hamlet	38	3	4	31	33	107	10

1967-68

Enfield	38	28	8	2	85	22	64
Sutton United	38	22	11	5	89	27	55
Hendon	38	23	6	9	90	36	52
Leytonstone	38	21	10	7	78	41	52
St Albans City	38	20	8	10	78	41	48
Walthamstow Avenue	38	19	9	10	81	64	47
Wealdstone	38	19	8	11	80	45	46
Tooting & Mitcham United	38	19	5	14	57	45	43
Barking	38	17	8	13	75	57	42
Oxford City	38	17	4	17	59	58	38
Kingstonian	38	14	10	14	56	61	38
Hitchin Town	38	14	9	15	61	73	37
Bromley	38	12	10	16	58	80	34
Wycombe Wanderers	38	13	5	20	73	85	31
Dulwich Hamlet	38	10	7	21	39	66	27
Clapton	38	10	7	21	51	88	27
Woking	38	8	8	22	50	90	24
Corinthian Casuals	38	7	10	21	40	80	24
Ilford	38	7	7	24	41	77	21
Maidstone United	38	3	4	31	26	131	10

1968-69

Enfield	38	27	7	4	103	28	61
Hitchin Town	38	23	10	5	67	41	56
Sutton United	38	22	9	7	83	29	53
Wycombe Wanderers	38	23	6	9	70	37	52
Wealdstone	38	20	11	7	73	48	51
Hendon	38	22	5	11	69	47	49
St Albans City	38	17	13	8	75	44	47
Barking	38	20	7	11	69	46	47
Oxford City	38	18	8	12	76	64	44
Tooting & Mitcham United	38	16	10	12	68	55	42
Leytonstone	38	18	4	16	71	53	40
Kingstonian	38	15	8	15	62	56	38
Walthamstow Avenue	38	10	10	18	47	71	30
Maidstone United	38	10	8	20	47	75	28
Clapton	38	10	7	21	52	76	27
Woking	38	8	7	23	45	77	23
Bromley	38	8	7	23	52	95	23
Dulwich Hamlet	38	6	9	23	31	77	21
Ilford	38	6	8	24	33	77	20
Corinthian Casuals	38	2	4	32	23	120	8

1969-70

Enfield	38	27	8	3	91	26	62
Wycombe Wanderers	38	25	11	2	85	24	61
Sutton United	38	24	9	5	75	35	57
Barking	38	21	9	8	93	47	51
Hendon	38	19	12	7	77	44	50
St Albans City	38	21	8	9	69	40	50
Hitchin Town	38	19	10	9	71	40	48
Tooting & Mitcham United	38	19	5	14	88	62	43
Leytonstone	38	17	7	14	57	41	41
Wealdstone	38	15	10	13	53	48	40
Oxford City	38	15	7	16	61	78	37
Kingstonian	38	13	9	16	55	57	35
Ilford	38	8	15	15	42	73	31
Dulwich Hamlet	38	8	12	18	46	66	28
Woking	38	10	7	21	46	69	27
Walthamstow Avenue	38	11	5	22	52	81	27
Clapton	38	9	7	22	45	87	25
Maidstone United	38	7	8	23	48	84	22
Corinthian Casuals	38	6	3	29	30	99	15
Bromley	38	3	4	31	28	111	10

1970-71

Wycombe Wanderers	38	28	6	4	93	32	62
Sutton United	38	29	3	6	76	35	61
St Albans City	38	23	10	5	87	26	56
Enfield	38	24	7	7	67	24	55
Ilford	38	21	7	10	74	51	49
Hendon	38	18	11	9	81	37	47
Barking	38	20	4	14	89	59	44
Leytonstone	38	17	10	11	68	50	44
Woking	38	18	6	14	57	50	42
Walthamstow Avenue	38	14	11	13	63	52	39
Oxford City	38	13	10	15	51	48	36
Hitchin Town	38	12	9	17	46	60	33
Wealdstone	38	12	8	18	45	64	32
Tooting & Mitcham United	38	11	9	18	44	66	31
Kingstonian	38	11	8	19	53	71	30
Bromley	38	10	6	22	34	77	26
Dulwich Hamlet	38	7	10	21	30	66	24
Maidstone United	38	7	6	25	42	84	20
Clapton	38	5	7	26	33	101	17
Corinthian Casuals	38	2	8	28	23	103	12

1971-72

Wycombe Wanderers	40	31	3	6	102	20	65
Enfield	40	26	8	6	90	41	60
Walton & Hersham	40	24	8	8	69	25	56
Hendon	40	23	10	7	79	35	56
Bishop's Stortford	40	24	5	11	61	37	53
Sutton United	40	21	10	9	77	43	52
St Albans City	40	23	4	13	74	47	50
Ilford	40	17	11	12	62	52	45
Barking	40	20	4	16	65	61	44
Hitchin Town	40	17	10	13	68	66	44
Bromley	40	16	10	14	67	64	42
Hayes	40	14	12	14	50	48	40
Oxford City	40	13	9	18	67	74	35
Woking	40	11	10	19	52	58	32
Kingstonian	40	10	12	18	49	59	32
Walthamstow Avenue	40	12	8	20	58	71	32
Leytonstone	40	11	8	21	48	68	30
Tooting & Mitcham United	40	6	9	25	38	93	21
Clapton	40	7	7	26	45	118	21
Dulwich Hamlet	40	4	12	24	35	81	20
Corinthian Casuals	40	3	4	33	21	116	10

1972-73

Hendon	42	34	6	2	88	18	74
Walton & Hersham	42	25	11	6	60	25	61
Leatherhead	42	23	10	9	76	32	56
Wycombe Wanderers	42	25	6	11	66	32	56
Walthamstow Avenue	42	20	12	10	66	48	52
Tooting & Mitcham United	42	20	11	11	73	39	51
Sutton United	42	21	9	12	69	48	51
Kingstonian	42	20	10	12	60	49	50
Enfield	42	20	8	14	90	54	48
Bishop's Stortford	42	18	12	12	58	51	48
Hayes	42	19	8	15	69	42	46
Dulwich Hamlet	42	18	9	15	59	52	45
Ilford	42	18	9	15	61	59	45
Leytonstone	42	17	11	14	55	54	45
Woking	42	18	8	16	61	56	44
Hitchin Town	42	15	9	18	52	64	39
Barking	42	8	7	27	45	88	23
St Albans City	42	5	12	25	34	76	22
Oxford City	42	6	7	29	30	101	19
Bromley	42	4	10	28	31	70	18
Clapton	42	3	11	28	31	100	17
Corinthian Casuals	42	3	8	31	30	106	14

1973-74

First Division

Wycombe Wanderers	42	27	9	6	96	34	90
Hendon	42	25	13	4	63	20	88
Bishop's Stortford	42	26	9	7	78	26	87
Dulwich Hamlet	42	22	11	9	71	38	77
Leatherhead	42	23	6	13	81	44	75
Walton & Hersham	42	20	12	10	68	50	72
Woking	42	22	6	14	63	55	72
Leytonstone	42	20	9	13	63	44	69
Ilford	42	20	8	14	60	44	68
Hayes	42	17	14	11	65	43	65
Oxford City	42	15	16	11	45	47	61
Sutton United	42	13	16	13	51	52	55
Hitchin Town	42	15	10	17	68	73	55
Barking	42	14	12	16	57	58	54
Kingstonian	42	12	15	15	47	46	51
Tooting & Mitcham United	42	14	9	19	57	62	51
Enfield	42	13	11	18	50	57	50
Walthamstow Avenue	42	11	13	18	46	62	46
Bromley	42	7	9	26	37	81	30
Clapton	42	8	3	31	36	128	27
St Albans City	42	4	7	31	30	92	19
Corinthian Casuals	42	3	4	35	31	107	13

Second Division

Dagenham	30	22	4	4	68	23	70
Slough Town	30	18	6	6	46	23	60
Hertford Town	30	17	5	8	46	29	56
Chesham Town	30	16	6	8	61	43	54
Aveley	30	16	5	9	50	28	53
Tilbury	30	14	5	11	47	36	47
Maidenhead United	30	12	11	7	36	30	47
Horsham	30	12	9	9	47	35	45
Harwich & Parkeston	30	11	9	10	46	41	42
Staines Town	30	10	8	12	34	41	38
Carshalton Athletic	30	8	8	14	34	51	32
Hampton	30	6	10	14	33	51	28
Harlow Town	30	6	9	15	33	48	27
Finchley	30	6	7	17	29	52	25
Southall	30	3	10	17	17	52	19
Wokingham Town	30	3	8	19	30	74	17

1974-75

First Division

Wycombe Wanderers	42	28	11	3	93	30	95
Enfield	42	29	8	5	78	26	95
Dagenham	42	28	5	9	95	44	89
Tooting & Mitcham United	42	25	9	8	78	46	84
Dulwich Hamlet	42	24	10	8	75	38	82
Leatherhead	42	23	10	9	83	42	79
Ilford	42	23	10	9	98	51	79
Oxford City	42	17	9	16	63	56	60
Slough Town	42	17	6	19	68	52	57
Sutton United	42	17	6	19	68	63	57
Bishop's Stortford	42	17	6	19	56	64	57
Hitchin Town	42	15	10	17	57	71	55
Hendon	42	15	7	20	59	74	52
Walthamstow Avenue	42	13	9	20	56	62	48
Woking	42	12	10	20	53	73	46
Hayes	42	10	14	18	52	66	44
Barking	42	12	8	22	57	81	44
Leytonstone	42	12	7	23	42	61	43
Kingstonian	42	13	4	25	48	73	43
Clapton	42	12	4	26	46	96	40
Walton & Hersham	42	9	4	29	37	108	31
Bromley	42	6	3	33	25	110	21

Second Division

Staines Town	34	23	2	9	65	23	71
Southall	34	20	3	11	55	41	63
Tilbury	34	19	5	10	64	36	60
Harwich & Parkeston	34	18	4	12	52	44	58
Chesham United	34	17	6	11	59	39	57
St Albans City	34	15	11	8	42	37	56
Harlow Town	34	16	6	12	53	47	54
Horsham	34	16	5	13	59	49	53
Maidenhead United	34	13	7	14	38	40	46
Hampton	34	12	7	15	44	42	43
Croydon	34	11	10	13	48	55	43
Hertford Town	34	10	7	17	35	52	37
Boreham Wood	34	7	15	12	41	49	36
Wokingham Town	34	10	6	18	32	43	36
Finchley	34	9	9	16	36	53	36
Carshalton Athletic	34	9	9	16	38	58	36
Aveley	34	9	7	18	34	63	34
Corinthian Casuals	34	8	9	17	35	59	33

Tilbury had 2 points deducted

1975-76

First Division

Enfield	42	26	9	7	83	38	87
Wycombe Wanderers	42	24	10	8	71	41	82
Dagenham	42	25	6	11	89	55	81
Ilford	42	22	10	10	58	39	76
Dulwich Hamlet	42	22	5	15	67	41	71
Hendon	42	20	11	11	60	41	71
Tooting & Mitcham United	42	19	11	12	73	49	68
Leatherhead	42	19	10	13	63	53	67
Staines Town	42	19	9	14	46	37	66
Slough Town	42	17	12	13	58	45	63
Sutton United	42	17	11	14	71	60	62
Bishop's Stortford	42	15	12	15	51	47	57
Walthamstow Avenue	42	14	11	17	47	60	53
Woking	42	14	9	19	58	62	51
Barking	42	15	6	21	57	70	51
Hitchin Town	42	13	11	18	45	57	50
Hayes	42	10	19	13	44	48	49
Kingstonian	42	13	8	21	53	87	47
Southall & Ealing Borough	42	11	9	22	56	69	42
Leytonstone	42	10	10	22	41	63	40
Oxford City	42	9	8	25	29	65	35
Clapton	42	3	3	36	19	112	12

Second Division

Tilbury	42	32	6	4	97	30	102
Croydon	42	28	14	0	81	27	98
Carshalton Athletic	42	28	6	8	75	37	90
Chesham United	42	21	12	9	91	51	75
Harwich & Parkeston	42	21	11	10	78	56	74
Hampton	42	21	9	12	72	52	72
St Albans City	42	18	12	12	59	48	66
Boreham Wood	42	17	12	13	68	50	63
Harrow Borough	42	15	12	15	71	74	57
Hornchurch	42	15	11	16	61	61	56
Horsham	42	14	13	15	60	55	55
Wembley	42	14	13	15	51	54	55
Wokingham Town	42	13	16	13	45	52	55
Walton & Hersham	42	14	12	16	61	56	54
Finchley	42	14	11	17	52	53	53
Bromley	42	11	11	20	64	86	44
Aveley	42	11	9	22	34	51	42
Harlow Town	42	11	9	22	50	73	42
Maidenhead United	42	6	17	19	32	65	35
Ware	42	7	12	23	50	95	33
Hertford Town	42	5	9	28	32	87	24
Corinthian Casuals	42	4	7	31	42	113	19

1976-77

First Division

Enfield	42	24	12	6	63	34	84
Wycombe Wanderers	42	25	8	9	71	34	83
Dagenham	42	23	10	9	80	39	79
Hendon	42	19	10	13	60	48	67
Tilbury	42	18	13	11	57	49	67
Tooting & Mitcham	42	18	10	14	85	72	64
Walthamstow Avenue	42	19	7	16	61	55	64
Slough Town	42	18	9	15	51	46	63
Hitchin Town	42	19	6	17	60	66	63
Leatherhead	42	18	7	17	61	47	61
Staines Town	42	16	13	13	52	48	61
Leytonstone	42	16	11	15	59	57	59
Barking	42	16	9	17	63	61	57
Southall & Ealing Borough	42	15	8	19	52	64	53
Croydon	42	13	10	19	38	52	49
Sutton United	42	14	7	21	40	55	49
Kingstonian	42	13	7	22	45	60	46
Hayes	42	12	10	20	49	69	46
Woking	42	11	12	19	47	61	45
Bishop's Stortford	42	11	11	20	51	71	44
Dulwich Hamlet	42	11	8	23	52	68	41
Ilford	42	10	8	24	32	73	38

Second Division

Boreham Wood	42	35	4	5	80	26	103
Carshalton Athletic	42	25	12	5	80	33	87
Harwich & Parkeston	42	23	8	11	93	61	77
Wembley	42	23	8	11	82	58	77
Harrow Borough	42	21	12	9	78	44	75
Horsham	42	23	5	14	67	56	74
Bromley	42	20	10	12	71	46	70
Oxford City	42	20	8	14	73	55	68
Hampton	42	20	8	14	62	45	68
Wokingham Town	42	16	14	12	60	44	62
Hornchurch	42	18	7	17	62	53	61
Chesham United	42	17	10	15	63	66	61
St Albans City	42	16	12	14	59	53	60
Walton & Hersham	42	17	9	16	57	56	60
Aveley	42	14	8	20	49	62	50
Corinthian Casuals	42	13	6	23	52	75	45
Harlow Town	42	11	8	23	39	77	41
Hertford Town	42	9	9	24	45	80	36
Maidenhead United	42	8	8	26	36	73	32
Clapton	42	7	9	28	43	87	30
Finchley	42	5	13	24	36	82	28
Ware	42	5	8	29	43	98	23

1977-78

Premier Division

Enfield	42	35	5	2	96	27	110
Dagenham	42	24	7	11	78	55	79
Wycombe Wanderers	42	22	9	11	66	41	75
Tooting & Mitcham United	42	22	8	12	64	49	74
Hitchin Town	42	20	9	13	69	53	69
Sutton United	42	18	12	12	66	57	66
Leatherhead	42	18	11	13	62	48	65
Croydon	42	18	10	14	61	52	64
Walthamstow Avenue	42	17	12	13	64	61	63
Barking	42	17	7	18	76	66	58
Carshalton Athletic	42	15	11	16	60	62	56
Hayes	42	15	11	16	46	53	56
Hendon	42	16	7	19	57	55	55
Woking	42	14	11	17	62	62	53
Boreham Wood	42	15	8	19	48	65	53
Slough Town	42	14	8	20	52	69	0
Staines Town	42	12	13	17	46	60	49
Tilbury	42	11	12	19	57	68	45
Kingstonian	42	8	13	21	43	65	37
Leytonstone	42	7	15	20	44	71	36
Southall & Ealing Borough	42	6	15	21	43	74	33
Bishop's Stortford	42	7	8	27	36	83	29

First Division

Dulwich Hamlet	42	28	9	5	91	25	93
Oxford City	42	26	5	11	85	44	83
Bromley	42	23	13	6	74	41	82
Walton & Hersham	42	22	11	9	69	41	77
Ilford	42	21	14	7	57	47	77
St Albans City	42	22	10	10	83	46	76
Wokingham Town	42	19	12	11	69	48	69
Harlow Town	42	19	8	15	63	49	65
Harrow Borough	42	17	10	15	59	54	61
Maidenhead United	42	16	13	13	55	54	61
Hertford Town	42	15	14	13	57	51	59
Chesham United	42	14	13	15	69	70	55
Hampton	42	13	13	16	49	53	52
Harwich & Parkeston	42	12	13	17	68	79	49
Wembley	42	15	3	24	56	82	48
Horsham	42	12	10	20	41	57	46
Finchley	42	11	13	18	41	68	46
Aveley	42	13	7	22	47	75	46
Ware	42	8	13	21	61	95	37
Clapton	42	10	6	26	46	78	36
Hornchurch	42	8	10	24	47	81	34
Corinthian Casuals	42	3	10	29	40	88	19

Second Division

Epsom & Ewell	32	21	5	6	65	34	68
Metropolitan Police	32	19	6	7	53	30	63
Farnborough Town	32	19	4	9	68	40	61
Molesey	32	17	8	7	47	27	59
Egham Town	32	15	9	8	52	34	54
Tring Town	32	14	11	7	62	32	53
Letchworth Garden City	32	14	11	7	67	48	53
Lewes	32	13	7	12	52	51	46
Rainham Town	32	13	6	13	42	50	45
Worthing	32	11	9	12	40	45	42
Eastbourne United	32	10	8	14	40	50	38
Cheshunt	32	9	6	17	43	60	33
Feltham	32	7	9	16	30	49	30
Camberley Town	32	6	11	15	32	49	29
Hemel Hempstead	32	6	9	17	33	50	27
Epping Town	32	7	6	19	37	64	27
Willesden	32	7	3	22	38	88	24

1978-79

Premier Division

Barking	42	28	9	5	92	50	93
Dagenham	42	25	6	11	83	63	81
Enfield	42	22	11	9	69	37	77
Dulwich Hamlet	42	21	13	8	69	39	76
Slough Town	42	20	12	10	61	44	72
Wycombe Wanderers	42	20	9	13	59	44	69
Woking	42	18	14	10	79	59	68
Croydon	42	19	9	14	61	51	66
Hendon	42	16	14	12	55	48	62
Leatherhead	42	17	9	16	57	45	60
Sutton United	42	17	9	16	62	51	60
Tooting & Mitcham United	42	15	14	13	52	52	59
Walthamstow Avenue	42	15	6	21	61	69	51
Tilbury	42	13	1	18	60	76	50
Boreham Wood	42	13	10	19	50	67	49
Hitchin Town	42	12	11	19	59	71	47
Carshalton Athletic	42	10	16	16	49	69	46
Hayes	42	9	18	15	45	58	45
Oxford City	42	12	7	23	50	80	43
Staines Town	42	6	16	20	40	64	34
Leytonstone	42	8	7	27	36	75	31
Kingstonian	42	3	15	24	35	72	24

First Division

Harlow Town	42	31	7	4	93	32	100
Harrow Borough	42	26	8	8	85	49	86
Maidenhead United	42	25	6	11	72	50	81
Bishop's Stortford	42	22	11	9	68	40	77
Horsham	42	23	7	12	63	47	76
Hertford Town	42	21	11	10	62	41	74
Harwich & Parkeston	42	22	5	15	90	57	71
Bromley	42	18	12	12	76	50	66
Hampton	42	17	11	14	59	47	62
Epsom & Ewell	42	18	7	17	69	41	61
Wembley	42	15	14	13	57	57	59
Aveley	42	17	6	19	57	67	57
Wokingham Town	42	17	8	17	64	68	56
Clapton	42	15	8	19	67	80	53
Metropolitan Police	42	12	13	17	58	55	49
Walton & Hersham	42	12	9	21	47	71	45
Ilford	42	13	5	24	48	80	44
Ware	42	11	10	21	46	69	43
Chesham United	42	11	9	22	46	66	42
Finchley	42	7	15	20	43	75	36
St Albans City	42	7	7	28	43	90	28
Southall & Ealing Borough	42	5	5	32	41	114	20

Wokingham Town had 3 points deducted

Second Division

Farnborough Town	34	26	3	5	77	34	81
Camberley Town	34	21	8	5	71	32	71
Molesey	34	19	11	4	55	33	68
Lewes	34	19	6	9	66	50	63
Feltham	34	16	7	11	47	36	55
Letchworth Garden City	34	14	10	10	56	48	52
Eastbourne United	34	16	4	14	47	45	52
Hemel Hempstead	34	13	11	10	46	37	50
Epping Town	34	14	7	13	49	44	49
Rainham Town	34	13	10	11	42	41	49
Cheshunt	34	11	8	15	43	49	41
Hungerford Town	34	11	8	15	48	58	41
Worthing	34	9	8	17	40	50	35
Hornchurch	34	9	8	17	39	62	35
Egham Town	34	7	12	15	48	54	33
Tring Town	34	6	8	20	33	56	26
Willesden	34	6	8	20	41	77	26
Corinthian Casuals	34	4	7	23	23	65	19

1979-80

Premier Division

Enfield	42	25	9	8	74	32	84
Walthamstow Avenue	42	24	9	9	87	48	81
Dulwich Hamlet	42	21	16	5	66	37	79
Sutton United	42	20	13	9	67	40	73
Dagenham	42	20	13	9	82	56	73
Tooting & Mitcham United	42	21	6	15	62	59	69
Barking	42	19	10	13	72	51	67
Harrow Borough	42	17	15	10	64	51	66
Woking	42	17	13	12	78	59	64
Wycombe Wanderers	42	17	13	12	72	53	64
Harlow Town	42	14	12	16	55	61	54
Hitchin Town	42	13	15	14	55	69	54
Hendon	42	12	13	17	50	57	49
Slough Town	42	13	10	19	54	71	49
Boreham Wood	42	13	10	19	50	69	49
Staines Town	42	14	6	22	46	67	48
Hayes	42	12	9	21	48	68	45
Leatherhead	42	11	11	20	51	60	44
Carshalton Athletic	42	12	7	23	48	78	43
Croydon	42	10	10	22	51	59	40
Oxford City	42	10	9	23	49	87	39
Tilbury	42	7	11	24	41	90	30

Tilbury had 2 points deducted

First Division

Leytonstone & Ilford	42	31	6	5	83	35	99
Bromley	42	24	10	8	93	44	82
Maidenhead United	42	24	8	10	81	46	80
Bishop's Stortford	42	24	8	10	74	47	80
Kingstonian	42	22	8	12	59	44	74
Chesham United	42	18	13	11	68	56	67
St Albans City	42	17	13	12	65	47	64
Farnborough Town	42	19	7	16	70	57	64
Epsom & Ewell	42	18	7	17	62	57	61
Camberley Town	42	16	10	16	43	38	58
Walton & Hersham	42	15	12	15	61	50	57
Wembley	42	16	8	18	46	52	56
Wokingham Town	42	14	11	17	45	49	53
Hertford Town	42	13	11	18	71	74	50
Aveley	42	12	13	17	45	55	49
Hampton	42	14	7	21	57	74	49
Finchley	42	13	9	20	44	59	48
Metropolitan Police	42	13	8	21	46	67	47
Ware	42	11	12	19	45	61	45
Clapton	42	14	3	25	48	77	45
Harwich & Parkeston	42	11	6	25	51	84	38
Horsham	42	6	4	32	29	113	22

Harwich & Parkeston had 1 point deducted

Second Division

Billericay Town	36	31	3	2	100	18	96
Lewes	36	24	7	5	82	33	79
Hungerford Town	36	21	8	7	78	36	71
Eastbourne United	36	21	6	9	77	45	69
Letchworth Garden City	36	21	6	9	63	32	69
Hornchurch	36	21	6	9	66	39	69
Molesey	36	15	9	12	67	60	54
Barton Rovers	36	15	7	14	49	49	52
Worthing	36	14	9	13	58	54	51
Cheshunt	36	13	7	16	47	52	46
Rainham Town	36	12	7	17	54	65	43
Egham Town	36	11	9	16	47	53	42
Southall & Ealing Borough	36	11	6	19	43	69	39
Feltham	36	8	11	17	23	49	35
Tring Town	36	7	13	16	38	55	34
Epping Town	36	10	4	22	44	69	34
Willesden	36	9	6	21	32	83	33
Hemel Hempstead	36	4	9	23	33	72	21
Corinthian Casuals	36	6	3	27	24	92	21

1980-81

Premier Division

Slough Town	42	23	13	6	73	34	82
Enfield	42	23	11	8	81	43	80
Wycombe Wanderers	42	22	9	11	76	49	75
Leytonstone & Ilford	42	19	12	11	78	57	69
Sutton United	42	19	12	11	82	65	69
Hendon	42	18	10	14	66	58	64
Dagenham	42	17	11	14	79	66	62
Hayes	42	18	8	16	45	50	62
Harrow Borough	42	16	11	15	57	52	59
Bromley	42	16	9	17	63	69	57
Staines Town	42	15	9	18	60	61	54
Tooting & Mitcham United	42	15	8	19	49	53	53
Hitchin Town	42	14	10	18	64	62	52
Croydon	42	12	15	15	51	51	51
Dulwich Hamlet	42	13	12	17	62	67	51
Leatherhead	42	12	14	16	36	50	50
Carshalton Athletic	42	14	8	20	57	82	50
Barking	42	13	12	17	58	72	49
Harlow Town	42	11	15	16	53	66	48
Walthamstow Avenue	42	13	7	22	50	81	46
Boreham Wood	42	10	13	19	46	69	43
Woking	42	11	7	24	40	69	37

Barking had 1 point deducted
Woking had 3 points deducted

First Division

Bishop's Stortford	42	30	6	6	84	28	96
Billericay Town	42	29	6	7	67	34	93
Epsom & Ewell	42	24	12	6	80	36	84
Farnborough Town	42	23	11	8	75	39	80
St Albans City	42	24	5	13	85	61	77
Kingstonian	42	20	9	13	63	52	66
Oxford City	42	18	9	15	71	48	63
Wokingham Town	42	16	15	11	70	56	63
Metropolitan Police	42	18	7	17	61	58	61
Chesham United	42	17	7	18	64	64	58
Lewes	42	17	7	18	72	83	58
Maidenhead United	42	16	7	19	58	62	55
Walton & Hersham	42	12	15	15	46	53	51
Hertford Town	42	13	11	18	46	65	50
Hampton	42	12	13	17	46	53	49
Aveley	42	13	9	20	54	55	48
Wembley	42	13	8	21	47	61	47
Clapton	42	12	8	22	53	86	44
Ware	42	9	13	20	50	69	40
Tilbury	42	10	8	24	42	84	35
Camberley Town	42	8	7	27	42	88	31
Finchley	42	6	11	25	36	77	29

Kingstonian and Tilbury both had 3 points deducted

Second Division

Feltham	38	24	10	4	65	30	82
Hornchurch	38	25	6	7	74	35	81
Hungerford Town	38	23	10	5	84	29	79
Barton Rovers	38	19	11	8	61	25	68
Worthing	38	19	11	8	74	43	68
Cheshunt	38	19	11	8	57	33	68
Letchworth Garden City	38	18	7	13	49	40	61
Southall	38	14	11	13	48	52	53
Dorking Town	38	13	12	13	47	45	51
Horsham	38	16	3	19	47	47	51
Hemel Hempstead	38	14	7	17	47	54	49
Egham Town	38	13	9	16	45	62	48
Harwich & Parkeston	38	12	11	15	57	58	47
Rainham Town	38	11	13	14	44	45	46
Epping Town	38	12	7	19	37	50	43
Eastbourne United	38	11	10	17	59	75	43
Willesden	38	11	8	19	57	68	41
Tring Town	38	11	6	21	40	71	39
Molesey	38	4	9	25	31	83	21
Corinthian Casuals	38	1	8	29	17	95	11

1981-82

Premier Division

Leytonstone & Ilford	42	26	5	11	91	52	83
Sutton United	42	22	9	11	72	49	75
Wycombe Wanderers	42	21	10	11	63	48	73
Staines Town	42	21	9	12	58	45	72
Walthamstow Avenue	42	21	7	14	81	62	70
Harrow Borough	42	18	13	11	77	55	67
Tooting & Mitcham United	42	19	10	13	58	47	67
Slough Town	42	17	13	12	64	54	64
Leatherhead	42	16	12	14	57	52	60
Hayes	42	16	10	16	58	52	58
Croydon	42	16	9	17	59	57	57
Barking	42	14	14	14	53	51	56
Hendon	42	13	13	16	56	65	52
Dulwich Hamlet	42	14	10	18	47	59	52
Bishop's Stortford	42	15	5	22	50	70	50
Carshalton Athletic	42	14	8	20	58	86	50
Billericay Town	42	11	16	15	41	50	49
Hitchin Town	42	12	11	19	56	77	47
Bromley	42	13	7	22	63	79	46
Woking	42	11	13	18	57	75	46
Harlow Town	42	10	11	21	50	73	41
Boreham Wood	42	8	13	21	47	58	37

First Division

Wokingham Town	40	29	5	6	86	30	92
Bognor Regis Town	40	23	10	7	65	34	79
Metropolitan Police	40	22	11	7	75	48	77
Oxford City	40	21	11	8	82	47	74
Feltham	40	20	8	12	65	49	68
Lewes	40	19	7	14	73	66	64
Hertford Town	40	16	10	14	62	54	58
Wembley	40	14	15	11	69	55	57
Farnborough Town	40	15	11	14	71	57	56
Epsom & Ewell	40	16	8	16	52	44	56
Kingstonian	40	16	7	17	57	56	55
Hampton	40	15	9	16	52	52	54
Hornchurch	40	13	15	12	42	50	54
Aveley	40	14	10	16	46	58	54
St Albans City	40	14	9	17	55	55	51
Maidenhead United	40	11	10	19	49	70	43
Tilbury	40	9	15	16	49	66	42
Walton & Hersham	40	10	11	19	43	65	41
Chesham United	40	9	9	22	41	71	36
Clapton	40	9	7	24	44	75	34
Ware	40	5	2	33	29	105	17

Second Division

Worthing	40	29	6	5	95	25	93
Cheshunt	40	25	7	8	79	33	82
Hungerford Town	40	22	10	8	89	42	74
Barton Rovers	40	22	8	10	65	32	74
Windsor & Eton	40	22	6	12	69	49	72
Corinthian Casuals	40	19	12	9	67	50	69
Harwich & Parkeston	40	19	12	9	64	47	69
Letchworth Garden City	40	15	11	14	67	55	56
Dorking Town	40	13	17	10	52	44	56
Hemel Hempstead	40	15	9	16	54	49	54
Basildon United	40	16	5	19	64	51	53
Finchley	40	14	9	17	57	68	51
Southall	40	12	14	14	36	42	50
Epping Town	40	12	11	17	48	62	47
Molesey	40	13	7	20	61	73	46
Egham Town	40	11	9	20	56	64	42
Rainham Town	40	11	9	20	53	83	42
Tring Town	40	9	13	18	49	78	40
Eastbourne United	40	9	12	19	51	73	39
Horsham	40	10	9	21	42	79	39
Camberley Town	40	3	2	35	21	140	11

Hungerford Town had 2 points deducted

1982-83

Premier Division

Wycombe Wanderers	42	26	7	9	79	47	85
Leytonstone & Ilford	42	24	9	9	71	39	81
Harrow Borough	42	24	7	11	91	58	79
Hayes	42	23	9	10	63	41	78
Sutton United	42	20	8	14	96	71	68
Dulwich Hamlet	42	18	14	10	59	52	68
Slough Town	42	18	13	11	73	36	67
Bognor Regis Town	42	19	8	15	53	48	65
Tooting & Mitcham United	42	18	9	15	65	62	63
Billericay Town	42	17	10	15	54	51	61
Croydon	42	17	9	16	68	58	60
Hendon	42	18	6	18	68	61	60
Bishop's Stortford	42	17	9	16	61	58	60
Barking	42	14	14	14	47	55	56
Bromley	42	14	12	16	51	50	54
Carshalton Athletic	42	15	9	18	58	60	54
Wokingham Town	42	13	9	20	37	51	48
Walthamstow Avenue	42	12	11	19	48	64	47
Staines Town	42	12	11	19	62	79	47
Hitchin Town	42	11	9	22	49	77	42
Woking	42	6	6	30	30	79	24
Leatherhead	42	4	5	33	35	121	17

First Division

Worthing	40	25	6	9	76	39	81
Harlow Town	40	21	11	8	84	55	74
Farnborough Town	40	20	13	7	69	39	73
Hertford Town	40	20	11	9	70	61	71
Oxford City	40	19	13	8	70	49	70
Boreham Wood	40	21	6	13	62	42	69
Metropolitan Police	40	19	9	12	77	57	66
Walton & Hersham	40	17	6	17	65	59	57
Hampton	40	15	10	15	62	60	55
Wembley	40	14	10	16	62	61	52
Aveley	40	15	7	18	52	62	52
Kingstonian	40	13	12	15	53	53	51
Tilbury	40	12	10	18	41	47	46
Feltham	40	11	12	17	45	54	45
Chesham United	40	13	6	21	43	70	45
Epsom & Ewell	40	10	14	16	44	49	44
Lewes	40	12	8	20	47	71	44
Cheshunt	40	10	13	17	41	49	43
Hornchurch	40	11	8	21	45	74	41
Maidenhead United	40	10	10	20	57	87	40
St Albans City	40	10	9	21	52	79	37

St Albans City had 2 points deducted

Second Division

Clapton	42	30	4	8	96	46	94
Windsor & Eton	42	27	7	8	98	43	88
Barton Rovers	42	26	6	10	86	48	84
Leyton Wingate	42	25	8	9	111	41	83
Basildon United	42	23	13	6	92	42	82
Uxbridge	42	22	12	8	80	42	78
Hungerford Town	42	22	10	10	82	39	76
Corinthian Casuals	42	23	6	13	95	48	75
Egham Town	42	21	8	13	77	67	71
Tring Town	42	20	10	12	86	59	70
Letchworth Garden City	42	18	13	11	68	53	66
Southall	42	18	7	17	81	80	61
Molesey	42	17	9	16	73	56	60
Dorking Town	42	15	9	18	56	75	54
Hemel Hempstead	42	12	14	16	53	59	50
Rainham Town	42	14	4	24	57	94	46
Eastbourne United	42	10	6	26	54	104	36
Epping Town	42	6	8	28	29	89	26
Ware	42	6	6	30	34	97	24
Finchley	42	4	12	26	28	92	24
Horsham	42	5	7	30	32	106	22
Harwich & Parkeston	42	5	7	30	42	130	22

Letchworth Garden City had 1 point deducted

1983-84 Premier Division

Harrow Borough	42	25	13	4	73	42	88
Worthing	42	20	11	11	89	72	71
Slough Town	42	20	9	13	73	56	69
Sutton United	42	18	12	12	67	45	66
Hayes	42	17	13	12	56	41	64
Hitchin Town	42	16	15	11	58	57	63
Wycombe Wanderers	42	16	14	12	63	52	62
Wokingham Town	42	18	10	14	78	55	61
Hendon	42	17	10	15	62	51	61
Dulwich Hamlet	42	16	11	15	61	64	59
Bishop's Stortford	42	15	13	14	56	57	58
Harlow Town	42	15	11	16	64	70	56
Bognor Regis Town	42	14	13	15	62	69	55
Staines Town	42	15	9	18	63	72	54
Billericay Town	42	15	8	19	53	73	53
Barking	42	13	13	16	60	64	52
Croydon	42	14	10	18	52	58	52
Walthamstow Avenue	42	13	10	19	53	67	49
Leytonstone & Ilford	42	13	9	20	54	67	48
Carshalton Athletic	42	11	10	21	59	72	43
Tooting & Mitcham United	42	10	13	19	50	63	43
Bromley	42	7	11	24	33	72	32

Wokingham Town had 3 points deducted

First Division

Windsor & Eton	42	26	7	9	89	44	85
Epsom & Ewell	42	23	9	10	73	51	78
Wembley	42	21	11	10	65	32	74
Maidenhead United	42	22	8	12	67	42	74
Boreham Wood	42	22	7	13	74	43	73
Farnborough Town	42	18	12	12	78	60	66
Hampton	42	18	12	12	65	49	66
Metropolitan Police	42	20	5	17	79	64	65
Chesham United	42	18	8	16	64	57	62
Tilbury	42	17	10	15	54	64	61
Leatherhead	42	15	10	17	67	56	55
Aveley	42	15	10	17	49	53	55
Woking	42	16	7	19	66	73	55
Hertford Town	42	15	9	18	56	73	54
Oxford City	42	14	9	19	57	56	51
Lewes	42	13	12	17	49	65	51
Walton & Hersham	42	13	10	19	52	70	49
Hornchurch	42	13	10	19	43	65	49
Kingstonian	42	13	9	20	47	67	48
Clapton	42	12	11	19	49	67	47
Cheshunt	42	12	8	22	45	64	44
Feltham	42	7	4	31	31	106	25

Second Division

Basildon United	42	30	7	5	88	27	97
St Albans City	42	29	9	5	100	46	96
Leyton Wingate	42	29	4	9	97	41	91
Tring Town	42	23	11	8	89	44	80
Corinthian Casuals	42	23	11	8	75	47	80
Hungerford Town	42	21	12	9	94	47	75
Uxbridge	42	18	15	9	61	36	69
Grays Athletic	42	20	9	13	72	57	69
Dorking	42	21	5	16	66	54	68
Southall	42	20	8	14	79	60	65
Egham Town	42	16	15	11	59	49	63
Epping Town	42	15	16	11	61	50	61
Molesey	42	13	14	15	59	68	53
Barton Rovers	42	15	8	19	54	64	53
Letchworth Garden City	42	15	7	20	48	66	52
Newbury Town	42	14	5	23	60	82	47
Hemel Hempstead	42	12	9	21	63	69	45
Rainham Town	42	7	5	30	38	114	26
Finchley	42	5	9	28	28	78	24
Eastbourne United	42	7	3	32	36	98	24
Ware	42	6	6	30	48	114	24
Horsham	42	7	4	31	40	104	23

Southall had 2 points deducted
Horsham had 3 points deducted

1984-85

Premier Division

Sutton United	42	23	15	4	115	55	84
Worthing	42	24	8	10	89	59	80
Wycombe Wanderers	42	24	6	12	68	46	78
Wokingham Town	42	20	13	9	74	54	73
Windsor & Eton	42	19	10	13	65	55	67
Bognor Regis Town	42	20	6	16	67	58	66
Dulwich Hamlet	42	16	17	9	82	57	65
Harrow Borough	42	18	8	16	70	56	62
Hayes	42	17	8	17	60	56	59
Tooting & Mitcham United	42	16	11	15	64	66	59
Walthamstow Avenue	42	15	11	16	64	65	56
Croydon	42	15	12	15	62	63	54
Epsom & Ewell	42	13	14	15	65	62	53
Slough Town	42	13	12	17	69	74	51
Carshalton Athletic	42	14	8	20	55	68	50
Bishop's Stortford	42	12	12	18	48	67	48
Hendon	42	9	19	14	62	65	46
Billericay Town	42	11	14	17	53	74	46
Barking	42	13	7	22	43	75	46
Hitchin Town	42	10	15	17	55	70	45
Leytonstone & Ilford	42	11	10	21	37	72	43
Harlow Town	42	5	12	25	45	95	27

Billercay Town had 1 point deducted
Croydon had 3 points deducted

First Division

Farnborough Town	42	26	8	8	101	45	86
Kingstonian	42	23	10	9	67	39	79
Leatherhead	42	23	10	9	109	61	76
Chesham United	42	22	8	12	78	46	74
Wembley	42	20	10	12	59	40	70
St Albans City	42	19	10	13	79	60	67
Tilbury	42	18	13	11	86	68	67
Bromley	42	18	9	15	71	64	63
Hampton	42	17	11	14	75	62	62
Staines Town	42	16	11	15	59	53	59
Maidenhead United	42	17	8	17	65	64	59
Walton & Hersham	42	16	8	18	60	69	55
Aveley	42	16	7	19	62	78	55
Oxford City	42	14	12	16	62	53	54
Lewes	42	15	9	18	70	72	54
Basildon United	42	15	8	19	55	61	53
Boreham Wood	42	15	7	20	72	83	52
Hornchurch	42	15	6	21	55	74	51
Woking	42	15	6	21	60	91	51
Metropolitan Police	42	10	12	20	65	92	42
Clapton	42	5	11	26	50	124	26
Hertford Town	42	5	10	27	36	97	25

Walton & Hersham had 1 point deducted
Leatherhead had 3 points deducted

Second Division North

Leyton Wingate	38	24	9	5	98	50	81
Finchley	38	24	8	6	66	31	79
Heybridge Swifts	38	22	9	7	71	33	75
Stevenage Borough	38	23	6	9	79	49	75
Saffron Walden Town	38	22	8	8	73	31	74
Tring Town	38	19	11	8	76	41	68
Chalfont St Peter	38	17	10	11	72	41	61
Flackwell Heath	38	16	11	11	54	40	59
Berkhamsted Town	38	15	12	11	50	42	57
Letchworth Garden City	38	17	6	15	66	69	57
Royston Town	38	13	9	16	47	77	48
Cheshunt	38	14	5	19	52	57	47
Marlow	38	13	6	19	64	81	45
Hemel Hempstead	38	11	7	20	49	65	40
Barton Rovers	38	9	8	21	40	62	35
Wolverton Town	38	9	8	21	38	77	35
Kingsbury Town	38	9	7	22	53	72	34
Harefield United	38	7	9	22	51	81	30
Haringey Borough	38	6	12	20	38	79	30
Ware	38	7	5	26	40	100	26

Finchley had 1 point deducted
The record of Epping Town was expunged

Second Division South

Grays Athletic	36	24	9	3	84	25	81
Uxbridge	36	22	10	4	81	20	76
Molesey	36	20	5	11	62	42	65
Hungerford Town	36	18	9	9	71	49	63
Whyteleafe	36	17	10	9	66	34	61
Egham Town	36	17	7	12	54	42	58
Southall	36	18	3	15	54	57	57
Bracknell Town	36	15	7	14	54	48	52
Banstead Athletic	36	14	8	14	63	70	50
Horsham	36	13	10	13	44	39	49
Ruislip Manor	36	13	10	13	48	49	49
Dorking	36	12	11	13	45	50	47
Rainham Town	36	12	8	16	58	61	44
Feltham	36	10	13	13	44	58	43
Camberley Town	36	10	12	14	44	54	42
Eastbourne United	36	10	9	17	66	72	39
Petersfield Town	36	9	5	22	41	80	32
Newbury Town	36	8	7	21	35	69	16
Chertsey Town	36	2	3	31	23	118	6

Chertsey Town had 3 points deducted
Newbury Town had 15 points deducted

1985-86

Premier Division

Sutton United	42	29	8	5	109	39	95
Yeovil Town	42	28	7	7	92	48	91
Farnborough Town	42	23	8	11	90	50	77
Croydon	42	23	7	12	70	50	76
Harrow Borough	42	21	8	13	76	66	71
Slough Town	42	18	8	16	66	68	62
Bishop's Stortford	42	17	10	15	55	61	61
Kingstonian	42	15	15	12	57	56	60
Dulwich Hamlet	42	17	9	16	64	79	60
Wokingham Town	42	16	10	16	67	64	58
Windsor & Eton	42	17	7	18	58	75	58
Tooting & Mitcham United	42	14	11	17	65	76	53
Walthamstow Avenue	42	12	14	16	69	70	50
Worthing	42	13	10	19	72	82	49
Bognor Regis Town	42	15	6	21	63	70	48
Hayes	42	10	17	15	36	42	47
Hitchin Town	42	11	14	17	53	69	47
Barking	42	11	13	18	45	55	46
Hendon	42	10	13	19	59	77	43
Carshalton Athletic	42	9	13	20	56	79	40
Billericay Town	42	9	12	21	59	78	39
Epsom & Ewell	42	8	12	22	63	90	36

Bognor Regis Town had 3 points deducted

First Division

St Albans City	42	23	11	8	92	61	80
Bromley	42	24	8	10	68	41	80
Wembley	42	22	12	8	59	30	78
Oxford City	42	22	11	9	75	51	77
Hampton	42	21	11	10	63	45	74
Leyton Wingate	42	21	10	11	77	56	73
Uxbridge	42	20	8	14	64	49	68
Staines Town	42	18	10	14	69	66	64
Boreham Wood	42	15	16	11	62	54	61
Walton & Hersham	42	16	10	16	68	71	58
Lewes	42	16	8	18	61	75	56
Leytonstone & Ilford	42	13	15	14	57	67	54
Finchley	42	12	17	13	61	59	53
Grays Athletic	42	13	11	18	69	75	50
Leatherhead	42	14	8	20	62	68	50
Tilbury	42	13	11	18	60	66	50
Maidenhead United	42	13	7	22	61	67	46
Basildon United	42	12	9	21	52	72	45
Hornchurch	42	11	11	20	44	59	44
Chesham United	42	12	6	24	51	87	42
Harlow Town	42	8	14	20	53	70	38
Aveley	42	8	6	28	59	98	30

Second Division North

Stevenage Borough	38	26	6	6	71	24	84
Kingsbury Town	38	25	8	5	84	35	83
Heybridge Swifts	38	20	8	10	65	46	68
Cheshunt	38	18	10	10	60	40	64
Hertford Town	38	17	7	14	60	50	58
Chalfont St Peter	38	15	11	12	53	50	56
Tring Town	38	14	13	11	58	46	55
Royston Town	38	13	13	12	59	57	52
Saffron Walden Town	38	13	12	13	61	65	51
Berkhamsted Town	38	14	8	16	45	52	50
Haringey Borough	38	14	7	17	49	51	49
Letchworth Garden City	38	13	8	17	46	52	47
Rainham Town	38	14	4	20	54	91	46
Hemel Hempstead	38	12	9	17	50	66	45
Ware	38	11	11	16	56	61	44
Vauxhall Motors	38	11	10	17	58	62	43
Barton Rovers	38	12	7	19	50	60	43
Harefield United	38	9	12	17	56	72	39
Clapton	38	10	7	21	51	90	37
Wolverton Town	38	8	11	19	42	58	35

Second Division South

Southwick	38	25	8	5	86	34	83
Bracknell Town	38	24	9	5	80	23	81
Woking	38	23	9	6	94	45	78
Newbury Town	38	22	7	9	86	53	73
Whyteleafe	38	21	10	7	61	41	73
Molesey	38	21	8	9	59	39	71
Metropolitan Police	38	20	6	12	72	48	66
Southall	38	19	7	12	76	58	64
Dorking	38	18	10	10	70	57	64
Feltham	38	16	7	15	65	60	55
Banstead Athletic	38	15	8	15	60	66	53
Petersfield United	38	12	9	17	61	71	45
Hungerford Town	38	11	6	21	57	78	39
Flackwell Heath	38	11	6	21	46	72	39
Eastbourne United	38	9	8	21	51	81	35
Camberley Town	38	9	7	22	53	64	34
Egham Town	38	7	8	23	41	83	29
Horsham	38	6	10	22	33	74	28
Ruislip Manor	38	5	12	21	44	87	27
Marlow	38	6	5	27	47	108	23

1986-87

Premier Division

Wycombe Wanderers	42	32	5	5	103	32	101
Yeovil Town	42	28	8	6	71	27	92
Slough Town	42	23	8	11	70	44	77
Hendon	42	22	7	13	67	53	73
Bognor Regis Town	42	20	10	12	85	61	70
Harrow Borough	42	20	10	12	68	44	70
Croydon	42	18	10	14	51	48	64
Barking	42	16	14	12	76	56	62
Farnborough Town	42	17	11	14	66	72	62
Bishop's Stortford	42	15	15	12	62	57	60
Bromley	42	16	11	15	63	72	59
Kingstonian	42	16	9	17	58	50	57
Windsor & Eton	42	13	15	14	47	52	54
St Albans City	42	14	9	19	61	70	51
Carshalton Athletic	42	13	9	20	55	68	48
Wokingham Town	42	14	6	22	47	61	48
Hayes	42	12	12	18	45	68	48
Dulwich Hamlet	42	12	10	20	62	71	46
Tooting & Mitcham United	42	12	9	21	51	53	45
Hitchin Town	42	13	5	24	56	69	44
Worthing	42	8	9	25	58	107	33
Walthamstow Avenue	42	4	6	32	36	113	18

First Division

Leytonstone & Ilford	42	30	5	7	78	29	95
Leyton Wingate	42	23	13	6	68	31	82
Bracknell Town	42	24	9	9	92	48	81
Southwick	42	23	7	12	80	66	76
Wembley	42	21	9	12	61	47	72
Grays Athletic	42	19	10	13	76	64	67
Kingsbury Town	42	20	7	15	69	67	67
Boreham Wood	42	20	6	16	59	52	66
Uxbridge	42	18	9	15	60	59	63
Leatherhead	42	17	11	14	45	48	62
Hampton	42	18	5	19	57	55	59
Basildon United	42	16	10	16	58	60	58
Billericay Town	42	14	12	16	57	52	54
Staines Town	42	13	13	16	40	51	52
Lewes	42	15	6	21	55	65	51
Stevenage Borough	42	12	11	19	61	67	47
Oxford City	42	11	10	21	64	72	43
Walton & Hersham	42	11	10	21	53	74	43
Tilbury	42	12	7	23	46	70	43
Epsom & Ewell	42	12	7	23	44	68	43
Maidenhead United	42	11	4	27	44	76	37
Finchley	42	6	11	25	44	90	29

Second Division North

Chesham United	42	28	6	8	81	48	90
Wolverton Town	42	23	14	5	74	32	83
Haringey Borough	42	22	13	7	86	40	79
Heybridge Swifts	42	21	11	10	81	54	74
Aveley	42	19	13	10	68	50	70
Letchworth Garden City	42	19	11	12	77	62	68
Barton Rovers	42	18	11	13	49	39	65
Tring Town	42	19	7	16	69	49	64
Collier Row	42	19	5	18	67	65	62
Ware	42	17	8	17	51	50	59
Saffron Walden Town	42	14	14	14	56	54	56
Wivenhoe Town	42	15	11	16	61	61	56
Vauxhall Motors	42	15	10	17	61	57	55
Hornchurch	42	13	16	13	60	60	55
Hertford Town	42	14	13	15	52	53	55
Berkhamsted Town	42	12	16	14	62	64	52
Harlow Town	42	13	11	18	45	55	50
Rainham Town	42	12	11	19	53	70	47
Clapton	42	10	11	21	45	63	41
Hemel Hempstead	42	9	12	21	48	77	39
Royston Town	42	4	12	26	37	109	24
Cheshunt	42	5	6	31	43	114	21

Second Division South

Woking	40	27	7	6	110	32	88
Marlow	40	28	4	8	78	36	88
Dorking	40	24	12	4	78	30	84
Feltham	40	25	3	12	79	34	78
Ruislip Manor	40	22	10	8	85	47	76
Chertsey Town	40	18	11	11	56	44	65
Metropolitan Police	40	16	13	11	70	61	61
Chalfont St Peter	40	17	10	13	60	55	61
Hungerford Town	40	14	14	12	55	48	56
Harefield United	40	14	14	12	53	47	56
Eastbourne United	40	15	10	15	72	59	55
Whyteleafe	40	12	15	13	52	63	51
Horsham	40	14	8	18	54	61	50
Egham Town	40	14	6	20	45	77	48
Camberley Town	40	13	3	24	62	89	42
Flackwell Heath	40	9	11	20	34	63	38
Banstead Athletic	40	7	15	18	44	61	36
Petersfield United	40	9	8	23	45	84	34
Molesey	40	7	12	21	37	89	33
Newbury Town	40	6	14	20	51	83	32
Southall	40	6	6	28	28	85	24

1987-88

Premier Division

Yeovil Town	42	24	9	9	66	34	81
Bromley	42	23	7	12	68	40	76
Slough Town	42	21	9	12	67	41	72
Leytonstone & Ilford	42	20	11	11	59	43	71
Wokingham Town	42	21	7	14	62	52	70
Hayes	42	20	9	13	62	48	69
Windsor & Eton	42	16	17	9	59	43	65
Farnborough Town	42	17	11	14	63	60	62
Carshalton Athletic	42	16	13	13	49	41	61
Hendon	42	16	12	14	62	58	60
Tooting & Mitcham United	42	15	14	13	57	59	59
Harrow Borough	42	15	11	16	53	58	56
Bishop's Stortford	42	15	10	17	55	58	55
Kingstonian	42	14	12	16	47	53	54
St Albans City	42	15	6	21	60	69	51
Bognor Regis Town	42	14	9	19	41	57	51
Leyton Wingate	42	14	8	20	58	64	50
Croydon	42	11	13	18	40	52	46
Barking	42	11	12	19	44	57	45
Dulwich Hamlet	42	10	11	21	46	64	41
Hitchin Town	42	10	8	24	46	79	38
Basingstoke Town	42	6	17	19	37	71	35

First Division

Marlow	42	32	5	5	100	44	101
Grays Athletic	42	30	10	2	74	25	100
Woking	42	25	7	10	91	52	82
Boreham Wood	42	21	9	12	65	45	72
Staines Town	42	19	11	12	71	48	68
Wembley	42	18	11	13	54	46	65
Basildon United	42	18	9	15	65	58	63
Walton & Hersham	42	15	16	11	53	44	61
Hampton	42	17	10	15	59	54	61
Leatherhead	42	16	11	15	64	53	59
Southwick	42	13	12	17	59	63	51
Oxford City	42	13	12	17	70	77	51
Worthing	42	14	8	20	67	73	50
Kingsbury Town	42	11	17	14	62	69	50
Walthamstow Avenue	42	13	11	18	53	63	50
Lewes	42	12	13	17	83	77	49
Uxbridge	42	11	16	15	41	47	49
Chesham United	42	12	10	20	69	77	46
Bracknell Town	42	12	9	21	54	80	45
Billericay Town	42	11	11	20	58	88	44
Stevenage Borough	42	11	9	22	36	64	42
Wolverton Town	42	3	3	36	23	124	12

Second Division North

Wivenhoe Town	42	26	10	6	105	42	88
Collier Row	42	22	13	7	71	39	79
Tilbury	42	18	15	9	61	40	69
Berkhamsted Town	42	19	12	11	71	53	69
Harlow Town	42	17	16	9	67	36	67
Ware	42	17	15	10	63	58	66
Witham Town	42	17	14	11	69	47	65
Vauxhall Motors	42	16	17	9	56	42	65
Heybridge Swifts	42	17	13	12	56	50	64
Tring Town	42	18	6	18	69	67	60
Letchworth Garden City	42	18	5	19	59	64	59
Finchley	42	16	10	16	67	54	58
Clapton	42	14	15	13	50	62	57
Hornchurch	42	13	15	14	56	65	54
Barton Rovers	42	13	10	19	43	60	49
Rainham Town	42	12	12	18	63	66	48
Royston Town	42	13	8	21	49	70	47
Saffron Waldon Town	42	13	7	22	34	67	46
Hemel Hempstead	42	11	12	19	38	71	45
Haringey Borough	42	11	8	23	54	78	41
Aveley	42	8	13	21	42	65	37
Hertford Town	42	8	4	30	45	92	28

Second Division South

Chalfont St Peter	42	26	9	7	81	35	87
Metropolitan Police	42	23	17	2	80	32	86
Dorking	42	25	11	6	86	39	86
Feltham	42	21	12	9	74	41	75
Epsom & Ewell	42	21	11	10	71	49	74
Chertsey Town	42	22	7	13	63	47	73
Whyteleafe	42	20	11	11	84	55	71
Hungerford Town	42	21	7	14	66	54	70
Ruislip Manor	42	21	5	16	74	57	68
Yeading	42	19	10	13	83	56	67
Maidenhead United	42	18	12	12	69	54	66
Eastbourne United	42	18	10	14	67	57	64
Harefield Town	42	18	6	18	59	60	60
Egham Town	42	12	12	18	45	55	48
Horsham	42	12	10	20	45	66	46
Southall	42	13	7	22	45	72	46
Molesey	42	11	11	20	42	63	44
Newbury Town	42	8	13	21	40	81	37
Camberley Town	42	9	9	24	51	94	36
Flackwell Heath	42	6	8	28	42	96	26
Banstead Athletic	42	6	7	29	34	81	25
Petersfield United	42	6	7	29	45	102	25

1988-89

Premier Division

Leytonstone & Ilford	42	26	11	5	76	36	89
Farnborough Town	42	24	9	9	85	61	81
Slough Town	42	24	6	12	72	42	78
Carshalton Athletic	42	19	15	8	59	36	72
Grays Athletic	42	19	13	10	62	47	70
Kingstonian	42	19	11	12	54	37	68
Bishop's Stortford	42	20	6	16	70	56	66
Hayes	42	18	12	12	6	47	66
Bognor Regis Town	42	17	11	14	38	49	62
Barking	42	16	13	13	49	45	61
Wokingham Town	42	15	11	16	60	54	56
Hendon	42	13	17	12	51	68	56
Windsor & Eton	42	14	13	15	52	50	55
Bromley	42	13	15	14	61	48	54
Leyton Wingate	42	13	15	14	55	56	54
Dulwich Hamlet	42	12	12	18	58	57	48
St Albans City	42	12	9	21	51	59	45
Dagenham	42	11	12	19	53	68	45
Harrow Borough	42	9	13	20	53	75	40
Marlow	42	9	11	22	48	83	38
Tooting & Mitcham United	42	10	6	26	41	81	36
Croydon	42	4	9	29	27	81	21

First Division

Staines Town	40	26	9	5	79	29	87
Basingstoke Town	40	25	8	7	85	36	83
Woking	40	24	10	6	72	30	82
Hitchin Town	40	21	11	8	60	32	74
Wivenhoe Town	40	22	6	12	62	44	72
Lewes	40	21	8	11	72	54	71
Walton & Hersham	40	21	7	12	56	36	70
Kingsbury Town	40	20	7	13	65	41	67
Uxbridge	40	19	7	14	60	54	64
Wembley	40	18	6	16	45	58	60
Boreham Wood	40	16	9	15	57	52	57
Leatherhead	40	14	8	18	56	58	50
Metropolitan Police	40	13	9	18	52	68	48
Chesham United	40	12	9	19	54	67	45
Southwick	40	9	15	16	44	58	42
Chalfont St Peter	40	11	9	20	56	82	42
Hampton	40	7	14	19	37	62	35
Worthing	40	8	10	22	49	80	32
Collier Row	40	8	7	25	37	82	31
Bracknell Town	40	8	6	26	38	70	30
Basildon Town	40	6	7	27	34	77	25

Worthing had 2 points deducted.

Second Division North

Harlow Town	42	27	9	6	83	38	90
Purfleet	42	22	12	8	60	42	78
Tring Town	42	22	10	10	65	44	76
Stevenage Borough	42	20	13	9	84	55	73
Heybridge Swifts	42	21	9	12	64	43	72
Billericay Town	42	19	11	12	65	52	68
Clapton	42	18	11	13	65	56	65
Barton Rovers	42	18	11	13	58	50	65
Aveley	42	18	10	14	54	52	64
Hertford Town	42	16	13	13	62	49	59
Ware	42	17	8	17	60	65	59
Hemel Hempstead	42	16	10	16	55	58	58
Witham Town	42	16	7	19	69	67	55
Vauxhall Motors	42	15	9	18	53	57	54
Berkhamsted Town	42	14	10	18	57	70	52
Hornchurch	42	11	16	15	59	61	49
Tilbury	42	13	10	19	53	60	49
Royston Town	42	12	7	23	46	72	43
Rainham Town	42	9	15	18	49	62	42
Saffron Walden Town	42	8	16	18	54	72	40
Letchworth Garden City	42	4	18	20	34	71	30
Wolverton Town	42	5	7	30	42	95	13

Hertford Town 2 points deducted, Wolverton Town 9 points deducted.

Second Division South

Dorking	40	32	4	4	109	35	100
Whyteleafe	40	25	9	6	86	41	84
Finchley	40	21	9	10	70	45	72
Molesey	40	19	13	8	58	42	70
Harefield United	40	19	7	14	56	45	64
Hungerford Town	40	17	13	10	55	45	64
Ruislip Manor	40	16	9	15	56	43	57
Feltham	40	16	9	15	58	53	57
Epsom & Ewell	40	16	8	16	55	55	56
Egham Town	40	16	7	17	54	58	55
Eastbourne United	40	15	9	16	68	61	54
Chertsey Town	40	13	14	13	55	58	53
Flackwell Heath	40	13	11	16	51	49	50
Camberley Town	40	15	5	20	51	71	50
Yeading	40	13	9	18	47	63	46
Banstead Athletic	40	12	8	20	50	65	44
Maidenhead United	40	10	13	17	44	61	43
Southall	40	11	10	19	41	73	43
Newbury Town	40	11	8	21	47	65	41
Horsham	40	7	14	19	36	68	35
Petersfield United	40	5	7	28	36	87	22

Yeading had 2 points deducted.

1989-90 Premier Division

Slough Town	42	27	11	4	85	38	92
Wokingham Town	42	26	11	5	67	34	89
Aylesbury United	42	25	9	8	86	30	84
Kingstonian	42	24	9	9	87	51	81
Grays Athletic	42	19	13	10	59	44	70
Dagenham	42	17	15	10	54	43	66
Leyton Wingate	42	20	6	16	54	48	66
Basingstoke Town	42	18	9	15	65	55	63
Bishop's Stortford	42	19	6	17	60	59	63
Carshalton Athletic	42	19	5	18	63	59	59
Redbridge Forest	42	16	11	15	65	62	59
Hendon	42	15	10	17	54	63	55
Windsor & Eton	42	13	15	14	51	47	54
Hayes	42	14	11	17	61	59	53
St Albans City	42	13	10	19	49	59	49
Staines Town	42	14	6	22	53	69	48
Marlow	42	11	13	18	42	59	46
Harrow Borough	42	11	10	21	51	79	43
Bognor Regis Town	42	9	14	19	37	67	41
Barking	42	7	11	24	53	86	32
Bromley	42	7	11	24	32	69	32
Dulwich Hamlet	42	6	8	28	32	80	26

Carshalton Athletic had 3 points deducted.

First Division

Wivenhoe Town	42	31	7	4	94	36	100
Woking	42	30	8	4	102	29	98
Southwick	42	23	15	4	68	30	84
Hitchin Town	42	22	13	7	60	30	79
Walton & Hersham	42	20	10	12	68	50	70
Dorking	42	19	12	11	66	41	69
Boreham Wood	42	17	13	12	60	59	64
Harlow Town	42	16	13	13	60	53	61
Metropolitan Police	42	16	11	15	54	59	59
Chesham United	42	15	12	15	46	49	57
Chalfont St Peter	42	14	13	15	50	59	55
Tooting & Mitcham United	42	14	13	15	42	51	55
Worthing	42	15	8	19	56	63	53
Whyteleafe	42	11	16	15	50	65	49
Lewes	42	12	11	19	55	65	47
Wembley	42	11	10	21	57	68	43
Croydon	42	9	16	17	43	57	43
Uxbridge	42	11	10	21	52	75	43
Hampton	42	8	13	21	28	51	37
Leatherhead	42	7	10	25	34	77	31
Purfleet	42	7	8	27	33	78	29
Kingsbury Town	42	8	10	24	45	78	25

Kingsbury Town had 9 points deducted

Second Division North

Heybridge Swifts	42	26	9	7	79	29	87
Aveley	42	23	16	3	68	24	85
Hertford Town	42	24	11	7	92	51	83
Stevenage Borough	42	21	16	5	70	31	79
Barton Rovers	42	22	6	14	60	45	72
Tilbury	42	20	9	13	68	54	69
Basildon United	42	13	20	9	50	44	59
Collier Row	42	15	13	14	43	45	58
Royston Town	42	15	11	16	63	72	56
Saffron Walden Town	42	15	11	16	60	73	56
Vauxhall Motors	42	14	13	15	55	54	55
Clapton	42	13	16	13	50	46	54
Ware	42	14	11	17	53	59	53
Hemel Hempstead	42	12	15	15	58	70	51
Billericay Town	42	13	11	18	49	58	50
Hornchurch	42	12	12	18	49	64	48
Berkhamsted Town	42	9	16	17	44	68	43
Finchley	42	11	10	21	50	75	43
Tring Town	42	10	9	23	48	70	39
Witham Town	42	8	14	20	44	56	38
Rainham Town	42	9	11	22	48	75	38
Letchworth Garden City	42	7	12	23	30	68	33

Clapton had 1 point deducted

Second Division South

Yeading	40	29	4	7	86	37	91
Molesey	40	24	11	5	76	30	83
Abingdon Town	40	22	9	9	64	39	75
Ruislip Manor	40	20	12	8	60	32	72
Maidenhead United	40	20	12	8	66	39	72
Southall	40	22	5	13	56	33	71
Newbury Town	40	21	7	12	50	36	70
Flackwell Heath	40	16	11	13	69	65	59
Hungerford Town	40	14	16	10	54	51	58
Egham Town	40	12	14	14	39	38	50
Banstead Athletic	40	14	8	18	46	47	50
Harefield United	40	13	9	18	44	46	48
Chertsey Town	40	13	9	18	53	58	48
Epsom & Ewell	40	13	9	18	49	54	48
Malden Vale	40	13	7	20	36	67	46
Eastbourne United	40	11	10	19	47	65	43
Camberley Town	40	11	9	20	44	66	42
Feltham	40	11	7	22	47	80	40
Bracknell Town	40	10	9	21	40	57	39
Petersfield United	40	10	8	22	48	93	38
Horsham	40	4	8	28	29	70	20

1990-91

Premier Division

Redbridge Forest	42	29	6	7	74	43	93
Enfield	42	26	11	5	83	30	89
Aylesbury United	42	24	11	7	90	47	83
Woking	42	24	10	8	84	39	82
Kingstonian	42	21	12	9	86	57	75
Grays Athletic	42	20	8	14	66	53	68
Marlow	42	18	13	11	72	49	67
Hayes	42	20	5	17	60	57	65
Carshalton Athletic	42	19	7	16	80	67	64
Wivenhoe Town	42	16	11	15	69	66	59
Wokingham Town	42	15	13	14	58	54	58
Windsor & Eton	42	15	10	17	48	63	55
Bishop's Stortford	42	14	12	16	54	49	54
Dagenham	42	13	11	18	62	68	50
Hendon	42	12	10	20	48	62	46
St Albans City	42	11	12	19	60	74	45
Bognor Regis Town	42	12	8	22	44	71	44
Basingstoke Town	42	12	7	23	57	95	43
Staines Town	42	10	10	22	46	79	39
Harrow Borough	42	10	8	24	57	84	38
Barking	42	8	10	24	41	85	34
Leyton Wingate	42	7	7	28	44	91	28

Staines Town had 1 point deducted

First Division

Chesham United	42	27	8	7	102	37	89
Bromley	42	22	14	6	62	37	80
Yeading	42	23	8	11	75	45	77
Aveley	42	21	9	12	76	43	72
Hitchin Town	42	21	9	12	78	50	72
Tooting & Mitcham United	42	20	12	10	71	48	72
Walton & Hersham	42	21	8	13	73	48	71
Molesey	42	22	5	15	65	46	71
Whyteleafe	42	21	6	15	62	53	69
Dorking	42	20	5	17	78	67	65
Chalfont St Peter	42	19	5	18	56	63	62
Dulwich Hamlet	42	16	11	15	67	54	59
Harlow Town	42	17	8	17	73	64	59
Boreham Wood	42	15	8	19	46	53	53
Wembley	42	13	12	17	62	59	51
Uxbridge	42	15	5	22	45	61	50
Croydon	42	15	5	22	44	85	50
Heybridge Swifts	42	13	10	19	46	59	49
Southwick	42	13	8	21	49	75	47
Lewes	42	10	8	24	49	82	38
Metropolitan Police	42	9	6	27	55	76	33
Worthing	42	2	4	36	28	157	10

Second Division North

Stevenage Borough	42	34	5	3	122	29	107
Vauxhall Motors	42	24	10	8	82	50	82
Billericay Town	42	22	8	12	70	41	74
Ware	42	22	8	12	78	51	74
Berkhamsted Town	42	19	11	12	60	51	68
Witham Town	42	19	10	13	70	59	67
Purfleet	42	17	14	11	68	57	65
Rainham Town	42	19	7	16	57	46	64
Hemel Hempstead	42	16	14	12	62	56	62
Barton Rovers	42	17	10	15	61	58	61
Saffron Walden Town	42	16	13	13	72	77	61
Collier Row	42	16	11	15	63	63	59
Kingsbury Town	42	17	8	17	64	72	59
Edgware Town	42	17	7	18	73	65	58
Hertford Town	42	16	10	16	69	70	58
Royston Town	42	14	15	13	78	62	57
Tilbury	42	14	6	22	70	79	48
Basildon United	42	11	10	21	61	90	43
Hornchurch	42	10	9	23	53	87	39
Clapton	42	9	10	23	54	93	34
Finchley	42	6	7	29	50	112	24
Tring Town	42	1	9	32	30	99	12

Finchley had 1 point deducted
Clapton had 3 points deducted

Second Division South

Abingdon Town	42	29	7	6	95	28	94
Maidenhead United	42	28	8	6	85	33	92
Egham Town	42	27	6	9	100	46	87
Malden Vale	42	26	5	11	72	44	83
Ruislip Manor	42	25	5	12	93	44	80
Southall	42	23	10	9	84	43	79
Harefield United	42	23	10	9	81	56	79
Newbury Town	42	23	8	11	71	45	77
Hungerford Town	42	16	13	13	84	69	61
Leatherhead	42	17	9	16	82	55	60
Banstead Athletic	42	15	13	14	58	62	58
Hampton	42	14	15	13	62	43	57
Epsom & Ewell	42	15	12	15	49	50	57
Chertsey Town	42	15	9	18	76	72	54
Horsham	42	14	7	21	58	67	49
Flackwell Heath	42	11	11	20	56	78	44
Bracknell Town	42	11	7	24	60	97	40
Feltham	42	10	8	24	45	80	38
Cove	42	10	7	25	51	94	37
Eastbourne United	42	10	7	25	53	109	37
Petersfield United	42	6	3	33	35	119	21
Camberley Town	42	1	6	35	27	143	9

1991-92

Premier Division

Woking	42	30	7	5	96	25	97
Enfield	42	24	7	11	59	45	79
Sutton United	42	19	13	10	88	51	70
Chesham United	42	20	10	12	67	48	70
Wokingham Town	42	19	10	13	73	58	67
Marlow	42	20	7	15	56	50	67
Ayelsbury United	42	16	17	9	69	46	65
Carshalton Athletic	42	18	8	16	64	67	62
Dagenham	42	15	16	11	70	59	61
Kingstonian	42	17	8	17	71	65	59
Windsor & Eton	42	15	11	16	56	56	56
Bromley	42	14	12	16	51	57	54
St Albans City	42	14	11	17	66	70	53
Basingstoke Town	42	14	11	17	56	65	53
Grays Athletic	42	14	11	17	53	68	53
Wivenhoe Town	42	16	4	22	56	81	52
Hendon	42	13	9	20	59	73	48
Harrow Borough	42	11	13	18	58	78	46
Hayes	42	10	14	18	52	63	44
Staines Town	42	11	10	21	43	73	43
Bognor Regis Town	42	9	11	22	51	89	38
Bishop's Stortford	42	7	12	23	41	68	33

First Division

Stevenage Borough	40	30	6	4	95	37	96
Yeading	40	24	10	6	83	34	82
Dulwich Hamlet	40	22	9	9	71	40	75
Boreham Wood	40	22	7	11	65	40	73
Wembley	40	21	6	13	54	43	69
Abingdon Town	40	19	8	13	60	47	65
Tooting & Mitcham United	40	16	13	11	57	45	61
Hitchin Town	40	17	10	13	55	45	61
Walton & Hersham	40	15	13	12	62	50	58
Molesey	40	16	9	15	55	61	57
Dorking	40	16	7	17	68	65	55
Barking	40	14	11	15	51	54	53
Chalfont St Peter	40	15	6	19	62	70	51
Leyton Wingate	40	13	11	16	53	56	50
Uxbridge	40	13	8	19	47	62	47
Maidenhead United	40	13	7	20	52	61	46
Harlow Town	40	11	9	20	50	70	42
Croydon	40	11	6	23	44	68	39
Heybridge Swifts	40	8	9	23	33	71	33
Whyteleafe	40	7	10	23	42	78	31
Aveley	40	8	3	29	33	95	27

Second Division

Purfleet	42	27	8	7	97	48	89
Lewes	42	23	14	5	74	36	83
Billericay Town	42	24	8	10	75	44	80
Leatherhead	42	23	6	13	68	40	75
Ruislip Manor	42	20	9	13	74	51	69
Egham Town	42	19	12	11	81	62	69
Metropolitan Police	42	20	9	13	76	58	69
Saffron Walden Town	42	19	11	12	86	67	68
Hemel Hempstead	42	18	10	14	63	50	64
Hungerford Town	42	18	7	17	53	58	61
Barton Rovers	42	17	8	17	61	64	59
Worthing	42	17	8	17	67	72	59
Witham Town	42	16	11	15	56	61	59
Banstead Athletic	42	16	10	16	69	58	58
Malden Vale	42	15	12	15	63	48	57
Rainham Town	42	14	13	15	53	48	55
Ware	42	14	9	19	58	62	51
Berkhamsted Town	42	13	11	18	56	57	50
Harefield United	42	11	7	24	47	66	40
Southall	42	8	7	27	39	93	31
Southwick	42	6	2	34	29	115	20
Newbury Town	42	4	8	30	30	117	20

Third Division

Edgware Town	40	30	3	7	106	44	93
Chertsey Town	40	29	4	7	115	44	91
Tilbury	40	26	9	5	84	40	87
Hampton	40	26	5	9	93	35	83
Horsham	40	23	8	9	92	51	77
Cove	40	21	9	10	74	49	72
Flackwell Heath	40	19	12	9	78	50	69
Thame United	40	19	7	14	73	46	64
Epsom & Ewell	40	17	11	12	55	50	62
Collier Row	40	17	9	14	67	59	60
Royston Town	40	17	7	16	59	58	58
Kingsbury Town	40	12	10	18	54	61	46
Hertford Town	40	12	10	18	55	73	46
Petersfield United	40	12	9	19	45	67	45
Camberley Town	40	11	8	21	52	69	41
Feltham & Hounslow	40	11	2	22	53	78	40
Bracknell Town	40	10	7	23	48	90	37
Hornchurch	40	8	7	25	40	87	31
Tring Town	40	9	4	27	35	94	31
Clapton	40	9	3	28	47	92	30
Eastbourne United	40	5	5	30	34	121	20

1992-93

Premier Division

Chesham United	42	30	8	4	104	34	98
St Albans City	42	28	9	5	103	50	93
Enfield	42	25	6	11	94	48	81
Carshalton Athletic	42	22	10	10	96	56	76
Sutton United	42	18	14	10	74	57	68
Grays Athletic	42	18	11	13	61	64	65
Stevenage Borough	42	8	8	16	62	60	62
Harrow Borough	42	16	14	12	59	60	62
Hayes	42	16	13	13	64	59	61
Aylesbury United	42	18	6	18	70	77	60
Hendon	42	12	18	12	52	54	54
Basingstoke Town	42	12	17	13	49	45	53
Kingstonian	42	14	10	18	59	58	52
Dulwich Hamlet	42	12	14	16	52	66	50
Marlow	42	12	11	19	72	73	47
Wokingham Town	42	11	13	18	62	81	46
Bromley	42	11	13	18	51	72	46
Wivenhoe Town	42	13	7	22	41	75	46
Yeading	42	11	12	19	58	66	45
Staines Town	42	10	13	19	59	77	43
Windsor & Eton	42	8	7	27	40	90	31
Bognor Regis Town	42	5	10	27	46	106	25

First Division

Hitchin Town	40	25	7	8	67	29	82
Molesey	40	23	11	6	81	38	80
Dorking	40	23	9	8	73	40	78
Purfleet	40	19	12	9	67	42	69
Bishop's Stortford	40	19	10	11	63	42	67
Abingdon Town	40	17	13	10	65	47	64
Tooting & Mitcham United	40	17	12	11	68	46	63
Billericay Town	40	18	6	16	67	61	60
Wembley	40	14	15	11	44	34	57
Walton & Hersham	40	14	12	14	58	54	54
Boreham Wood	40	12	14	14	44	43	50
Maidenhead United	40	10	18	12	45	50	48
Leyton	40	11	14	15	56	61	47
Whyteleafe	40	12	10	18	63	71	46
Uxbridge	40	11	13	16	50	59	46
Heybridge Swifts	40	11	9	20	47	65	42
Croydon	40	11	9	20	54	82	42
Chalfont St Peter	40	7	17	16	48	70	38
Barking	40	10	8	22	42	80	38
Lewes	40	9	10	21	34	80	37
Aveley	40	9	7	24	45	87	34

Second Division

Worthing	42	28	7	7	105	50	91
Ruislip Manor	42	25	12	5	78	33	87
Berkhamsted Town	42	24	8	10	77	55	80
Hemel Hempstead	42	22	12	8	84	52	78
Metropolitan Police	42	22	6	14	84	51	72
Malden Vale	42	20	9	13	78	54	69
Chertsey Town	42	20	7	15	84	60	67
Saffron Walden Town	42	19	10	13	63	49	67
Newbury Town	42	14	18	10	53	51	60
Hampton	42	16	11	15	59	59	59
Edgware Town	42	16	10	16	84	75	58
Egham Town	42	16	9	17	60	71	57
Banstead Athletic	42	14	13	15	67	52	55
Leatherhead	42	14	11	17	66	61	53
Ware	42	12	11	19	68	76	47
Witham Town	42	10	16	16	54	65	46
Tilbury	42	12	8	22	55	101	44
Barton Rovers	42	9	14	19	40	66	41
Hungerford Town	42	11	8	23	37	93	41
Rainham Town	42	9	10	23	56	80	37
Harefield United	42	10	7	25	37	72	37
Southall	42	7	7	28	43	106	28

Third Division

Aldershot Town	38	28	8	2	90	35	92
Thame United	38	21	11	6	84	38	74
Collier Row	38	21	11	6	68	30	74
Leighton Town	38	21	10	7	89	47	73
Cove	38	21	8	9	69	42	71
Northwood	38	19	11	8	84	68	68
Royston Town	38	17	8	13	59	42	59
East Thurrock United	38	17	7	14	69	58	58
Kingsbury Town	38	15	9	14	62	59	54
Hertford Town	38	14	10	14	61	64	52
Flackwell Heath	38	15	6	17	82	76	51
Tring Town	38	12	11	15	59	63	47
Hornchurch	38	11	13	14	53	52	46
Horsham	38	12	7	19	63	72	43
Epsom & Ewell	38	10	11	17	52	67	41
Bracknell Town	38	7	13	18	52	94	34
Clapton	38	8	7	23	46	74	31
Camberley Town	38	8	7	23	37	72	31
Petersfield United	38	6	12	20	36	90	30
Feltham & Hounslow	38	5	4	29	47	119	19

1993-94

Premier Division

Stevenage Borough	42	31	4	7	88	39	97
Enfield	42	28	8	6	80	28	92
Marlow	42	25	7	10	90	67	82
Chesham United	42	24	8	10	73	45	80
Sutton United	42	23	10	9	77	31	79
Carshalton Athletic	42	22	7	13	81	53	73
St Albans City	42	21	10	11	81	54	73
Hitchin Town	42	21	7	14	81	56	70
Harrow Borough	42	18	11	13	54	56	65
Kingstonian	42	18	9	15	101	64	63
Hendon	42	18	9	15	61	51	63
Aylesbury United	42	17	7	18	64	67	58
Hayes	42	15	8	19	63	72	53
Grays Athletic	42	15	5	22	56	69	50
Bromley	42	14	7	21	56	69	49
Dulwich Hamlet	42	13	8	21	52	74	47
Yeading	42	11	13	18	58	66	46
Molesey	42	11	11	20	44	62	44
Wokingham Town	42	11	6	25	38	67	39
Dorking	42	9	4	29	58	104	31
Basingstoke Town	42	5	12	25	38	86	27
Wivenhoe Town	42	5	3	34	38	152	18

First Division

Bishop's Stortford	42	24	13	5	83	31	85
Purfleet	42	22	12	8	70	44	78
Walton & Hersham	42	22	11	9	81	53	77
Tooting & Mitcham United	42	21	12	9	66	37	75
Heybridge Swifts	42	20	11	11	72	45	71
Billericay Town	42	20	11	11	70	51	71
Abingdon Town	42	20	10	12	61	50	70
Worthing	42	19	11	12	79	46	68
Leyton	42	20	8	14	88	66	68
Boreham Wood	42	17	15	10	69	50	66
Staines Town	42	18	9	15	85	56	63
Bognor Regis Town	42	15	14	13	57	48	59
Wembley	42	16	10	16	66	52	58
Barking	42	15	11	16	63	69	56
Uxbridge	42	15	8	19	57	58	53
Whyteleafe	42	15	6	21	71	90	51
Maidenhead United	42	12	13	17	52	48	49
Berkhamsted Town	42	12	9	21	65	77	45
Ruislip Manor	42	10	8	24	42	79	38
Chalfont St Peter	42	7	10	25	40	79	31
Windsor & Eton	42	8	7	27	47	94	31
Croydon	42	3	3	36	37	198	12

Second Division

Newbury Town	42	32	7	3	115	36	103
Chertsey Town	42	33	3	6	121	48	102
Aldershot Town	42	30	7	5	78	27	97
Barton Rovers	42	25	8	9	68	37	83
Witham Town	42	21	10	11	68	51	73
Malden Vale	42	20	10	12	70	49	70
Thame United	42	19	12	11	87	51	69
Metropolitan Police	42	20	9	13	75	54	69
Banstead Athletic	42	19	9	14	56	53	66
Aveley	42	19	5	18	60	66	62
Edgware Town	42	16	10	16	88	75	58
Saffron Walden Town	42	17	7	18	61	62	58
Hemel Hempstead	42	14	11	17	47	43	53
Egham Town	42	14	8	20	48	65	50
Ware	42	14	7	21	48	76	49
Hungerford Town	42	13	7	22	56	66	46
Tilbury	42	13	3	26	59	81	42
Hampton	42	12	5	25	42	70	41
Leatherhead	42	10	6	26	46	92	36
Lewes	42	8	11	24	38	85	34
Collier Row	42	7	8	27	37	88	29
Rainham Town	42	4	2	36	24	116	14

Third Division

Bracknell Town	40	25	8	7	78	29	83
Cheshunt	40	23	12	5	62	34	81
Oxford City	40	24	6	10	94	55	78
Harlow Town	40	22	11	7	61	36	77
Southall	40	17	12	11	66	53	63
Camberley Town	40	18	7	15	56	50	61
Hertford Town	40	18	6	16	67	65	60
Royston Town	40	15	11	14	44	41	56
Northwood	40	15	11	14	78	77	56
Epsom & Ewell	40	15	9	16	63	62	54
Harefield United	40	12	15	13	45	55	51
Cove	40	15	6	19	59	74	51
Kingsbury Town	40	12	14	14	57	54	50
Feltham & Hounslow	40	14	7	19	60	63	49
Leighton Town	40	12	11	17	51	64	47
East Thurrock Town	40	10	15	15	65	64	45
Clapton	40	12	9	19	51	65	45
Hornchurch	40	12	8	20	42	60	44
Tring Town	40	10	11	19	48	64	41
Flackwell Heath	40	9	11	20	44	83	38
Horsham	40	6	8	26	43	86	26

1994-95

Premier Division

Enfield	42	26	9	5	106	43	93
Slough Town	42	22	13	7	82	56	79
Hayes	42	20	14	8	66	47	74
Aylesbury United	42	21	6	15	86	59	69
Hitchin Town	42	18	12	12	68	59	66
Bromley	42	18	11	13	76	67	65
St Albans City	42	17	13	12	96	81	64
Molesey	42	18	8	16	65	61	62
Yeading	42	14	15	13	60	59	57
Harrow Borough	42	17	6	19	64	67	57
Dulwich Hamlet	42	16	9	17	70	82	57
Carshalton Athletic	42	16	9	17	69	84	57
Kingstonian	42	16	8	18	62	57	56
Walton & Hersham	42	14	11	17	75	73	53
Sutton United	42	13	12	17	74	69	51
Purfleet	42	13	12	17	76	90	51
Hendon	42	12	14	16	57	65	50
Grays Athletic	42	11	16	15	57	61	49
Bishop's Stortford	42	12	11	19	53	76	47
Chesham United	42	12	9	21	60	87	45
Marlow	42	10	9	23	52	84	39
Wokingham Town	42	6	9	27	39	86	27

First Division

Boreham Wood	42	31	5	6	90	38	98
Worthing	42	21	13	8	93	49	76
Chertsey Town	42	21	11	10	109	57	74
Aldershot Town	42	23	5	14	80	53	74
Billericay Town	42	20	9	13	68	52	69
Staines Town	42	17	12	13	83	65	63
Basingstoke Town	42	17	10	15	81	71	61
Tooting & Mitcham United	42	15	14	13	58	48	59
Wembley	42	16	11	15	70	61	59
Abingdon Town	42	16	11	15	67	69	59
Whyteleafe	42	17	7	18	70	78	58
Maidenhead United	42	15	12	15	73	76	57
Uxbridge	42	15	11	16	54	62	56
Leyton	42	15	10	17	67	66	55
Barking	42	16	7	19	74	77	55
Heybridge Swifts	42	16	6	20	73	78	54
Ruislip Manor	42	14	11	17	70	75	53
Bognor Regis Town	42	13	14	15	57	63	53
Berkhamsted Town	42	14	10	18	54	70	52
Newbury Town	42	12	15	15	58	71	51
Wivenhoe Town	42	8	7	27	47	94	31
Dorking	42	3	3	36	40	163	12

Second Division

Thame United	42	30	3	9	97	49	93
Barton Rovers	42	25	7	10	93	51	82
Oxford City	42	24	8	10	86	47	80
Bracknell Town	42	23	9	10	86	47	78
Metropolitan Police	42	19	12	11	81	65	69
Hampton	42	20	9	13	79	74	69
Croydon	42	20	5	17	85	65	65
Banstead Athletic	42	18	10	14	73	59	64
Saffron Walden Town	42	17	13	12	64	59	64
Chalfont St Peter	42	17	12	13	67	54	63
Witham Town	42	18	9	15	75	64	63
Leatherhead	42	16	12	14	71	75	60
Edgware Town	42	16	10	16	70	66	58
Tilbury	42	15	9	18	62	82	54
Cheshunt	42	13	13	16	66	81	52
Ware	42	14	7	21	61	81	49
Egham Town	42	11	14	17	60	65	47
Hemel Hempstead	42	10	11	21	45	76	41
Hungerford Town	42	11	7	24	55	81	40
Windsor & Eton	42	10	8	24	58	84	38
Aveley	42	9	5	28	48	95	32
Malden Vale	42	5	9	28	46	108	24

Third Division

Collier Row	40	30	5	5	86	23	95
Canvey Island	40	28	4	8	88	42	88
Bedford Town	40	22	11	7	90	50	77
Northwood	40	22	8	10	80	47	74
Horsham	40	22	6	12	84	61	72
Southall	40	21	8	11	87	59	71
Leighton Town	40	20	8	12	66	43	68
Camberley Town	40	19	8	13	59	39	65
Kingsbury Town	40	18	11	1	72	54	65
Hornchurch	40	17	8	15	64	63	59
Clapton	40	14	11	15	69	61	53
Tring Town	40	13	12	15	68	69	51
East Thurrock United	40	14	8	18	60	79	50
Epsom & Ewell	40	13	10	17	58	62	49
Harlow Town	40	13	8	19	53	83	47
Harefield United	40	12	8	20	51	79	44
Hertford Town	40	11	10	19	56	78	43
Feltham & Hounslow	40	13	4	23	64	87	43
Flackwell Heath	40	8	4	28	50	99	28
Lewes	40	6	5	29	34	104	23
Cove	40	3	5	32	37	94	14

1995-96

Premier Division

Hayes	42	24	14	4	76	32	86
Enfield	42	26	8	8	78	35	86
Boreham Wood	42	24	1	7	69	29	83
Yeovil Town	42	23	11	8	83	51	80
Dulwich Hamlet	42	23	11	8	85	59	80
Carshalton Athletic	42	22	8	12	68	49	74
St Albans City	42	20	12	10	70	41	72
Kingstonian	42	20	11	11	62	38	71
Harrow Borough	42	19	10	13	70	56	67
Sutton United	42	17	14	11	71	56	65
Aylesbury United	42	17	12	13	71	58	63
Bishop's Stortford	42	16	9	17	61	62	57
Yeading	42	11	14	17	48	60	47
Hendon	42	12	10	20	52	65	46
Chertsey Town	42	13	6	23	45	71	45
Purfleet	42	12	8	22	48	67	44
Grays Athletic	42	11	11	20	43	63	44
Hitchin Town	42	10	10	22	41	74	40
Bromley	42	10	7	25	52	91	37
Molesey	42	9	9	24	46	81	36
Walton & Hersham	42	9	7	26	42	79	34
Worthing	42	4	7	31	42	106	19

First Division

Oxford City	42	28	7	7	98	60	91
Heybridge Swifts	42	27	7	8	97	43	88
Staines Town	42	23	11	8	82	59	80
Leyton Pennant	42	22	7	13	77	57	73
Aldershot Town	42	21	9	12	81	46	72
Billericay Town	42	19	9	14	58	58	66
Bognor Regis Town	42	18	11	13	71	53	65
Marlow	42	19	5	18	72	75	62
Basingstoke Town	42	16	13	13	70	60	61
Uxbridge	42	16	12	14	46	49	60
Wokingham Town	42	16	10	16	62	65	58
Chesham United	42	15	12	15	51	44	57
Thame United	42	14	13	15	64	73	55
Maidenhead United	42	12	14	16	50	63	50
Whyteleafe	42	12	13	17	71	81	49
Abingdon Town	42	13	9	20	63	80	48
Barton Rovers	42	12	10	20	69	87	46
Berkhamsted Town	42	11	11	20	52	68	44
Tooting & Mitcham United	42	11	10	21	45	64	43
Ruislip Manor	42	11	9	22	55	77	42
Wembley	42	11	8	23	49	66	41
Barking	42	4	12	26	35	90	24

Second Division

Canvey Island	40	25	12	3	91	36	87
Croydon	40	25	6	9	78	42	81
Hampton	40	23	10	7	74	44	79
Banstead Athletic	40	21	11	8	72	36	74
Collier Row	40	21	11	8	73	41	74
Wivenhoe Town	40	21	8	11	82	57	71
Metropolitan Police	40	18	10	12	57	45	64
Bedford Town	40	18	10	12	69	59	64
Bracknell Town	40	18	8	14	69	50	62
Edgware Town	40	16	9	15	72	67	57
Tilbury	40	12	11	17	52	62	47
Ware	40	13	8	19	55	80	47
Chalfont St Peter	40	11	13	16	58	63	46
Leatherhead	40	12	10	18	71	77	46
Saffron Walden Town	40	11	12	17	56	58	45
Cheshunt	40	10	12	18	56	90	42
Hemel Hempstead	40	10	10	20	46	62	40
Egham Town	40	12	3	25	42	74	39
Witham Town	40	8	10	22	35	68	34
Hungerford Town	40	9	7	24	44	79	34
Dorking	40	8	5	27	44	104	29

Third Division

Horsham	40	29	5	6	95	40	92
Leighton Town	40	28	5	7	95	34	89
Windsor & Eton	40	27	6	7	117	46	87
Wealdstone	40	23	8	9	104	39	77
Harlow Town	40	22	10	8	85	62	76
Northwood	40	20	9	11	76	56	69
Epsom & Ewell	40	18	14	8	95	57	68
Kingsbury Town	40	15	16	9	61	48	61
East Thurrock United	40	17	8	15	61	50	59
Aveley	40	16	10	14	62	53	58
Wingate & Finchley	40	16	7	17	74	70	55
Lewes	40	14	7	19	56	72	49
Flackwell Heath	40	14	5	21	60	84	47
Hornchurch	40	11	8	21	55	77	41
Harefield United	40	11	7	22	49	89	40
Tring Town	40	10	8	22	40	78	38
Camberley Town	40	9	9	22	45	81	36
Hertford Town	40	10	5	25	72	103	35
Cove	40	8	10	22	37	89	34
Clapton	40	9	6	25	48	89	33
Southall	40	9	5	26	34	104	32

1996-97

Premier Division

Yeovil Town	42	31	8	3	83	34	101
Enfield	42	28	11	3	91	29	98
Sutton United	42	18	13	11	87	70	67
Dagenham & Redbridge	42	18	11	13	57	43	65
Yeading	42	17	14	11	58	47	65
St Albans City	42	18	11	13	65	55	65
Aylesbury United	42	18	11	13	64	54	65
Purfleet	42	17	11	14	67	63	62
Heybridge Swifts	42	16	14	12	62	62	62
Boreham Wood	42	15	13	14	56	52	58
Kingstonian	42	16	8	18	79	79	56
Dulwich Hamlet	42	14	13	15	57	57	55
Carshalton Athletic	42	14	11	17	51	56	53
Hitchin Town	42	15	7	20	67	73	52
Oxford City	42	14	10	18	67	83	52
Hendon	42	13	12	17	53	59	51
Harrow Borough	42	12	14	16	58	62	50
Bromley	42	13	9	20	67	72	48
Bishop's Stortford	42	10	13	19	43	64	43
Staines Town	42	10	8	24	46	71	38
Grays Athletic	42	8	9	25	43	78	33
Chertsey Town	42	8	7	27	40	98	31

First Division

Chesham United	42	27	6	9	80	46	87
Basingstoke Town	42	22	13	7	81	38	79
Walton & Hersham	42	21	13	8	67	41	76
Hampton	42	21	12	9	62	39	75
Billericay Town	42	21	12	9	69	49	75
Bognor Regis Town	42	21	9	12	63	44	72
Aldershot Town	42	19	14	9	67	45	71
Uxbridge	42	15	17	10	65	48	62
Whyteleafe	42	18	7	17	71	68	61
Molesey	42	17	9	16	50	53	60
Abingdon Town	42	15	11	16	44	42	56
Leyton Pennant	42	14	12	16	71	72	54
Maidenhead United	42	15	10	17	57	57	52
Wokingham Town	42	14	10	18	41	45	52
Thame United	42	13	10	19	57	69	49
Worthing	42	11	11	20	58	77	44
Barton Rovers	42	11	11	20	61	58	44
Croydon	42	11	10	21	40	57	43
Berkhamsted Town	42	11	9	22	47	66	42
Canvey Island	42	9	14	19	52	71	41
Marlow	42	11	6	25	41	84	39
Tooting & Mitcham United	42	8	8	26	40	85	32

Maidenhead United had 3 points deducted

Second Division

Collier Row & Romford	42	28	12	2	93	33	96
Leatherhead	42	30	5	7	116	45	95
Wembley	42	23	11	8	92	45	80
Barking	42	22	13	7	69	40	79
Horsham	42	22	11	9	78	48	77
Edgware Town	42	20	14	8	74	50	74
Bedford Town	42	21	8	13	77	43	71
Banstead Athletic	42	21	5	16	75	52	68
Windsor & Eton	42	17	13	12	65	62	64
Leighton Town	42	17	12	13	64	52	63
Bracknell Town	42	17	9	16	78	71	60
Wivenhoe Town	42	17	9	16	69	62	60
Chalfont St Peter	42	14	13	15	53	61	55
Hungerford Town	42	14	13	15	68	77	55
Metropolitan Police	42	14	7	21	72	75	49
Tilbury	42	14	7	21	68	77	49
Witham Town	42	11	10	21	39	67	43
Egham Town	42	10	9	23	47	86	39
Cheshunt	42	9	3	30	37	101	30
Ware	42	7	8	27	44	80	29
Dorking	42	7	6	29	40	100	27
Hemel Hempstead	42	5	6	31	34	125	21

Third Division

Wealdstone	32	24	3	5	72	24	75
Braintree Town	32	23	5	4	99	29	74
Northwood	32	18	10	4	60	31	64
Harlow Town	32	19	4	9	60	41	61
Aveley	32	17	6	9	64	39	57
East Thurrock United	32	16	6	10	58	51	54
Camberley Town	32	15	6	11	55	44	51
Wingate & Finchley	32	11	7	14	52	63	40
Hornchurch	32	11	6	15	35	51	39
Clapton	32	11	6	15	31	49	39
Lewes	32	10	8	14	45	53	38
Kingsbury Town	32	11	4	17	41	54	37
Hertford Town	32	10	6	16	55	65	36
Epsom & Ewell	32	8	5	19	62	78	29
Flackwell Heath	32	8	5	19	36	71	29
Tring Town	32	7	3	22	33	74	24
Southall	32	6	4	22	28	69	22

1997-98

Premier Division

Kingstonian	42	25	12	5	84	35	87
Boreham Wood	42	23	11	8	81	42	80
Sutton United	42	22	12	8	83	56	78
Dagenham & Redbridge	42	21	10	11	73	50	73
Hendon	42	21	10	11	69	50	73
Heybridge Swifts	42	18	11	13	74	62	65
Enfield	42	18	8	16	66	58	62
Basingstoke Town	42	17	11	14	56	60	62
Walton & Hersham	42	18	6	18	50	70	60
Purfleet	42	15	13	14	57	58	58
St Albans City	42	17	7	18	54	59	58
Harrow Borough	42	15	10	17	60	67	55
Gravesend & Northfleet	42	15	8	19	65	67	53
Chesham United	42	14	10	18	71	70	52
Bromley	42	13	13	16	53	53	52
Dulwich Hamlet	42	13	11	18	56	67	50
Carshalton Athletic	42	13	9	20	54	77	48
Aylesbury United	42	13	8	21	55	70	47
Bishop's Stortford	42	14	5	23	53	69	47
Yeading	42	12	11	19	49	65	47
Hitchin Town	42	8	15	19	45	62	39
Oxford City	42	7	9	26	35	76	30

First Division

Aldershot Town	42	28	8	6	89	36	92
Billericay Town	42	25	6	11	78	44	81
Hampton	42	22	15	5	75	47	81
Maidenhead United	42	25	5	12	76	37	80
Uxbridge	42	23	6	13	66	59	75
Grays Athletic	42	21	10	11	79	49	73
Romford	42	21	8	13	92	59	71
Bognor Regis Town	42	20	9	13	77	45	69
Leatherhead	42	18	11	13	70	51	65
Leyton Pennant	42	17	11	14	66	58	62
Chertsey Town	42	16	13	13	83	70	61
Worthing	42	17	6	19	64	71	57
Berkhamsted Town	42	15	8	19	59	69	53
Staines Town	42	13	10	19	54	74	49
Croydon	42	13	10	19	47	64	49
Barton Rovers	42	11	13	18	53	72	46
Wembley	42	10	15	17	38	61	45
Molesey	42	10	11	21	47	65	41
Whyteleafe	42	10	10	22	48	83	40
Wokingham Town	42	7	10	25	41	74	31
Abingdon Town	42	9	4	29	47	101	31
Thame United	42	7	9	25	33	96	30

Second Division

Canvey Island	42	30	8	4	116	41	98
Braintree Town	42	29	11	2	117	45	98
Wealdstone	42	24	11	7	81	46	83
Bedford Town	42	22	12	8	55	25	78
Metropolitan Police	42	21	8	13	80	65	71
Wivenhoe Town	42	18	12	12	84	66	66
Edgware Town	42	18	10	14	81	65	64
Chalfont St Peter	42	17	13	12	63	60	64
Northwood	42	17	11	14	65	69	62
Windsor & Eton	42	17	7	18	75	72	58
Tooting & Mitcham United	42	16	9	17	58	56	57
Barking	42	15	12	15	62	75	57
Banstead Athletic	42	15	9	18	60	63	54
Marlow	42	16	5	21	64	78	53
Horsham	42	13	9	20	67	75	48
Bracknell Town	42	13	8	21	68	93	47
Leighton Town	42	13	6	23	45	78	45
Hungerford Town	42	11	11	20	66	77	44
Witham Town	42	9	13	20	55	68	40
Tilbury	42	9	12	21	57	88	39
Egham Town	42	9	5	28	47	101	32
Cheshunt	42	4	10	28	31	90	32

Third Division

Hemel Hempstead	38	27	6	5	86	28	87
Hertford Town	38	26	5	7	77	31	83
Harlow Town	38	24	11	3	81	43	83
Camberley Town	38	24	7	7	93	43	79
Ford United	38	23	9	6	90	34	78
East Thurrock United	38	23	7	8	70	40	76
Epsom & Ewell	38	17	6	15	69	57	57
Ware	38	17	6	15	69	57	57
Aveley	38	16	7	15	65	57	55
Corinthian Casuals	38	16	6	16	59	57	54
Hornchurch	38	12	9	17	55	68	45
Clapton	38	13	6	19	46	61	45
Flackwell Heath	38	12	9	17	50	76	45
Croydon Athletic	38	12	7	19	58	63	43
Tring Town	38	12	7	19	51	69	43
Southall	38	10	6	22	41	85	46
Dorking	38	9	6	23	49	94	33
Wingate & Finchley	38	7	8	23	46	80	29
Lewes	38	7	5	26	34	88	26
Kingsbury Town	38	5	3	30	35	93	18

1998-99

Premier Division

Sutton United	42	27	7	8	89	39	88
Aylesbury United	42	23	8	11	67	38	77
Dagenham & Redbridge	42	20	13	9	71	44	73
Purfleet	42	22	7	13	71	54	73
Enfield	42	21	9	12	73	49	72
St Albans City	42	17	17	8	71	52	68
Aldershot Town	42	16	14	12	83	48	62
Basingstoke Town	42	17	10	15	63	53	61
Harrow Borough	42	17	9	16	72	66	60
Gravesend & Northfleet	42	18	6	18	54	53	60
Slough Town	42	16	11	15	60	53	59
Billericay Town	42	15	13	14	54	56	58
Hendon	42	16	9	17	70	71	57
Boreham Wood	42	14	15	13	59	63	57
Chesham United	42	15	9	18	58	79	54
Dulwich Hamlet	42	14	8	20	53	63	50
Heybridge Swifts	42	13	9	20	51	85	48
Walton & Hersham	42	12	7	23	50	77	43
Hampton	42	10	12	20	41	71	42
Carshalton Athletic	42	10	10	22	47	82	40
Bishops Stortford	42	9	10	23	49	90	37
Bromley	42	8	11	23	50	72	35

First Division

Canvey Island	42	28	6	8	76	41	90
Hitchin Town	42	25	10	7	75	38	85
Wealdstone	42	26	6	10	75	48	84
Braintree Town	42	20	10	12	75	48	70
Bognor Regis Town	42	20	8	14	63	44	68
Grays Athletic	42	19	11	12	56	42	68
Oxford City	42	16	14	12	58	51	62
Croydon	42	16	13	13	53	53	61
Chertsey Town	42	14	16	12	57	57	58
Romford	42	14	15	13	58	63	57
Maidenhead United	42	13	15	14	50	46	54
Worthing	42	13	13	16	47	61	52
Leyton Pennant	42	13	12	17	62	70	51
Uxbridge	42	13	11	18	54	51	50
Barton Rovers	42	11	15	16	43	49	48
Yeading	42	12	10	20	51	55	46
Leatherhead	42	12	9	21	48	59	45
Whyteleafe	42	13	6	23	51	72	45
Staines Town	42	10	15	17	33	57	45
Molesey	42	8	20	14	35	52	44
Wembley	42	10	10	22	36	71	40
Berkhamsted Town	42	10	7	25	53	81	37

Second Division

Bedford Town	42	29	7	6	89	31	94
Harlow Town	42	27	8	7	100	47	89
Thame United	42	26	8	8	89	50	86
Hemel Hempstead	42	21	12	9	90	50	75
Windsor & Eton	42	22	6	14	87	55	72
Banstead Athletic	42	21	8	13	83	62	71
Northwood	42	20	7	15	67	68	67
Tooting & Mitcham United	42	19	9	14	63	62	66
Chalfont St Peter	42	16	12	14	70	71	60
Metropolitan Police	42	17	8	17	61	58	59
Leighton Town	42	16	10	16	60	64	58
Horsham	42	17	6	19	74	67	57
Marlow	42	16	9	17	72	68	57
Edgware Town	42	14	10	18	65	68	52
Witham Town	42	12	15	15	64	64	51
Hungerford Town	42	13	12	17	59	61	51
Wivenhoe Town	42	14	8	20	71	83	50
Wokingham Town	42	14	4	24	44	79	46
Barking	42	10	11	21	50	75	41
Hertford Town	42	11	2	29	44	96	35
Bracknell Town	42	7	10	25	48	92	31
Abingdon Town	42	6	6	30	48	124	24

Third Division

Ford United	38	27	5	6	110	42	86
Wingate & Finchley	38	25	5	8	79	38	80
Cheshunt	38	23	10	5	70	41	79
Lewes	38	25	3	10	86	45	78
Epsom & Ewell	38	19	5	14	61	51	62
Ware	38	19	4	15	79	60	61
Tilbury	38	17	8	13	74	52	59
Croydon Athletic	38	16	10	12	82	59	58
East Thurrock United	38	15	13	10	74	56	58
Egham Town	38	16	8	14	65	58	56
Corinthian Casuals	38	16	7	15	70	71	55
Southall	38	14	9	15	68	66	51
Camberley Town	38	14	8	16	66	77	50
Aveley	38	12	7	19	50	67	43
Flackwell Heath	38	11	9	18	59	70	42
Hornchurch	38	10	9	19	48	73	39
Clapton	38	11	6	21	48	89	39
Dorking	38	8	7	23	52	98	31
Kingsbury Town	38	6	3	29	40	98	21
Tring Town	38	5	6	27	38	108	21

1999-2000

Premier Division

Dagenham & Redbridge	42	32	5	5	97	35	101
Aldershot Town	42	24	5	13	71	51	77
Chesham United	42	20	10	12	64	50	70
Purfleet	42	18	15	9	70	48	69
Canvey Island	42	21	6	15	70	53	69
St Albans City	42	19	10	13	75	55	67
Billericay Town	42	18	12	12	62	62	66
Hendon	42	18	8	16	61	64	62
Slough Town	42	17	9	16	61	59	60
Dulwich Hamlet	42	17	5	20	62	68	56
Gravesend & Northfleet	42	15	10	17	66	67	55
Farnborough Town	42	14	11	17	52	55	53
Hampton & Richmond Borough	42	13	13	16	49	57	52
Enfield	42	13	11	18	64	68	50
Heybridge Swifts	42	13	11	18	57	65	50
Hitchin Town	42	13	11	18	59	72	50
Carshalton Athletic	42	12	12	18	55	65	48
Basingstoke Town	42	13	9	20	56	71	48
Harrow Borough	42	14	6	22	54	70	48
Aylesbury United	42	13	9	20	64	81	48
Boreham Wood	42	11	10	21	44	71	43
Walton & Hersham	42	11	8	23	44	70	41

First Division

Croydon	42	25	9	8	85	47	84
Grays Athletic	42	21	12	9	80	44	75
Maidenhead United	42	20	15	7	72	45	75
Thame United	42	20	13	9	61	38	73
Worthing	42	19	12	11	80	60	69
Staines Town	42	19	12	11	63	52	69
Whyteleafe	42	20	9	13	60	49	69
Bedford Town	42	17	12	13	59	52	63
Bromley	42	17	9	16	63	65	60
Uxbridge	42	15	13	14	60	44	58
Bishop's Stortford	42	16	10	16	57	62	58
Barton Rovers	42	16	8	18	64	83	56
Oxford City	42	17	4	21	57	55	55
Braintree Town	42	15	10	17	65	74	55
Yeading	42	12	18	12	53	54	54
Wealdstone	42	13	12	17	51	58	51
Bognor Regis Town	42	12	13	17	47	53	49
Harlow Town	42	11	13	18	62	76	46
Romford	42	12	9	21	51	70	45
Leatherhead	42	9	13	20	47	70	40
Chertsey Town	42	9	5	28	50	84	32
Leyton Pennant	42	7	9	26	34	85	30

Second Division

Hemel Hempstead	42	31	8	3	98	27	101
Northwood	42	29	9	4	109	40	96
Ford United	42	28	8	6	108	41	92
Berkhamsted Town	42	22	8	12	75	52	74
Windsor & Eton	42	20	13	9	73	53	73
Wivenhoe Town	42	20	9	13	61	47	69
Barking	42	18	13	11	70	51	67
Marlow	42	20	4	18	86	66	64
Metropolitan Police	42	18	7	17	75	71	61
Banstead Athletic	42	16	11	15	55	56	59
Tooting & Mitcham United	42	16	7	19	72	74	55
Wokingham Town	42	15	9	18	58	80	54
Wembley	42	14	11	17	47	53	53
Edgware Town	42	13	11	18	72	71	50
Hungerford Town	42	13	10	19	61	78	49
Cheshunt	42	12	12	18	53	65	48
Horsham	42	13	8	21	66	81	47
Leighton Town	42	13	8	21	65	84	47
Molesey	42	10	12	20	54	69	42
Wingate & Finchley	42	11	7	24	54	97	40
Witham Town	42	7	9	26	39	110	30
Chalfont St Peter	42	2	8	32	39	124	14

Third Division

East Thurrock United	40	26	7	7	89	42	85
Great Wakering Rovers	40	25	7	8	81	41	82
Tilbury	40	21	12	7	67	39	75
Hornchurch	40	19	12	9	72	57	69
Croydon Athletic	40	19	11	10	85	52	68
Epsom & Ewell	40	18	12	10	67	46	66
Lewes	40	18	10	12	73	51	64
Bracknell Town	40	15	16	9	81	64	61
Aveley	40	17	10	13	73	64	61
Corinthian Casuals	40	16	10	14	59	51	58
Flackwell Heath	40	17	6	17	74	76	57
Ware	40	16	8	16	74	62	56
Egham Town	40	14	13	13	48	43	55
Hertford Town	40	15	10	15	63	60	55
Abingdon Town	40	10	12	18	48	64	42
Kingsbury Town	40	11	8	21	55	86	41
Camberley Town	40	11	7	22	44	79	40
Tring Town	40	10	9	21	37	64	39
Dorking	40	9	10	21	53	69	37
Clapton	40	9	7	24	50	93	34
Southall	40	3	5	32	33	123	14

2000-2001

Premier Division

Farnborough Town	42	31	6	5	86	27	99
Canvey Island	42	27	8	7	79	41	89
Basingstoke Town	42	22	13	7	73	40	79
Aldershot Town	41	21	11	9	73	39	74
Chesham United	42	22	6	14	78	52	72
Gravesend & Northfleet	42	22	5	15	62	45	71
Heybridge Swifts	42	18	13	11	74	60	67
Billericay Town	41	18	13	10	62	54	67
Hampton & Richmond Borough	42	18	12	12	73	60	66
Hitchin Town	42	18	5	19	72	69	59
Purfleet	42	14	13	15	55	55	55
Hendon	42	16	6	18	62	62	54
Sutton United	41	14	11	16	74	70	53
St Albans City	42	15	5	22	50	69	50
Grays Athletic	42	14	8	20	49	68	50
Maidenhead United	42	15	2	25	47	63	47
Croydon	42	12	10	20	55	77	46
Enfield	42	12	9	21	48	74	45
Harrow Borough	41	10	11	20	61	90	41
Slough Town	42	10	9	23	40	62	39
Carshalton Athletic	42	10	6	26	40	85	36
Dulwich Hamlet	42	4	10	28	33	84	22

First Division

Boreham Wood	42	26	7	9	82	49	85
Bedford Town	42	22	16	4	81	40	82
Braintree Town	42	25	6	11	112	60	81
Bishop's Stortford	42	24	6	12	103	76	78
Thame United	42	22	8	12	86	54	74
Ford United	42	19	12	11	70	58	69
Uxbridge	42	21	5	16	73	55	68
Northwood	42	20	8	14	89	81	68
Whyteleafe	42	20	6	16	62	69	66
Oxford City	42	16	13	13	64	49	61
Harlow Town	42	15	16	11	70	66	61
Worthing	42	16	9	17	69	69	57
Staines Town	42	16	8	18	60	66	56
Aylesbury United	42	17	4	21	65	55	55
Yeading	42	15	9	18	72	74	54
Bognor Regis Town	42	13	11	18	71	71	50
Walton & Hersham	42	14	8	20	59	80	50
Bromley	42	14	6	22	63	86	48
Wealdstone	42	12	9	21	54	73	45
Leatherhead	42	12	4	26	37	87	40
Romford	42	9	4	29	53	113	31
Barton Rovers	42	2	9	31	30	94	15

Second Division

Tooting & Mitcham United	42	26	11	5	92	35	89
Windsor	42	24	10	8	70	40	82
Barking	42	23	13	6	82	54	82
Berkhamsted Town	42	24	8	10	99	49	80
Wivenhoe Town	42	23	11	8	78	52	80
Hemel Hempstead	42	22	10	10	74	44	76
Horsham	42	19	9	14	84	61	66
Chertsey Town	42	18	9	15	59	59	63
Great Wakering Rovers	42	16	13	13	69	59	61
Tilbury	42	18	6	18	61	67	60
Banstead Athletic	42	17	8	17	69	58	59
East Thurrock United	42	16	11	15	72	64	59
Metropolitan Police	42	18	4	20	64	77	58
Marlow	42	15	11	16	62	61	56
Molesey	42	14	9	19	53	61	51
Wembley	42	12	10	20	39	63	46
Hungerford Town	42	11	9	22	40	73	42
Leyton Pennant	42	10	11	21	47	74	41
Cheshunt	42	11	6	25	48	77	39
Edgware Town	42	9	9	24	41	77	36
Leighton Town	42	8	10	24	44	87	34
Wokingham Town	42	3	12	27	39	94	20

Wokingham Town had 1 point deducted

Third Division

Arlesey Town	42	34	6	2	138	37	108
Lewes	41	25	11	5	104	34	86
Ashford Town	42	26	7	9	102	49	85
Flackwell Heath	42	24	10	8	93	51	82
Corinthian Casuals	42	24	10	8	83	50	82
Aveley	42	24	3	15	85	61	75
Epsom & Ewell	42	23	4	15	76	52	73
Witham Town	42	21	9	12	76	57	72
Bracknell Town	41	19	10	12	90	70	67
Croydon Athletic	41	15	12	14	78	63	57
Ware	42	17	6	19	75	76	57
Tring Town	42	16	9	17	60	71	57
Egham Town	42	15	11	16	60	60	56
Hornchurch	42	14	13	15	73	60	55
Wingate & Finchley	42	15	7	20	75	75	52
Kingsbury Town	42	11	8	23	74	100	41
Abingdon Town	42	12	7	23	53	102	40
Dorking	42	10	9	23	59	99	39
Hertford Town	41	9	8	24	57	97	35
Camberley Town	42	8	8	26	53	107	32
Clapton	42	5	9	28	48	121	24
Chalfont St Peter	42	4	1	37	30	150	13

Abingdon Town had 3 points deducted

2001-2002

Premier Division

Gravesend & Northfleet	42	31	6	5	90	33	99
Canvey Island	42	30	5	7	107	41	95
Aldershot Town	42	22	7	13	76	51	73
Braintree Town	42	23	4	15	66	61	73
Purfleet	42	19	15	8	67	44	72
Grays Athletic	42	20	10	12	65	55	70
Chesham United	42	19	10	13	69	53	67
Hendon Town	42	19	5	18	66	54	62
Billericay Town	42	16	13	13	59	60	61
St Albans City	42	16	9	17	71	60	57
Hitchin Town	42	15	10	17	73	81	55
Sutton Albion	42	13	15	14	62	62	54
Heybridge Swifts	42	15	9	18	68	85	54
Kingstonian	42	13	13	16	50	56	52
Boreham Wood	42	15	6	21	49	62	51
Maidenhead United	42	15	5	22	51	63	50
Bedford Town	42	12	12	18	64	69	48
Basingstoke Town	42	11	15	16	50	68	48
Enfield	42	11	9	22	48	77	42
Hampton & Richmond Borough	42	9	13	20	51	71	40
Harrow Borough	42	8	10	24	50	89	34
Croydon	42	7	5	30	36	93	26

First Division

Ford United	42	27	7	8	92	56	88
Bishop's Stortford	42	26	9	7	104	51	87
Aylesbury United	42	23	10	9	96	64	79
Bognor Regis Town	42	20	13	9	74	55	73
Northwood	42	19	11	12	92	64	68
Carshalton Athletic	42	17	16	9	64	53	67
Harlow Town	42	19	9	14	77	65	66
Slough Town	42	17	11	14	68	51	62
Uxbridge	42	18	6	18	68	65	60
Oxford City	42	17	9	16	59	66	60
Thame United	42	15	14	13	75	61	59
Tooting & Mitcham United	42	16	11	15	70	70	59
Walton & Hersham	42	16	10	16	75	70	58
Yeading	42	16	10	16	84	90	58
Worthing	42	15	8	19	69	65	53
Staines Town	42	12	11	19	45	60	47
Dulwich Hamlet	42	11	13	18	64	76	46
Wealdstone	42	11	12	19	60	82	45
Bromley	42	10	11	21	44	74	41
Whyteleafe	42	10	11	21	46	86	41
Barking & East Ham United	42	8	7	27	61	123	31
Windsor & Eton	42	7	5	30	53	93	26

Second Division

Lewes	42	29	9	4	108	31	96
Horsham	42	27	9	6	104	44	90
Berkhamstead Town	42	23	10	9	82	51	79
Arlesey Town	42	23	6	13	89	55	75
Banstead Athletic	42	22	8	12	83	54	74
Leyton Pennant	42	22	8	12	84	60	74
Great Wakering Rovers	42	21	8	13	64	37	71
East Thurrock United	42	21	8	13	67	59	71
Marlow	42	18	13	11	73	63	67
Hemel Hempstead Town	42	18	10	14	82	66	64
Leatherhead	42	17	6	19	72	62	57
Ashford Town	42	15	11	16	58	71	56
Metropolitan Police	42	16	7	19	84	84	55
Barton Rovers	42	15	9	18	54	60	54
Hungerford Town	42	14	9	19	56	75	51
Tilbury	42	15	6	21	55	74	51
Chertsey Town	42	10	14	18	79	112	44
Wembley	42	9	10	23	51	82	37
Molesey	42	10	6	26	40	93	36
Cheshunt	42	7	13	22	51	84	34
Wivenhoe Town	42	8	9	25	55	111	33
Romford	42	4	7	31	42	105	19

Third Division

Croydon Athletic	42	30	5	7	138	41	95
Hornchurch	42	25	11	6	96	46	86
Aveley	42	26	6	10	109	55	84
Bracknell Town	42	25	8	9	96	54	83
Epsom & Ewell	42	20	15	7	79	51	75
Egham Town	42	21	11	10	72	59	74
Wingate & Finchley	42	20	9	13	80	60	69
Dorking	42	18	14	10	77	66	68
Tring Town	42	19	11	12	64	62	68
Corinthian-Casuals	42	18	13	11	69	44	67
Hertford Town	42	20	7	15	88	74	67
Witham Town	42	15	10	17	66	72	55
Ware	42	14	10	18	74	76	52
Chalfont St Peter	42	15	4	23	69	92	49
Wokingham Town	42	14	6	22	79	105	48
Abingdon Town	42	13	7	22	61	75	46
Leighton Town	42	8	12	22	56	95	36
Kingsbury Town	42	8	11	23	58	91	35
Edgware Town	42	9	7	26	65	101	34
Flackwell Heath	42	9	8	25	53	99	32
Clapton	42	9	4	29	45	118	31
Camberley Town	42	7	9	26	37	95	30

NORTHERN PREMIER LEAGUE

1968-69

Macclesfield Town	38	27	6	5	82	38	60
Wigan Athletic	38	18	12	8	59	41	48
Morecambe	38	16	14	8	64	37	46
Gainsborough Trinity	38	19	8	11	64	43	46
South Shields	38	19	8	11	78	56	46
Bangor City	38	18	9	11	102	64	45
Hyde United	38	16	10	12	71	65	42
Goole Town	38	15	10	13	80	78	40
Altrincham	38	14	10	14	69	52	38
Fleetwood	38	16	6	16	58	58	38
Gateshead	38	14	9	15	42	48	37
South Liverpool	38	12	13	13	56	66	37
Northwich Victoria	38	16	5	17	59	82	37
Boston United	38	14	8	16	59	65	36
Runcorn	38	12	11	15	59	63	35
Netherfield	38	12	4	22	51	69	28
Scarborough	38	9	10	19	49	68	28
Ashington	38	10	8	20	48	74	28
Chorley	38	8	9	21	46	75	25
Worksop Town	38	6	8	24	34	88	20

1969-70

Macclesfield Town	38	22	8	8	72	41	52
Wigan Athletic	38	20	12	6	56	32	52
Boston United	38	21	8	9	65	33	50
Scarborough	38	20	10	8	74	39	50
South Shields	38	19	7	12	66	43	45
Gainsborough Trinity	38	16	11	11	64	49	43
Stafford Rangers	38	16	7	15	59	52	39
Bangor City	38	15	9	14	68	63	39
Northwich Victoria	38	15	8	15	60	66	38
Netherfield	38	14	9	15	56	54	37
Hyde United	38	15	7	16	59	59	37
Altincham	38	14	8	16	62	65	36
Fleetwood	38	13	10	15	53	60	36
Runcorn	38	11	13	14	57	72	35
Morecambe	38	10	13	15	41	51	33
South Liverpool	38	11	11	16	44	55	33
Great Harwood	38	10	9	19	63	92	29
Matlock Town	38	8	12	18	52	67	28
Goole Town	38	10	6	22	50	71	26
Gateshead	38	5	12	21	37	94	22

1970-71

Wigan Athletic	42	27	13	2	91	32	67
Stafford Rangers	42	27	7	8	87	51	61
Scarborough	42	23	12	7	83	40	58
Boston United	42	22	12	8	69	31	56
Macclesfield Town	42	23	10	9	84	45	56
Northwich Victoria	42	22	5	15	71	55	49
Bangor City	42	19	10	13	72	61	48
Altrincham	42	19	10	13	80	76	48
South Liverpool	42	15	15	12	67	57	45
Chorley	42	14	14	14	58	61	42
Gainsborough Trinity	42	15	11	16	65	63	41
Morecambe	42	14	11	17	67	79	39
South Shields	42	12	14	16	67	66	38
Bradford Park Avenue	42	15	8	19	54	73	38
Lancaster City	42	12	12	18	53	76	36
Netherfield	42	13	9	20	59	57	35
Matlock Town	42	10	13	19	58	80	33
Fleetwood	42	10	11	21	56	90	31
Great Harwood	42	8	13	21	66	98	29
Runcorn	42	10	5	27	58	84	25
Kirkby Town	42	6	13	23	57	93	25
Goole Town	42	10	4	28	44	98	24

1971-72

Stafford Rangers	46	30	11	5	91	32	71
Boston United	46	28	13	5	87	37	69
Wigan Athletic	46	27	10	9	70	43	64
Scarborough	46	21	15	10	75	46	57
Northwich Victoria	46	20	14	12	65	59	54
Macclesfield Town	46	18	15	13	61	50	51
Gainsborough Trinity	46	21	9	16	93	79	51
South Shields	46	18	14	14	75	57	50
Bangor City	46	20	8	18	93	74	48
Altrincham	46	18	11	17	72	58	47
Skelmersdale United	46	19	9	18	61	58	47
Matlock Town	46	20	7	19	67	75	47
Chorley	46	17	12	17	66	59	46
Lancaster City	46	15	14	17	84	84	44
Great Harwood	46	15	14	17	60	74	44
Ellesmere Port Town	46	17	9	20	67	71	43
Morecambe	46	15	10	21	51	64	40
Bradford Park Avenue	46	13	13	20	54	71	39
Netherfield	46	16	5	25	51	73	37
Fleetwood	46	11	15	20	43	67	37
South Liverpool	46	12	12	22	61	73	36
Runcorn	46	8	14	24	48	80	30
Goole Town	46	9	10	27	51	97	28
Kirkby Town	46	6	12	28	38	104	24

1972-73

Boston United	46	27	16	3	88	34	70
Scarborough	46	26	9	11	72	39	61
Wigan Athletic	46	23	14	9	69	38	60
Altrincham	46	22	16	8	75	55	60
Bradford Park Avenue	46	19	17	10	63	50	55
Stafford Rangers	46	20	11	15	63	46	51
Gainsborough Trinity	46	18	13	15	70	50	49
Northwich Victoria	46	17	15	14	74	62	49
Netherfield	46	20	9	17	68	65	49
Macclesfield Town	46	16	16	14	58	47	48
Ellesmere Port Town	46	18	11	17	52	56	47
Skelmersdale United	46	15	16	15	58	59	46
Bangor City	46	16	13	17	70	60	45
Mossley	46	17	11	18	70	73	45
Morecambe	46	17	11	18	62	70	45
Great Harwood	46	14	15	17	63	74	43
South Liverpool	46	12	19	15	47	57	43
Runcorn	46	15	12	19	75	78	42
Goole Town	46	13	13	20	64	73	39
South Shields	46	17	4	25	64	81	38
Matlock Town	46	11	11	24	42	80	33
Lancaster City	46	10	11	25	53	78	31
Barrow	46	12	6	28	52	101	30
Fleetwood	46	5	15	26	31	77	25

1973-74

Boston United	46	27	11	8	69	32	65
Wigan Athletic	46	28	8	10	96	39	64
Altrincham	46	26	11	9	77	34	63
Stafford Rangers	46	27	9	10	101	45	63
Scarborough	46	22	14	10	62	43	58
South Shields	46	25	6	15	87	48	56
Runcorn	46	21	14	11	72	47	56
Macclesfield Town	46	18	15	13	48	47	51
Bangor City	46	19	11	16	65	56	49
Gainsborough Trinity	46	18	11	17	77	64	47
South Liverpool	46	16	15	15	55	47	47
Skelmersdale United	46	16	13	17	50	59	45
Goole Town	46	14	15	17	60	69	43
Fleetwood	46	14	15	17	48	68	43
Mossley	46	15	11	20	53	65	41
Northwich Victoria	46	14	13	19	68	75	41
Morecambe	46	13	13	20	62	84	39
Buxton	46	14	10	22	45	71	38
Matlock Town	46	11	14	21	50	79	36
Great Harwood	46	10	14	22	52	74	34
Bradford Park Avenue	46	9	15	22	42	84	33
Barrow	46	13	7	26	46	94	33
Lancaster City	46	10	12	24	52	67	32
Netherfield	46	11	5	30	42	88	27

1974-75

Wigan Athletic	46	33	6	7	94	38	72
Runcorn	46	30	8	8	102	42	68
Altrincham	46	26	12	8	87	43	64
Stafford Rangers	46	25	13	8	81	39	63
Scarborough	46	24	12	10	73	45	60
Mossley	46	23	11	12	78	52	57
Gateshead United	46	22	12	12	74	48	56
Goole Town	46	19	12	15	75	71	50
Northwich Victoria	46	18	12	16	83	71	48
Great Harwood	46	17	14	15	69	66	48
Matlock Town	46	19	8	19	87	79	46
Boston United	46	16	14	16	64	63	46
Morecambe	46	14	15	17	71	87	43
Worksop Town	46	14	14	18	69	66	42
South Liverpool	46	14	14	18	59	71	42
Buxton	46	11	17	18	50	77	39
Macclesfield Town	46	11	14	21	46	62	36
Lancaster City	46	13	10	23	53	76	36
Bangor City	46	13	9	24	56	67	35
Gainsborough Trinity	46	10	15	21	46	79	35
Skelmersdale United	46	13	7	26	63	93	33
Barrow	46	9	15	22	45	72	33
Netherfield	46	12	8	26	42	91	32
Fleetwood	46	5	10	31	26	97	20

1975-76

Runcorn	46	29	10	7	95	42	68
Stafford Rangers	46	26	15	5	81	41	67
Scarborough	46	26	10	10	84	43	62
Matlock Town	46	26	9	11	96	63	61
Boston United	46	27	6	13	95	58	60
Wigan Athletic	46	21	15	10	81	42	57
Altrincham	46	20	14	12	77	57	54
Bangor City	46	21	12	13	80	70	54
Mossley	46	21	11	14	70	58	53
Goole Town	46	20	13	13	58	49	53
Northwich Victoria	46	17	17	12	79	59	51
Lancaster City	46	18	9	19	61	70	45
Worksop Town	46	17	10	19	63	56	44
Gainsborough Trinity	46	13	17	16	58	69	43
Macclesfield Town	46	15	12	19	50	64	42
Gateshead United	46	17	7	22	64	63	41
Buxton	46	11	13	22	37	62	35
Skelmersdale United	46	12	10	24	45	74	34
Netherfield	46	11	11	24	55	76	33
Morecambe	46	11	11	24	47	67	33
Great Harwood	46	13	7	26	58	86	33
South Liverpool	46	12	9	25	45	78	33
Barrow	46	12	9	25	47	84	33
Fleetwood	46	3	9	34	36	131	15

1976-77

Boston United	44	27	11	6	82	35	65
Northwich Victoria	44	27	11	6	85	43	65
Matlock Town	44	26	11	7	108	57	63
Bangor City	44	22	11	11	87	52	55
Scarborough	44	21	12	11	77	66	54
Goole Town	44	23	6	15	64	50	52
Lancaster City	44	21	9	14	71	58	51
Gateshead United	44	18	12	14	80	64	48
Mossley	44	17	14	13	74	59	48
Altrincham	44	19	9	16	60	53	47
Stafford Rangers	44	16	14	14	60	55	46
Runcorn	44	15	14	15	57	49	44
Worksop Town	44	16	12	16	50	58	44
Wigan Athletic	44	14	15	15	62	54	43
Morecambe	44	13	11	20	59	75	37
Gainsborough Trinity	44	13	10	21	58	74	36
Great Harwood	44	11	14	19	63	84	36
Buxton	44	11	13	20	48	63	35
Macclesfield Town	44	8	15	21	41	68	31
Frickley Athletic	44	11	8	25	53	93	30
Barrow	44	11	6	27	56	87	28
South Liverpool	44	10	8	26	51	104	28
Netherfield	44	9	8	27	47	92	26

1977-78

Boston United	46	31	9	6	85	35	71
Wigan Athletic	46	25	15	6	83	45	65
Bangor City	46	26	10	10	92	50	62
Scarborough	46	26	10	10	80	39	62
Altrincham	46	22	15	9	84	49	59
Northwich Victoria	46	22	14	10	83	55	50
Stafford Rangers	46	22	13	11	71	41	57
Runcorn	46	19	18	9	70	44	56
Mossley	46	22	11	13	85	73	55
Matlock Town	46	21	12	13	79	60	54
Lancaster City	46	15	14	17	66	82	44
Frickley Athletic	46	15	12	19	77	81	42
Barrow	46	14	12	20	50	61	40
Goole Town	46	15	9	22	60	68	39
Great Harwood	46	13	13	20	66	83	39
Gainsborough Trinity	46	14	10	22	61	74	38
Gateshead	46	16	5	25	65	74	37
Netherfield	46	11	13	22	50	80	35
Workington	46	13	8	25	48	80	34
Worksop Town	46	12	10	24	45	84	34
Morecambe	46	11	11	24	67	92	33
Macclesfield Town	46	12	9	25	60	92	33
Buxton	46	13	6	27	60	95	32
South Liverpool	46	9	7	30	53	111	25

1978-79

Mossley	44	32	5	7	117	48	69
Altrincham	44	25	11	8	93	39	61
Matlock Town	44	24	8	12	100	59	56
Scarborough	44	19	14	11	61	44	52
Southport	44	19	14	11	62	49	52
Boston United	44	17	18	9	40	33	52
Runcorn	44	21	9	14	79	54	51
Stafford Rangers	44	18	14	12	67	41	50
Goole Town	44	17	15	12	56	61	49
Northwich Victoria	44	18	11	15	64	52	47
Lancaster City	44	17	12	15	62	54	46
Bangor City	44	15	14	15	65	66	44
Worksop Town	44	13	14	17	55	67	40
Workington	44	16	7	21	62	74	39
Netherfield	44	13	11	20	39	69	37
Barrow	44	14	9	21	47	78	37
Gainsborough Trinity	44	12	12	20	52	67	36
Morecambe	44	11	13	20	55	65	35
Frickley Athletic	44	13	9	22	58	70	35
South Liverpool	44	12	10	22	48	85	34
Gateshead	44	11	11	22	42	63	33
Buxton	44	11	9	24	50	84	31
Macclesfield Town	44	8	10	26	40	92	26

1979-80

Mossley	42	28	9	5	96	41	65
Witton Albion	42	28	8	6	89	30	64
Frickley Athletic	42	24	13	5	93	48	61
Burton Albion	42	25	6	11	83	42	56
Matlock Town	42	18	17	7	87	53	53
Buxton	42	21	9	12	61	48	51
Worksop Town	42	20	10	12	65	52	50
Macclesfield Town	42	18	11	13	67	53	47
Grantham	42	18	8	16	71	65	44
Marine	42	16	10	16	65	57	42
Goole Town	42	14	13	15	61	63	41
Lancaster City	42	13	13	16	74	77	39
Oswestry Town	42	12	14	16	44	60	38
Gainsborough Trinity	42	14	8	20	64	75	36
Runcorn	42	11	11	20	46	63	33
Gateshead	42	11	11	20	50	77	33
Morecambe	42	10	12	20	40	59	32
Netherfield	42	7	15	20	37	66	29
Southport	42	8	13	21	30	75	29
South Liverpool	42	7	14	21	51	84	28
Workington	42	8	12	22	50	85	28
Tamworth	42	8	9	25	26	77	25

1980-81

Runcorn	42	32	7	3	99	22	71
Mossley	42	24	7	11	95	55	55
Marine	42	22	10	10	60	41	54
Buxton	42	21	7	14	64	50	49
Gainsborough Trinity	42	17	13	12	50	57	47
Burton Albion	42	19	8	15	63	54	46
Witton Albion	42	19	8	15	70	62	46
Goole Town	42	14	16	12	56	50	44
South Liverpool	42	19	6	17	59	64	44
Workington	42	15	13	14	57	48	43
Gateshead	42	12	18	12	65	61	42
Worksop Town	42	15	11	16	66	61	41
Macclesfield Town	42	13	13	16	52	69	39
Grantham	42	14	9	19	57	74	37
Matlock Town	42	12	12	18	57	80	36
Lancaster City	42	13	9	20	48	70	35
Netherfield	42	11	12	19	73	81	34
Oswestry Town	42	13	8	21	54	67	34
King's Lynn	42	8	18	16	46	65	34
Southport	42	11	11	26	42	68	33
Morecambe	42	11	8	23	42	74	30
Tamworth	42	9	12	21	38	76	30

1981-82

Bangor City	42	27	8	7	108	60	62
Mossley	42	24	11	7	76	43	59
Witton Albion	42	22	10	10	75	44	54
Gateshead	42	19	14	9	65	49	52
King's Lynn	42	19	12	11	61	36	50
Grantham	42	18	13	11	65	53	49
Burton Albion	42	19	9	14	71	62	47
Southport	42	16	14	12	63	55	46
Marine	42	17	12	13	64	57	46
Macclesfield Town	42	17	9	16	67	58	43
Workington	42	18	7	17	62	60	43
Worksop Town	42	15	13	14	52	60	43
South Liverpool	42	13	13	16	55	57	39
Goole Town	42	13	13	16	56	60	39
Oswestry Town	42	14	11	17	55	59	39
Buxton	42	14	11	17	48	56	39
Lancaster City	42	13	12	17	47	50	38
Gainsborough Trinity	42	10	13	19	60	69	33
Tamworth	42	10	9	23	31	56	29
Morecambe	42	9	11	22	43	86	29
Matlock Town	42	7	12	23	38	72	26
Netherfield	42	5	9	28	31	91	19

1982-83

Gateshead	42	32	4	6	114	43	100
Mossley	42	25	9	8	77	42	84
Burton Albion	42	24	9	9	81	53	81
Chorley	42	23	11	8	77	49	80
Macclesfield Town	42	24	8	10	71	49	80
Marine	42	17	17	8	81	57	68
Workington	42	19	10	13	71	55	67
Hyde United	42	18	12	12	91	63	66
King's Lynn	42	17	13	12	62	44	64
Matlock Town	42	18	10	14	70	65	64
Witton Albion	42	17	12	13	82	52	63
Buxton	42	17	9	16	60	62	60
Morecambe	42	16	11	15	75	66	59
Grantham	42	15	13	14	49	50	58
Southport	42	11	14	17	58	65	47
Goole Town	42	13	7	22	52	66	46
Gainsborough Trinity	42	11	9	22	60	71	42
Oswestry Town	42	10	8	24	56	99	38
South Liverpool	42	7	15	20	57	91	36
Tamworth	42	7	8	27	44	97	29
Worksop Town	42	5	10	27	50	98	25
Netherfield	42	2	9	31	28	129	15

1983-84

Barrow	42	29	10	3	92	38	97
Matlock Town	42	23	8	11	72	48	77
South Liverpool	42	22	11	9	55	44	77
Grantham	42	20	8	14	64	51	68
Burton Albion	42	17	13	12	61	47	64
Macclesfield Town	42	18	10	14	65	55	64
Rhyl	42	19	6	17	64	55	63
Horwich	42	18	9	15	64	59	63
Gainsborough Trinity	42	17	11	14	82	66	62
Stafford Rangers	42	15	17	10	65	52	62
Hyde United	42	17	8	17	61	63	59
Marine	42	16	10	16	63	68	58
Witton Albion	42	14	14	14	64	57	56
Chorley	42	14	11	17	68	65	53
Workington	42	14	9	19	53	57	51
Southport	42	14	8	20	57	74	50
Worksop Town	42	13	8	21	57	74	47
Goole Town	42	12	10	20	59	80	46
Morecambe	42	11	12	19	59	75	45
Oswestry Town	42	11	8	23	66	97	41
Buxton	42	11	6	25	52	91	39
Mossley	42	9	9	24	47	74	33

Mossley had 3 points deducted

1984-85

Stafford Rangers	42	26	8	8	81	40	86
Macclesfield Town	42	23	13	6	67	39	82
Witton Albion	42	22	8	12	57	39	74
Hyde United	42	21	8	13	68	52	71
Marine	42	18	15	9	59	34	69
Burton Albion	42	18	15	9	70	49	69
Worksop Town	42	19	10	13	68	56	67
Workington	42	18	9	15	59	53	53
Horwich	42	16	14	12	67	50	62
Bangor City	42	17	9	16	70	61	60
Gainsborough Trinity	42	14	14	14	72	73	56
Southport	42	15	9	18	65	66	54
Matlock Town	42	14	9	19	56	66	51
Oswestry Town	42	14	9	19	59	75	51
Mossley	42	14	9	19	45	65	51
Goole Town	42	13	11	18	60	65	50
Rhyl	42	11	14	17	52	63	47
Morecambe	42	11	14	17	51	67	47
Chorley	42	12	10	20	47	63	46
South Liverpool	42	9	15	18	43	71	42
Grantham	42	8	13	21	41	69	36
Buxton	42	8	6	28	38	79	30

Grantham had 1 point deducted

1985-86

Gateshead	42	24	10	8	85	51	82
Marine	42	23	11	8	63	35	80
Morecambe	42	17	17	8	59	39	68
Gainsborough Trinity	42	18	14	10	66	52	68
Burton Albion	42	18	12	12	64	47	66
Southport	42	17	11	14	70	66	62
Worksop Town	42	17	10	15	51	48	61
Workington	42	14	18	10	54	46	59
Macclesfield Town	42	17	8	17	67	65	59
Hyde United	42	14	15	13	63	62	57
Witton Albion	42	15	13	14	56	59	57
Mossley	42	13	16	13	56	60	55
Bangor City	42	13	15	14	51	51	54
Rhyl	42	14	10	18	65	71	52
South Liverpool	42	11	17	14	43	44	50
Horwich	42	15	6	21	53	63	50
Caernarfon Town	42	11	17	14	51	63	50
Oswestry Town	42	12	13	17	51	60	49
Buxton	42	11	12	19	55	76	45
Chorley	42	9	15	18	56	64	42
Matlock Town	42	9	15	18	59	75	42
Goole Town	42	7	11	24	37	78	31

Workington, Witton Albion, Horwich & Goole Town – 1 point deducted.

1986-87

Macclesfield Town	42	26	10	6	80	47	88
Bangor City	42	25	12	5	74	35	87
Caernarfon Town	42	20	16	6	67	40	76
Marine	42	21	10	11	70	43	73
South Liverpool	42	21	10	11	58	40	73
Morecambe	42	20	12	10	68	49	72
Matlock Town	42	20	10	12	81	67	70
Southport	42	19	11	12	67	49	68
Chorley	42	16	12	14	58	59	60
Mossley	42	15	12	15	57	52	57
Hyde United	42	15	10	17	81	70	55
Burton Albion	42	16	6	20	56	68	54
Buxton	42	13	14	15	71	68	53
Witton Albion	42	15	8	19	68	79	53
Barrow	42	15	7	20	42	57	52
Goole Town	42	13	12	17	58	62	51
Oswestry Town	42	14	8	20	55	83	50
Rhyl	42	10	15	17	56	74	45
Worksop Town	42	9	13	20	56	74	40
Gainsborough Trinity	42	9	10	23	53	77	37
Workington	42	5	14	23	38	70	28
Horwich RMI	42	3	12	27	36	85	20

Workington and Horwich RMI both had 1 point deducted.

1987-88 Premier Division

Chorley	42	26	10	6	78	35	88
Hyde United	42	25	10	7	91	52	85
Caernarfon Town	42	22	10	10	56	34	76
Morecambe	42	19	15	8	61	41	72
Barrow	42	21	8	13	70	41	71
Worksop Town	42	20	11	11	74	55	71
Bangor City	42	20	10	12	71	55	70
Rhyl	42	18	13	11	70	42	67
Marine	42	19	10	13	67	45	67
Frickley Athletic	42	18	11	13	61	55	65
Witton Albion	42	16	12	14	61	47	60
Goole Town	42	17	9	16	71	61	60
Horwich	42	17	9	16	46	42	60
Southport	42	15	12	15	43	48	57
South Liverpool	42	10	19	13	56	64	49
Buxton	42	11	14	17	72	76	47
Mossley	42	11	11	20	54	75	44
Gateshead	42	11	7	24	52	71	40
Matlock Town	42	10	8	24	58	89	38
Gainsborough Trinity	42	8	10	24	38	81	34
Oswestry Town	42	6	10	26	44	101	28
Workington	42	6	3	33	28	113	21

First Division

Fleetwood Town	36	22	7	7	85	45	73
Stalybridge Celtic	36	22	6	8	72	42	72
Leek Town	36	20	10	6	63	38	70
Accrington Stanley	36	21	6	9	71	39	69
Farsley Celtic	36	18	9	9	64	48	60
Droylsden	36	16	10	10	63	48	58
Eastwood Hanley	36	14	12	10	50	37	54
Winsford United	36	15	6	15	59	47	51
Congleton Town	36	12	16	8	43	39	51
Harrogate Town	36	13	9	14	51	50	48
Alfreton Town	36	13	8	15	53	54	47
Radcliffe Borough	36	11	13	12	66	62	46
Irlam Town	36	12	10	14	39	45	46
Penrith	36	11	11	14	46	51	44
Sutton Town	36	11	5	20	51	96	38
Lancaster City	36	10	6	20	45	72	36
Eastwood Town	36	8	10	18	45	65	34
Curzon Ashton	36	8	4	24	43	73	28
Netherfield	36	4	4	28	35	93	16

Congleton Town had 1 point deducted
Farsley Celtic had 3 points deducted

1988-89

Premier Division

Barrow	42	26	9	7	89	35	87
Hyde United	42	24	8	10	77	44	80
Witton Albion	42	22	13	7	67	39	79
Bangor City	42	22	10	10	77	48	76
Marine	42	23	7	12	69	48	76
Goole Town	42	22	7	13	75	60	73
Fleetwood Town	42	19	16	7	53	44	73
Rhyl	42	18	10	14	75	65	64
Frickley Athletic	42	17	10	15	64	53	61
Mossley	42	17	9	16	56	58	60
South Liverpool	42	15	13	14	65	57	58
Caernarfon Town	42	15	10	17	49	53	55
Matlock Town	42	16	5	21	65	73	53
Southport	42	13	12	17	66	52	51
Buxton	42	12	14	16	61	63	50
Morecambe	42	13	9	20	55	60	47
Gainsborough Trinity	42	12	11	19	56	73	47
Shepshed Charterhouse	42	14	8	20	19	80	44
Stalybridge Celtic	42	9	13	20	16	81	40
Horwich	42	7	14	21	12	70	35
Gateshead	42	7	13	22	36	70	34
Worksop Town	42	6	5	31	42	103	23

Morecambe had 1 point deducted
Shepshed C'House had 6 points deducted

First Division

Colne Dynamo	42	30	11	1	102	21	98
Bishop Auckland	42	28	5	9	78	28	89
Leek Town	42	25	11	6	74	41	85
Droylsden	42	25	9	8	84	48	84
Whitley Bay	42	23	6	13	77	49	75
Accrington Stanley	42	21	10	11	81	60	73
Lancaster City	42	21	8	13	76	54	71
Harrogate Town	42	19	7	16	68	61	64
Newtown	42	15	12	15	65	59	57
Congleton Town	42	15	11	16	62	66	56
Workington	42	17	3	22	59	74	54
Eastwood Town	42	14	10	13	55	61	52
Curzon Ashton	42	13	11	18	74	72	50
Farsley Celtic	42	12	13	17	52	73	49
Irlam Town	42	11	14	17	53	63	47
Penrith	42	14	5	23	61	91	47
Radcliffe Borough	42	12	10	20	62	86	46
Eastwood Hanley	42	11	12	10	46	67	45
Winsford United	42	13	6	23	58	93	35
Alfreton Town	42	8	11	23	44	92	35
Netherfield	42	8	9	25	57	90	32
Sutton Town	42	7	6	29	70	109	23

Leek Town and Netherfield both had 1 point deducted
Colne Dynamo had 3 points deducted
Sutton Town had 4 points deducted

1989-90

Premier Division

Colne Dynamoes	42	32	6	4	86	40	102
Gateshead	42	22	10	10	78	58	76
Witton Albion	42	22	7	13	67	39	73
Hyde United	42	21	8	13	73	50	71
South Liverpool	42	20	9	13	89	79	69
Matlock Town	42	18	12	12	61	42	66
Southport	42	17	14	11	54	48	65
Fleetwood Town	42	17	12	13	73	66	63
Marine	42	16	14	12	59	55	62
Bangor City	42	15	15	12	64	58	60
Bishop Auckland	42	17	8	17	72	64	59
Frickley Athletic	42	16	8	18	56	61	56
Horwich	42	15	13	14	66	69	55
Morecambe	42	15	9	18	58	70	54
Gainsborough Trinity	42	16	8	18	59	55	53
Buxton	42	15	8	19	59	72	53
Stalybridge Celtic	42	12	9	21	48	61	45
Mossley	42	11	10	21	61	82	43
Goole Town	42	12	5	25	54	77	41
Shepshed	42	11	7	24	55	82	40
Caernarfon Town	42	10	8	24	56	86	38
Rhyl	42	7	10	25	43	77	30

Rhyl had 1 point deducted
Horwich and Gainsborough Trinity both had 3 points deducted

First Division

Leek Town	42	26	8	8	70	31	86
Droylsden	42	27	6	9	81	46	80
Accrington Stanley	42	22	10	10	80	53	76
Whitley Bay	42	21	11	10	93	59	74
Emley	42	20	9	13	70	42	69
Congleton Town	42	20	12	10	65	53	69
Winsford United	42	18	10	14	65	53	64
Curzon Ashton	42	17	11	14	66	60	62
Harrogate Town	42	17	9	16	68	62	60
Lancaster City	42	15	14	13	73	54	59
Eastwood Town	42	16	11	15	61	64	59
Farsley Celtic	42	17	6	19	71	75	57
Rossendale United	42	15	9	18	73	69	54
Newtown	42	14	12	16	49	62	54
Irlam Town	42	14	11	17	61	66	53
Workington	42	14	8	20	56	64	50
Radcliffe Borough	42	14	7	21	47	63	49
Alfreton Town	42	13	8	21	59	85	47
Worksop Town	42	13	5	24	56	95	44
Netherfield	42	11	6	25	56	89	39
Eastwood Hanley	42	10	6	26	45	76	36
Penrith	42	9	9	24	44	88	36

Congleton Town 3 points deducted. Droylsden 7 points deducted.

1990-91

Premier Division

Witton Albion	40	28	9	3	81	31	93
Stalybridge Celtic	40	22	11	7	44	26	77
Morecambe	40	19	16	5	72	44	73
Fleetwood Town	40	20	9	11	69	44	69
Southport	40	18	14	8	66	48	68
Marine	40	18	11	11	56	39	65
Bishop Auckland	40	17	10	13	62	56	61
Buxton	40	17	11	12	66	61	59
Leek Town	40	15	11	14	48	44	56
Frickley Athletic	40	16	6	18	64	62	54
Hyde United	40	14	11	15	73	63	53
Goole Town	40	14	10	16	68	74	52
Droylsden	40	12	11	17	67	70	47
Chorley	40	12	10	18	55	55	46
Mossley	40	13	10	17	55	68	45
Horwich	40	13	6	21	62	81	45
Matlock Town	40	12	7	21	52	70	43
Bangor City	40	9	12	19	52	70	39
South Liverpool	40	10	9	21	58	92	39
Gainsborough Trinity	40	9	11	20	57	84	38
Shepshed Charterhouse	40	6	7	27	38	83	25

First Division

Whitley Bay	42	25	10	7	95	38	85
Emley	42	24	12	6	78	37	84
Worksop Town	42	25	7	10	85	56	82
Accrington Stanley	42	21	13	8	83	57	76
Rhyl	42	21	7	14	62	63	70
Eastwood Town	42	17	11	14	70	60	62
Warrington Town	42	17	10	15	68	52	61
Lancaster City	42	19	8	15	58	56	61
Bridlington Town	42	15	15	12	72	52	60
Curzon Ashton	42	14	14	14	49	57	56
Congleton Town	42	14	12	16	57	71	54
Netherfield	42	14	11	17	67	66	53
Newtown	42	13	12	17	68	75	51
Caernarfon Town	42	13	10	19	51	64	49
Rossendale United	42	12	13	17	66	67	48
Radcliffe Borough	42	12	12	18	50	69	48
Irlam Town	42	12	11	19	55	76	47
Winsford United	42	11	13	18	51	66	46
Harrogate Town	42	11	13	18	55	73	46
Workington	42	11	11	20	54	67	41
Farsley Celtic	42	11	9	22	49	78	39
Alfreton Town	42	7	12	23	41	84	33

1991-92 Premier Division

Stalybridge Celtic	42	26	14	2	84	33	92
Marine	42	23	9	10	64	32	78
Morecambe	42	21	13	8	70	44	76
Leek Town	42	21	10	11	62	49	73
Buxton	42	21	9	12	65	47	72
Emley	42	18	11	13	69	47	65
Southport	42	16	17	9	57	48	65
Accrington Stanley	42	17	12	13	78	62	63
Hyde United	42	17	9	16	69	67	60
Fleetwood United	42	17	8	17	67	64	59
Bishop Auckland	42	16	9	17	48	58	57
Goole Town	42	15	9	18	60	72	54
Horwich	42	13	14	15	44	52	53
Frickley Athletic	42	12	16	14	61	57	52
Droylsden	42	12	14	16	62	72	50
Mossley	42	15	4	23	51	73	49
Whitley Bay	42	13	9	20	53	79	48
Gainsborough Trinity	42	11	13	18	48	63	46
Matlock Town	42	12	9	21	59	87	45
Bangor City	42	11	10	21	46	57	43
Chorley	42	11	9	22	61	82	42
Shepshed Albion	42	6	8	28	46	79	26

First Division

Colwyn Bay	42	30	4	8	99	49	94
Winsford United	42	29	6	7	96	41	93
Worksop Town	42	25	5	12	101	54	80
Guiseley	42	22	12	8	93	56	78
Caernarfon Town	42	23	9	10	78	47	78
Bridlington Town	42	22	9	11	86	46	75
Warrington Town	42	20	8	14	79	64	68
Knowsley United	42	18	10	14	69	52	64
Netherfield	42	18	7	17	54	61	61
Harrogate Town	42	14	16	12	73	69	58
Curzon Ashton	42	15	9	18	71	83	54
Farsley Celtic	42	15	9	18	79	101	53
Radcliffe Borough	42	15	9	18	67	72	51
Newtown	42	15	6	21	60	95	51
Eastwood Town	42	13	11	18	59	70	50
Lancaster City	42	10	19	13	55	62	49
Congleton Town	42	14	5	23	59	81	47
Rhyl	42	11	10	21	59	69	43
Rossendale United	42	9	11	22	61	90	38
Alfreton Town	42	12	2	28	63	98	38
Irlam Town	42	9	7	26	45	95	33
Workington	42	7	8	27	45	99	28

Farsley Celtic 1 point deducted. Radcliffe Borough 3 points deducted.

1992-93 Premier Division

Southport	42	29	9	4	103	31	96
Winsford United	42	27	9	6	91	43	90
Morecambe	42	25	11	6	93	51	86
Marine	42	26	8	8	83	47	86
Leek Town	42	21	11	10	86	51	74
Accrington Stanley	42	20	13	9	79	45	73
Frickley Athletic	42	21	6	15	62	52	69
Barrow	42	18	11	13	71	55	65
Hyde United	42	17	13	12	87	71	64
Bishop Auckland	42	17	11	14	63	52	62
Gainsborough Trinity	42	17	8	17	63	66	59
Colwyn Bay	42	16	6	20	80	79	54
Horwich	42	14	10	18	72	79	52
Buxton	42	13	10	19	60	75	49
Matlock Town	42	13	11	18	56	79	47
Emley	42	13	6	23	62	91	45
Whitley Bay	42	11	8	23	57	96	41
Chorley	42	10	10	22	52	93	40
Fleetwood Town	42	10	7	25	50	77	37
Droylsden	42	10	7	25	47	84	37
Mossley	42	7	8	27	53	95	29
Goole Town	42	6	9	27	47	105	27

Matlock Town had 3 points deducted

First Division

Bridlington Town	40	25	11	4	84	35	86
Knowsley United	40	23	7	10	86	48	76
Ashton United	40	22	8	10	81	54	74
Guiseley	40	20	10	10	90	64	70
Warrington Town	40	19	10	11	85	57	67
Gretna	40	17	12	11	64	47	63
Curzon Ashton	40	16	15	9	69	63	63
Great Harwood Town	40	17	9	14	66	57	60
Alfreton Town	40	15	9	16	80	80	54
Harrogate Town	40	14	12	14	77	81	54
Worksop Town	40	15	9	16	66	70	54
Radcliffe Borough	40	13	14	13	66	69	53
Workington	40	13	13	14	51	61	52
Eastwood Town	40	3	11	16	49	52	50
Netherfield	40	11	14	15	68	63	47
Caernarfon Town	40	13	8	19	66	74	47
Farsley Celtic	40	12	8	20	64	77	44
Lancaster City	40	10	12	18	49	76	42
Shepshed Albion	40	9	12	19	46	66	39
Congleton Town	40	10	7	23	58	95	37
Rossendale United	40	5	5	30	50	126	20

1993-94

Premier Division

Marine	42	27	9	6	106	62	90
Leek Town	42	27	8	7	79	50	89
Boston United	42	23	9	10	90	43	78
Bishop Auckland	42	23	9	10	73	58	78
Frickley Athletic	42	21	12	9	90	51	75
Colwyn Bay	42	18	14	10	74	51	68
Morecambe	42	20	7	15	90	56	67
Barrow	42	18	10	14	59	51	64
Hyde United	42	17	10	15	80	71	61
Chorley	42	17	10	15	70	67	61
Whitley Bay	42	17	9	16	61	72	60
Gainsborough Trinity	42	15	11	16	64	66	56
Emley	42	12	16	14	63	71	52
Matlock Town	42	13	12	17	71	76	51
Buxton	42	13	10	19	67	73	49
Accrington Stanley	42	14	7	21	63	85	49
Droylsden	42	11	14	17	57	82	47
Knowsley United	42	11	11	20	52	66	44
Winsford United	42	9	11	22	50	74	38
Horwich RMI	42	8	12	22	50	75	35
Bridlington Town	42	7	10	25	41	91	28
Fleetwood Town	42	7	7	28	55	114	28

Horwich RMI 1 point deducted. Bridlington Town 3 points deducted

First Division

Guiseley	40	29	6	5	87	37	93
Spennymoor United	40	25	6	9	95	50	81
Ashton United	40	24	7	9	85	41	79
Lancaster City	40	20	10	10	74	46	70
Netherfield	40	20	6	14	68	60	66
Alfreton Town	40	18	10	12	83	70	64
Warrington Town	40	17	11	12	52	48	62
Goole Town	40	16	11	13	72	58	59
Great Harwood Town	40	15	14	11	56	60	59
Gretna	40	16	7	17	64	65	55
Workington	40	14	10	16	70	74	52
Worksop Town	40	14	9	17	79	87	51
Bamber Bridge	40	13	11	16	62	59	50
Curzon Ashton	40	13	8	19	62	71	47
Congleton Town	40	12	9	19	53	68	45
Radcliffe Borough	40	10	14	16	62	75	44
Mossley	40	10	12	18	44	68	39
Caernarfon Town	40	9	11	20	54	88	38
Farsley Celtic	40	6	16	18	42	77	34
Harrogate Town	40	8	9	23	40	86	33
Eastwood Town	40	7	11	22	47	63	32

Mossley had 3 points deducted

1994-95

Premier Division

Marine	42	29	11	2	83	27	98
Morecambe	42	28	10	4	99	34	94
Guiseley	42	28	9	5	96	50	93
Hyde United	42	22	10	10	89	59	76
Boston United	42	20	11	11	80	43	71
Spennymoor United	42	20	11	11	66	52	71
Buxton	42	18	9	15	65	62	63
Gainsborough Trinity	42	16	13	13	69	61	61
Bishop Auckland	42	16	12	14	68	55	57
Witton Albion	42	14	14	14	54	56	56
Barrow	42	17	5	20	68	71	56
Colwyn Bay	42	16	8	18	71	80	56
Emley	42	14	13	15	62	68	55
Matlock Town	42	15	5	22	62	72	50
Accrington Stanley	42	12	13	17	55	77	49
Knowsley United	42	11	14	17	64	83	47
Winsford United	42	10	11	21	56	75	41
Chorley	42	11	7	24	64	87	40
Frickley Athletic	42	10	10	22	53	79	40
Droylsden	42	10	8	24	56	93	38
Whitley Bay	42	8	8	26	46	97	32
Horwich RMI	42	9	4	29	49	94	31

Bishop Auckland had 3 points deducted

First Division

Blyth Spartans	42	26	9	7	95	55	87
Bamber Bridge	42	25	10	7	101	51	85
Warrington Town	42	25	9	8	74	40	84
Alfreton Town	42	25	7	10	94	49	82
Lancaster City	42	23	10	9	81	44	79
Worksop Town	42	19	14	9	95	68	71
Radcliffe Borough	42	18	10	14	76	70	64
Ashton United	42	18	8	16	80	70	62
Netherfield	42	17	7	118	54	56	58
Eastwood Town	42	14	13	15	67	61	55
Gretna	42	14	13	15	64	66	55
Atherton Laburnum Rovers	42	14	8	20	60	67	50
Harrogate Town	42	14	8	20	57	78	50
Caernarfon Town	42	13	10	19	59	62	49
Curzon Ashton	42	10	16	16	64	80	46
Great Harwood Town	42	11	13	18	66	87	46
Congleton Town	42	11	13	18	52	75	46
Fleetwood	42	12	11	19	51	74	44
Farsley Celtic	42	12	7	23	66	100	43
Workington	42	12	6	24	61	91	42
Goole Town	42	11	7	24	46	81	40
Mossley	42	11	5	26	52	90	37

Mossley had 1 point deducted
Fleetwood had 3 points deducted

1995-96

Premier Division

Bamber Bridge	42	20	16	6	81	49	76
Boston United	42	23	6	13	86	59	75
Hyde United	42	21	11	10	86	51	74
Barrow	42	20	13	9	69	42	73
Gainsborough Trinity	42	20	13	9	60	41	73
Blyth Spartans	42	17	13	12	75	61	64
Accrington Stanley	42	17	14	11	62	54	62
Emley	42	17	10	15	57	53	61
Spennymoor United	42	14	18	10	67	61	60
Guiseley	42	15	14	13	62	57	59
Bishop Auckland	42	16	11	15	60	55	59
Marine	42	15	14	13	59	54	59
Witton Albion	42	17	8	17	60	62	59
Chorley	42	14	9	19	67	74	48
Knowsley United	42	14	6	22	61	89	48
Winsford United	42	10	16	16	56	79	46
Leek Town	42	10	15	17	52	55	45
Colwyn Bay	42	8	21	13	43	57	45
Frickley Athletic	42	11	14	17	63	87	44
Buxton	42	9	11	22	43	72	38
Droylsden	42	10	8	24	58	100	38
Matlock Town	42	8	11	23	71	86	35

Accrington Stanley, Chorley & Frickley Town all had 3 points deducted

First Division

Lancaster City	40	24	11	5	79	38	83
Alfreton Town	40	23	9	8	79	47	78
Lincoln United	40	22	7	11	80	56	73
Curzon Ashton	40	20	7	13	73	53	67
Farsley Celtic	40	19	9	12	66	61	66
Radcliffe Borough	40	17	13	10	70	48	64
Eastwood Town	40	18	9	13	60	47	63
Whitley Bay	40	18	8	14	72	62	62
Ashton United	40	19	7	14	73	65	60
Atherton Laburnum Rovers	40	15	12	13	60	61	57
Worksop Town	40	16	8	16	84	90	56
Gretna	40	13	13	14	75	65	52
Warrington Town	40	13	10	17	75	72	49
Leigh	40	14	7	19	53	59	49
Netherfield	40	13	10	17	64	73	49
Workington	40	11	12	17	50	62	45
Bradford Park Avenue	40	9	14	17	57	72	41
Congleton Town	40	11	11	18	36	59	41
Great Harwood Town	40	9	7	24	44	78	33
Fleetwood	40	7	10	23	41	81	31
Harrogate Town	40	7	10	23	54	96	31

Great Harwood Town had 1 point deducted
Congleton Town had 3 points deducted
Ashton United had 4 points deducted

1996-97

Premier Division

Leek Town	44	28	9	7	71	35	93
Bishop Auckland	44	23	14	7	88	43	83
Hyde United	44	22	16	6	93	46	82
Emley	44	23	12	9	89	54	81
Barrow	44	23	11	10	71	45	80
Boston United	44	22	13	9	74	47	79
Blyth Spartans	44	22	11	11	74	49	77
Marine	44	20	15	9	53	37	75
Guiseley	44	20	11	13	63	54	71
Gainsborough Trinity	44	18	12	14	65	46	66
Accrington Stanley	44	18	12	14	77	70	66
Runcorn	44	15	15	14	63	62	60
Chorley	44	16	9	19	69	66	57
Winsford United	44	13	14	17	50	56	53
Knowsley United	44	12	14	18	58	79	49
Colwyn Bay	44	11	13	20	60	76	46
Lancaster City	44	12	9	23	48	75	45
Frickley Athletic	44	12	8	24	62	91	44
Spennymoor United	44	10	10	24	52	68	40
Bamber Bridge	44	11	7	26	59	99	40
Alfreton Town	44	8	13	23	45	83	37
Witton Albion	44	5	14	25	41	91	39
Buxton	44	5	12	27	33	86	27

Knowsley United had 1 point deducted

First Division

Radcliffe Borough	42	26	7	9	77	33	85
Leigh	42	24	11	7	65	33	83
Lincoln United	42	25	8	9	78	47	83
Farsley Celtic	42	23	8	11	75	48	77
Worksop Town	42	20	12	10	68	38	69
Stocksbridge Park Steels	42	19	11	12	66	54	68
Bradford Park Avenue	42	20	8	14	58	50	68
Ashton United	42	17	14	11	73	52	65
Great Harwood Town	42	16	12	14	56	46	60
Droylsden	42	15	14	13	69	67	59
Matlock Town	42	16	10	16	61	69	58
Whitley Bay	42	14	12	16	47	54	54
Flixton	42	15	7	20	57	72	52
Netherfield	42	12	14	16	54	56	50
Eastwood Town	42	12	14	16	42	50	50
Gretna	42	10	18	14	55	68	48
Harrogate Town	42	13	8	21	55	76	47
Congleton Town	42	12	9	21	47	64	45
Workington	42	10	12	20	45	63	42
Curzon Ashton	42	8	10	24	48	79	34
Warrington Town	42	5	18	19	42	79	33
Atherton Laburnum Rovers	42	7	9	26	45	85	30

Worksop Town had 3 points deducted

1997-98

Premier Division

Barrow	42	25	8	9	61	29	83
Boston United	42	22	12	8	55	40	78
Leigh RMI	42	21	13	8	63	41	76
Runcorn	42	22	9	11	80	50	75
Gainsborough Trinity	42	22	9	11	60	39	75
Emley	42	22	8	12	81	61	74
Winsford United	42	19	12	11	54	43	69
Altrincham	42	18	11	13	76	44	65
Guiseley	42	16	16	10	61	53	64
Bishop Auckland	42	17	12	13	78	60	63
Marine	42	15	11	16	56	59	56
Hyde United	42	13	16	13	60	55	55
Colwyn Bay	42	15	9	18	53	57	54
Spennymoor United	42	14	11	17	58	72	52
Chorley	42	14	7	21	51	70	49
Frickley Athletic	42	12	12	18	45	62	48
Lancaster City	42	13	8	21	55	74	47
Blyth Spartans	42	12	13	17	52	63	39
Bamber Bridge	42	9	12	21	51	74	39
Accrington Stanley	42	8	14	20	49	68	38
Radcliffe Borough	42	6	12	24	39	70	30
Alfreton Town	42	3	13	26	32	86	22

Spennymoor United had 1 point deducted
Blyth Spartans had 10 points deducted

First Division

Whitby Town	42	30	8	4	99	48	98
Worksop Town	42	28	7	7	93	44	91
Ashton Town	42	26	9	7	93	43	87
Droylsden	42	24	8	10	70	49	80
Lincoln United	42	20	11	11	76	62	71
Farsley Celtic	42	20	10	12	72	66	70
Witton Albion	42	19	9	14	77	55	66
Eastwood Town	42	18	12	12	68	51	66
Bradford Park Avenue	42	18	11	13	62	46	65
Belper Town	42	18	7	17	68	66	61
Stocksbridge Park Steels	42	17	9	16	68	63	60
Trafford	42	16	6	20	59	61	54
Whitley Bay	42	14	12	16	60	63	54
Matlock Town	42	14	11	17	68	65	53
Gretna	42	13	9	20	58	64	48
Netherfield	42	12	11	19	55	75	47
Flixton	42	10	12	20	45	73	42
Congleton Town	42	11	8	23	65	101	41
Harrogate Town	42	8	14	20	57	80	38
Great Harwood Town	42	8	12	22	42	88	36
Workington	42	8	7	27	38	84	31
Buxton	42	7	3	32	41	87	24

1998-99

Premier Division

Altrincham	42	23	11	8	67	33	80
Worksop Town	42	22	10	10	66	48	76
Guiseley	42	21	9	12	64	47	72
Bamber Bridge	42	18	15	9	63	48	69
Gateshead	42	18	11	13	69	58	65
Gainsborough Trinity	42	19	8	15	65	59	65
Whitby Town	42	17	13	12	77	62	64
Leigh	42	16	15	11	63	54	63
Hyde United	42	16	11	15	61	48	59
Stalybridge Celtic	42	16	11	15	71	63	59
Winsford United	42	14	15	13	56	52	57
Runcorn	42	12	19	11	46	49	55
Emley	42	12	17	13	47	49	53
Blyth Spartans	42	14	9	19	56	64	51
Colwyn Bay	42	12	13	17	60	71	49
Frickley Athletic	42	11	15	16	55	71	48
Marine	42	10	17	15	61	69	47
Spennymoor United	42	12	11	19	52	71	47
Lancaster City	42	11	13	18	50	62	46
Bishop Auckland	42	10	15	17	49	67	45
Chorley	42	8	15	19	45	68	39
Accrington Stanley	42	9	9	24	47	77	36

First Division

Droylsden	42	26	8	8	97	55	86
Hucknall Town	42	26	11	5	80	38	86
Ashton United	42	22	12	8	79	46	78
Lincoln United	42	20	12	10	94	65	72
Eastwood Town	42	20	8	14	65	69	68
Radcliffe Borough	42	19	8	15	78	62	65
Burscough	42	19	8	15	67	61	65
Witton Albion	42	18	9	15	70	63	63
Bradford Park Avenue	42	17	11	14	64	55	62
Stocksbridge Park Steels	42	16	13	13	64	60	61
Harrogate Town	42	17	7	18	75	77	58
Gretna	42	16	10	16	73	80	58
Belper Town	42	15	11	16	58	57	56
Trafford	42	14	11	17	50	58	53
Netherfield Kendal	42	13	10	19	51	64	49
Flixton	42	12	12	18	50	64	48
Matlock Town	42	14	6	22	53	72	48
Farsley Celtic	42	11	13	18	56	73	46
Whitley Bay	42	10	9	23	53	77	39
Congleton Town	42	8	15	19	65	91	39
Great Harwood Town	42	10	8	24	51	73	38
Alfreton Town	42	9	8	25	53	86	35

Hucknall Town had 3 points deducted

1999-2000

Premier Division

Leigh	44	28	8	8	91	45	92
Hyde United	44	24	13	7	77	44	85
Gateshead	44	23	13	8	79	41	82
Marine	44	21	16	7	78	46	79
Emley	44	20	12	12	54	41	72
Lancaster City	44	20	11	13	65	55	71
Stalybridge Celtic	44	18	12	14	64	54	66
Bishop Auckland	44	18	11	15	63	61	65
Runcorn	44	18	10	16	64	55	64
Worksop Town	44	19	6	19	78	65	63
Gainsborough Trinity	44	16	15	13	59	49	63
Whitby Town	44	15	13	16	66	66	58
Barrow	44	14	15	15	65	59	57
Blyth Spartans	44	15	9	20	62	67	54
Droylsden	44	14	12	18	53	60	54
Frickley Athletic	44	15	9	20	64	85	54
Bamber Bridge	44	14	11	19	70	67	53
Hucknall Town	44	14	11	19	55	61	53
Leek Town	44	14	10	20	58	79	52
Colwyn Bay	44	12	12	20	46	85	48
Spennymoor United	44	10	13	21	41	71	42
Guiseley	44	8	17	19	52	72	41
Winsford United	44	3	7	34	40	116	16

Spennymoor United had 1 point deducted

First Division

Accrington Stanley	42	25	9	8	96	43	84
Burscough	42	22	18	2	81	35	84
Witton Albion	42	23	15	4	88	46	84
Bradford Park Avenue	42	23	9	10	77	48	78
Radcliffe Borough	42	22	12	8	71	48	78
Farsley Celtic	42	19	11	12	66	52	68
Matlock Town	42	17	16	9	72	55	67
Ossett Town	42	17	8	17	77	55	59
Stocksbridge Park Steels	42	16	8	18	55	70	56
Eastwood Town	42	15	11	16	64	65	55
Harrogate Town	42	14	12	16	65	67	54
Congleton Town	42	14	12	16	63	73	54
Chorley	42	13	15	14	53	64	54
Ashton United	42	12	16	14	65	67	52
Workington	42	13	13	16	49	55	52
Lincoln United	42	13	12	17	52	80	51
Belper Town	42	13	11	18	59	72	50
Trafford	42	11	12	19	55	63	45
Gretna	42	11	7	24	48	78	40
Netherfield Kendal	42	8	9	25	46	82	33
Flixton	42	7	9	26	47	85	30
Whitley Bay	42	7	9	26	41	87	30

Eastwood Town had 1 point deducted

2000-2001

Premier Division

Stalybridge Celtic	44	31	9	4	96	32	102
Emley	44	31	8	5	86	42	101
Bishop Auckland	44	26	7	11	89	53	85
Lancaster City	44	24	9	11	84	60	81
Worksop Town	44	20	13	11	102	60	73
Barrow	44	21	9	14	83	53	72
Altrincham	44	20	10	14	80	59	70
Gainsborough Trinity	44	17	14	13	59	56	65
Accrington Stanley	44	18	10	16	72	65	64
Hucknall Town	44	17	12	15	57	63	63
Gateshead	44	16	12	16	67	61	60
Bamber Bridge	44	17	8	19	63	65	59
Runcorn	44	15	10	19	56	71	55
Blyth Spartans	44	15	9	20	61	64	54
Burscough	44	14	10	20	59	68	52
Hyde United	44	13	12	19	72	79	51
Whitby Town	44	13	11	20	60	76	50
Marine	44	12	13	19	62	78	49
Colwyn Bay	44	12	10	22	68	102	46
Frickley Athletic	44	10	15	19	50	79	45
Droylsden	44	13	6	25	50	80	45
Leek Town	44	12	8	24	45	70	44
Spennymoor United	44	4	5	35	32	108	17

First Division

Bradford Park Avenue	42	28	5	9	83	40	89
Vauxhall Motors	42	23	10	9	95	50	79
Ashton United	42	23	9	10	91	49	78
Stocksbridge Park Steels	42	19	13	10	80	60	70
Trafford	42	20	9	13	70	62	68
Belper Town	42	18	11	13	71	62	65
Witton Albion	42	15	16	11	51	50	61
Ossett Town	42	16	12	14	66	58	60
Radcliffe Borough	42	17	8	17	72	71	59
Chorley	42	15	14	13	71	70	59
Harrogate Town	42	15	10	17	60	70	55
Matlock Town	42	14	10	18	70	74	52
North Ferriby United	42	14	10	18	64	73	52
Workington	42	13	12	17	53	60	51
Lincoln United	42	13	12	17	60	75	51
Gretna	42	12	12	18	72	82	48
Guiseley	42	11	15	16	37	50	48
Kendal Town	42	12	12	18	60	69	47
Farsley Celtic	42	12	11	19	53	71	47
Eastwood Town	42	12	8	21	40	63	47
Winsford United	42	13	11	18	61	70	44
Congleton Town	42	13	6	28	43	94	30

Trafford and Kendal Town both had 1 point deducted
Winsford United had 6 points deducted

2001-2002

Premier Division

Burton Albion	44	31	11	2	106	30	104
Vauxhall Motors	44	27	8	9	86	55	89
Lancaster City	44	23	9	12	80	57	78
Worksop Town	44	23	9	12	74	51	78
Emley	44	22	9	13	69	55	75
Accrington Stanley	44	21	9	14	89	64	72
Runcorn FC Halton	44	21	8	15	76	53	71
Barrow	44	19	10	15	75	59	67
Altrincham	44	19	9	16	66	58	66
Bradford Park Avenue	44	18	5	21	77	76	59
Droylsden	44	17	8	19	65	78	59
Blyth Spartans	44	14	16	14	59	62	58
Frickley Athletic	44	16	11	17	63	69	58
Gateshead	44	14	14	16	58	71	56
Whitby Town	44	15	8	21	61	76	53
Hucknall Town	44	14	9	21	50	68	51
Marine	44	11	17	16	62	71	50
Burscough	44	15	5	24	69	86	50
Gainsborough Trinity	44	13	10	21	61	76	49
Colwyn Bay	44	12	11	21	49	82	47
Bishop Auckland	44	12	8	24	46	68	44
Hyde United	44	10	10	24	61	87	40
Bamber Bridge	44	7	10	27	38	88	30

First Division

Harrogate Town	42	25	11	6	80	35	86
Ossett Town	42	21	13	8	73	44	76
Ashton United	42	21	12	9	90	63	75
Spennymoor United	42	22	6	14	75	73	72
Radcliffe Borough	42	20	8	14	73	51	68
Leek Town	42	20	8	14	67	51	68
Gretna	42	19	7	16	66	66	63
Eastwood Town	42	17	11	14	61	59	62
Rossendale United	42	17	10	15	69	58	61
Witton Albion	42	17	10	15	72	68	61
Guiseley	42	18	7	17	60	67	61
North Ferriby United	42	14	16	12	71	60	58
Chorley	42	16	9	17	59	57	57
Matlock Town	42	15	9	18	49	48	54
Trafford	42	14	9	19	64	80	51
Workington	42	12	12	18	51	57	48
Farsley Celtic	42	12	11	19	64	78	47
Belper Town	42	12	11	19	49	66	47
Lincoln United	42	11	14	17	62	80	47
Stocksbridge Park Steels	42	12	9	21	55	76	45
Kendal Town	42	9	9	24	52	76	36
Ossett Albion	42	8	8	26	43	92	32

MIDLAND LEAGUE

1889-90

Lincoln City	20	16	2	2	75	19	34
Derby Midland	19	11	3	5	41	30	25
Rotherham Town	20	11	3	6	44	27	25
Burton Wanderers	20	11	3	6	42	40	25
Staveley	20	9	4	7	46	28	22
Warwick County	20	9	4	7	36	28	22
Gainsborough Trinity	19	8	5	6	47	32	21
Derby Junction	18	7	2	9	32	49	16
Leek	20	3	2	15	26	64	8
Notts Rangers	15	1	4	10	11	36	6
Sheffield	19	2	2	15	19	66	6

Notts Rangers did not play Derby Junction, home and away, or Derby Midland, Gainsborough Trinity and Sheffield at home. Notts Rangers were expelled for not fulfilling their fixtures, but their record was allowed to stand. Derby Midland were placed second, allowing for their unplayed match. Leek and Sheffield were not re-elected.

1890-91

Gainsborough Trinity	18	10	4	4	58	21	24
Long Eaton Rangers	18	10	2	6	50	33	22
Lincoln City	18	7	6	5	34	21	20
Derby Midland	18	8	4	6	28	28	20
Sheffield United	18	8	3	7	32	25	19
Burton Wanderers	18	7	4	7	25	33	18
Rotherham Town	18	7	4	7	20	28	18
Burslem Port Vale	18	7	2	9	35	43	16
Derby Junction	18	5	5	8	18	30	15
Staveley	18	2	4	12	19	57	8

Warwick County were expelled for not fulfilling their fixtures and their record was deleted. Kidderminster resigned during the season and their record was also deleted. Derby Midland amalgamated with Derby County, thus leaving the league. Lincoln City and Sheffield City also resigned from the League.

1891-92

Rotherham Town	20	13	1	6	70	41	27
Gainsborough Trinity	20	12	2	6	49	31	26
Burslem Port Vale	20	11	1	8	49	33	23
Wednesbury Old Athletic	20	9	5	6	49	41	23
Burton Wanderers	20	10	2	8	48	32	22
Doncaster Rovers	20	8	5	7	30	36	21
Grantham Rovers	20	6	6	8	29	37	18
Loughborough Town	20	8	1	11	42	46	17
Long Eaton Rangers	20	5	7	8	32	46	17
Derby Junction	20	4	5	11	21	41	13
Leicester Fosse	20	5	3	12	21	56	13

Staveley resigned from the League during the season and their record was deleted. Burslem Port Vale also resigned.

1892-93

Rotherham Town	24	19	3	2	80	28	41
Burton Wanderers	24	15	4	5	49	33	34
Loughborough Town	24	15	3	6	64	30	33
Leicester Fosse	24	12	3	9	50	37	27
Doncaster Rovers	24	11	4	9	47	44	26
Gainsborough Trinity	24	12	1	11	51	34	25
Kettering	24	11	3	10	48	41	25
Grantham Rovers	24	10	2	12	46	43	22
Wednesbury Old Athletic	24	8	3	13	41	51	19
Long Eaton Rangers	24	6	6	12	34	53	18
Mansfield Town	24	7	2	15	26	70	16
Newark	24	6	3	15	34	62	15
Derby Junction	24	3	5	16	32	76	11

Derby Junction did not seek re-election. Rotherham Town and Wednesbury Old Athletic both resigned from the League.

1893-94

Burton Wanderers	20	17	3	0	82	12	35
Leicester Fosse	20	15	2	3	49	13	32
Loughborough Town	20	12	6	2	52	22	30
Grantham Rovers	20	9	4	7	35	33	22
Mansfield Greenhaigh's	20	9	3	8	43	54	21
Long Eaton Rangers	20	7	4	9	43	44	18
Doncaster Rovers	20	5	4	11	27	48	14
Newark	20	6	2	12	28	55	14
Kettering	20	4	5	11	26	59	13
Gainsborough Trinity	20	5	1	14	28	46	11
Mansfield Town	20	2	4	14	27	54	8

Burton Wanderers had 2 points deducted for playing an ineligible player. Mansfield Town and Mansfield Greenhaigh's combined to form Mansfield. Burton Wanderers and Leicester Fosse both resigned from the League.

1894-95

Loughborough Town	26	19	4	3	84	25	42
Stoke Swifts	26	14	7	5	90	33	35
Derby County Reserves	26	12	8	6	46	27	32
Gainsborough Trinity	26	14	4	8	55	36	32
Kettering	26	13	6	7	59	45	32
Ilkeston Town	26	13	5	8	53	46	31
Mansfield	26	12	5	9	46	37	29
Heanor Town	26	9	5	12	49	48	23
Rushden Town	26	10	3	13	47	70	23
Long Eaton Rangers	26	7	5	14	41	55	19
Newark	26	6	6	14	37	63	18
Doncaster Rovers	26	6	6	14	35	70	18
Grantham Rovers	26	6	5	15	27	59	17
Matlock	26	3	7	16	37	92	13

Derby County Reserves, Loughborough Town and Stoke Swifts all resigned from the League.

1895-96

Kettering	28	20	5	3	74	28	45
Gainsborough Trinity	28	17	6	5	59	26	40
Walsall	28	17	6	5	91	47	40
Long Eaton Rangers	28	18	3	7	68	39	39
Rushden Town	28	14	4	10	61	46	32
Heanor Town	28	12	7	9	70	45	31
Ilkeston Town	28	14	2	12	62	41	30
Barnsley Saint Peter's	28	13	3	12	62	52	29
Grantham Rovers	28	11	5	12	64	47	27
Doncaster Rovers	28	10	6	12	44	56	26
Dresden United	28	9	6	13	44	49	24
Wellingborough	28	10	4	14	44	71	24
Mansfield	28	9	2	17	35	68	20
Newark	28	6	1	21	36	78	13
Matlock	28	0	0	28	9	130	0

Mansfield, Matlock and Newark did not seek re-election. Gainsborough Trinity and Walsall resigned from the League.

1896-97

Doncaster Rovers	28	17	5	6	77	40	39
Glossop North End	27	15	4	8	67	39	36
Long Eaton Rangers	28	15	2	11	55	39	32
Chesterfield	28	13	6	9	74	53	32
Kettering	28	13	5	10	51	40	31
Wellingborough	28	12	7	9	52	46	31
Burslem Port Vale	28	13	3	11	62	56	31
Heanor Town	28	12	6	10	55	47	30
Ilkeston Town	28	11	7	10	60	57	29
Dresden United	28	12	5	11	48	63	29
Barnsley Saint Peter's	28	10	4	14	57	71	24
Rushden Town	28	9	5	14	43	53	23
Mexborough Town	28	7	7	14	39	50	21
Worksop Town	28	6	5	17	27	63	17
Grantham Rovers	27	6	3	18	26	76	15

Glossop North End vs Grantham Rovers was not played. Glossop North End were awarded 2 points. Grantham Rovers and Worksop Town did not seek re-election. Dresden United and Heanor Town both resigned from the League. After this season, only the bottom two clubs had to retire each season, still being eligible for re-election.

1897-98

Mexborough Town	22	15	3	4	53	30	33
Barnsley Saint Peter's	22	14	3	5	47	29	31
Chesterfield	22	11	7	4	54	23	29
Ilkeston Town	22	9	6	7	37	39	24
Burslem Port Vale	22	10	3	9	46	32	23
Rushden Town	22	9	5	8	35	44	23
Kettering	22	7	5	10	19	28	19
Long Eaton Rangers	22	7	5	10	26	44	19
Glossop North End	22	8	2	12	41	47	18
Doncaster Rovers	22	5	6	11	33	35	16
Burton Wanderers	22	5	6	11	31	44	16
Wellingborough	22	5	3	14	21	48	13

Barnsley Saint Peter's, Burslem Port Vale and Glossop North End all resigned from the League.

1898-99

Doncaster Rovers	26	14	5	7	56	47	33
Ilkeston Town	26	15	2	9	55	37	32
Kettering	26	12	7	7	47	32	31
Chesterfield	26	14	3	9	59	42	31
Wellingborough	26	11	6	9	49	34	28
Burton Wanderers	26	11	5	10	49	38	27
Rushden Town	26	12	3	11	44	42	27
Derby County Reserves	26	10	5	11	61	47	25
Sheffield United Reserves	26	9	7	10	45	45	25
The Wednesday Reserves	26	10	5	11	42	52	25
Heanor Town	26	8	5	13	35	53	21
Leicester Fosse Reserves	26	9	2	15	34	59	20
Long Eaton Rangers	26	9	2	15	37	65	20
Mexborough Town	26	8	3	15	33	54	19

Chesterfield, Long Eaton Rangers, Mexborough Town, Sheffield United Reserves, and The Wednesday Reserves all resigned from the League.

1899-1900

Kettering	24	16	5	3	57	24	37
Wellingborough	24	6	4	4	64	38	36
Northampton	24	16	2	6	66	36	34
Derby County Reserves	24	11	5	8	63	46	27
Lincoln City Reserves	24	11	3	10	45	46	25
Heanor Town	24	9	7	8	31	36	25
Doncaster Rovers	24	9	6	9	51	42	24
Ilkeston Town	24	9	6	9	43	44	24
Newark	24	10	1	13	51	59	21
Burton Wanderers	24	6	6	12	40	62	18
Rushden Town	24	7	2	15	38	56	16
Barnsley Reserves	24	5	6	13	39	68	16
Leicester Fosse Reserves	24	3	3	18	34	74	9

Barnsley previously were League members as Barnsley Saint Peter's. Barnsley Reserves did not seek re-election. Heanor Town and Kettering both resigned from the League.

1900-01

Sheffield United Reserves	26	21	3	2	78	23	45
Doncaster Rovers	26	17	2	7	87	32	36
Northampton	26	13	7	6	65	43	33
Derby County Reserves	26	14	4	8	74	45	32
Hinckley Town	26	12	6	8	55	44	30
Newark	26	13	2	11	56	50	28
Wellingborough	26	12	4	10	44	46	28
Ilkeston Town	26	10	4	12	70	50	24
Leicester Fosse Reserves	26	11	1	14	60	64	23
Lincoln City Reserves	26	7	7	12	46	49	21
Rushden Town	26	8	5	13	35	61	21
Worksop Town	26	8	4	14	50	75	20
Coalville Town	26	5	2	19	30	102	12
Burton Wanderers	26	4	3	19	33	99	11

Loughborough Town were elected to the League, but shortly afterwards resigned, without playing a game. Burton Wanderers combined with Burton Swifts at the end of the season, to form Burton United. Burton United Reserves were subsequently elected to the League. Northampton, Rushden Town and Wellingborough all resigned from the League.

1901-02

Barnsley Reserves	28	19	4	5	72	46	42
Sheffield United Reserves	28	18	3	7	92	31	39
The Wednesday Reserves	28	13	11	4	82	32	37
Grimsby Town Reserves	28	16	3	9	72	38	35
Walsall	28	14	7	7	51	37	35
Newark	28	13	5	10	58	45	31
Whitwick White Cross	28	14	3	11	71	56	31
Lincoln City Reserves	28	12	5	11	53	57	29
Hinckley Town	28	11	4	13	59	55	26
Worksop Town	28	9	7	12	61	67	25
Derby County Reserves	28	10	2	16	57	90	22
Ilkeston Town	28	9	1	18	48	80	19
Leicester Fosse Reserves	28	7	5	16	38	70	19
Burton United Reserves	28	7	4	17	41	77	18
Coalville Town	28	5	2	21	32	106	12

Doncaster Rovers were elected to the Football League to fill the vacancy caused by the resignation of New Brighton Tower, after playing their first Midland League fixture. They declined to fulfil the rest of their fixtures, which were taken over by Barnsley Reserves. Coalville Town did not seek re-election.

1902-03

The Wednesday Reserves	32	24	3	5	98	26	51
Derby County Reserves	32	17	10	5	63	44	44
Worksop Town	32	19	5	8	69	51	43
Sheffield United Reserves	32	16	7	9	56	48	39
Barnsley Reserves	32	16	6	10	55	43	38
Hinckley Town	32	14	7	11	61	51	35
Whitwick White Cross	32	13	8	11	56	48	34
Doncaster Rovers Reserves	32	13	5	14	52	46	31
Walsall	32	12	7	13	52	48	31
Newark	32	14	3	15	60	57	31
Chesterfield Town Reserves	32	12	6	14	48	49	30
Grimsby Town Reserves	32	12	4	16	51	47	28
Burton United Reserves	32	11	6	15	54	72	28
Denaby United	32	9	8	15	40	59	26
Lincoln City Reserves	32	9	2	21	44	73	20
Gainsborough Trinity Reserves	32	6	7	19	38	78	19
Leicester Fosse Reserves	32	6	4	22	30	87	16

Ilkeston Town refused to fulfil their fixtures, and were expelled from the League in February 1903. Their record was deleted. Chesterfield Town were previously known as Chesterfield. Burton United Reserves, Leicester Fosse Reserves and Walsall all resigned from the League.

1903-04

Sheffield United Reserves	34	26	4	4	101	24	56
The Wednesday Reserves	34	25	5	4	104	28	55
Newark	34	17	5	12	64	45	39
Nottingham Forest Reserves	34	15	9	10	57	50	39
Rotherham Town	34	15	8	11	67	49	38
Chesterfield Town Reserves	34	14	10	10	57	50	38
Derby County Reserves	34	15	6	13	63	53	36
Barnsley Reserves	34	16	2	16	66	70	34
Grimsby Town Reserves	34	15	4	15	56	62	34
Hinckley Town	34	15	4	15	61	73	34
Doncaster Rovers	34	13	5	16	58	55	31
Thornhill United	34	10	9	15	49	59	29
Gresley Rovers	34	10	8	16	60	84	28
Denaby United	34	8	11	15	40	75	27
Whitwick White Cross	34	10	6	18	47	66	26
Worksop Town	34	10	6	18	57	83	26
Gainsborough Trinity Reserves	34	7	9	18	52	89	23
Lincoln City Reserves	34	7	5	22	48	92	19

Grimsby Town Reserves, Hinckley Town and Whitwick White Cross all resigned from the League.

1904-05

Sheffield United Reserves	32	22	4	6	107	33	48
Nottingham Forest Reserves	32	20	5	7	85	49	45
Newark	32	16	12	4	61	30	44
The Wednesday Reserves	32	18	6	8	8	43	42
Thornhill United	32	18	5	9	58	41	41
Rotherham Town	32	17	6	9	74	46	40
Notts County Reserves	32	17	5	10	79	48	39
Gainsborough Trinity Reserves	32	14	3	15	67	70	31
Worksop Town	32	11	8	13	63	62	30
Denaby United	32	12	5	15	45	50	29
Stockport County	32	12	4	16	47	83	28
Barnsley Reserves	32	12	3	17	56	63	27
Chesterfield Town Reserves	32	9	6	17	34	55	24
Derby County Reserves	32	9	5	18	53	99	23
Gresley Rovers	32	8	6	18	46	73	22
Lincoln City Reserves	32	7	7	18	38	72	21
Doncaster Rovers Reserves	32	3	4	25	29	105	10

Chesterfield Town Reserves, Derby County Reserves and Stockport County all resigned from the League.

1905-06

The Wednesday Reserves	34	25	5	4	111	28	55
Grimsby Town Reserves	34	24	6	4	89	35	54
Sheffield United Reserves	34	19	7	8	102	43	45
Rotherham Town	34	18	9	7	90	45	45
Mexborough Town	34	16	8	10	73	45	40
Barnsley Reserves	34	18	4	12	61	60	40
Denaby United	34	16	7	11	76	47	39
Newark	34	13	9	12	46	45	35
Nottingham Forest Reserves	34	15	4	15	78	72	34
Rotherham County	34	14	3	17	65	58	31
Lincoln City Reserves	34	12	7	15	65	91	29
Leeds City Reserves	34	10	8	16	60	81	28
Notts County Reserves	34	9	9	16	51	72	27
Doncaster Rovers	34	10	6	18	47	78	26
Worksop Town	34	10	6	18	43	85	26
Gainsborough Trinity Reserves	34	8	9	17	43	74	25
Gresley Rovers	34	7	4	23	42	114	18
Grantham Avenue	34	3	7	24	34	102	13

Lincoln City Reserves had 2 points deducted for playing an ineligible player. Rotherham County were previously known as Thornhill United. Gresley Rovers did not seek re-election.

1906-07

Sheffield United Reserves	38	31	2	5	126	41	64
Grimsby Town Reserves	38	25	7	6	92	46	57
The Wednesday Reserves	38	25	5	8	84	44	55
Rotherham Town	38	24	4	10	110	43	52
Denaby United	38	19	10	9	78	46	48
Mexborough Town	38	20	7	11	71	51	47
Newark	38	17	10	11	61	71	44
Leeds City Reserves	38	16	10	12	67	64	42
Bradford City Reserves	38	17	7	14	98	74	41
Rotherham County	38	13	8	17	57	63	34
Hull City Reserves	38	15	4	19	66	75	34
Lincoln City Reserves	38	10	12	16	46	81	32
Barnsley Reserves	38	12	7	19	72	77	31
Worksop Town	38	14	2	22	66	91	30
Grantham Avenue	38	10	10	18	58	86	30
Chesterfield Town Reserves	38	10	7	21	68	93	27
Doncaster Rovers	38	10	7	21	52	82	27
Gainsborough Trinity Reserves	38	10	6	22	53	104	26
Nottingham Forest Reserves	38	6	9	23	59	103	21
Notts County Reserves	38	6	6	26	43	92	18

Notts County Reserves did not seek re-election.

1907-08

The Wednesday Reserves	38	27	2	9	106	37	56
Denaby United	38	23	8	7	90	51	54
Rotherham Town	38	21	8	9	74	50	50
Sheffield United Reserves	38	23	3	12	89	44	49
Grimsby Town Reserves	38	19	7	12	69	56	45
Newark	38	16	10	12	62	59	42
Hull City Reserves	38	15	9	14	56	48	39
Leicester Fosse Reserves	38	17	5	16	72	70	39
Worksop Town	38	15	8	15	74	85	38
Barnsley Reserves	38	15	7	16	62	65	37
Leeds City Reserves	38	14	9	15	61	72	37
Nottingham Forest Reserves	38	14	8	16	70	70	36
Bradford City Reserves	38	13	6	19	65	67	32
Chesterfield Town Reserves	38	12	8	18	63	70	32
Doncaster Rovers	38	14	4	20	48	65	32
Gainsborough Trinity Reserves	38	12	7	19	64	85	31
Mexborough Town	38	12	7	19	57	78	31
Lincoln City Reserves	38	8	12	18	55	82	28
Rotherham County	38	9	8	21	46	88	26
Grantham Avenue	38	8	10	20	36	77	26

Grantham Avenue were not re-elected.

1908-09

Lincoln City	38	29	5	4	86	38	63
Rotherham Town	38	22	6	10	78	53	50
Bradford City Reserves	38	20	7	11	76	51	47
Barnsley Reserves	38	16	12	10	68	53	44
Denaby United	38	18	8	12	59	49	44
The Wednesday Reserves	38	17	8	13	80	45	42
Hull City Reserves	38	17	7	14	79	66	41
Sheffield United Reserves	38	16	8	14	76	63	40
Rotherham County	38	19	2	17	77	67	40
Grimsby Town Reserves	38	17	5	16	69	66	39
Doncaster Rovers	38	18	3	17	50	58	39
Mexborough Town	38	13	8	17	57	88	34
Leicester Fosse Reserves	38	13	7	18	87	70	33
Nottingham Forest Reserves	38	15	2	21	66	92	32
Newark	38	10	11	17	51	79	31
Notts County Reserves	38	12	6	20	64	74	30
Gainsborough Trinity Reserves	38	10	9	19	54	62	29
Leeds City Reserves	38	12	4	22	56	90	28
Chesterfield Town Reserves	38	9	10	19	55	101	28
Worksop Town	38	10	6	22	73	96	26

Before the 1909-1910 season began, Newark resigned from the League. Castleford Town were elected to take over their fixtures.

1909-10

Chesterfield Town	42	27	7	8	102	44	61
Hull City Reserves	42	27	3	12	113	65	57
Bradford Park Avenue Reserves	42	23	8	11	117	64	54
The Wednesday Reserves	42	20	11	11	110	66	51
Huddersfield Town	42	22	6	14	92	76	50
Nottingham Forest Reserves	42	20	9	13	96	79	49
Sheffield United Reserves	42	17	10	15	77	56	44
Grimsby Town Reserves	42	20	4	18	105	85	44
Barnsley Reserves	42	20	3	19	90	71	43
Notts County Reserves	42	17	8	17	78	74	42
Rotherham County	42	17	8	17	68	80	42
Leeds City Reserves	42	18	6	18	60	75	42
Denaby United	42	16	7	19	74	67	39
Doncaster Rovers	42	14	11	17	51	66	39
Worksop Town	42	14	10	18	68	88	38
Lincoln City Reserves	42	16	5	21	74	96	37
Rotherham Town	42	14	8	20	82	97	36
Leicester Fosse Reserves	42	13	10	19	76	93	36
Bradford City Reserves	42	13	7	22	63	89	33
Mexborough Town	42	15	3	24	67	101	33
Castleford Town	42	9	12	21	46	101	30
Gainsborough Trinity Reserves	42	10	4	28	65	141	24

Bradford City Reserves and Bradford Park Avenue Reserves both resigned from the League.

1910-11

Grimsby Town	38	25	7	6	93	32	57
The Wednesday Reserves	38	24	8	6	86	41	56
Doncaster Rovers	38	23	4	11	106	63	50
Hull City Reserves	38	20	9	9	105	63	49
Chesterfield Town	38	20	5	13	80	61	45
Rotherham County	38	19	7	12	81	72	45
Huddersfield Town Reserves	38	18	5	15	81	65	41
Barnsley Reserves	38	15	8	15	82	70	38
Notts County Reserves	38	18	2	18	88	81	38
Mexborough Town	38	13	10	15	70	65	36
Gainsborough Trinity Reserves	38	15	6	17	49	65	36
Leeds City Reserves	38	13	9	16	66	68	35
Lincoln City Reserves	38	15	5	18	60	89	35
Sheffield United Reserves	38	14	4	20	76	89	32
Castleford Town	38	14	3	21	72	110	31
Rotherham Town	38	11	7	20	57	72	29
Denaby United	38	13	3	22	60	92	29
Leicester Fosse Reserves	38	11	7	20	62	100	29
Nottingham Forest Reserves	38	10	7	21	56	83	27
Worksop Town	38	10	2	26	55	104	22

Nottingham Forest Reserves resigned from the League.

1911-12

Rotherham County	36	23	5	8	92	56	51
Rotherham Town	36	19	11	6	75	49	49
Doncaster Rovers	36	21	6	9	79	42	48
Leicester Fosse Reserves	36	17	8	11	90	54	42
Leeds City Reserves	36	18	6	12	57	49	42
Grimsby Town Reserves	36	17	5	14	69	84	39
Barnsley Reserves	36	16	6	14	72	62	38
The Wednesday Reserves	36	15	8	13	68	64	38
Mexborough Town	36	15	8	13	54	66	38
Castleford Reserves	36	15	7	14	66	58	37
Notts County Reserves	36	15	6	15	63	58	36
Chesterfield Town	36	14	8	14	63	62	36
Lincoln City	36	13	6	17	62	67	32
Huddersfield Town Reserves	36	13	6	17	53	66	32
Sheffield United Reserves	36	11	8	17	64	57	30
Gainsborough Trinity Reserves	36	10	9	17	52	46	29
Hull City Reserves	36	9	7	20	53	66	25
Worksop Town	36	9	6	21	47	88	24
Denaby United	36	7	4	25	38	123	18

Barnsley Reserves, Huddersfield Town Reserves and Leicester City Fosse Reserves all resigned from the League.

1912-13

Rotherham County	38	28	5	5	111	37	61
Chesterfield Town	38	20	11	7	78	41	51
Gainsborough Trinity	38	22	6	10	84	40	50
Doncaster Rovers	38	21	7	10	67	43	49
Leeds City Reserves	38	18	7	13	68	52	43
Goole Town	38	14	14	10	52	49	42
The Wednesday Reserves	38	16	7	15	78	69	39
Grimsby Town Reserves	38	15	9	14	65	67	39
Sheffield United Reserves	38	15	8	15	68	57	38
York City	38	16	6	16	69	80	38
Rotherham Town	38	17	4	17	55	67	38
Hull City Reserves	38	17	3	18	65	73	37
Lincoln City Reserves	38	16	3	19	81	73	35
Halifax Town	38	14	7	17	68	67	35
Scunthorpe United	38	13	8	17	55	78	34
Castleford Town	38	12	9	17	55	56	33
Worksop Town	38	12	5	21	47	91	29
Notts County Reserves	38	10	6	22	67	85	26
Mexborough Town	38	11	3	24	42	77	25
Denaby United	38	7	4	27	39	112	18

Denaby United did not seek re-election. Notts County Reserves resigned from the League.

1913-14

Rotherham County	34	25	2	7	92	38	52
Gainsborough Trinity	34	22	6	6	76	36	50
Chesterfield Town	34	19	4	11	80	43	42
The Wednesday Reserves	34	17	6	11	68	50	40
Goole Town	34	16	6	12	52	39	38
Grimsby Town Reserves	34	16	6	12	68	56	38
Scunthorpe United	34	16	4	14	55	55	36
Castleford Town	34	15	4	15	54	51	34
Rotherham Town	34	13	8	13	46	61	34
Sheffield United Reserves	34	11	10	13	60	62	32
Lincoln City Reserves	34	11	9	14	49	60	31
York City	34	13	5	16	48	60	31
Worksop Town	34	13	3	18	51	61	29
Halifax Town	34	11	6	17	38	51	28
Hull City Reserves	34	11	5	18	37	55	27
Doncaster Rovers	34	12	2	20	30	51	26
Mexborough Town	34	10	4	20	41	85	24
Leeds City Reserves	34	8	4	22	45	75	20

1914-15

Rotherham County	38	23	8	7	104	42	54
Leeds City Reserves	38	24	5	9	99	42	53
Chesterfield Town	38	20	10	8	76	41	50
Goole Town	38	20	7	11	103	58	47
The Wednesday Reserves	38	20	7	11	92	56	47
Gainsborough Trinity	38	19	8	11	78	46	46
Grimsby Town Reserves	38	21	3	14	73	54	45
Worksop Town	38	17	11	10	70	55	45
Rotherham Town	38	20	4	14	112	65	44
Halifax Town	38	16	9	13	49	57	41
Bradford Park Avenue Reserves	38	16	6	16	83	66	38
Sheffield United Reserves	38	15	6	17	57	46	36
Scunthorpe United	38	13	9	16	70	79	35
Lincoln City Reserves	38	12	9	17	76	74	33
Doncaster Rovers	38	14	3	21	58	82	31
York City	38	12	7	19	45	72	31
Mexborough Town	38	10	8	20	37	89	28
Castleford Town	38	9	9	20	50	103	27
Hull City Reserves	38	8	2	28	39	105	18
Heckmondwike	38	5	1	32	30	169	11

Heckmondwike were expelled for failing to fulfil fixtures on their arranged dates. Leeds City Reserves resigned from the League. Barnsley Reserves were elected to the competition.

During the war, Bradford Park Avenue Reserves, Chesterfield Town, Doncaster Rovers, Gainsborough Trinity, Goole Town, Halifax Town, Hull City Reserves, Mexborough Town, and York City all resigned from the League.

For 1919-20, the ten remaining members elected Chesterfield Municipal, Gainsborough Trinity, Mexborough, Notts County Reserves, and Silverwood Colliery to the League. Subsequently, Halifax Town were elected to make a League of 16 clubs. Hull City Reserves and Leeds United joined the League shortly after the start of the season to bring the total membership to 18.

1919-20

Chesterfield Municipal	34	24	5	5	78	35	53
Sheffield United Reserves	34	20	11	3	73	28	51
Scunthorpe United	34	18	7	9	71	39	43
Worksop Town	34	20	3	11	71	52	43
Mexborough	34	18	6	10	60	45	42
The Wednesday Reserves	34	16	6	12	50	44	38
Rotherham Town	34	14	8	12	83	71	36
Castleford Town	34	14	8	12	53	46	36
Hull City Reserves	34	16	2	16	74	59	34
Grimsby Town Reserves	34	14	5	15	66	64	33
Rotherham County Reserves	34	13	5	16	60	57	31
Leeds United	34	11	9	14	56	56	31
Notts County Reserves	34	10	11	13	50	56	31
Halifax Town	34	13	4	17	52	70	30
Lincoln City Reserves	34	8	7	19	43	83	23
Barnsley Reserves	34	6	9	19	46	72	21
Silverwood Colliery	34	6	7	21	38	89	19
Gainsborough Trinity	34	7	3	24	37	95	17

Silverwood Colliery were not re-elected.

1920-21

Lincoln City	38	27	3	8	95	40	57
Notts County Reserves	38	22	9	7	80	45	53
Chesterfield	38	18	11	9	70	46	47
Scunthorpe United	38	18	9	11	64	43	45
Rotherham Town	38	18	8	12	68	48	44
Sheffield United Reserves	38	16	10	12	73	63	42
Rotherham County Reserves	38	16	9	13	57	37	41
Castleford Town	38	17	6	15	61	56	40
The Wednesday Reserves	38	16	7	15	66	50	39
Worksop Town	38	16	7	15	62	55	39
Halifax Town	38	17	5	16	54	62	39
Leeds United Reserves	38	15	8	15	49	51	38
Gainsborough Trinity	38	14	8	16	58	60	36
Nottingham Forest Reserves	38	13	10	15	69	77	36
Hull City Reserves	38	12	9	17	52	68	33
Doncaster Rovers	38	11	10	17	38	54	32
Mexborough	38	10	11	17	39	61	31
Grimsby Town Reserves	38	11	6	21	45	72	28
Barnsley Reserves	38	9	8	21	55	86	26
Denaby United	38	4	6	28	37	118	14

Chesterfield were previously known as Chesterfield Municipal. Chesterfield, Halifax Town, Leeds United Reserves and Sheffield United Reserves all resigned from the League.

1921-22

Worksop Town	42	26	9	7	70	41	61
Grimsby Town Reserves	42	24	9	9	87	56	57
The Wednesday Reserves	42	23	10	9	98	49	56
Scunthorpe United	42	22	8	12	87	60	52
Barnsley Reserves	42	20	9	13	81	50	49
Mexborough	42	19	9	14	67	40	47
Castleford Town	42	18	11	13	69	54	47
Mansfield Town	42	20	7	15	68	57	47
Nottingham Forest Reserves	42	19	6	17	69	60	44
Rotherham County Reserves	42	17	8	17	80	79	42
Rotherham Town	42	15	11	16	65	66	41
Wombwell	42	16	9	17	60	66	41
Doncaster Rovers	42	17	6	19	52	66	40
Denaby United	42	14	11	17	67	67	39
Gainsborough Trinity	42	15	9	18	63	65	39
Notts County Reserves	42	15	7	20	64	57	37
Boston	42	15	7	20	66	73	37
Wath Athletic	42	13	8	21	50	71	34
Harrogate	42	14	6	22	49	88	34
Hull City Reserves	42	10	8	24	55	83	28
Wakefield City	42	9	9	24	39	103	27
Lincoln City Reserves	42	6	13	23	53	97	25

Harrogate and Wakefield City both resigned from the League.

1922-23

The Wednesday Reserves	42	28	7	7	88	37	63
Doncaster Rovers	42	26	9	7	72	28	61
Worksop Town	42	26	5	11	86	45	57
Denaby United	42	24	9	9	76	48	57
Grimsby Town Reserves	42	21	9	12	77	58	51
Scunthorpe United	42	18	13	11	65	58	49
Wath Athletic	42	18	10	14	59	38	46
Notts County Reserves	42	16	12	14	76	55	44
Boston	42	18	8	16	61	46	44
Nottingham Forest Reserves	42	16	11	15	74	60	43
Rotherham County Reserves	42	18	6	18	56	52	42
Hull City Reserves	42	14	13	15	63	63	41
Mansfield Town	42	17	6	19	79	64	40
Barnsley Reserves	42	14	12	16	67	65	40
Wombwell	42	12	14	16	50	63	38
Castleford Town	42	15	6	21	61	70	36
Chesterfield Reserves	42	14	8	20	56	79	36
Mexborough	42	11	13	18	44	63	35
York City	42	11	12	19	56	70	34
Gainsborough Trinity	42	8	8	26	42	111	24
Rotherham Town	42	8	6	28	45	105	22
Lincoln City Reserves	42	7	7	28	39	114	21

The Wednesday Reserves resigned from the League.

1923-24

Mansfield Town	42	31	6	5	98	31	68
Grimsby Town Reserves	42	25	6	11	99	46	56
Worksop Town	42	25	4	13	93	54	54
Mexborough	42	22	7	13	78	64	51
Notts County Reserves	42	21	8	13	83	51	50
Scunthorpe United	42	21	7	14	55	49	49
Sutton Town	42	21	6	15	86	68	48
Denaby United	42	21	6	15	78	62	48
Hull City Reserves	42	19	8	15	70	48	46
Nottingham Forest Reserves	42	18	9	15	52	52	45
Chesterfield Reserves	42	19	5	18	64	64	43
Boston	42	15	10	16	64	62	42
Gainsborough Trinity	42	16	8	18	55	62	40
Barnsley Reserves	42	15	9	18	58	57	39
Doncaster Rovers Reserves	42	14	9	19	58	63	37
Rotherham County Reserves	42	15	7	20	60	75	37
Wath Athletic	42	14	8	20	57	85	36
Wombwell	42	12	10	20	47	74	34
York City	42	10	13	19	48	71	33
Lincoln City Reserves	42	13	3	26	46	81	29
Castleford Town	42	8	5	29	39	116	21
Rotherham Town	42	7	4	31	42	95	18

Barnsley Reserves, Chesterfield Reserves, Doncaster Rovers Reserves, Grimsby Town Reserves, Hull City Reserves, Nottingham Forest Reserves, Notts County Reserves and Rotherham County Reserves all resigned from the League.

1924-25

Mansfield Town	28	20	4	4	82	27	44
Boston	28	17	5	6	56	36	39
Gainsborough Trinity	28	14	7	7	47	38	35
Worksop Town	28	14	4	10	51	42	32
Lincoln City Reserves	28	14	4	10	40	40	32
York City	28	10	10	8	39	36	30
Scunthorpe United	28	12	5	11	45	41	29
Mexborough	28	9	9	10	49	49	27
Denaby United	28	9	8	11	41	38	26
Wath Athletic	28	10	4	14	43	49	24
Castleford Town	28	9	6	13	47	61	24
Rotherham Town	28	10	2	16	43	46	22
Frickley Colliery	28	5	10	13	35	61	20
Sutton Town	28	7	4	17	40	66	18
Wombwell	28	5	8	15	31	59	18

Rotherham Town amalgamated with Rotherham County to form Rotherham United. They resigned from the League.

1925-26

Mexborough	40	25	7	8	111	53	57
Mansfield Town	40	23	7	10	120	54	53
Boston	40	21	10	9	98	43	52
Lincoln City Reserves	40	20	10	10	102	57	50
Denaby United	40	20	7	13	95	63	47
Wath Athletic	40	19	9	12	98	72	47
Scunthorpe United	40	19	9	12	86	78	47
Newark Town	40	16	9	15	94	88	41
Alfreton Town	40	17	7	16	99	102	41
Loughborough Corinthians	40	17	5	18	86	82	39
Worksop Town	40	14	10	16	82	82	38
Wombwell	40	14	9	17	73	89	37
Long Eaton	40	14	8	18	82	94	36
Grantham	40	15	6	19	71	94	36
Sutton Town	40	15	6	19	68	102	36
York City	40	14	7	19	74	94	35
Gainsborough Trinity	40	13	8	19	58	85	34
Shirebrook	40	14	4	22	81	106	32
Ilkeston United	40	12	7	21	57	91	31
Frickley Colliery	40	11	7	22	61	99	29
Castleford Town	40	10	2	28	62	130	22

Mansfield Town resigned from the League. Castleford Town did not seek re-election.

1926-27

Scunthorpe United	38	28	4	6	121	44	60
Boston	38	21	7	10	128	64	49
Gainsborough Trinity	38	22	5	11	85	63	49
Wath Athletic	38	21	4	13	76	63	46
Mexborough Athletic	38	20	6	12	97	81	46
York City	38	16	13	9	96	68	45
Loughborough Corinthians	38	20	5	13	94	76	45
Lincoln City Reserves	38	18	7	13	94	70	43
Denaby United	38	18	4	16	88	59	40
Shirebrook	38	19	2	17	112	96	40
Worksop Town	38	17	5	16	95	87	39
Frickley Colliery	38	14	9	15	90	84	37
Ilkeston United	38	13	7	18	73	95	33
Grantham	38	12	8	18	84	76	32
Heanor Town	38	13	6	19	70	99	32
Newark Town	38	13	6	19	67	95	32
Long Eaton	38	12	7	19	72	105	31
Alfreton Town	38	8	5	25	58	143	21
Wombwell	38	7	6	25	57	111	20
Sutton Town	38	8	4	26	67	136	20

Mexborough Athletic were previously known as Mexborough. Long Eaton resigned from the League. Alfreton Town resigned and disbanded, but subsequently re-formed, applying unsuccessfully for re-election. Sutton Town failed to gain re-election.

1927-28

Gainsborough Trinity	44	29	7	8	141	62	65
Scarborough	44	26	7	11	108	61	59
Nottingham Forest Reserves	44	23	8	13	127	84	54
Notts County Reserves	44	24	5	15	143	81	53
Lincoln City Reserves	44	23	7	14	126	99	53
Wath Athletic	44	24	4	16	94	74	52
York City	44	22	7	15	97	73	51
Shirebrook	44	23	5	16	108	89	51
Scunthorpe United	44	23	4	17	118	85	50
Mansfield Town	44	19	11	14	118	97	49
Worksop Town	44	20	9	15	97	101	49
Grimsby Town Reserves	44	20	8	16	93	83	48
Grantham	44	17	11	16	88	102	45
Denaby United	44	19	6	19	76	82	44
Boston	44	16	11	17	79	87	43
Staveley Town	44	16	10	18	98	109	42
Mexborough Athletic	44	14	9	21	84	112	37
Frickley Colliery	44	15	5	24	84	107	35
Loughborough Corinthians	44	14	7	23	76	104	35
Wombwell	44	12	7	25	70	107	31
Heanor Town	44	10	5	29	66	155	25
Ilkeston Town	44	8	5	31	75	133	21
Newark Town	44	8	4	32	60	139	20

Heanor Town resigned, but subsequently applied to be re-elected. However, it was decided to expel them from the League. Ilkeston United failed to gain re-election.

1928-29

Mansfield Town	50	31	10	9	133	72	72
Gainsborough Trinity	50	25	13	12	94	54	63
Lincoln City Reserves	50	29	5	16	118	86	63
Hull City Reserves	50	26	10	14	101	84	62
Grantham	50	25	10	15	113	79	60
Boston	50	27	5	18	96	72	59
Scarborough	50	25	8	17	115	91	58
Notts County Reserves	50	21	15	14	91	75	57
York City	50	22	13	15	106	99	57
Grimsby Town Reserves	50	24	6	20	109	95	54
Scunthorpe United	50	20	14	16	98	96	54
Barnsley Reserves	50	18	17	15	95	79	53
Nottingham Forest Reserves	50	20	12	18	101	74	52
Frickley Colliery	50	22	8	20	93	87	52
Denaby United	50	22	7	21	86	86	51
Chesterfield Reserves	50	19	9	22	69	81	47
Shirebrook	50	19	8	23	112	113	46
Doncaster Rovers	50	19	7	24	92	97	45
Wath Athletic	50	16	12	22	97	104	44
Mexborough Athletic	50	15	12	23	81	105	42
Newark Town	50	16	9	25	82	118	41
Rotherham United Reserves	50	18	4	28	99	125	40
Staveley Town	50	15	8	27	102	142	38
Loughborough Corinthians	50	13	6	31	75	117	32
Wombwell	50	12	8	30	80	136	32
Worksop Town	50	10	6	34	69	140	26

York City resigned from the League.

1929-30

Scarborough	50	36	9	5	143	44	81
Barnsley Reserves	50	33	9	8	137	69	75
Bradford Park Avenue Reserves	50	33	5	12	163	83	71
Grimsby Town Reserves	50	28	9	13	160	88	65
Lincoln City Reserves	50	27	9	14	131	83	63
Loughborough Corinthians	50	25	11	14	113	74	61
Scunthorpe United	50	26	6	18	124	98	58
Gainsborough Trinity	50	25	6	19	117	99	56
Nottingham Forest Reserves	50	24	8	18	117	103	56
Mansfield Town	50	25	4	21	126	98	54
Notts County Reserves	50	22	9	19	136	114	53
Boston	50	23	7	20	102	94	53
Grantham	50	23	6	21	100	93	52
Chesterfield Reserves	50	21	8	21	123	102	50
Rotherham United Reserves	50	22	4	24	101	122	48
Hull City Reserves	50	20	7	23	109	105	47
Shirebrook	50	16	13	21	87	109	45
Newark Town	50	17	11	22	93	125	45
Frickley Colliery	50	16	9	25	83	129	41
Mexborough Athletic	50	14	12	24	90	132	40
Wombwell	50	15	9	26	76	116	39
Denaby United	50	15	7	28	90	123	37
Doncaster Rovers Reserves	50	12	12	26	85	118	36
Worksop Town	50	13	6	31	114	162	32
Staveley Town	50	11	6	33	78	193	28
Wath Athletic	50	4	6	40	55	177	14

Staveley Town, Wath Athletic and Worksop Town all resigned from the League.

1930-31

Grimsby Town Reserves	46	32	6	8	174	73	70
Bradford City Reserves	46	32	6	8	141	76	70
Bradford Park Avenue Reserves	46	20	4	12	138	63	64
Barnsley Reserves	46	25	7	14	126	78	57
Nottingham Forest Reserves	46	25	7	14	152	108	57
Lincoln City Reserves	46	22	10	14	124	80	54
Grantham	46	21	10	15	85	85	52
Hull City Reserves	46	20	11	15	105	88	51
Gainsborough Trinity	46	22	5	19	131	117	49
Mansfield Town	46	19	11	16	103	95	49
Scunthorpe United	46	19	11	16	98	101	49
Newark Town	46	18	8	20	74	89	44
Boston	46	16	11	19	79	92	43
Denaby United	46	17	9	20	84	104	43
Chesterfield Reserves	46	17	8	21	91	111	42
Scarborough	46	16	9	21	93	110	41
Notts County	46	17	6	23	119	121	40
Shirebrook	46	15	10	21	100	116	40
Loughborough Corinthians	46	14	8	24	80	116	36
Mexborough Athletic	46	13	8	25	84	129	34
Rotherham United Reserves	46	14	6	26	85	145	34
Doncaster Rovers Reserves	46	10	13	23	54	95	33
Wombwell	46	9	9	28	74	129	27
Frickley Colliery	46	8	9	29	64	137	25

Championship play-off: Grimsby Town Reserves beat Bradford City Reserves 3-0 to win the Championship

Shirebrook resigned from the League.

1931-32

Bradford Park Avenue Reserves	46	36	3	7	189	63	75
Grimsby Town Reserves	46	36	3	7	178	60	75
Nottingham Forest Reserves	46	30	7	9	117	62	67
Notts County Reserves	46	24	11	11	115	81	59
Bradford City Reserves	46	20	11	15	111	93	51
Scarborough	46	22	7	17	81	83	51
York City Reserves	46	20	8	18	99	99	48
Chesterfield Reserves	46	18	9	19	100	98	45
Scunthorpe United	46	18	9	19	83	99	45
Mansfield Town Reserves	46	16	12	18	86	86	44
Newark Town	46	18	8	20	85	90	44
Gainsborough Trinity	46	17	10	19	76	86	44
Loughborough Corinthians	46	18	8	20	88	113	44
Doncaster Rovers Reserves	46	16	11	19	96	100	43
Boston	46	16	10	20	87	112	42
Mexborough Athletic	46	18	5	23	92	121	41
Hull City Reserves	46	17	7	22	76	112	41
Barnsley Reserves	46	14	12	20	97	108	40
Lincoln City Reserves	46	15	7	24	103	112	37
Wombwell	46	14	9	23	81	99	37
Denaby United	46	10	14	22	101	127	34
Grantham	46	12	9	25	80	121	33
Frickley Colliery	46	13	7	26	86	135	33
Rotherham United Reserves	46	12	7	27	59	106	31

Championship play-off: Bradford Park Avenue Reserves beat Grimsby Town Reserves 2-1 to win the Championship.
Nottingham Forest Reserves resigned from the League.

1932-33

Grimsby Town Reserves	44	36	1	7	184	66	73
Lincoln City Reserves	44	30	6	8	161	73	66
Bradford Park Avenue Reserves	44	28	8	8	146	52	64
Chesterfield Reserves	44	28	4	12	131	67	60
Scarborough	44	25	9	10	137	81	59
Bradford City Reserves	44	24	10	10	112	63	58
Barnsley Reserves	44	24	5	15	116	83	53
Scunthorpe United	44	23	5	16	104	100	51
Notts County Reserves	44	20	10	14	104	76	50
Gainsborough Trinity	44	18	10	16	95	90	46
Denaby United	44	20	5	19	78	93	45
Doncaster Rovers Reserves	44	16	12	16	83	89	44
Mansfield Town Reserves	44	16	9	19	108	97	41
Frickley Colliery	44	16	7	21	80	118	39
Loughborough Corinthians	44	14	10	20	92	110	38
Hull City Reserves	44	17	4	23	104	131	38
Grantham	44	12	11	21	91	110	35
Boston	44	15	4	25	94	109	34
Newark Town	44	14	4	26	92	132	32
York City Reserves	44	13	4	27	74	129	30
Mexborough Athletic	44	11	6	27	73	139	28
Rotherham United Reserves	44	9	4	31	66	153	22
Wombwell	44	2	2	40	32	196	6

Frickley Colliery, Grantham, Loughborough Corinthians, Mansfield Town Reserves, Newark Town and Wombwell all resigned from the League.

1933-34

Grimsby Town Reserves	32	25	4	3	127	47	54
Bradford City Reserves	32	23	3	6	107	47	49
Bradford Park Avenue Reserves	32	21	2	9	90	43	44
Chesterfield Reserves	32	15	4	13	66	56	34
Lincoln City Reserves	32	14	6	12	83	75	34
Hull City Reserves	32	15	3	14	74	70	33
Scunthorpe United	32	14	5	13	76	73	33
Scarborough	32	12	8	12	57	67	32
Denaby United	32	11	9	12	58	76	31
Barnsley Reserves	32	12	5	15	71	80	29
Notts County Reserves	32	13	2	17	64	64	28
York City Reserves	32	10	7	15	69	88	27
Doncaster Rovers Reserves	32	10	5	17	57	58	25
Boston United	32	11	3	18	54	96	25
Gainsborough Trinity	32	10	4	18	54	79	24
Mexborough Athletic	32	10	2	20	53	85	22
Rotherham United Reserves	32	8	4	20	46	102	20

Boston United were previously known as Boston. York City Reserves resigned from the League.

1934-35

Barnsley Reserves	38	28	5	5	120	56	61
Norwich City Reserves	38	22	8	8	97	36	52
Grimsby Town Reserves	38	20	8	10	114	54	48
Bradford Park Avenue Reserves	38	19	9	10	94	64	47
Boston United	38	19	8	11	85	71	46
Bradford City Reserves	38	19	7	12	104	65	45
Notts County Reserves	38	17	11	10	69	59	45
Gainsborough Trinity	38	18	8	12	80	73	44
Grantham	38	15	11	12	86	67	41
Peterborough United	38	15	10	13	81	84	40
Scunthorpe United	38	17	3	18	67	82	37
Doncaster Rovers Reserves	38	14	8	16	64	70	36
Chesterfield Reserves	38	14	7	17	77	76	35
Lincoln City Reserves	38	15	5	18	83	89	35
Mexborough Athletic	38	14	4	20	69	96	32
Hull City Reserves	38	13	5	20	73	91	31
Rotherham United Reserves	38	6	13	19	65	97	25
Denaby United	38	8	8	22	67	104	24
Frickley Colliery	38	5	11	22	57	137	21
Scarborough	38	2	11	25	32	113	15

1935-36

Barnsley Reserves	40	28	3	9	127	59	59
Bradford Park Avenue Reserves	40	22	8	10	107	51	52
Gainsborough Trinity	40	24	4	12	92	49	52
Grantham	40	20	7	13	83	60	47
Doncaster Rovers Reserves	40	20	6	14	73	70	46
Norwich City Reserves	40	17	10	13	92	59	44
Boston United	40	19	4	17	64	69	42
Grimsby Town Reserves	40	16	8	16	88	70	40
Rotherham United Reserves	40	16	8	16	71	70	40
Burton Town	40	15	10	15	95	94	40
Scunthorpe United	40	16	8	16	73	77	40
Notts County Reserves	40	14	11	15	68	69	39
Scarborough	40	15	9	16	61	70	39
Chesterfield Reserves	40	16	5	19	99	91	37
Bradford City Reserves	40	14	7	19	74	77	35
Denaby United	40	12	10	18	73	111	34
Peterborough United	40	13	8	19	52	86	34
Lincoln City Reserves	40	15	3	22	85	106	33
Frickley Colliery	40	14	5	21	76	109	33
Hull City Reserves	40	12	8	20	63	99	32
Mexborough Athletic	40	7	8	25	46	117	22

Mexborough Athletic and Norwich City Reserves resigned from the League.

1936-37

Barnsley Reserves	42	27	7	8	121	68	61
Bradford Park Avenue Reserves	42	26	8	8	124	62	60
Grimsby Town Reserves	42	23	7	12	108	61	53
Chesterfield Reserves	42	23	4	15	117	79	50
Bradford City Reserves	42	23	4	15	104	75	50
Doncaster Rovers Reserves	42	21	8	13	84	63	50
Nottingham Forest Reserves	42	23	3	16	109	67	49
Gainsborough Trinity	42	22	5	15	110	82	49
Grantham	42	19	7	16	91	72	45
Boston United	42	19	7	16	85	76	45
Rotherham United Reserves	42	20	5	17	94	94	45
Hull City Reserves	42	19	6	17	64	62	44
Burton Town	42	17	8	17	75	89	42
Scunthorpe United	42	19	3	10	77	86	41
Notts County Reserves	42	17	5	20	92	106	39
Peterborough United	42	16	6	20	75	97	38
Lincoln City Reserves	42	16	4	22	77	85	36
Newark Town	42	15	4	23	80	97	34
Mansfield Town Reserves	42	11	9	22	57	100	31
Denaby United	42	12	4	26	73	134	28
Scarborough	42	10	6	26	55	99	26
Frickley Colliery	42	3	2	37	39	157	8

Chesterfield Reserves resigned from the League.

1937-38

Shrewsbury Town	42	25	9	8	111	50	59
Grantham	42	25	6	11	89	63	56
Scarborough	42	23	7	12	70	46	53
Doncaster Rovers Reserves	42	21	9	12	80	48	51
Grimsby Town Reserves	42	22	5	15	87	57	49
Scunthorpe United	42	22	5	15	109	78	49
Lincoln City Reserves	42	22	5	15	107	90	49
Barnsley Reserves	42	19	10	13	93	59	48
Boston United	42	20	8	14	79	74	48
Frickley Colliery	42	19	8	15	77	79	46
Burton Town	42	18	8	16	74	66	44
Notts County Reserves	42	16	9	17	70	72	41
Nottingham Forest Reserves	42	16	8	18	90	81	40
Bradford Park Avenue Reserves	42	16	7	19	95	72	39
Mansfield Town Reserves	42	18	3	21	69	67	39
Gainsborough Trinity	42	16	7	19	90	109	39
Hull City Reserves	42	17	4	21	73	83	38
Bradford City Reserves	42	16	6	20	81	105	38
Peterborough United	42	7	13	22	67	105	27
Newark Town	42	10	7	25	57	106	27
Rotherham United Reserves	42	10	7	25	51	107	27
Denaby United	42	6	5	31	57	159	17

1938-39

Scunthorpe United	42	28	8	6	133	57	64
Barnsley Reserves	42	27	4	11	130	73	68
Shrewsbury Town	42	25	5	12	125	95	55
Nottingham Forest Reserves	42	21	13	8	102	70	55
Grimsby Town Reserves	42	23	6	13	120	74	52
Burton Town	42	22	6	14	115	75	50
Bradford City Reserves	42	20	7	15	107	77	47
Boston United	42	21	5	16	95	90	47
Scarborough	42	18	10	14	79	81	46
Peterborough United	42	20	4	18	99	77	44
Rotherham United Reserves	42	17	9	16	76	83	43
Lincoln City Reserves	42	18	5	19	93	90	41
Doncaster Rovers Reserves	42	18	4	20	95	87	40
Grantham	42	17	6	19	103	118	40
Gainsborough Trinity	42	18	3	21	102	92	39
Bradford Park Avenue Reserves	42	18	3	21	91	83	39
Frickley Colliery	42	19	1	22	96	111	39
Hull City Reserves	42	15	3	24	76	90	33
Mansfield Town Reserves	42	11	7	24	80	112	29
Notts County Reserves	42	11	6	25	60	121	28
Newark Town	42	11	5	26	82	149	27
Denaby United	42	2	4	36	34	218	8

1939-40

The competition was suspended due to outbreak of war.

Emergency Wartime Competition

First Competition

Scunthorpe United	14	9	3	2	53	27	21
Peterborough United	14	8	3	3	49	29	19
Frickley Colliery	13	7	2	4	45	30	16
Newark Town	14	6	2	6	45	51	14
Boston United	14	6	2	6	28	39	14
Denaby United	14	4	4	6	30	39	12
Grantham	14	3	3	8	28	43	9
Gainsborough Trinity	13	2	1	10	25	45	5

Gainsborough Trinity v Frickley Colliery was not played.

The First Competition counted as the Championship.

Second Competition

Peterborough United	14	11	2	1	56	24	24
Scunthorpe United	13	10	1	2	49	18	21
Denaby United	12	5	2	5	24	23	12
Newark Town	12	5	0	7	29	22	10
Boston United	10	5	0	5	21	30	10
Frickley Colliery	9	1	3	5	20	24	5
Grantham	8	1	0	7	6	40	2
Gainsborough Trinity	6	0	0	6	7	31	0

The fixtures were not completed, and this competition was abandoned. Peterborough United beat Scunthorpe United 3-2 in an unofficial match to decide the Championship.

When in 1945-46 the competition was revived with 19 clubs, Bradford City Reserves, Hull City Reserves, Newark Town and Scarborough had left the League. Ollerton Colliery and Ransome & Marles (Newark) had joined the League.

1945-46

Shrewsbury Town	36	25	6	4	133	43	58
Ransome & Marles (Newark)	36	26	5	5	90	39	57
Barnsley Reserves	36	23	6	7	91	50	52
Rotherham United Reserves	36	15	11	10	85	62	41
Grantham	36	18	5	13	91	69	41
Scunthorpe United	36	17	5	13	82	65	40
Frickley Colliery	36	16	6	14	83	72	38
Boston United	36	16	6	14	76	80	38
Peterborough United	36	17	3	16	63	74	37
Grimsby Town Reserves	35	15	4	16	59	64	34
Doncaster Rovers Reserves	36	13	8	15	65	88	34
Gainsborough Trinity	36	15	3	18	100	95	33
Lincoln City Reserves	36	12	6	18	81	101	30
Denaby United	36	10	9	17	70	94	29
Bradford Park Avenue Reserves	36	8	10	18	83	116	26
Nottingham Forest Reserves	35	9	7	19	76	81	25
Ollerton Colliery	36	10	4	22	71	114	24
Notts County Reserves	36	6	11	19	59	110	23
Mansfield Town Reserves	36	7	8	21	66	104	22

Grimsby Town Reserves v Nottingham Forest Reserves was not played.

1946-47

Grimsby Town Reserves	42	29	8	5	133	54	66
Nottingham Forest Reserves	42	26	8	8	119	60	60
Bradford Park Avenue Reserves	42	28	2	12	131	68	58
Scunthorpe United	42	24	9	9	121	61	57
Barnsley Reserves	42	24	8	10	100	57	56
Shrewsbury Town	42	25	4	13	117	77	54
Doncaster Rovers Reserves	42	21	8	13	101	71	50
Grantham	42	19	10	13	102	71	48
Peterborough United	42	18	12	12	90	77	48
Gainsborough Trinity	42	19	9	14	96	79	47
Ransome & Marles (Newark)	42	19	6	17	79	75	44
Denaby United	42	19	6	17	107	104	44
Boston United	42	16	10	16	96	107	42
Scarborough	42	15	9	18	73	83	39
Rotherham United Reserves	42	15	6	21	93	109	36
Notts County Reserves	42	16	4	12	90	113	36
Hull City Reserves	42	12	7	23	68	108	31
Lincoln City Reserves	42	13	4	25	77	113	30
Ollerton Colliery	42	8	5	29	68	130	21
Mansfield Town Reserves	42	7	6	29	84	126	20
Bradford City Reserves	42	7	5	30	66	150	19
Frickley Colliery	42	7	4	31	54	172	18

Barnsley Reserves resigned from the League.

1947-48

Shrewsbury Town	42	28	6	8	98	51	62
Scunthorpe United	42	23	9	10	89	57	55
Nottingham Forest Reserves	42	23	8	11	112	59	54
Bradford Park Avenue Reserves	42	25	2	15	138	97	52
Lincoln City Reserves	42	22	5	15	97	53	49
Peterborough United	42	22	4	16	88	78	48
Gainsborough Trinity	42	19	10	13	88	80	48
Ransome & Marles (Newark)	42	19	9	14	85	76	47
Grimsby Town Reserves	42	18	10	14	101	88	46
Grantham	42	10	6	16	110	99	46
Boston United	42	21	4	17	89	32	46
Doncaster Rovers Reserves	42	17	11	14	93	66	45
Hull City Reserves	42	19	6	17	86	71	44
Denaby United	42	16	9	17	82	84	41
Notts County Reserves	42	16	6	20	72	95	38
York City Reserves	42	13	10	19	69	109	36
Scarborough	42	12	9	21	67	52	33
Mansfield Town Reserves	42	12	9	21	63	82	33
Rotherham United Reserves	42	12	8	22	75	93	32
Frickley Colliery	42	11	9	22	85	119	31
Bradford City Reserves	42	9	5	28	59	111	23
Ollerton Colliery	42	7	1	34	57	168	15

Ollerton Colliery did not seek re-election.

1948-49

Gainsborough Trinity	42	26	8	8	93	69	60
Bradford Park Avenue Reserves	42	26	4	12	117	67	56
Nottingham Forest Reserves	42	25	5	12	116	53	55
Scunthorpe United	42	24	6	12	104	56	54
Grimsby Town Reserves	42	21	9	12	86	65	51
Notts County Reserves	42	18	14	10	79	60	50
Rotherham United Reserves	42	21	7	14	81	60	49
Shrewsbury Town	42	19	7	16	82	70	45
Hull City Reserves	42	16	12	14	86	67	44
Goole Town	42	19	6	17	86	86	44
Lincoln City Reserves	42	18	7	17	89	86	43
Grantham	42	15	12	15	89	79	42
Boston United	42	15	10	17	83	108	40
York City Reserves	42	15	10	17	68	98	40
Ransome & Marles (Newark)	42	15	7	20	82	98	37
Peterborough United	42	15	6	21	58	86	36
Bradford City Reserves	42	12	10	20	72	84	34
Doncaster Rovers Reserves	42	13	8	21	47	63	34
Scarborough	42	11	9	22	49	90	31
Denaby United	42	13	4	25	67	96	30
Mansfield Town Reserves	42	9	8	25	49	81	26
Frickley Colliery	42	8	7	27	51	115	23

1949-50

Nottingham Forest Reserves	46	31	8	7	105	44	78
Grimsby Town Reserves	46	29	7	10	98	58	65
Scunthorpe United	46	29	6	11	99	44	64
Peterborough United	46	23	10	13	91	71	56
Hull City Reserves	46	22	11	13	91	64	55
York City Reserves	46	25	5	16	103	81	55
Rotherham United Reserves	46	20	12	14	79	59	52
Gainsborough Trinity	46	21	10	15	88	74	52
Goole Town	46	22	6	18	76	86	50
Shrewsbury Town	46	19	11	16	96	86	49
Bradford Park Avenue Reserves	46	19	10	17	99	84	48
Denaby United	46	18	12	16	90	72	48
Bradford City Reserves	46	18	12	16	91	84	48
Scarborough	46	18	8	20	106	96	44
Grantham	46	17	9	20	95	118	43
Notts County Reserves	46	15	10	21	84	82	40
Mansfield Town Reserves	46	16	6	23	66	93	40
Frickley Colliery	46	15	9	22	87	94	39
Lincoln City Reserves	46	14	11	21	69	82	39
Worksop Town	46	14	5	27	56	80	33
Halifax Town Reserves	46	10	11	25	66	99	31
Boston United	46	8	14	24	71	113	30
Ransome & Marles (Newark)	46	13	2	31	59	135	28
Doncaster Rovers Reserves	46	9	7	30	63	128	25

Shrewsbury Town resigned from the League. Ransome & Marles (Newark) did not seek re-election.

1950-51

Nottingham Forest Reserves	42	26	9	7	103	45	61
Rotherham United Reserves	42	19	14	9	80	52	52
Goole Town	42	20	12	10	79	57	52
Grimsby Town Reserves	42	23	5	14	84	61	51
Gainsborough Trinity	42	20	8	14	102	80	48
Grantham	42	20	8	14	92	74	48
Bradford City Reserves	42	18	12	12	80	72	48
Mansfield Town Reserves	42	17	13	12	69	50	47
Peterborough United	42	16	15	11	69	65	47
Doncaster Rovers Reserves	42	16	14	12	72	62	46
Scarborough	42	14	14	14	70	70	42
Worksop Town	42	15	12	15	68	70	42
Frickley Colliery	42	15	12	15	73	85	42
Notts County Reserves	42	15	10	17	59	58	40
Boston United	42	15	9	18	62	86	39
Bradford Park Avenue Reserves	42	12	12	18	72	82	36
Denaby United	42	13	10	19	64	77	36
Lincoln City Reserves	42	12	10	20	62	83	34
York City Reserves	42	11	11	20	68	87	33
Hull City Reserves	42	11	10	21	67	74	32
Scunthorpe United Reserves	42	10	11	21	51	90	31
Halifax Town Reserves	42	5	7	30	39	105	17

1951-52

Nottingham Forest Reserves	42	33	6	3	105	29	72
Notts County Reserves	42	30	3	9	108	54	63
Bradford City Reserves	42	25	4	13	96	71	54
Hull City Reserves	42	21	8	13	80	54	50
Peterborough United	42	20	10	12	90	71	50
Scarborough	42	19	10	13	92	76	48
Scunthorpe United Reserves	42	21	6	15	69	61	48
Gainsborough Trinity	42	16	16	10	81	74	48
Boston United	42	18	7	17	89	72	43
Worksop Town	42	15	12	15	72	82	42
Goole Town	42	15	10	17	66	76	40
Rotherham United Reserves	42	16	7	19	80	78	39
Frickley Colliery	42	14	11	17	65	73	39
Grimsby Town Reserves	42	15	7	20	73	73	37
Mansfield Town Reserves	42	12	13	17	63	65	37
Bradford Park Avenue Reserves	42	14	9	19	66	76	37
Doncaster Rovers Reserves	42	11	10	21	72	96	32
Halifax Town Reserves	42	12	8	22	71	96	32
Lincoln City Reserves	42	12	7	23	78	118	31
Grantham	42	13	3	26	65	95	29
Denaby United	42	11	7	24	51	90	29
York City Reserves	42	8	8	26	68	120	24

1952-53

Nottingham Forest Reserves	46	31	8	7	140	59	70
Corby Town	46	28	12	6	112	60	68
Grimsby Town Reserves	46	27	8	11	115	56	62
Hull City Reserves	46	22	15	9	101	62	59
Grantham	46	23	12	11	82	68	58
Lincoln City Reserves	46	24	8	14	119	93	56
Notts County Reserves	46	22	10	14	92	64	54
Peterborough United	46	18	15	13	76	55	51
Rotherham United Reserves	46	18	10	18	94	75	46
Goole Town	46	19	7	20	105	102	45
York City Reserves	46	16	12	18	92	95	44
Gainsborough Trinity	46	19	6	21	82	98	44
Bradford Park Avenue Reserves	46	17	9	20	101	104	43
Mansfield Town Reserves	46	16	10	20	86	95	42
Bradford City Reserves	46	17	8	21	80	112	42
Boston United	46	16	8	22	106	118	40
Scunthorpe United Reserves	46	13	13	20	71	92	39
Doncaster Rovers Reserves	46	16	7	23	68	98	39
Worksop Town	46	14	7	25	65	85	35
Scarborough	46	14	7	25	74	108	35
Frickley Colliery	46	14	6	26	78	112	34
Halifax Town Reserves	46	14	5	27	64	91	33
Denaby United	46	11	11	24	69	115	33
Wisbech Town	46	13	6	27	76	131	32

1953-54

Nottingham Forest Reserves	46	33	6	7	139	44	72
Peterborough United	46	27	8	11	111	73	62
Doncaster Rovers Reserves	46	26	8	12	93	56	60
Corby Town	46	26	8	12	115	76	60
Rotherham United Reserves	46	24	9	13	118	74	57
Hull City Reserves	46	23	8	15	103	71	54
Notts County Reserves	46	23	7	16	104	74	53
Grantham	46	23	6	17	100	85	52
Wisbech Town	46	20	11	15	92	79	51
Worksop Town	46	19	10	17	73	61	48
Grimsby Town Reserves	46	20	8	18	74	62	48
Lincoln City Reserves	46	18	7	21	94	88	43
Scunthorpe United Reserves	46	16	11	19	75	80	43
Boston United	46	18	7	21	93	112	43
Bradford Park Avenue Reserves	46	16	10	20	105	103	42
Gainsborough Trinity	46	17	8	21	82	98	42
Denaby United	46	16	10	20	68	90	42
Frickley Colliery	46	14	13	19	70	81	41
Scarborough	46	14	10	22	80	97	38
Mansfield Town Reserves	46	17	3	26	80	120	37
Goole Town	46	13	8	25	84	134	34
Bradford City Reserves	46	12	7	27	79	123	31
York City Reserves	46	12	5	29	72	125	29
Halifax Town Reserves	46	8	6	32	56	154	22

1954-55

Notts County Reserves	46	27	11	8	135	50	65
Rotherham United Reserves	46	28	7	11	98	55	63
Peterborough United	46	23	16	7	69	38	62
Hull City Reserves	46	26	8	12	102	60	60
Boston United	46	23	10	13	96	48	56
King's Lynn	46	24	8	14	109	83	56
Nottingham Forest Reserves	46	21	9	16	102	80	51
Grantham	46	19	13	14	83	67	51
Gainsborough Trinity	46	22	7	17	81	73	51
Scunthorpe United Reserves	46	19	12	15	82	70	50
Lincoln City Reserves	46	19	10	17	90	83	48
Corby Town	46	17	14	15	73	81	48
Bradford Park Avenue Reserves	46	19	9	18	87	70	47
Worksop Town	46	19	9	18	84	78	47
Doncaster Rovers Reserves	46	17	11	18	75	77	45
Goole Town	46	17	9	20	95	110	43
Grimsby Town Reserves	46	16	9	21	89	98	41
Wisbech Town	46	12	12	22	75	89	36
Mansfield Town Reserves	46	12	11	23	79	104	35
York City Reserves	46	12	11	23	74	106	35
Denaby United	46	12	9	25	69	110	33
Scarborough	46	12	8	26	62	122	32
Frickley Colliery	46	11	7	28	63	121	29
Bradford City Reserves	46	8	4	34	53	142	20

1955-56

Peterborough United	46	33	11	2	137	46	77
Boston United	46	34	4	8	107	42	72
Scunthorpe United Reserves	46	28	6	12	108	67	62
Rotherham United Reserves	46	25	10	11	125	78	60
King's Lynn	46	25	8	13	104	81	58
York City Reserves	46	25	7	14	96	90	57
Nottingham Forest Reserves	46	22	11	13	111	76	55
Notts County Reserves	46	21	12	13	106	72	54
Grantham	46	23	7	16	101	86	53
Wisbech Town	46	19	12	15	92	97	50
Doncaster Rovers Reserves	46	22	4	20	88	76	48
Gainsborough Trinity	46	16	15	15	70	77	47
Hull City Reserves	46	19	8	19	105	85	46
Grimsby Town Reserves	46	19	6	21	88	76	44
Denaby United	46	17	9	20	76	91	43
Worksop Town	46	15	11	20	78	82	41
Corby Town	46	14	12	20	88	101	40
Scarborough	46	13	10	23	90	113	36
Lincoln City Reserves	46	13	9	24	72	103	35
Bradford Park Avenue Reserves	46	12	7	27	78	108	31
Frickley Colliery	46	13	5	28	90	134	31
Mansfield Town Reserves	46	10	7	29	85	141	27
Bradford City Reserves	46	5	10	31	41	119	20
Goole Town	46	5	7	34	66	161	17

1956-57

[illegible]rough United	46	36	6	4	148	35	78
[illegible]n United Reserves	46	32	5	9	133	69	69
[illegible]d	46	23	11	12	97	64	57
[illegible]serves	46	22	9	15	85	63	53
[illegible]es	46	21	11	14	83	78	53
[illegible]	46	22	8	16	110	98	52
[illegible] Reserves	46	16	18	12	90	82	50
[illegible]	46	19	11	16	92	81	49
No[illegible] Reserves	46	20	8	18	97	73	48
Donca[illegible]Reserves	46	20	7	19	97	85	47
King's Lynn	46	18	11	17	96	93	47
Frickley Colliery	46	19	8	19	80	77	46
Grantham	46	15	16	15	94	93	46
Notts County Reserves	46	15	14	17	86	87	44
Grimsby Town Reserves	46	18	7	21	108	86	43
Denaby United	46	19	5	22	113	118	43
Bradford City Reserves	46	17	7	22	92	109	41
Bradford Park Avenue Reserves	46	17	6	23	69	97	40
Gainsborough Trinity	46	15	10	21	69	101	40
Wisbech Town	46	14	11	21	63	97	39
Goole Town	46	13	11	22	64	89	37
Hull City Reserves	46	12	11	23	84	116	35
Scarborough	46	13	7	26	86	128	33
Mansfield Town Reserves	46	4	6	36	55	173	14

1957-58

Peterborough United	46	35	5	6	160	46	75
Wisbech Town	46	31	6	9	123	69	68
Boston United	46	28	7	11	123	59	63
York City Reserves	46	21	12	13	94	73	54
Grimsby Town Reserves	46	22	10	14	88	75	54
King's Lynn	46	21	19	16	91	69	51
Scarborough	46	20	10	16	80	70	50
Corby Town	46	21	7	18	106	111	49
Nottingham Forest Reserves	46	21	6	19	96	83	48
Frickley Colliery	46	16	16	13	80	87	48
Scunthorpe United Reserves	46	20	6	20	80	95	46
Gainsborough Trinity	46	19	8	19	89	99	46
Lincoln City Reserves	46	17	11	18	76	81	45
Mansfield Town Reserves	46	18	8	20	108	105	44
Notts County Reserves	46	20	3	23	97	95	43
Hull City Reserves	46	16	10	20	78	84	42
Goole Town	46	14	13	19	78	98	41
Grantham	46	15	10	21	89	112	40
Bradford City Reserves	46	12	13	21	95	114	37
Doncaster Rovers Reserves	46	12	11	23	89	119	35
Bradford Park Avenue Reserves	46	12	11	23	74	101	35
Rotherham United Reserves	46	13	9	24	72	99	35
Denaby United	46	9	10	27	62	117	28
Worksop Town	46	8	11	27	70	127	27

Boston United, Bradford City Reserves, Bradford Park Avenue Reserves, Corby Town, Doncaster Rovers Reserves, Grimsby Town Reserves, Hull City Reserves, King's Lynn, Lincoln City Reserves, Mansfield Town Reserves, Nottingham Forest Reserves, Notts County Reserves, Rotherham United Reserves, Wisbech Town and York City Reserves all resigned from the League.

1958-59

Peterborough United	36	32	4	0	137	26	68
Ashington	36	28	4	4	125	40	60
North Shields	36	21	6	9	82	49	48
South Shields	36	19	8	9	79	45	46
Blyth Spartans	36	18	10	8	79	52	46
Skegness Town	36	17	7	12	73	71	41
Horden Colliery	36	15	10	11	68	73	40
Consett	36	16	4	16	72	72	36
Scarborough	36	13	9	14	63	79	35
Frickley Colliery	36	12	9	15	70	75	33
Goole Town	36	12	7	17	72	90	31
Gainsborough Trinity	36	10	10	16	70	77	30
Sutton Town	36	10	9	17	69	98	29
Spennymoor United	36	8	12	16	55	92	28
Scunthorpe United Reserves	36	8	10	18	58	70	26
Denaby United	36	10	3	23	57	107	23
Stockton	36	7	8	21	65	106	22
Grantham	36	7	7	22	66	90	21
Worksop Town	36	10	1	25	50	98	21

Grantham and Scunthorpe United Reserves resigned from the League.

1959-60

Peterborough United	32	23	6	3	108	37	52
North Shields	32	22	5	5	76	27	49
Ashington	32	19	7	6	90	40	45
South Shields	32	16	8	8	65	41	40
Blyth Spartans	32	13	10	9	74	51	36
Stockton	32	12	8	12	53	66	32
Goole Town	32	13	5	14	62	78	31
Consett	32	13	4	15	54	65	30
Spennymoor United	32	12	6	14	47	57	30
Horden Colliery	32	12	5	15	46	62	29
Gainsborough Trinity	32	7	14	11	41	60	28
Skegness Town	32	9	9	14	50	64	27
Scarborough	32	9	8	15	48	65	26
Worksop Town	32	10	4	18	41	70	24
Sutton Town	32	6	11	15	44	76	23
Denaby United	32	8	6	18	44	68	22
Frickley Colliery	32	7	6	19	54	70	20

1960-61

No competition.

1961-62

Matlock Town	34	23	5	6	99	52	51
Retford Town	34	20	6	8	88	66	46
Ilkeston Town	34	18	7	9	65	38	43
Worksop Town	34	20	3	11	88	60	43
Denaby United	34	17	7	10	60	48	41
Sutton Town	34	18	4	12	71	53	40
Belper Town	34	15	8	11	78	50	38
Grantham	34	14	7	13	71	58	35
Goole Town	34	13	7	14	68	63	33
Gainsborough Trinity	34	14	5	15	65	64	33
Loughborough United	34	13	7	14	61	61	33
Bourne Town	34	10	9	15	59	71	29
Heanor Town	34	11	7	16	54	66	29
Long Eaton United	34	12	5	17	53	75	29
Skegness Town	34	10	6	18	55	82	26
Stamford	34	10	6	18	47	97	26
Spalding United	34	9	3	22	47	83	21
Alfreton Town	34	6	4	24	48	100	16

1962-63

Loughborough United	38	25	10	3	114	43	60
Worksop Town	38	25	7	6	101	40	57
Matlock Town	38	22	7	9	102	59	51
Ilkeston Town	38	18	14	6	61	64	50
Alfreton Town	38	18	14	6	83	50	50
Boston United	38	19	12	7	89	66	50
Belper Town	38	20	8	10	79	52	48
Grantham	38	19	9	10	95	67	47
Sutton Town	38	19	8	11	75	69	46
Goole Town	38	14	10	14	72	62	38
Heanor Town	38	15	7	16	73	74	37
Bourne Town	38	15	7	16	75	88	37
Denaby United	38	15	5	18	63	69	35
Retford Town	38	12	6	20	72	82	30
Gainsborough Trinity	38	12	3	23	69	94	27
Stamford	38	12	1	25	61	112	25
Skegness Town	38	8	6	24	42	95	22
Long Eaton United	38	8	5	25	51	86	21
Holbeach United	38	6	7	25	42	96	19
Spalding United	38	3	4	31	28	109	10

Holbeach United failed to gain re-election.

1963-64

Grantham	42	33	6	3	152	56	72
Scarborough	42	26	11	5	107	45	63
Lockheed-Leamington	42	23	8	11	114	60	54
Alfreton Town	42	22	10	10	88	56	54
Retford Town	42	22	8	12	94	70	52
Gainsborough Trinity	42	22	4	16	92	81	48
Heanor Town	42	20	6	15	76	71	47
Long Eaton United	42	17	10	15	70	82	44
Worksop Town	42	16	11	15	93	66	43
Goole Town	42	18	7	17	94	99	43
Boston United	42	20	2	20	91	92	42
Belper Town	42	16	10	16	87	94	42
Ilkeston Town	42	15	11	16	73	75	41
Spalding United	42	15	10	17	80	69	40
Sutton Town	42	17	6	19	79	78	40
Arnold	42	14	12	16	70	84	40
Loughborough United	42	15	6	21	92	94	36
Matlock Town	42	14	4	24	80	105	32
Bourne Town	42	11	6	25	94	136	28
Skegness Town	42	8	11	23	57	87	27
Bourne Town	42	8	7	27	52	123	23
Denaby United	42	4	5	33	45	157	13

Boston United resigned from the League.

1964-65

Lockheed-Leamington	42	28	9	5	113	[illegible]	[illegible]
Grantham	42	28	5	9	110	[illegible]	[illegible]
Heanor Town	42	25	8	9	[illegible]	[illegible]	[illegible]
Ashton United	42	23	8	11	[illegible]	[illegible]	[illegible]
Scarborough	42	22	10	10	[illegible]	[illegible]	[illegible]
Goole Town	42	24	5	[illegible]	[illegible]	[illegible]	[illegible]
Alfreton Town	42	21	8	[illegible]	[illegible]	[illegible]	[illegible]
Long Eaton United	42	20	7	[illegible]	[illegible]	[illegible]	[illegible]
Retford Town	42	18	8	[illegible]	[illegible]	[illegible]	44
Belper Town	42	18	8	[illegible]	[illegible]	[illegible]	44
Gainsborough Trinity	42	16	11	15	83	74	43
Arnold	42	18	7	17	75	76	43
Sutton Town	42	14	14	14	61	61	42
Stamford	42	16	6	20	71	81	38
Spalding United	42	14	9	19	71	87	37
Loughborough United	42	12	12	18	66	86	36
Matlock Town	42	13	9	20	74	90	35
Worksop Town	42	13	9	20	67	82	35
Ilkeston Town	42	10	6	26	58	110	26
Skegness Town	42	10	6	26	45	110	26
Bourne Town	42	6	6	30	64	125	[illegible]
Denaby United	42	4	7	31	54	153	15

Bourne Town did not seek re-election.
Denaby United did not gain re-election.

1965-66

Worksop Town	42	28	7	7	155	71	63
Heanor Town	42	27	5	10	112	59	59
Grantham	42	26	7	9	115	63	59
Ilkeston Town	42	24	9	9	115	71	57
Lockheed-Leamington	42	21	12	9	126	81	54
Gainsborough Trinity	42	23	5	14	80	64	51
Arnold	42	20	10	12	104	90	50
Retford Town	42	20	6	16	93	86	46
Goole Town	42	19	7	16	95	75	45
Alfreton Town	42	19	7	16	100	87	45
Scarborough	42	19	7	16	89	80	45
Scunthorpe United Reserves	42	16	8	18	93	90	40
Belper Town	42	17	6	19	82	91	40
Matlock Town	42	14	11	17	63	81	39
Loughborough United	42	13	11	18	84	93	37
Lincoln City Reserves	42	12	7	23	83	119	31
Ashton United	42	12	7	23	75	108	31
Stamford	42	11	8	23	66	110	30
Long Eaton United	42	9	11	22	49	90	29
Spalding United	42	10	9	23	51	97	29
Sutton Town	42	10	8	24	61	97	28
Skegness Town	42	7	2	33	64	152	16

Ashton United resigned from the League.

1966-67

Gainsborough Trinity	42	30	5	7	105	42	65
Worksop Town	42	30	5	7	102	52	65
Grantham	42	26	5	11	106	68	57
Arnold	42	24	6	12	106	68	54
Lockheed-Leamington	42	23	6	13	105	80	52
Scarborough	42	22	7	13	89	59	51
Heanor Town	42	21	7	14	97	65	49
Alfreton Town	42	20	7	15	77	74	47
Goole Town	42	18	10	14	87	66	46
Ilkeston Town	42	20	5	17	97	83	45
Spalding United	42	19	6	17	86	82	44
Retford Town	42	15	9	18	76	82	39
Long Eaton United	42	11	14	17	51	68	36
Skegness Town	42	13	8	21	74	111	34
Grimsby Town Reserves	42	14	5	23	76	83	33
Matlock Town	42	13	7	22	60	90	33
Lincoln City Reserves	42	11	10	21	65	92	32
Belper Town	42	11	10	21	55	79	32
Stamford	42	10	9	23	64	127	29
Sutton Town	42	10	8	24	55	93	28
Scunthorpe United Reserves	42	12	3	27	69	99	27
Loughborough United	42	8	10	24	66	105	26

1967-68

Ilkeston Town	40	22	11	7	66	35	55
Heanor Town	40	25	5	10	90	51	55
Arnold	40	20	12	8	100	62	52
Gainsborough Trinity	40	21	9	10	80	47	51
Goole Town	40	19	10	11	71	61	48
Grantham	40	19	10	11	79	68	48
Scarborough	40	21	4	15	67	52	46
Long Eaton United	40	17	11	12	48	36	45
Worksop Town	40	16	13	11	76	68	45
Alfreton Town	40	18	6	16	84	71	42
Matlock Town	40	18	6	16	74	71	42
Sutton Town	40	15	11	14	64	60	41
Lockheed-Leamington	40	16	6	18	66	69	38
Retford Town	40	14	7	19	70	64	35
Belper Town	40	13	9	18	70	69	35
Grimsby Town Reserves	40	10	11	19	53	61	31
Stamford	40	11	9	20	53	89	31
Scunthorpe United Reserves	40	10	10	20	49	90	30
Skegness Town	40	9	9	22	56	94	27
Loughborough United	40	6	13	21	43	78	25
Spalding United	40	6	6	28	50	113	18

1968-69

Matlock Town	34	22	7	5	84	33	51
Sutton Town	34	21	9	4	61	33	51
Arnold	34	18	9	7	73	52	45
Grantham	34	16	10	8	78	47	42
Skegness Town	34	16	10	8	57	40	42
Ilkeston Town	34	17	6	11	61	35	40
Alfreton Town	34	13	13	8	62	46	39
Long Eaton United	34	15	8	11	49	56	38
Warley	34	13	8	13	51	42	34
Lockheed-Leamington	34	12	8	14	53	64	32
Heanor Town	34	12	7	15	67	51	31
Stamford	34	11	8	15	50	57	30
Ashby	34	10	6	18	44	69	26
Boston	34	7	11	16	38	53	25
Retford Town	34	9	6	19	39	69	24
Loughborough United	34	9	6	19	44	82	24
Barton Town	34	7	7	20	35	78	21
Belper Town	34	5	7	22	40	79	17

1969-70

Alfreton Town	34	30	3	1	119	19	63
Grantham	34	21	7	6	81	40	49
Arnold	34	18	9	7	80	48	45
Ashby	34	17	11	6	59	42	45
Sutton Town	34	18	7	9	66	34	43
Worksop Town	34	17	6	11	76	45	40
Ilkeston Town	34	17	5	12	65	51	39
Heanor Town	34	17	3	14	72	53	37
Lockheed-Leamington	34	16	4	14	65	59	36
Retford Town	34	16	3	15	65	65	35
Skegness Town	34	13	8	13	54	44	34
Stamford	34	13	4	17	63	79	30
Warley	34	8	7	19	37	81	23
Boston	34	8	6	20	32	72	22
Loughborough United	34	9	3	22	51	93	21
Long Eaton United	34	5	10	19	45	79	20
Barton Town	34	7	4	23	38	92	18
Belper Town	34	4	4	26	31	104	12

Barton Town did not seek re-election.

1970-71

Grantham	34	26	6	2	100	28	58
Arnold	34	21	8	5	78	45	50
Frickley Colliery	34	19	11	4	68	38	49
Ilkeston Town	34	18	10	6	53	31	46
Alfreton Town	34	18	6	10	83	39	42
Lockheed-Leamington	34	18	6	10	64	41	42
Worksop Town	34	13	10	11	65	72	36
Skegness Town	34	9	14	11	39	44	32
Sutton Town	34	13	5	16	52	52	31
Retford Town	34	13	5	16	65	88	31
Belper Town	34	10	9	15	38	44	29
Long Eaton United	34	11	6	17	50	63	28
Heanor Town	34	7	13	14	46	60	27
Loughborough United	34	7	13	14	37	53	27
Ashby	34	7	12	15	39	60	26
Boston	34	7	11	16	36	54	25
Stamford	34	3	12	19	31	72	18
Warley	34	5	5	24	33	93	15

Ilkeston Town and Lockheed-Leamington resigned from the League.
Warley did not seek re-election.

1971-72

Grantham	34	25	5	4	106	32	55
Alfreton Town	34	22	5	7	85	39	49
Skegness Town	34	18	8	8	62	34	44
Long Eaton United	34	16	10	8	49	38	42
Belper Town	34	16	9	9	46	33	41
Worksop Town	34	17	7	10	70	53	41
Arnold	34	18	4	12	70	54	40
Gateshead	34	17	5	12	60	53	39
Frickley Athletic	34	13	8	13	46	43	34
Boston	34	13	7	14	44	48	33
Sutton Town	34	10	11	13	47	52	31
Retford Town	34	11	8	15	61	69	30
Eastwood Town	34	9	9	16	50	65	27
Ashby	34	10	7	17	47	62	27
Heanor Town	34	11	5	18	51	68	27
Kimberley Town	34	7	8	19	31	72	22
Stamford	34	5	8	20	33	71	19
Loughborough United	34	5	1	28	27	98	11

Frickley Athletic were previously known as Frickley Colliery. Stamford did not seek re-election. Grantham and Heanor Town resigned from the League.

1972-73

Worksop Town	34	26	3	5	101	35	55
Frickley Athletic	34	22	6	6	75	26	50
Kimberley Town	34	20	5	9	66	38	45
Alfreton Town	34	17	10	7	80	44	44
Sutton Town	34	16	12	6	55	33	44
Belper Town	34	17	9	8	52	31	43
Boston	34	16	10	8	62	30	42
Long Eaton United	34	14	7	13	51	56	35
Gateshead	34	14	6	14	72	68	34
Arnold	34	12	10	12	57	57	34
Skegness Town	34	13	6	15	67	52	32
Ashby	34	11	8	15	54	52	30
Eastwood Town	34	10	9	15	51	56	29
Bridlington Trinity	34	9	5	20	58	74	23
Hednesford Town	34	11	1	22	49	93	23
Stockton	34	6	10	18	43	50	22
Retford Town	34	7	8	19	36	81	22
Loughborough United	34	2	1	31	24	167	5

Loughborough United did not seek re-election. Stockton resigned from the League.

1973-74

Alfreton Town	32	22	5	5	77	37	49
Worksop Town	32	21	4	7	90	29	46
Ashby	32	19	7	6	52	28	45
Arnold	32	19	7	6	50	31	45
Frickley Athletic	32	15	6	11	71	61	36
Sutton Town	32	13	8	11	35	34	34
Boston	32	12	7	13	47	46	31
Kimberley Town	32	12	7	13	40	49	31
Long Eaton United	32	11	8	13	41	47	30
Belper Town	32	10	9	13	26	33	29
Eastwood Town	32	9	10	13	34	51	28
Retford Town	32	12	4	16	35	55	28
Bridlington Trinity	32	12	3	17	50	62	27
Ilkeston Town	32	9	9	14	41	54	27
Skegness Town	32	8	7	17	32	45	23
Clifton	32	8	6	18	30	55	22
Hednesford Town	32	4	5	23	30	64	13

Gateshead withdrew beforethe season began. Hednesford Town did not seek re-election. Worksop Town resigned from the League.

1974-75

Boston	34	21	11	2	70	25	53
Eastwood Town	34	23	7	4	67	36	53
Alfreton Town	34	22	6	6	80	40	50
Skegness Town	34	18	11	5	67	37	47
Arnold	34	17	9	8	61	37	43
Mexborough Town Athletic	34	17	5	12	54	48	39
Frickley Athletic	34	12	9	13	52	56	33
Heanor Town	34	11	11	12	41	46	33
Sutton Town	34	11	9	14	44	43	31
Ashby	34	9	13	12	41	46	31
Retford Town	34	9	12	13	32	36	30
Belper Town	34	6	17	11	30	37	29
Ilkeston Town	34	9	11	14	29	49	29
Long Eaton United	34	8	12	14	42	54	28
Kimberley Town	34	8	9	17	38	61	25
Louth United	34	5	10	19	24	62	20
Clifton	34	4	14	19	33	62	19
Bridlington Town	34	6	7	21	31	61	19

The 18 teams listed above became the Premier Division with a First Division of 16 new clubs formed. Goal difference replaced goal average for season 1975-76.

1975-76

Premier Division

Eastwood Town	34	23	6	5	70	36	52
Arnold	34	20	9	5	74	44	49
Long Eaton United	34	17	12	5	47	31	46
Alfreton Town	34	19	6	9	76	41	44
Bridlington Trinity	34	18	6	10	56	36	42
Mexborough Town Athletic	34	15	10	9	71	45	40
Boston	34	14	8	12	54	47	36
Frickley Athletic	34	10	16	8	50	45	36
Belper Town	34	14	8	12	36	32	36
Kimberley Town	34	14	6	14	47	56	34
Ilkeston Town	34	12	8	14	52	61	32
Skegness Town	34	11	9	14	41	40	31
Louth United	34	10	10	14	57	60	30
Sutton Town	34	9	12	13	39	46	30
Clifton	34	5	12	17	37	63	22
Retford Town	34	6	7	21	37	79	19
Heanor Town	34	4	9	21	33	69	17
Ashby	34	4	8	22	28	74	16

Frickley Athletic resigned from the League.

First Division

Brimington	28	20	4	4	63	18	44
Arnold Kingswell	28	18	6	4	81	26	42
Long Eaton Grange	28	17	8	3	56	22	42
Linby Colliery	28	17	5	6	61	37	39
Staveley Works	28	12	11	5	63	32	35
Oakham United	28	11	5	12	49	45	27
Clifton Reserves	28	11	5	12	43	52	27
Clay Cross	28	9	9	10	45	57	27
Eastwood Reserves	28	9	6	13	29	46	24
Arnold Reserves	28	9	5	14	40	54	23
Long Eaton United Reserves	28	7	7	14	37	47	21
Sutton Town Reserves	28	7	7	14	42	55	21
Belper Town Reserves	28	8	5	15	37	62	21
Retford Town Reserves	28	7	3	18	39	76	17
Kimberley Town Reserves	28	4	2	22	29	85	10

Worksop Town Reserves resigned during the season and their record was expunged. Kimberley Town Reserves and Retford Town Reserves also resigned from the League.

1976-77

Premier Division

Alfreton Town	34	24	5	5	79	33	53
Long Eaton United	34	20	6	8	66	36	46
Brigg Town	34	16	13	5	54	32	45
Arnold	34	18	6	10	63	38	42
Eastwood Town	34	14	11	9	57	41	39
Mexborough Town Athletic	34	14	11	9	50	37	39
Boston	34	14	10	10	42	26	38
Louth United	34	14	8	12	61	55	36
Sutton Town	34	12	11	11	39	45	35
Bridlington Trinity	34	12	8	14	43	51	32
Kimberley Town	34	12	6	16	40	54	30
Heanor Town	34	10	9	15	38	59	29
Skegness Town	34	10	7	17	29	42	27
Belper Town	34	8	10	16	31	48	26
Ilkeston Town	34	9	8	17	41	66	26
Clifton	34	6	13	15	28	51	25
Retford Town	34	7	8	19	39	59	22
Ashby	34	6	10	18	34	61	22

First Division

Long Eaton Grange	32	22	6	4	77	18	50
Staveley Works	32	21	7	4	64	31	49
Arnold Kingswell	32	19	9	4	69	24	47
Linby Colliery	32	20	6	6	72	35	46
Clay Cross	32	16	8	8	66	48	40
Carr Vale United	32	16	7	9	60	49	39
Brimington	32	13	11	8	44	31	37
Attenborough	32	12	9	11	59	54	33
Clifton Reserves	32	13	6	13	61	67	32
Dinnington Colliery	32	10	8	14	45	43	28
Oakham United	32	11	5	16	64	66	27
Arnold Reserves	32	9	7	16	42	66	23
Eastwood Town Reserves	32	6	11	15	35	67	23
Long Eaton United Reserves	32	8	5	19	39	66	21
Ilkeston Town Reserves	32	7	4	21	34	68	18
Sutton Town Reserves	32	6	3	23	27	86	15
Belper Town Reserves	32	4	6	22	23	62	14

Arnold Reserves had 2 points deducted.
Brimington and Sutton Town Reserves both resigned from the League.

1977-78

Premier Division

Brigg Town	32	26	5	1	70	23	57
Eastwood Town	32	10	5	7	66	29	45
Louth United	32	18	8	6	77	54	44
Alfreton Town	32	20	2	10	52	37	42
Mexborough Town Athletic	32	14	9	9	55	41	37
Boston	32	15	5	12	50	37	35
Skegness Town	32	12	9	11	52	48	33
Long Eaton United	32	12	8	12	45	34	32
Belper Town	32	9	13	10	39	42	31
Arnold	32	11	8	13	42	51	30
Sutton Town	32	10	9	13	43	50	29
Heanor Town	32	8	11	13	40	50	27
Bridlington Trinity	32	7	10	15	30	55	24
Retford Town	32	8	6	18	49	74	22
Ashby	32	5	10	17	40	64	20
Ilkeston Town	32	5	9	18	46	74	19
Kimberley Town	32	5	7	20	33	66	17

Clifton resigned during the season, and their record was expunged.

First Division

Staveley Works	32	21	5	6	87	26	47
Linby Colliery	32	21	4	7	78	29	46
Long Eaton Grange	32	19	8	5	65	23	46
Carr Vale United	32	17	8	7	63	34	42
Ripley Town	32	17	7	8	56	38	41
T.I. Chesterfield	32	17	7	8	57	43	41
Oakham United	32	17	3	12	50	43	37
Clay Cross Works	32	15	5	12	52	47	35
Arnold Reserves	32	14	6	12	71	58	34
Arnold Kingswell	32	12	8	12	47	42	32
Long Eaton United Reserves	32	14	4	14	42	40	32
Attenborough	32	12	4	16	55	54	28
Eastwood Reserves	32	7	5	20	52	81	19
Dinnington Colliery	32	7	5	20	34	65	19
Ilkeston Town Reserves	32	7	4	21	31	71	18
Belper Town Reserves	32	5	5	22	38	90	15
Kimberley Town Reserves	32	4	4	24	28	122	12

Clifton Reserves resigned during the season and their record was expunged. Clay Cross Works was previously known as Clay Cross. Belper Town Reserves, Dinnington Colliery and Ilkeston Town Reserves also resigned from the League.

1978-79

Premier Division

Boston	36	24	6	6	71	27	54
Skegness Town	36	23	8	5	65	31	54
Mexborough Town Athletic	36	21	8	7	57	35	50
Eastwood Town	36	19	10	7	56	35	48
Bridlington Trinity	36	16	11	9	76	43	43
Arnold	36	14	14	8	56	50	42
Sutton Town	36	16	7	13	53	50	39
Long Eaton United	36	16	6	14	51	40	38
Brigg Town	36	12	9	15	52	54	33
Ashby	36	13	7	16	36	48	33
Retford Town	36	12	8	16	49	49	32
Appleby Frodingham Athletic	36	13	6	17	55	63	32
Ilkeston Town	36	11	9	16	52	61	31
Kimberley Town	36	7	16	13	46	54	30
Louth United	36	10	7	19	43	72	27
Spalding United	36	7	12	17	44	68	26
Alfreton Town	36	6	13	17	39	61	25
Heanor Town	36	7	10	19	37	64	24
Belper Town	36	6	11	19	43	76	23

Louth United resigned from the League.

First Division

Long Eaton Grange	30	22	4	4	51	23	48
Arnold Kingswell	30	21	4	5	79	30	46
Oakham United	30	17	7	6	70	36	41
Creswell Colliery	30	14	10	6	53	37	38
Linby Colliery	30	14	7	9	58	36	35
Staveley Works	30	13	9	8	42	33	35
Grantham Reserves	30	9	12	9	40	37	30
Long Eaton United Reserves	30	13	2	15	43	50	28
Eastwood Town Reserves	30	9	8	13	45	52	26
Attenborough	30	11	4	15	45	60	26
T.I. Chesterfield	30	8	9	13	36	39	25
Arnold Reserves	30	8	9	13	32	49	25
Clay Cross Works	30	8	5	17	27	54	21
Carr Vale United	30	6	8	16	27	54	20
Kimberley Town Reserves	30	5	9	16	34	53	19
Ripley Town	30	5	7	18	21	60	17

T.I. Chesterfield, Clay Cross Works, Kimberley Town Reserves and Ripley Town all resigned from the League.

1979-80

Premier Division

Belper Town	34	18	11	5	50	25	47
Bridlington Trinity	34	19	9	6	56	34	47
Boston	34	18	8	8	60	28	44
Long Eaton United	34	17	9	8	50	32	43
Mexborough Town Athletic	34	13	13	8	46	38	39
Eastwood Town	34	16	6	12	57	43	38
Arnold	34	13	11	10	54	42	37
Heanor Town	34	14	9	11	53	49	37
Brigg Town	34	13	10	11	45	45	36
Alfreton Town	34	11	13	10	45	46	35
Skegness Town	34	11	11	12	46	45	33
Ashby	34	12	7	15	43	52	31
Ilkeston Town	34	9	12	13	36	37	30
Kimberley Town	34	11	8	15	38	53	30
Appleby Frodingham Athletic	34	9	10	15	55	61	28
Spalding United	34	5	13	16	32	51	23
Sutton Town	34	6	10	18	33	58	22
Retford Town	34	3	6	25	23	83	12

Retford Town were not re-elected.

First Division

Arnold Kingswell	30	17	11	2	76	37	45
Oakham United	30	19	5	6	63	34	43
Staveley Works	30	15	9	6	51	30	39
Borrowash Victoria	30	14	10	6	53	26	38
Long Eaton Grange	30	13	11	6	55	31	37
Linby Colliery	30	14	8	8	59	51	36
Creswell Colliery	30	13	8	9	51	43	34
Sutton Trinity	30	14	5	11	60	51	33
Eastwood Town Reserves	30	11	6	13	49	49	28
Arnold Reserves	30	10	8	12	34	39	28
Grantham Reserves	30	11	4	15	31	39	26
Carr Vale United	30	7	8	15	39	60	22
Attenborough	30	9	2	19	39	60	20
Long Eaton United Reserves	30	6	7	17	48	95	19
Retford Rail	30	6	5	19	27	65	17
Rolls Royce (Hucknall)	30	5	5	20	52	77	15

Grantham Reserves resigned from the League.

1980-81

Premier Division

Boston	34	23	9	2	70	18	55
Alfreton Town	34	16	10	8	73	40	42
Eastwood Town	34	16	9	9	63	41	41
Bridlington Trinity	34	15	10	9	63	40	40
Guisborough Town	34	16	7	11	60	48	39
Belper Town	34	15	8	11	44	43	38
Arnold	34	14	8	12	55	47	36
Heanor Town	34	13	10	11	57	52	36
Skegness Town	34	12	11	11	49	52	35
Long Eaton United	34	13	8	13	54	51	34
Appleby Frodingham Athletic	34	12	10	12	56	56	34
Sutton Town	34	12	10	12	48	51	34
Mexborough Town Athletic	34	12	5	17	42	67	29
Spalding United	34	10	7	17	28	47	27
Ashby	34	12	3	19	40	60	27
Ilkeston Town	34	7	9	18	44	65	23
Brigg Town	34	6	10	18	42	63	22
Kimberley Town	34	6	8	20	34	81	20

Kimberley Town were not re-elected to the Premier Division but did gain election to the First Division.

First Division

Borrowash Victoria	30	22	6	2	79	32	50
Staveley Works	30	20	6	4	67	24	46
Arnold Kingswell	30	17	8	5	71	37	42
Sutton Trinity	30	17	5	8	52	27	39
Folk House Old Boys	30	15	6	9	42	28	36
Long Eaton Grange	30	13	7	10	42	40	33
Oakham United	30	11	10	9	43	45	32
Linby Colliery	30	10	7	13	41	44	27
Creswell Colliery	30	8	9	13	37	53	25
Long Eaton United Reserves	30	10	4	16	41	57	24
Retford Hall	30	9	5	16	40	50	23
Eastwood Town Reserves	30	6	11	13	45	61	23
Carr Vale United	30	9	5	16	38	56	23
Arnold Reserves	30	7	7	16	42	58	21
Rolls Royce (Hucknall)	30	8	4	18	39	60	20
Attenborough	30	6	4	20	25	72	16

Carr Vale United and Linby Colliery resigned from the League.

1981-82

Premier Division

Shepshed Charterhouse	34	22	7	5	78	26	51
Alfreton Town	34	20	7	7	64	24	47
Eastwood Town	34	19	8	7	62	34	46
Spalding United	34	14	14	6	49	34	42
Guisborough Town	34	16	9	9	49	37	41
Appleby Frodingham Athletic	34	16	8	10	53	50	40
Heanor Town	34	12	15	7	40	32	39
Mexborough Town Athletic	34	14	8	12	45	41	36
Boston	34	12	11	11	45	35	35
Skegness Town	34	12	11	11	32	37	35
Long Eaton United	34	11	12	11	44	50	34
Belper Town	34	10	13	11	47	49	33
Bridlington Trinity	34	10	9	15	48	56	29
Ilkeston Town	34	8	9	17	35	46	25
Brigg Town	34	6	11	17	30	61	23
Arnold	34	9	4	21	46	74	22
Sutton Town	34	5	8	21	27	67	18
Ashby	34	4	8	22	24	65	16

Division One

Staveley Works	30	21	7	2	70	18	49
Arnold Kingswell	30	22	5	3	66	22	49
Kimberley Town	30	19	7	4	72	38	45
Rolls Royce (Hucknall)	30	15	7	8	55	38	37
Oakham United	30	14	5	11	46	37	33
Sutton Trinity	30	12	9	9	34	30	33
Graham Street Prims	30	13	6	11	52	41	32
Creswell Colliery	30	14	3	13	48	50	31
Arnold Reserves	30	12	6	12	50	47	30
Borrowash Victoria	30	10	10	10	41	38	30
Folk House Old Boys	30	10	8	12	37	51	28
Attenborough	30	7	5	18	30	57	19
Eastwood Town Reserves	30	6	6	18	37	79	18
Long Eaton Grange	30	5	7	18	34	57	17
Retford Rail	30	4	8	18	35	66	16
Long Eaton United Reserves	30	3	7	20	33	71	13

ATHENIAN LEAGUE

1912-13

Catford Southend	16	11	3	2	50	15	25
Barnet & Alston	16	9	3	4	36	17	21
Tufnell Park	16	8	5	3	25	13	21
Finchley	16	8	4	4	19	11	20
Grays Athletic	16	4	6	6	18	23	14
Chelmsford	16	5	3	8	21	36	13
Enfield	16	3	6	7	18	28	12
Chesham Town	16	3	4	9	21	42	10
Romford Town	16	2	4	10	17	40	8

1913-14

Tufnell Park	22	15	3	4	61	24	33
Luton Clarence	22	15	2	5	64	34	32
Grays Athletic	22	13	3	6	43	27	29
Metrogas	22	11	3	8	62	52	25
Enfield	22	10	3	9	52	37	23
Barnet & Alston	22	9	4	9	32	28	22
Catford Southend	22	7	7	8	35	41	21
Romford Town	22	8	5	9	47	65	21
Finchley	22	8	3	11	53	47	19
Hastings & St Leonards	22	7	2	13	38	59	16
Chelmsford	22	6	1	15	32	68	13
Chesham Town	22	4	2	16	24	61	10

1914-15

Chesham Town, Grays Athletic, Hastings & St Leonards and Romford Town left the League. Hampstead Town, Old Kingstonians, Summerstown and Tooting joined the League.
No Competition was held due to World War I.

1915-16 to 1918-19

No competition was held due to World War I.

1919-20

Luton Clarence	22	16	5	1	71	13	37
Metrogas	22	12	5	5	63	43	29
Barnet	22	11	4	7	53	31	26
Hampstead Town	22	19	6	6	43	37	26
Bromley	22	10	4	8	41	35	24
Summerstown	22	9	6	7	31	29	24
Wimbledon	22	8	5	9	44	43	21
Kingstonian	22	7	4	11	49	53	18
Chelmsford	22	7	3	12	38	51	17
Southall	22	7	1	14	28	51	15
Uxbridge Town	22	7	1	14	24	69	15
Cheshunt	22	4	1	14	42	71	12

1920-21

St Albans City	22	14	5	3	53	29	33
Wimbledon	22	14	3	5	41	22	31
Hampstead Town	22	12	4	6	46	41	28
Metrogas	22	11	4	7	46	31	26
Luton Clarence	22	11	2	9	57	40	24
Barnet	22	11	2	9	49	35	24
Bromley	22	8	4	10	38	42	20
Summerstown	22	9	2	11	38	42	20
Chelmsford	22	8	3	11	39	42	19
Southall	22	6	6	10	31	48	18
Kingstonian	22	6	4	12	30	49	16
West London Old Boys	22	1	3	18	14	61	5

1921-22

St Albans City	26	18	5	3	71	23	41
Metrogas	26	14	8	4	55	36	36
Summerstown	26	12	7	7	40	35	31
Hampstead Town	26	12	5	9	40	38	29
Southall	26	11	5	10	46	49	27
Bromley	26	11	5	10	31	35	27
Cheshunt	26	11	4	11	47	52	26
Sutton United	26	11	3	12	57	56	25
Enfield	26	8	7	11	48	48	23
Luton Clarence	26	8	5	13	50	53	21
Guildford	26	6	9	11	39	52	21
Barnet	26	6	8	12	29	45	20
Chelmsford	26	6	7	13	26	44	19
Kingstonian	26	6	6	14	34	47	18

1922-23

Bromley	24	18	4	2	64	25	40
St Albans City	24	15	4	5	69	31	34
Southall	24	13	6	5	48	31	32
Kingstonian	24	13	3	8	60	42	29
Enfield	24	12	5	7	38	35	29
Barnet	24	11	5	8	43	40	27
Sutton United	24	10	6	8	46	39	26
Hampstead Town	24	9	2	13	48	53	20
Summerstown	24	7	5	12	37	43	19
Windsor & Eton	24	6	6	12	36	53	18
Luton Clarence	24	6	4	14	37	68	16
Cheshunt	24	4	4	16	37	64	12
Guildford	24	4	2	18	32	71	10

1923-24

Kingstonian	24	17	2	5	63	32	36
Redhill	24	14	5	5	63	39	33
Southall	24	12	7	5	51	28	31
Barnet	24	11	6	7	48	29	28
Hampstead Town	24	10	6	8	49	37	26
Summerstown	24	9	7	8	46	40	25
Bromley	24	11	2	11	60	44	24
Barking	24	8	8	8	44	46	24
Windsor & Eaton	24	8	5	11	43	51	21
Sutton United	24	9	3	12	32	48	21
Cheshunt	24	7	5	12	33	51	19
Enfield	24	6	2	16	38	63	14
Luton Clarence	24	4	2	18	31	99	10

1924-25

Redhill	26	19	3	4	99	35	41
Barking	26	15	5	6	58	35	35
Kingstonian	26	15	4	7	48	34	34
Southall	26	16	1	9	62	29	33
Hampstead Town	26	10	11	5	55	34	31
Barnet	26	10	7	9	35	38	27
Enfield	26	8	9	9	46	42	25
Summerstown	26	9	7	10	41	42	25
Cheshunt	26	8	7	11	43	57	23
Uxbridge Town	26	8	6	12	43	70	22
Bromley	26	7	4	15	47	50	18
Windsor & Eton	26	4	10	12	47	77	18
Sutton	26	5	8	13	37	64	18
West Norwood	26	5	4	17	30	75	14

1925-26

Kingstonian	26	22	0	4	80	40	44
Redhill	26	18	2	6	91	46	38
Barking Town	26	17	2	7	94	53	36
Hampstead Town	26	15	1	10	66	46	31
Uxbridge Town	26	13	3	10	75	64	29
Barnet	26	12	4	10	74	57	28
Bromley	26	10	5	11	66	65	25
Southall	26	10	4	12	49	49	24
Windsor & Eton	26	10	4	12	66	70	24
Cheshunt	26	10	2	14	73	83	22
West Norwood	26	7	5	14	44	69	19
Enfield	26	8	3	15	49	77	19
Summerstown	26	6	5	15	41	70	17
Sutton United	26	3	2	21	37	116	8

1926-27

Southall	26	18	3	5	76	40	39
Kingstonian	26	16	2	8	85	54	34
Barking Town	26	14	5	7	76	61	33
Enfield	26	14	2	10	86	63	30
Cheshunt	26	13	3	10	82	74	29
Uxbridge Town	26	10	6	10	70	58	26
Barnet	26	10	6	10	48	40	26
Redhill	26	11	3	12	79	70	26
Windsor & Eton	26	11	3	12	63	85	26
Bromley	26	8	8	10	56	60	25
Sutton United	26	10	4	12	54	65	25
Summerstown	26	9	3	14	57	66	24
Hampstead	26	7	2	17	59	78	14
West Norwood	26	3	6	17	38	110	12

1927-28

Sutton United	26	20	3	3	83	35	43
Redhill	26	19	3	4	76	43	41
Barking Town	26	17	2	7	90	44	36
Leyton	26	17	1	8	77	40	35
Kingstonian	26	13	5	8	80	61	31
Enfield	26	13	3	10	70	61	29
Southall	26	11	5	10	55	50	27
Barnet	26	11	5	10	68	63	27
Bromley	26	10	2	14	60	85	22
Summerstown	26	7	7	12	51	64	21
Hampstead	26	6	4	16	44	76	16
Windsor & Eton	26	6	3	17	52	93	15
Uxbridge Town	26	5	2	19	59	99	12
Cheshunt	26	3	3	20	51	102	9

1928-29

Leyton	26	19	5	2	78	33	43
Hampstead	26	16	3	7	64	39	35
Sutton United	26	13	7	6	73	50	33
Southall	26	12	5	9	66	47	29
Enfield	26	11	7	8	47	51	29
Bromley	26	11	6	9	68	63	28
Barnet	26	12	3	11	67	55	27
Wealdstone	26	11	3	12	81	63	25
Redhill	26	9	6	11	70	59	24
Barking Town	26	11	2	13	52	55	24
Kingstonian	26	10	1	15	61	71	21
Uxbridge Town	26	7	3	16	59	71	17
Windsor & Eton	26	5	6	15	33	94	16
Cheshunt	26	4	5	17	53	120	13

1929-30

Walthamstow Avenue	26	19	3	4	94	39	41
Barnet	26	17	3	6	75	35	37
Leyton	26	15	7	4	58	35	37
Barking Town	26	14	3	9	66	60	31
Wealdstone	26	12	5	9	59	50	29
Enfield	26	11	5	10	53	50	27
Redhill	26	11	3	12	72	67	25
Sutton United	26	9	6	11	49	51	24
Uxbridge Town	26	11	2	13	60	65	24
Bromley	26	11	1	14	65	68	23
Hampstead	26	9	5	12	46	51	23
Finchley	26	7	5	14	53	74	19
Southall	26	5	4	17	45	74	14
Cheshunt	26	4	2	20	42	118	10

1930-31

Barnet	26	22	2	2	103	30	46
Walthamstow Avenue	26	14	6	6	73	47	34
Leyton	26	15	4	7	62	44	34
Enfield	26	12	5	9	73	52	29
Wealdstone	26	12	5	9	79	60	29
Southall	26	13	2	11	59	51	28
Hayes	26	12	4	10	66	58	28
Hampstead	26	11	6	9	68	60	28
Bromley	26	11	4	11	57	73	26
Barking Town	26	10	5	11	69	60	25
Sutton United	26	9	4	13	45	57	22
Uxbridge Town	26	6	4	16	53	88	16
Redhill	26	5	5	16	53	89	15
Cheshunt	26	1	2	23	32	125	4

1931-32

Barnet	26	17	5	4	90	56	39
Hayes	26	16	4	6	74	50	36
Leyton	26	15	4	7	74	46	34
Hampstead	26	14	4	8	72	52	32
Barking Town	26	13	6	7	71	54	32
Wealdstone	26	12	3	11	65	70	27
Enfield	26	12	2	12	81	65	26
Romford	26	10	6	10	64	61	26
Sutton United	26	9	7	10	65	56	25
Walthamstow Avenue	26	10	5	11	57	65	25
Southall	26	8	4	14	52	72	20
Redhill	26	7	3	16	59	83	19
Bromley	26	7	2	17	65	91	16
Uxbridge Town	26	4	1	21	29	97	9

1932-33

Walthamstow Avenue	26	19	6	4	80	29	38
Hampstead	26	15	6	5	82	35	36
Barnet	26	15	4	7	74	48	34
Barking	26	14	6	6	54	48	34
Leyton	26	8	11	7	58	54	27
Sutton United	26	10	5	11	54	66	25
Romford	26	8	8	10	50	66	24
Enfield	26	10	3	13	55	51	23
Redhill	26	9	5	12	53	66	23
Wealdstone	26	9	4	13	38	56	22
Southall	26	7	7	12	53	75	21
Hayes	26	7	6	13	53	57	20
Uxbridge Town	26	8	3	15	46	80	19
Bromley	26	7	4	15	68	87	18

1933-34

Walthamstow Avenue	26	20	1	5	80	34	41
Romford	26	16	4	6	61	39	36
Golders Green	26	16	2	8	80	37	34
Enfield	26	12	5	9	56	51	29
Barnet	26	13	2	11	66	55	28
Sutton United	26	12	2	12	58	56	26
Barking	26	12	2	12	59	64	26
Hayes	26	11	3	12	66	69	25
Leyton	26	10	4	12	55	60	24
Uxbridge Town	26	10	3	13	55	56	23
Southall	26	9	4	13	50	69	22
Redhill	26	9	3	14	55	71	21
Wealdstone	26	5	6	15	54	78	16
Bromley	26	4	5	17	42	98	13

1934-35

Barking	26	15	5	6	57	40	35
Enfield	26	15	3	8	51	33	33
Leyton	26	13	7	6	57	39	33
Walthamstow Avenue	26	13	5	8	50	38	31
Romford	26	11	7	8	62	46	29
Golders Green	26	12	5	9	70	56	29
Bromley	26	12	4	10	41	50	28
Southall	26	10	5	11	43	57	25
Sutton United	26	10	3	13	69	63	23
Barnet	26	9	3	14	41	53	21
Hayes	26	8	5	13	45	59	21
Uxbridge Town	26	7	6	13	54	66	20
Redhill	26	7	5	14	51	69	19
Wealdstone	26	5	7	14	47	72	17

1935-36

Romford	26	15	8	3	79	36	38
Bromley	26	16	5	5	52	26	37
Walthamstow Avenue	26	16	4	6	81	41	36
Enfield	26	13	6	7	49	42	32
Golders Green	26	13	5	8	73	60	31
Southall	26	13	3	10	57	60	29
Redhill	26	11	5	10	48	47	27
Leyton	26	10	6	10	45	49	26
Barking	26	8	7	11	65	48	23
Sutton United	26	9	5	12	40	61	23
Hayes	26	7	7	12	45	61	21
Barnet	26	6	3	17	53	83	15
Wealdstone	26	6	2	18	48	80	14
Uxbridge	26	3	6	17	45	86	12

1936-37

Romford	26	24	1	1	102	35	49
Walthamstow Avenue	26	16	5	4	101	45	39
Wealdstone	26	17	3	6	66	44	37
Sutton United	26	11	5	10	47	45	27
Bromley	26	12	3	11	51	63	27
Barnet	26	11	3	12	66	82	25
Leyton	26	10	4	12	56	51	24
Redhill	26	7	9	10	56	66	23
Hayes	26	7	9	10	49	58	23
Golders Green	26	8	5	13	58	56	21
Barking	26	9	2	15	56	64	20
Southall	26	8	4	14	54	76	20
Enfield	26	8	2	16	57	68	18
Uxbridge	26	3	5	18	31	97	11

1937-38

Walthamstow Avenue	26	19	4	3	96	32	42
Barnet	26	15	3	8	62	46	33
Romford	26	13	5	8	73	49	31
Wealdstone	26	11	7	8	58	45	29
Golders Green	26	11	6	9	61	56	28
Sutton United	26	10	6	10	56	63	26
Leyton	26	12	1	13	49	46	25
Bromley	26	10	4	12	38	49	24
Barking	26	8	7	11	39	41	23
Hayes	26	10	3	13	45	55	23
Redhill	26	9	4	13	50	67	22
Tooting & Mitcham	26	9	4	13	44	63	22
Enfield	26	5	8	13	38	62	18
Southall	26	7	4	15	40	75	18

1938-39

Walthamstow Avenue	26	19	4	3	70	28	42
Romford	26	18	1	7	81	35	37
Wealdstone	26	15	5	6	70	49	35
Hayes	26	14	6	6	63	36	34
Barnet	26	10	5	11	62	68	25
Barking	26	11	2	13	53	48	24
Bromley	26	8	8	10	50	49	24
Golders Green	26	9	6	11	42	57	24
Leyton	26	10	3	13	41	50	23
Sutton United	26	9	4	13	45	57	22
Tooting & Mitcham	26	8	3	13	38	50	19
Southall	26	7	5	14	31	66	19
Redhill	26	6	6	14	48	83	18
Enfield	26	6	6	14	33	63	18

1939-40

Romford and Walthamstow Avenue resigned from the League.
Finchley and Hitchin Town joined the League.

1939-40 to 1944-45

No competition due to World War II.

1945-46

Sutton United	26	17	6	3	100	44	40
Leyton	26	17	5	4	80	35	39
Tooting & Mitcham	26	17	2	7	103	53	36
Hayes	26	16	4	6	68	45	36
Bromley	26	16	1	9	92	55	33
Wealdstone	26	10	9	7	64	55	29
Southall	26	12	3	11	62	60	27
Barnet	26	10	5	11	73	70	25
Finchley	26	8	6	12	59	71	22
Hitchin Town	26	10	1	15	61	68	21
Enfield	26	7	4	15	55	84	18
Golders Green	26	7	3	16	56	84	17
Barking	26	5	3	18	40	93	13
Redhill	26	2	4	20	39	135	8

Athenian League 1946-1954

1946-47

Barnet	26	15	4	7	58	45	34
Sutton United	26	15	4	7	59	37	34
Bromley	26	13	4	9	79	54	30
Wealdstone	26	12	6	8	58	46	30
Southall	26	13	4	9	66	62	30
Hitchin Town	26	11	5	10	64	63	27
Tooting & Mitcham	26	12	3	11	72	78	27
Hendon	26	12	2	12	62	59	26
Hayes	26	11	3	12	48	63	25
Redhill	26	11	1	14	59	69	23
Finchley	26	9	4	13	59	67	22
Barking	26	8	6	12	42	52	22
Enfield	26	8	3	15	52	77	19
Leyton	26	6	3	17	36	72	15

Hendon were previously known as Golders Green.

1947-48

Barnet	26	18	2	6	86	38	38
Hendon	26	14	5	7	45	30	33
Bromley	26	12	6	8	60	50	30
Tooting & Mitcham	26	12	4	10	46	41	28
Wealdstone	26	9	8	9	44	36	26
Enfield	26	10	6	10	55	60	26
Hayes	26	9	7	10	43	43	25
Sutton United	26	9	7	10	32	38	25
Leyton	26	10	5	11	48	59	25
Finchley	26	10	5	11	38	52	25
Hitchin Town	26	10	4	12	43	61	24
Redhill	26	8	5	13	32	39	21
Barking	26	6	9	11	27	37	21
Southall	26	6	5	15	37	52	17

1948-49

Bromley	26	18	5	3	88	35	41
Hendon	26	15	7	4	55	33	37
Tooting & Mitcham	26	15	4	7	64	42	34
Wealdstone	26	12	5	9	56	54	29
Sutton United	26	9	8	9	32	33	26
Finchley	26	9	8	9	47	50	26
Hitchin Town	26	9	7	10	44	46	25
Hayes	26	9	7	10	48	52	25
Barnet	26	10	3	13	46	53	23
Barking	26	7	7	12	46	48	21
Redhill	26	9	2	15	51	64	20
Enfield	26	7	6	13	32	52	20
Southall	26	6	7	13	46	63	19
Leyton	26	7	4	15	37	67	18

1949-50

Tooting & Mitcham	26	16	7	3	51	26	39
Hayes	26	15	4	7	51	29	34
Bromley	26	12	9	5	59	39	33
Barking	26	14	5	7	51	46	33
Wealdstone	26	11	7	8	55	42	29
Hitchin Town	26	12	5	9	44	50	29
Hendon	26	13	2	11	54	48	28
Barnet	26	10	2	14	53	56	22
Finchley	26	8	6	12	40	49	22
Southall	26	7	8	11	36	51	22
Enfield	26	8	5	13	43	47	21
Sutton United	26	9	2	15	37	48	20
Redhill	26	6	4	16	39	56	16
Leyton	26	5	6	15	29	55	16

1950-51

Bromley	[illegible]	[illegible]	[illegible]	[illegible]	[illegible]	[illegible]	[illegible]
Walton & Hersham	[illegible]	[illegible]	[illegible]	[illegible]	[illegible]	[illegible]	[illegible]
Hayes	[illegible]	[illegible]	[illegible]	[illegible]	[illegible]	[illegible]	[illegible]
Hendon	[illegible]	[illegible]	[illegible]	[illegible]	[illegible]	[illegible]	[illegible]
Sutton United	[illegible]	[illegible]	[illegible]	[illegible]	[illegible]	[illegible]	[illegible]
Redhill	[illegible]	[illegible]	[illegible]	[illegible]	[illegible]	[illegible]	[illegible]
Tooting & Mitcham	30	[illegible]	[illegible]	[illegible]	[illegible]	[illegible]	30
Barnet	30	[illegible]	[illegible]	[illegible]	[illegible]	69	29
Wealdstone	30	[illegible]	[illegible]	14	52	52	27
Finchley	30	12	3	15	68	82	27
Southall	30	10	6	14	41	53	26
Barking	30	10	4	16	54	65	24
Cambridge City	30	8	7	15	49	74	23
Enfield	30	8	4	18	36	54	20
Hitchin Town	30	6	6	18	47	75	18
Leyton	30	4	4	22	36	89	12

1951-52

Wealdstone	30	23	4	3	81	29	50
Hendon	30	20	8	2	84	32	48
Bromley	30	15	8	7	74	53	38
Sutton United	30	15	8	7	70	53	38
Hayes	30	15	7	8	65	40	37
Southall	30	12	11	7	71	49	35
Walton & Hersham	30	14	4	12	56	51	32
Finchley	30	12	6	12	64	62	30
Redhill	30	12	6	12	55	63	30
Barking	30	11	4	15	56	86	26
Leyton	30	8	7	15	51	52	23
Barnet	30	7	8	15	53	72	22
Tooting & Mitcham	30	6	9	15	64	71	21
Cambridge City	30	6	8	16	44	70	20
Enfield	30	6	7	17	47	77	19
Hitchin Town	30	5	1	24	36	111	11

1952-53

Hendon	26	18	6	2	68	21	42
Wealdstone	26	17	3	6	58	35	37
Southall	26	17	2	7	55	28	36
Tooting & Mitcham	26	11	6	9	42	34	28
Leyton	26	12	4	10	59	58	28
Finchley	26	12	2	12	52	57	26
Walton & Hersham	26	11	3	12	42	36	25
Cambridge City	26	11	2	13	38	38	24
Barnet	26	10	3	13	39	46	23
Hayes	26	9	4	13	41	51	22
Hitchin Town	26	8	4	14	37	56	20
Enfield	26	7	5	14	51	65	19
Sutton United	26	7	4	15	44	60	18
Redhill	26	6	4	16	41	82	16

1953-54

Finchley	26	17	4	5	61	37	38
Hitchin Town	26	16	3	7	58	32	35
Southall	26	15	3	8	56	40	33
Tooting & Mitcham	26	12	5	9	49	35	29
Hendon	26	12	5	9	40	32	29
Hayes	26	9	10	7	49	42	28
Cambridge City	26	11	6	9	45	49	28
Sutton United	26	8	7	11	35	42	23
Redhill	26	9	4	13	44	40	22
Walton & Hersham	26	9	4	13	32	55	22
Leyton	26	9	3	14	38	56	21
Wealdstone	26	8	4	14	51	60	20
Barnet	26	8	4	14	36	54	20
Enfield	26	4	8	14	40	60	16

…55

…ting & Mitcham	26	15	8	3	65	32	38
Southall	26	16	5	5	64	39	37
Enfield	26	12	9	5	51	39	33
Sutton United	26	11	8	7	57	45	30
Hendon	26	8	11	7	51	45	27
Finchley	26	11	5	10	47	44	27
Hayes	26	9	7	10	47	43	25
Redhill	26	8	8	10	45	52	24
Leyton	26	10	4	12	36	47	24
Walton & Hersham	26	8	7	11	51	53	23
Barnet	26	6	11	9	39	48	23
Hitchin Town	26	6	9	11	44	60	21
Cambridge City	26	9	1	16	37	53	19
Wealdstone	26	4	5	17	36	70	13

1955-56

Hendon	28	18	5	5	63	35	41
Hounslow Town	28	15	8	5	67	42	38
Enfield	28	16	5	7	60	39	37
Tooting & Mitcham	28	17	2	9	60	47	36
Redhill	28	12	5	11	45	37	29
Walton & Hersham	28	13	3	12	59	68	29
Barnet	28	11	6	11	53	58	28
Finchley	28	8	12	8	52	62	28
Southall	28	10	7	11	50	46	27
Wealdstone	28	11	3	14	64	60	25
Hayes	28	8	6	14	55	56	22
Sutton United	28	9	4	15	56	64	22
Leyton	28	8	6	14	46	67	22
Cambridge City	28	7	4	17	39	61	18
Hitchin Town	28	7	4	17	47	74	18

1956-57

Hayes	28	18	4	6	73	38	40
Finchley	28	18	4	6	75	43	40
Hounslow Town	28	17	4	7	78	49	38
Hendon	28	15	4	9	85	51	34
Leyton	28	13	6	9	59	47	32
Southall	28	14	1	13	57	54	29
Enfield	28	9	9	10	46	58	27
Carshalton Athletic	28	9	8	11	53	59	26
Cambridge City	28	11	4	13	48	62	26
Hitchin Town	28	10	5	13	67	73	25
Sutton United	28	10	5	13	40	51	25
Redhill	28	7	9	12	46	65	23
Wealdstone	28	10	1	17	61	69	21
Walton & Hersham	28	8	3	17	43	74	19
Barnet	28	4	7	17	41	79	15

1957-58

Sutton United	30	18	7	5	64	37	43
Maidstone United	30	19	4	7	63	45	42
Hendon	30	15	7	8	73	40	37
Barnet	30	16	5	9	78	52	37
Hounslow Town	30	16	4	10	60	55	36
Finchley	30	13	9	8	64	46	35
Hayes	30	14	3	13	76	70	31
Wealdstone	30	11	8	11	64	65	30
Hitchin Town	30	12	6	12	52	65	30
Southall	30	13	3	14	66	55	29
Enfield	30	10	8	12	47	49	28
Carshalton Athletic	30	9	6	15	48	67	24
Leyton	30	9	6	15	59	80	24
Redhill	30	6	7	17	53	71	19
Cambridge City	30	7	5	18	47	82	19
Walton & Hersham	30	5	6	19	45	80	16

1958-59

Barnet	30	20	4	6	85	44	44
Wealdstone	30	19	6	5	74	39	44
Maidstone United	30	16	6	8	53	37	38
Hendon	30	15	6	9	69	56	36
Grays Athletic	30	11	11	8	67	52	33
Hounslow Town	30	13	7	10	62	49	33
Hayes	30	13	7	10	61	58	33
Finchley	30	13	3	14	61	70	29
Enfield	30	10	7	13	63	55	27
Sutton United	30	10	6	14	49	60	26
Carshalton Athletic	30	8	10	12	41	61	26
Southall	30	8	9	13	50	56	25
Leyton	30	10	4	16	49	65	24
Hitchin Town	30	8	8	14	37	52	24
Walton & Hersham	30	9	4	17	39	61	22
Redhill	30	5	6	19	35	80	16

1959-60

Hounslow Town	30	21	4	5	80	43	46
Barnet	30	17	9	4	79	35	43
Enfield	30	14	7	9	65	46	35
Wealdstone	30	16	3	11	64	51	35
Hornchurch	30	15	5	10	56	47	35
Sutton United	30	16	1	13	66	60	33
Southall	30	12	7	11	58	49	31
Hendon	30	9	12	9	48	39	30
Hayes	30	11	7	12	52	51	29
Hitchin Town	30	11	6	13	55	57	28
Grays Athletic	30	10	5	15	59	64	25
Redhill	30	9	6	15	45	66	24
Finchley	30	8	6	16	50	69	22
Walton & Hersham	30	8	6	16	49	75	22
Leyton	30	8	5	17	39	75	21
Carshalton Athletic	30	7	7	16	37	75	21

1960-61

Hendon	30	18	6	6	72	38	42
Wealdstone	30	18	5	7	78	44	41
Barnet	30	17	5	8	69	43	39
Sutton United	30	17	3	10	71	55	37
Hitchin Town	30	15	6	9	81	52	36
Enfield	30	14	6	10	76	49	34
Hounslow Town	30	16	2	12	73	66	34
Hornchurch	30	13	6	11	65	57	32
Walton & Hersham	30	11	8	11	66	57	30
Hayes	30	13	3	14	63	65	29
Southall	30	9	11	10	48	64	29
Leyton	30	8	6	16	45	79	22
Redhill	30	8	4	18	46	85	20
Grays Athletic	30	7	5	18	46	74	19
Finchley	30	8	3	19	43	81	19
Carshalton Athletic	30	8	1	21	50	83	17

1961-62

Enfield	30	25	2	3	97	36	52
Barnet	30	23	3	4	85	30	49
Wealdstone	30	16	5	9	76	52	37
Hayes	30	16	4	10	58	63	36
Walton & Hersham	30	14	6	10	70	55	34
Hitchin Town	30	15	4	11	85	71	34
Hendon	30	13	5	12	54	56	31
Grays Athletic	30	13	3	14	56	65	29
Sutton United	30	13	2	15	70	69	28
Hounslow Town	30	11	6	13	56	62	28
Finchley	30	10	7	13	49	46	27
Leyton	30	9	9	12	60	79	27
Redhill	30	7	4	19	51	75	18
Carshalton Athletic	30	6	5	19	45	71	17
Hornchurch	30	4	9	17	37	77	17
Southall	30	6	4	20	41	83	16

1962-63

Enfield	30	26	2	2	130	28	54
Barnet	30	22	3	5	90	39	47
Wealdstone	30	19	4	7	62	39	42
Sutton United	30	16	4	10	75	47	36
Hitchin Town	30	16	3	11	74	61	35
Walton & Hersham	30	15	4	11	66	49	34
Hendon	30	12	5	13	60	60	29
Finchley	30	13	2	15	55	46	28
Hayes	30	13	2	15	52	62	28
Hounslow Town	30	10	7	13	49	63	27
Hornchurch	30	12	3	15	59	77	27
Southall	30	9	6	15	48	53	24
Grays Athletic	30	9	3	18	54	88	21
Carshalton Athletic	30	7	3	20	34	95	17
Leyton	30	7	2	21	34	82	16
Redhill	30	6	3	21	36	89	15

1963-64

Premier Division

Barnet	26	17	4	5	82	34	38
Finchley	26	14	6	6	61	39	34
Carshalton Athletic	26	15	4	7	42	28	34
Hayes	26	9	12	5	50	39	30
Wealdstone	26	12	5	9	54	47	29
Dagenham	26	12	4	10	57	42	28
Walton & Hersham	26	13	2	11	52	54	28
Redhill	26	9	9	8	39	40	27
Maidenhead United	26	12	2	12	54	48	26
Hornchurch	26	7	8	11	35	49	22
Grays Athletic	26	9	4	13	27	43	22
Leyton	26	4	9	13	33	62	17
Hounslow Town	26	7	1	18	38	76	15
Southall	26	5	4	17	36	59	14

First Division

Leatherhead	26	18	3	5	86	45	39
Worthing	26	18	2	6	76	40	38
Edgware Town	26	17	4	5	72	40	38
Erith & Belvedere	26	12	8	6	46	30	32
Slough Town	26	15	2	9	54	37	32
Letchworth Town	26	12	6	8	80	52	30
Chesham United	26	14	2	10	75	57	30
Uxbridge	26	11	5	10	45	41	27
Wokingham Town	26	11	3	12	42	54	25
Wembley	26	8	4	14	48	67	20
Eastbourne	26	7	3	16	44	75	17
Dorking	26	7	2	17	44	74	15
Horsham	26	4	3	19	27	67	11
Epsom & Ewell	26	4	1	21	45	104	9

Second Division

Tilbury	28	18	6	4	90	44	42
Harrow Town	28	20	2	6	85	42	42
Harlow Town	28	17	6	5	74	34	40
Hertford Town	28	15	7	6	72	42	37
Hemel Hempstead Town	28	15	4	9	63	43	34
Aveley	28	14	5	9	70	40	31
Bishop's Stortford	28	14	3	11	67	40	31
Windsor & Eton	28	12	4	12	61	61	28
Ware	28	11	5	12	62	59	27
Brentwood	28	10	5	13	42	59	25
Berkhamsted	28	9	6	13	52	67	24
Edmonton	28	7	6	15	53	65	20
Aylesbury United	28	8	1	19	45	87	17
Wingate	28	5	5	13	36	79	15
Histon	28	2	1	25	25	142	5

1964-65

Premier Division

Barnet	30	23	4	3	107	29	50
Leyton	30	19	3	8	67	41	41
Finchley	30	19	1	10	67	45	39
Worthing	30	15	8	7	70	65	38
Walton & Hersham	30	16	3	11	69	55	35
Hayes	30	14	5	11	71	56	33
Hounslow	30	14	5	11	69	61	33
Carshalton Athletic	30	13	4	13	62	54	30
Maidenhead United	30	12	6	12	60	53	30
Leatherhead	30	13	3	14	51	54	29
Hornchurch	30	11	6	13	61	67	28
Dagenham	30	8	8	14	40	57	24
Edgware Town	30	8	5	17	33	78	21
Grays Athletic	30	8	4	18	48	75	20
Southall	30	7	5	18	37	67	19
Redhill	30	4	2	24	32	87	10

First Division

Slough Town	30	21	6	3	81	23	48
Hemel Hempstead Town	30	21	4	5	77	32	46
Chesham United	30	21	3	6	64	38	45
Horsham	30	17	3	10	74	47	37
Harrow Town	30	16	5	9	79	55	37
Hertford Town	30	16	3	11	51	41	35
Letchworth Town	30	16	3	11	68	60	35
Erith & Belvedere	30	14	5	11	48	49	33
Tilbury	30	13	4	13	57	49	30
Eastbourne	30	9	9	12	53	67	27
Wokingham Town	30	8	6	16	50	63	22
Uxbridge	30	6	9	15	48	59	21
Harlow Town	30	6	6	18	37	66	18
Wembley	30	5	5	19	31	66	16
Dorking	30	5	5	20	31	92	15
Epsom & Ewell	30	6	3	21	52	93	13

Epsom & Ewell had 2 points deducted.

Second Division

Harwich & Parkeston	30	24	2	4	95	33	50
Bishop's Stortford	30	20	8	2	71	35	48
Ware	30	21	5	4	81	42	47
Aveley	30	18	6	6	62	32	42
Windsor & Eton	30	17	4	9	80	45	38
Herne Bay	30	18	2	10	80	53	38
Croydon Amateurs	30	16	4	10	63	38	36
Eastbourne United	30	13	8	9	70	43	34
Cheshunt	30	13	7	10	60	41	33
Edmonton	30	10	4	16	40	64	24
Berkhamsted Town	30	8	5	17	44	79	21
Rainham Town	30	7	5	18	41	67	19
Aylesbury United	30	6	5	19	41	73	17
Wingate	30	6	2	22	39	77	14
Brentwood & Warley	30	4	5	21	32	79	13
Histon	30	2	2	26	27	125	6

1965-66

Premier Division

Leyton	30	21	6	3	76	28	48
Finchley	30	22	4	4	83	39	48
Maidenhead United	30	21	3	6	63	29	45
Leatherhead	30	14	9	7	41	34	37
Hounslow	30	15	4	11	66	60	34
Dagenham	30	14	4	12	61	49	32
Southall	30	13	4	13	38	57	30
Slough Town	30	12	5	13	69	50	29
Hemel Hempstead Town	30	11	6	13	57	51	28
Grays Athletic	30	8	10	12	41	54	26
Walton & Hersham	30	9	6	15	56	66	24
Worthing	30	10	4	16	51	66	24
Hayes	30	9	5	16	50	55	23
Edgware Town	30	8	7	15	37	62	23
Carshalton Athletic	30	7	2	21	48	93	16
Hornchurch	30	3	7	20	34	76	13

First Division

Bishop's Stortford	30	24	3	3	84	33	51
Harwich & Parkeston	30	23	0	7	66	36	46
Hertford	30	17	7	6	58	26	41
Letchworth	30	17	7	6	30	49	41
Wembley	30	15	7	8	56	48	37
Chesham	30	15	4	11	74	52	34
Erith & Belvedere	30	13	8	9	55	44	34
Redhill	30	16	0	14	56	44	32
Harlow	30	11	7	12	53	55	29
Tilbury	30	10	4	16	58	66	24
Dorking	30	11	1	18	50	75	23
Uxbridge	30	7	6	17	49	65	20
Wokingham	30	7	5	18	37	74	19
Harrow	30	7	5	18	32	71	19
Horsham	30	5	5	20	50	84	15
Eastbourne	30	6	3	21	45	81	15

Second Division

Croydon Amateurs	30	21	5	4	85	37	47
Cheshunt	30	22	3	5	82	38	47
Eastbourne United	30	19	3	8	83	46	41
Lewes	30	17	6	7	66	42	40
Herne Bay	30	18	3	9	74	45	39
Windsor & Eton	30	16	4	10	79	49	36
Aveley	30	15	6	9	68	44	36
Ware	30	15	5	10	77	71	35
Epsom & Ewell	30	12	7	11	57	49	31
Rainham Town	30	10	7	13	58	65	27
Edmonton	30	8	6	16	43	71	22
Berkhamsted Town	30	7	4	19	51	80	18
Marlow	30	5	7	18	41	79	17
Wingate	30	6	4	20	47	84	16
Aylesbury United	30	5	5	20	45	89	15
Ruislip Manor	30	5	3	22	37	104	13

1966-67

Premier Division

Leyton	30	18	7	5	73	32	43
Bishop's Stortford	30	19	5	6	58	33	43
Finchley	30	16	6	8	72	38	38
Leatherhead	30	17	3	10	53	42	37
Harwich & Parkeston	30	15	5	10	64	42	35
Hounslow	30	14	6	10	62	49	34
Slough Town	30	14	5	11	52	38	33
Dagenham	30	13	7	10	48	40	33
Hayes	30	13	6	11	51	45	32
Grays Athletic	30	11	7	12	45	50	29
Hemel Hempstead Town	30	8	11	11	39	42	27
Southall	30	8	9	14	43	47	25
Walton & Hersham	30	10	5	15	45	58	25
Maidenhead United	30	7	10	13	49	65	24
Worthing	30	5	4	21	32	85	14
Edgware	30	2	4	24	19	98	8

First Division

Hornchurch	30	20	6	4	51	24	46
Redhill	30	19	7	4	71	32	45
Chesham	30	17	5	8	57	34	39
Wembley	30	15	5	10	49	40	35
Croydon Amateurs	30	17	0	13	71	48	34
Erith & Belvedere	30	12	6	12	54	41	30
Hertford	30	13	4	13	41	42	30
Letchworth	30	12	5	13	70	64	29
Harlow	30	10	8	12	39	42	28
Carshalton	30	11	6	13	43	49	28
Tilbury	30	11	5	14	63	64	27
Cheshunt	30	9	7	14	41	45	25
Dorking	30	10	5	15	42	60	25
Wokingham	30	10	3	17	47	68	23
Uxbridge	30	9	5	16	35	72	23
Harrow	30	5	3	22	37	63	13

Second Division

Eastbourne United	30	22	6	2	83	25	50
Ware	30	19	8	3	79	33	46
Horsham	30	20	3	7	59	32	43
Marlow	30	16	5	9	57	58	37
Lewes	30	14	8	8	62	37	36
Aveley	30	14	4	12	49	51	32
Windsor & Eton	30	11	7	12	47	54	29
Herne Bay	30	12	4	14	64	57	28
Boreham Wood	30	8	9	13	56	59	25
Aylesbury United	30	11	3	16	46	59	25
Rainham Town	30	7	10	13	40	50	24
Epsom & Ewell	30	9	6	15	65	91	24
Eastbourne	30	9	5	16	51	61	23
Ruislip Manor	30	9	4	17	48	71	22
Edmonton	30	6	9	15	25	48	21
Wingate	30	5	5	20	34	74	15

1967-68

Premier Division

Slough Town	30	23	5	2	93	23	51
Dagenham	30	20	4	6	74	34	44
Bishop's Stortford	30	18	3	9	75	38	39
Hayes	30	15	5	10	57	40	35
Leatherhead	30	15	4	11	55	44	34
Maidenhead United	30	15	4	11	50	48	34
Hounslow	30	13	6	11	50	50	32
Walton & Hersham	30	13	5	12	51	39	31
Hornchurch	30	10	9	11	42	46	29
Redhill	30	11	7	12	43	48	29
Grays Athletic	30	11	6	13	45	54	28
Southall	30	9	8	13	34	65	26
Finchley	30	6	9	15	42	53	21
Harwich & Parkeston	30	7	5	18	36	60	19
Leyton	30	5	6	19	22	63	16
Hemel Hempstead Town	30	4	4	22	23	85	12

First Division

Cheshunt	30	18	6	6	59	30	42
Wembley	30	16	8	6	67	37	40
Tilbury	30	16	6	8	58	35	38
Erith & Belvedere	30	14	9	7	55	41	37
Hertford	30	15	7	8	49	38	37
Croydon Amateurs	30	11	14	5	47	27	36
Carshalton	30	15	6	9	54	38	36
Dorking	30	13	6	11	37	31	32
Ware	30	12	6	12	42	49	30
Eastbourne United	30	11	6	13	44	47	28
Chesham	30	8	12	10	33	38	28
Wokingham	30	11	5	14	53	70	27
Letchworth	30	11	3	16	50	52	25
Harlow	30	6	7	17	33	59	19
Worthing	30	6	5	19	35	58	17
Edgware	30	1	6	23	11	77	8

Second Division

Lewes	30	21	4	5	89	22	46
Aylesbury United	30	18	6	6	62	35	42
Horsham	30	16	6	8	61	36	38
Edmonton	30	17	2	11	73	49	36
Boreham Wood	30	15	4	11	63	38	34
Windsor & Eton	30	14	6	10	45	40	34
Rainham Town	30	12	7	11	55	54	31
Marlow	30	14	2	14	54	54	30
Ruislip Manor	30	11	8	11	42	50	30
Harrow Borough	30	12	6	12	41	49	30
Aveley	30	12	5	13	54	53	29
Herne Bay	30	13	2	15	50	50	28
Uxbridge	30	9	5	16	41	60	23
Epsom & Ewell	30	10	3	17	44	66	23
Eastbourne	30	5	3	22	37	94	13
Wingate	30	5	3	22	23	85	13

1968-69

Premier Division

Walton & Hersham	30	24	4	2	79	22	52
Slough Town	30	21	6	3	65	30	48
Southall	30	18	3	9	55	31	39
Leatherhead	30	16	6	8	48	32	38
Dagenham	30	15	7	8	51	34	37
Bishop's Stortford	30	14	6	10	57	44	34
Maidenhead United	30	10	11	9	42	35	31
Cheshunt	30	10	9	11	33	39	29
Wembley	30	11	7	12	35	45	29
Harwich & Parkeston	30	9	7	14	33	47	25
Redhill	30	10	5	15	31	51	25
Hayes	30	7	10	13	31	45	24
Grays Athletic	30	7	7	16	34	48	21
Finchley	30	5	10	15	19	39	20
Hornchurch	30	3	10	17	23	53	16
Hounslow	30	5	2	23	26	67	12

First Division

Tilbury	30	20	5	5	65	28	45
Eastbourne United	30	19	6	5	70	40	44
Lewes	30	15	9	6	57	39	39
Hertford	30	16	6	8	48	28	38
Wokingham	30	12	11	7	44	28	35
Dorking	30	13	7	10	54	51	33
Erith & Belvedere	30	9	13	8	48	48	31
Carshalton	30	11	8	11	47	40	30
Harlow	30	12	4	14	47	49	28
Croydon Amateurs	30	7	12	11	39	45	26
Aylesbury	30	8	10	12	45	64	26
Chesham	30	8	9	13	44	42	25
Letchworth	30	8	8	14	41	56	24
Ware	30	8	6	16	44	69	22
Hemel Hempstead Town	30	6	6	18	32	67	18
Leyton	30	5	6	19	37	68	16

Second Division

Boreham Wood	30	20	6	4	68	25	46
Aveley	30	20	6	4	77	32	46
Eastbourne	30	17	8	5	60	33	42
Herne Bay	30	15	10	5	60	34	40
Horsham	30	17	4	9	63	38	38
Edmonton	30	16	2	12	48	42	34
Worthing	30	15	4	11	51	51	34
Marlow	30	11	11	8	45	36	33
Wingate	30	12	5	13	45	41	29
Windsor & Eton	30	11	7	12	35	46	29
Uxbridge	30	10	7	13	45	58	27
Ruislip Manor	30	6	6	18	40	65	18
Edgware Town	30	7	4	19	30	61	18
Epsom & Ewell	30	5	7	18	25	63	17
Rainham Town	30	5	6	19	37	64	16
Harrow Borough	30	5	3	22	45	85	13

1969-70

Premier Division

Bishop's Stortford	30	20	5	5	72	33	45
Walton & Hersham	30	16	8	6	56	32	40
Dagenham	30	15	9	6	62	22	39
Slough Town	30	15	9	6	52	21	39
Leatherhead	30	15	9	6	51	29	39
Redhill	30	17	5	8	48	36	39
Hayes	30	11	9	10	47	45	31
Tilbury	30	10	9	11	48	43	29
Cheshunt	30	9	9	12	33	30	27
Harwich & Parkeston	30	7	12	11	44	43	26
Southall	30	10	6	14	32	47	26
Grays Athletic	30	9	8	13	26	40	26
Wembley	30	9	7	14	34	46	25
Maidenhead United	30	6	9	15	29	54	21
Finchley	30	7	5	18	30	73	19
Eastbourne United	30	3	3	24	27	97	9

First Division

Lewes	30	20	5	5	59	20	45
Boreham Wood	30	20	5	5	66	27	45
Erith & Belvedere	30	15	9	6	59	33	39
Aveley	30	16	5	9	65	44	37
Hertford Town	30	14	6	10	43	31	34
Harlow Town	30	15	4	11	53	47	34
Chesham United	30	11	10	9	53	43	32
Dorking	30	10	10	10	39	37	30
Carshalton Athletic	30	11	7	12	39	39	29
Hounslow	30	11	5	14	37	43	27
Aylesbury United	30	9	8	13	38	50	26
Hornchurch	30	8	9	13	30	36	25
Wokingham Town	30	9	7	14	34	51	25
Letchworth Town	30	8	5	17	41	74	21
Ware	30	4	9	17	35	81	17
Croydon Amateurs	30	5	4	21	28	63	14

Second Division

Horsham	30	19	9	2	68	30	47
Edmonton	30	20	4	6	85	34	44
Herne Bay	30	18	5	7	69	34	41
Eastbourne	30	17	7	6	48	26	41
Marlow	30	13	9	8	51	39	35
Uxbridge	30	13	8	9	49	40	34
Rainham Town	30	11	11	8	42	39	33
Edgware Town	30	10	10	10	38	38	30
Leyton	30	12	5	13	50	64	29
Worthing	30	9	9	12	39	44	27
Windsor & Eton	30	7	13	10	34	40	27
Hemel Hempstead Town	30	10	4	16	36	50	24
Wingate	30	7	8	15	36	56	22
Harrow Borough	30	4	8	18	33	67	16
Epsom & Ewell	30	5	6	19	22	55	16
Ruislip Manor	30	4	6	20	33	82	14

1970-71

Premier Division

Dagenham	30	23	5	2	54	19	51
Walton & Hersham	30	20	7	3	56	21	47
Slough Town	30	17	7	6	48	21	41
Cheshunt	30	18	3	9	48	34	39
Maidenhead United	30	14	8	8	53	29	36
Leatherhead	30	14	6	10	45	31	34
Tilbury	30	13	4	13	48	44	30
Haye	30	11	7	12	43	41	29
Lewes	30	11	6	13	42	42	28
Boreham Wood	30	9	9	12	39	41	27
Redhill	30	10	7	13	36	48	27
Bishop's Stortford	30	11	4	15	45	61	26
Harwich & Parkeston	30	8	6	16	43	62	22
Wembley	30	4	8	18	33	62	16
Grays Athletic	30	7	2	21	27	68	16
Southall	30	4	3	23	17	53	11

First Division

Aveley	30	18	8	4	59	24	44
Erith & Belvedere	30	19	6	5	67	34	44
Hornchurch	30	18	5	7	54	30	41
Horsham	30	16	6	8	62	36	38
Carshalton Athletic	30	15	6	9	51	35	36
Hertford Town	30	12	10	8	55	42	34
Wokingham Town	30	13	8	9	39	32	34
Edmonton	30	15	3	12	50	54	33
Dorking	30	11	9	10	36	40	31
Aylesbury United	30	11	7	12	45	47	29
Finchley	30	8	12	10	29	33	28
Harlow Town	30	6	9	15	35	54	21
Chesham United	30	7	5	18	37	57	19
Letchworth Town	30	7	4	19	30	62	18
Eastbourne United	30	5	6	19	26	57	16
Hounslow	30	4	6	20	25	63	14

Second Division

Herne Bay	30	22	3	5	77	39	47
Croydon Amateurs	30	20	4	6	79	25	44
Marlow	30	18	7	5	54	29	43
Windsor & Eton	30	14	7	9	52	39	35
Worthing	30	14	6	10	49	35	34
Ware	30	13	6	11	53	46	32
Uxbridge	30	14	4	12	54	50	32
Eastbourne	30	12	5	13	40	42	29
Rainham Town	30	9	8	13	39	46	26
Ruislip Manor	30	10	6	14	29	37	26
Edgware	30	9	8	13	44	58	26
Harrow Borough	30	8	9	13	32	39	25
Hemel Hempstead Town	30	9	7	14	43	56	25
Wingate	30	9	6	15	36	57	24
Leyton	30	9	4	17	40	61	22
Epsom & Ewell	30	3	4	23	23	86	10

1971-72

Premier Division

Slough	30	22	4	4	60	17	48
Dagenham	30	19	5	6	61	27	43
Leatherhead	30	16	8	6	56	29	40
Tilbury	30	15	9	6	62	46	39
Harwich & Parkeston	30	14	9	7	47	40	37
Maidenhead	30	13	8	9	38	31	34
Redhill	30	11	10	9	51	35	32
Cheshunt	30	10	11	9	43	37	31
Aveley	30	12	6	12	46	37	30
Hornchurch	30	10	8	12	39	38	28
Boreham Wood	30	11	6	13	40	45	28
Lewes	30	10	8	12	48	52	28
Erith & Belvedere	30	9	8	13	39	54	26
Southall	30	5	9	16	25	49	19
Wembley	30	3	5	22	26	58	11
Grays Athletic	30	1	4	25	25	111	6

First Division

Harlow Town	30	22	5	3	96	40	49
Croydon Amateurs	30	20	6	4	77	25	46
Horsham	30	17	6	7	59	34	40
Carshalton Athletic	30	16	7	7	57	37	39
Marlow	30	12	11	7	53	41	35
Hertford Town	30	16	3	11	58	49	35
Finchley	30	12	9	9	43	43	33
Chesham United	30	12	8	10	45	33	32
Eastbourne United	30	10	8	12	48	51	28
Herne Bay	30	10	8	12	43	51	28
Dorking	30	10	6	14	48	62	26
Edmonton	30	9	7	14	47	61	25
Wokingham Town	30	7	6	17	30	51	20
Letchworth Town	30	5	6	19	34	61	16
Aylesbury United	30	4	8	18	42	90	16
Hounslow	30	3	6	21	33	84	12

Second Division

Staines Town	30	22	7	1	76	24	51
Worthing	30	18	5	7	54	29	41
Hampton	30	17	6	7	57	32	40
Windsor & Eton	30	17	5	8	51	35	39
Addlestone	30	17	4	9	47	35	38
Ware	30	16	2	12	45	41	34
Hemel Hempstead Town	30	14	5	11	40	37	33
Edgware	30	13	5	12	56	46	31
Leyton	30	12	7	11	46	46	31
Uxbridge	30	10	8	12	34	36	28
Ruislip Manor	30	9	4	17	41	51	22
Eastbourne Town	30	5	12	13	24	42	22
Harrow Borough	30	7	6	17	27	47	20
Wingate	30	8	3	19	33	72	19
Rainham Town	30	5	7	18	34	60	17
Epsom & Ewell	30	5	4	21	26	58	14

1972-73

Premier Division

Slough Town	30	22	4	4	74	23	48
Dagenham	30	17	9	4	47	18	43
Tilbury	30	17	9	4	57	35	43
Harlow Town	30	18	5	7	54	31	41
Erith & Belvedere	30	14	8	8	35	28	36
Harwich & Parkestone	30	11	10	9	44	38	32
Aveley	30	11	10	9	34	34	32
Cheshunt	30	13	6	11	36	36	32
Maidenhead	30	12	6	12	43	41	30
Southall	30	12	5	13	30	38	29
Boreham Wood	30	9	7	14	30	34	25
Lewes	30	5	11	14	28	45	21
Croydon Amateurs	30	5	11	14	21	37	21
Hornchurch	30	6	6	18	23	45	18
Redhill	30	3	9	18	20	49	15
Wembley	30	4	6	20	26	70	14

First Division

Horsham	30	24	3	3	74	24	51
Staines Town	30	20	3	7	54	32	43
Grays Athletic	30	16	5	9	33	27	37
Hounslow	30	13	7	10	49	36	33
Wokingham Town	30	11	7	12	51	47	29
Carshalton Athletic	30	11	7	12	41	42	29
Eastbourne United	30	11	7	12	32	38	29
Letchworth Town	30	10	9	11	32	43	29
Marlow	30	11	6	13	40	38	28
Chesham United	30	11	5	14	41	41	27
Edmonton	30	9	9	12	41	45	27
Finchley	30	10	6	14	43	46	26
Herne Bay	30	10	6	14	45	62	26
Worthing	30	7	10	13	29	42	24
Aylesbury United	30	8	6	16	38	58	22
Dorking	30	6	8	16	26	48	20

Second Division

Ruislip Manor	26	18	6	2	51	20	42
Hampton	26	14	8	4	39	20	36
Ware	26	14	8	4	61	38	26
Leyton	26	14	7	5	52	22	35
Edgware	26	11	10	5	32	20	32
Rainham Town	26	10	11	5	46	36	31
Uxbridge	26	13	4	9	42	27	30
Addlestone	26	11	7	8	42	28	29
Harrow Borough	26	12	5	9	43	30	29
Hemel Hempstead Town	26	5	7	14	26	53	17
Windsor & Eton	26	5	4	17	29	54	14
Eastbourne Town	26	6	2	18	24	51	14
Epsom & Ewell	26	4	6	16	24	54	14
Wingate	26	2	1	23	21	79	5

1973-74

First Division

Boreham Wood	34	25	6	3	68	20	56
Cheshunt	34	18	11	5	58	24	47
Ruislip Manor	34	18	10	6	61	29	46
Ware	34	16	8	10	55	47	40
Hornchurch	34	15	9	10	48	44	39
Croydon	34	14	12	8	49	34	38
Erith & Belvedere	34	14	9	11	41	32	37
Edmonton & Haringey	34	12	12	10	40	35	36
Hounslow	34	13	9	12	55	46	35
Worthing	34	14	7	13	47	51	35
Lewes	34	11	12	11	50	43	34
Redhill	34	13	8	13	46	45	34
Grays Athletic	34	8	12	14	34	40	28
Wembley	34	11	6	17	42	55	28
Eastbourne United	34	8	9	17	34	60	25
Marlow	34	8	6	20	23	48	22
Letchworth Town	34	7	7	20	28	56	21
Herne Bay	34	1	7	26	16	86	9

Croydon had 2 points deducted. Croydon were previously known as Croydon Amateurs. Edmonton & Haringey were previously known as Edmonton.

Second Division

Alton Town	30	19	7	4	54	23	45
Rainham Town	30	17	7	6	48	33	41
Leyton	30	14	11	5	55	30	39
Uxbridge	30	14	11	5	36	23	39
Faversham Town	30	14	7	9	47	31	35
Wingate	30	15	5	10	42	37	35
Molesey	30	15	5	10	36	33	35
Harrow Borough	30	11	9	10	44	37	31
Addlestone	30	12	5	13	41	38	29
Aylesbury United	30	8	10	12	42	45	26
Hemel Hempstead Town	30	8	9	13	37	41	25
Edgware	30	9	6	15	33	54	24
Eastbourne Town	30	8	7	15	31	46	23
Feltham	30	7	5	18	29	50	19
Barking	30	5	7	18	38	67	17
Windsor & Eton	30	6	5	19	25	55	17

1974-75

First Division

Letchworth Town	34	21	7	6	63	32	49
Wembley	34	18	12	4	57	26	48
Grays	34	20	7	7	68	35	47
Cheshunt	34	16	10	8	57	43	42
Lewes	34	15	11	8	60	39	41
Alton	34	15	10	9	59	42	40
Hornchurch	34	14	11	9	48	39	39
Ruislip Manor	34	13	9	12	42	43	35
Erith & Belvedere	34	11	11	12	55	38	33
Redhill	34	11	10	13	45	44	32
Edmonton & Haringey	34	11	10	13	51	53	32
Ware	34	12	8	14	59	68	32
Marlow	34	9	12	13	33	50	30
Rainham	34	10	9	15	39	47	29
Hounslow	34	12	4	18	52	75	28
Worthing	34	10	7	17	46	64	27
Leyton	34	7	6	21	30	53	20
Eastbourne United	34	2	4	28	21	94	8

Second Division

Egham	28	18	5	5	51	22	41
Addlestone	28	18	4	6	54	23	40
Wingate	28	17	4	7	43	22	38
Willesden	28	13	10	5	43	20	36
Eastbourne Town	28	14	8	6	38	25	36
Molesey	28	14	5	9	39	27	33
Epping	28	12	4	12	43	38	28
Uxbridge	28	8	11	9	31	31	27
Harrow Borough	28	11	5	12	35	37	27
Hemel Hempstead Town	28	8	7	13	29	36	23
Aylesbury	28	7	7	14	33	49	21
Windsor & Eton	28	8	4	16	31	57	20
Edgware	28	9	1	18	33	44	19
Faversham	28	7	5	16	27	56	19
Feltham	28	2	8	18	19	62	12

1975-76

First Division

Cheshunt	30	18	5	7	66	31	41
Egham	30	16	7	7	46	28	39
Addlestone	30	15	7	8	40	30	37
Grays Athletic	30	15	6	9	39	29	36
Rainham	30	15	3	12	52	37	33
Erith & Belvedere	30	11	10	9	29	28	32
Alton Town	30	14	4	12	37	42	32
Worthing	30	12	7	11	42	35	31
Hounslow	30	11	7	12	50	43	29
Lewes	30	9	11	10	45	45	29
Letchworth Town	30	10	9	11	31	38	29
Redhill	30	10	7	13	31	34	27
Ruislip Manor	30	9	8	13	39	41	26
Leyton-Wingate	30	8	8	14	37	41	24
Marlow	30	6	6	18	27	61	18
Edmonton & Haringey	30	5	7	18	31	79	17

Leyton-Wingate was formed by the amalgamation of Leyton and Wingate.

Second Division

Epping	30	16	10	4	47	21	42
Epsom & Ewell	30	16	8	6	58	25	40
Edgware	30	14	10	6	36	29	38
Hemel Hempstead Town	30	15	6	9	46	36	36
Windsor & Eton	30	13	7	10	42	26	33
Tring	30	12	9	9	31	31	33
Eastbourne Town	30	11	9	10	45	42	31
Feltham	30	11	8	11	39	42	30
Aylesbury	30	8	12	10	36	40	28
Willesden	30	10	10	16	22	34	28
Molesley	30	10	7	13	36	39	27
Camberley	30	7	11	12	31	43	25
Uxbridge	30	7	10	13	22	31	24
Eastbourne United	30	7	8	15	29	43	22
Harefield	30	6	10	14	29	43	22
Faversham	30	8	3	19	28	54	19

Willesden had 2 points deducted.

1976-77

First Division

Leyton-Wingate	34	22	6	6	65	26	50
Letchworth Garden City	34	21	7	6	66	33	49
Addlestone	34	19	10	5	58	24	48
Lewes	34	18	8	8	63	43	44
Cheshunt	34	18	8	8	57	39	44
Epping	34	17	8	9	54	37	42
Alton Town	34	14	10	10	46	39	38
Rainham	34	12	13	9	63	56	37
Egham	34	14	7	13	46	45	35
Epsom & Ewell	34	12	9	13	46	42	33
Redhill	34	12	9	13	43	43	33
Haringey	34	11	8	15	42	47	30
Worthing	34	9	9	16	47	59	27
Hounslow	34	10	7	17	37	56	27
Erith & Belvedere	34	4	14	16	27	44	22
Grays Athletic	34	6	10	18	38	63	22
Marlow	34	5	8	21	42	90	18
Ruislip Manor	34	4	5	25	33	87	13

Second Division

Farnborough	28	19	5	4	65	33	43
Tring	28	16	8	4	49	30	40
Molesey	28	12	10	6	50	35	34
Hemel Hempstead Town	28	14	5	9	48	29	33
Chalfont St Peter	28	13	7	8	41	28	33
Harefield	28	8	13	7	45	35	29
Uxbridge	28	11	7	10	32	25	29
Feltham	28	11	7	10	34	40	27
Edgware	28	11	5	12	29	36	25
Eastbourne United	28	8	7	13	41	42	23
Kingsbury	28	9	5	14	28	38	23
Camberley	28	6	11	11	25	34	23
Windsor & Eton	28	5	11	12	34	42	19
Willesden	28	6	7	15	23	49	19
Chertsey	28	3	8	17	22	70	14

Feltham, Edgware and Windsor & Eton all had 2 points deducted.

1977-78

Billericay	34	23	7	4	80	21	53
Leyton-Wingate	34	21	8	5	73	42	50
Grays Athletic	34	20	8	6	72	31	48
Burnham	34	20	8	6	69	33	48
Chalfont St Peter	34	20	5	9	59	31	45
Edgware	34	14	14	6	54	29	42
Alton Town	34	13	12	9	50	33	38
Marlow	34	14	7	13	61	59	35
Windsor & Eton	34	13	8	13	47	44	34
Harefield	34	10	13	11	37	50	33
Haringey	34	9	12	13	49	48	30
Uxbridge	34	10	9	15	30	37	29
Hoddesdon Town	34	8	12	14	41	54	28
Ruislip Manor	34	10	8	16	44	58	28
Chertsey	34	8	8	18	47	77	24
Kingsbury	34	6	9	19	33	60	21
Erith & Belvedere	34	6	6	22	34	82	18
Redhill	34	2	4	28	19	110	8

1978-79

Billericay	36	26	5	5	86	29	57
Burnham	36	22	10	4	86	37	54
Edgware	36	19	11	6	83	34	49
Windsor & Eton	36	21	6	9	62	30	48
Haringey Borough	36	16	15	5	60	42	47
Uxbridge	36	17	12	7	45	22	46
Welling United	36	17	9	10	60	46	43
Leyton-Wingate	36	16	10	10	67	48	42
Grays Athletic	36	17	8	11	55	46	42
Alton Town	36	15	9	12	51	45	39
Hoddesdon Town	36	13	7	16	63	60	33
Chalfont St Peter	36	12	8	16	41	58	32
Harefield United	36	11	7	18	53	70	29
Dorking Town	36	10	7	19	39	64	27
Marlow	36	9	4	23	48	92	22
Ruislip Manor	36	8	4	24	35	71	20
Fleet Town	36	6	7	23	37	73	19
Redhill	36	6	7	23	29	79	19
Chertsey Town	36	4	8	24	36	90	16

1979-80

Windsor & Eton	38	26	6	6	72	26	58
Burnham	38	24	8	6	73	28	56
Leyton-Wingate	38	22	8	8	86	48	52
Dorking Town	38	20	8	10	61	41	48
Welling United	38	20	7	11	86	46	47
Uxbridge	38	20	7	11	49	41	47
Grays Athletic	38	20	2	16	69	48	42
Ruislip Manor	38	16	10	12	55	46	42
Marlow	38	16	10	12	66	58	42
Edgware	38	15	11	12	62	63	41
Redhill	38	15	9	14	55	46	39
Banstead Athletic	38	15	9	14	57	54	39
Woodford Town	38	13	9	16	57	60	35
Hoddesdon Town	38	12	7	19	56	55	31
Chalfont St Peter	38	10	10	18	50	67	30
Harefield United	38	10	8	20	41	60	28
Fleet Town	38	10	6	22	43	80	26
Haringey Borough	38	9	7	22	41	83	25
Alton Town	38	8	5	25	43	101	21
Chertsey Town	38	4	3	31	33	104	11

1980-81

Windsor & Eton	38	27	6	5	100	32	60
Basildon United	38	24	11	3	71	24	59
Banstead	38	23	10	5	73	32	56
Grays Athletic	38	23	7	8	81	42	53
Edgware	38	20	8	10	77	38	48
Leyton-Wingate	38	18	12	8	72	46	48
Welling	38	19	8	11	62	48	46
Woodford Town	38	18	9	11	84	53	45
Burnham	38	20	4	14	62	45	44
Harefield United	38	16	10	12	67	51	42
Ruislip Manor	38	14	13	11	49	51	41
Uxbridge	38	11	13	14	38	39	35
Fleet Town	38	8	13	17	50	65	29
Haringey Borough	38	9	10	19	41	68	28
Redhill	38	8	11	19	45	59	27
Hoddesdon Town	38	10	6	22	53	80	26
Chertsey Town	38	9	7	22	30	84	25
Marlow	38	7	10	21	43	85	24
Chalfont St Peter	38	5	5	28	39	89	15
Alton Town	38	2	5	31	33	139	9

1981-82

Leyton-Wingate	36	28	8	0	87	19	64
Edgware	36	20	10	6	76	52	50
Uxbridge	36	20	9	7	56	27	49
Burnham	36	19	7	10	64	44	45
Redhill	36	14	13	9	43	38	41
Harefield United	36	14	12	10	52	47	40
Ruislip Manor	36	15	9	12	58	55	39
Banstead Athletic	36	13	12	11	51	35	38
Chertsey Town	36	11	14	11	43	44	36
Woodford Town	36	13	8	15	48	45	34
Marlow	36	12	8	16	40	46	32
Kingsbury Town	36	11	10	15	43	52	32
Whyteleafe	36	8	15	13	30	41	31
Horley Town	36	10	10	16	40	45	30
Hoddesdon Town	36	11	7	18	50	57	29
Grays Athletic	36	10	8	18	41	62	28
Chalfont St Peter	36	8	10	18	42	50	26
Fleet Town	36	7	9	20	38	76	23
Haringey Borough	36	4	9	23	27	90	17

1982-83

Newbury Town	38	27	5	6	97	42	59
Grays Athletic	38	25	3	10	79	27	53
Redhill	38	22	9	7	68	38	53
Marlow	38	21	8	9	67	40	50
Chalfont St Peter	38	18	12	8	64	40	48
Burnham	38	17	13	8	80	46	47
Banstead Athletic	38	16	10	12	62	50	42
Whyteleafe	38	15	12	11	46	39	42
Harefield United	38	15	12	11	54	55	42
Kingsbury Town	38	16	10	12	56	40	41
Hoddesdon Town	38	15	10	13	58	54	40
Flackwell Heath	38	11	13	14	45	50	35
Horley Town	38	10	13	15	45	58	33
Edgware	38	12	7	19	48	62	31
Chertsey Town	38	10	10	18	61	88	30
Ruislip Manor	38	12	4	22	55	70	28
Fleet Town	38	8	10	20	38	65	25
Thatcham Town	38	8	6	24	30	85	22
Haringey Town	38	5	9	24	27	82	19
Camberley Town	38	4	10	24	31	80	16

1983-84

Redhill	40	28	9	3	73	28	93
Chalfont St Peter	40	27	10	3	88	32	91
Burnham	40	27	7	6	80	29	88
Whyteleafe	40	24	8	8	63	32	80
Flackwell Heath	40	21	7	12	57	37	70
Harefield United	40	20	8	12	62	47	68
Banstead Athletic	40	19	10	11	63	48	67
Marlow	40	17	7	16	65	63	58
Hoddesdon Town	40	15	13	12	53	52	58
Ruislip Manor	40	16	9	15	59	44	57
Kingsbury Town	40	15	12	13	58	52	57
Wolverton Town	40	12	12	16	59	65	48
Edgware	40	13	8	19	47	51	47
Harwich & Parkeston	40	13	9	18	54	66	45
Chertsey Town	40	12	6	22	41	63	42
Berkhamsted Town	40	10	11	19	50	63	41
Thatcham Town	40	8	14	18	65	79	35
Horley Town	40	9	6	25	34	83	33
Haringey Borough	40	8	8	24	44	80	32
Fleet Town	40	6	8	26	31	82	26
Camberley Town	40	4	6	26	35	85	22

Harwich & Parkeston and Thatcham Town both had 3 points deducted.

NORTHERN LEAGUE

1889-90

Darlington St Augustine's	18	12	2	4	39	17	26
Newcastle West End	18	12	2	4	44	24	26
Stockton	18	10	4	4	41	18	24
Newcastle East End	18	9	3	6	32	28	21
Darlington	18	7	6	5	46	20	20
Middlesbrough	18	8	3	7	42	37	19
South Bank	18	6	2	10	33	60	14
Auckland Town	18	4	4	10	41	49	12
Birtley	18	3	3	12	28	48	9
Elswick Rangers	18	2	5	11	21	66	9

Darlington St Augustine's won championship on goal-average.

1890-91

Ironopolis (Middlesbrough)	14	9	2	3	37	24	20
Middlesbrough	14	8	3	3	33	17	19
Sunderland Albion	14	7	3	4	33	16	17
Stockton	14	8	1	5	38	19	17
Darlington	14	7	0	7	25	29	14
Newcastle East End	14	5	2	7	25	39	12
Newcastle West End	14	3	4	7	21	38	10
Darlington St Augustine's	14	0	3	11	14	44	3

1891-92

Ironopolis (Middlesbrough)	16	14	1	1	49	13	29
Middlesbrough	16	13	0	3	33	13	26
Sheffield United	16	10	2	4	49	21	22
Newcastle East End	16	9	2	5	37	20	20
Stockton	16	6	2	8	31	34	14
Sunderland Albion	16	5	0	11	36	38	10
South Bank	16	3	2	11	21	50	8
Newcastle West End	16	4	0	12	21	56	8
Darlington	16	2	3	11	17	49	7

1892-93

Ironopolis (Middlesbrough)	10	9	1	0	22	6	19
Newcastle United	10	5	1	4	30	19	11
Sheffield United	10	4	2	4	18	16	10
Middlesbrough	10	4	0	6	17	17	8
Stockton	10	3	1	6	24	27	7
Darlington	10	2	1	7	11	37	5

Newcastle East End officially changed their name during the season to Newcastle United on 9th December 1892.

1893-94

Middlesbrough	14	11	1	2	51	16	23
Stockton	14	10	1	3	41	23	21
South Bank	14	8	0	6	36	34	16
Darlington	14	7	1	6	30	25	15
Bishop Auckland	14	6	0	8	41	39	12
Whitby	14	5	2	7	45	43	12
North Skelton Rovers	14	3	1	10	25	52	7
Darlington St Augustine's	14	3	0	11	25	62	6

1894-95

Middlesbrough	18	12	5	1	58	17	29
South Bank	18	11	4	3	64	23	26
Tow Law	18	10	3	5	59	30	23
Darlington	18	11	0	7	56	30	22
Whitby	18	8	2	8	43	45	18
Stockton	18	8	1	9	44	37	17
Bishop Auckland	18	7	2	9	42	39	16
Howden Rangers	18	6	1	11	40	56	13
Darlington St Augustine's	18	5	3	10	38	66	13
North Skelton Rovers	18	1	1	16	16	117	3

1895-96

Darlington	16	10	4	2	53	24	24
South Bank	16	9	2	5	44	20	20
Middlesbrough	16	8	4	4	28	22	20
Bishop Auckland	16	7	3	6	42	32	17
Tow Law	16	5	5	6	23	28	15
Whitby	16	6	3	7	23	38	15
Stockton	16	5	3	8	26	30	13
Howden-le-Wear	16	4	3	9	19	36	11
Saltburn Swifts	16	4	1	11	12	40	9

1896-97

Middlesbrough	16	11	4	1	36	15	26
Darlington	16	10	2	4	54	35	22
South Bank	16	10	1	5	32	25	21
Stockton	16	7	3	6	37	24	17
Tow Law	16	7	1	8	29	25	15
Bishop Auckland	16	6	3	7	23	34	15
Crook Town	16	4	2	10	35	42	10
Leadgate Park	16	4	1	11	27	45	9
Darlington St Augustine's	16	5	9	9	26	54	7

Darlington St Augustine's had 2 points deducted.
Saltburn Swifts withdrew from the league on 3rd April 1897.

Playing record	13	3	4	6	21	33	10

1897-98

First Division

Stockton	16	11	2	3	37	20	24
Middlesbrough	16	9	4	3	42	22	22
Darlington	16	8	2	6	41	31	18
Bishop Auckland	16	6	4	6	33	35	16
Darlington St Augustine's	16	7	2	7	29	32	16
Leadgate Park	16	5	4	7	23	34	14
South Bank	16	5	3	8	34	38	13
Tow Law	16	4	4	8	16	24	12
Crook Town	16	3	3	10	17	36	9

Owing to a smallpox epidemic in the Middlesbrough area the 1897-98 season was not completed until the following season. The three games were played as follows: –
10th September 1898 – Middlesbrough v Crook Town
17th September 1898 – Middlesbrough v Darlington
8th October 1898 – Tow Law v Middlesbrough

Second Division

Howden-le-Wear	10	5	2	3	17	14	12
Darlington Rise Carr Rangers	10	5	1	4	22	18	11
Loftus	10	5	1	4	18	17	11
Leadgate Exiles	10	5	0	5	17	17	10
Shildon United	10	4	1	5	15	17	9
Brotton	10	3	1	6	14	20	7

Britannia Rovers "were struck out of the competition" on 31st March 1898. Their playing record was: – 6 0 1 5 6 25 1

1898-99

First Division

Bishop Auckland	16	9	7	0	35	16	25
Darlington	16	10	3	3	50	29	23
Middlesbrough	16	7	4	5	29	27	18
South Bank	16	6	6	4	20	21	18
Darlington St Augustine's	16	5	5	6	19	23	15
Leadgate Park	16	4	4	8	25	30	12
Stockton	16	4	4	8	25	31	12
Tow Law	16	3	6	7	18	25	12
Crook Town	16	4	1	11	25	44	9

Second Division

Stockton St John's	18	11	5	2	38	11	27
Thornaby Utopians	18	10	4	4	45	21	24
Thornaby	18	10	1	7	42	28	21
Brotton	17	9	2	6	33	22	20
Stockton Vulcan	17	10	0	7	29	30	20
Shildon United	16	7	1	8	21	20	15
West Hartlepool	18	6	1	11	23	48	13
Scarborough	16	5	1	10	21	37	11
Loftus	17	4	3	10	18	41	11
Howden-le-Wear	17	4	2	11	21	33	10

The following matches were not played: – Howden-le-Wear v Brotton; Stockton Vulcan v Loftus; Scarborough v Shildon United (both home and away matches).
The above table shows many discrepancies from the tables which appeared in newspapers.
The Scarborough v Shildon United games home and away were counted as 0-0 draws, yet were not played! Stockton St John's final record was given as: 18 10 6 2 39 13 26
but at the League AGM on 12th June 1899 the League Secretary officially gave their correct record as above. To add to the chaos five games were replayed following protests but these tables were not amended in various newspapers.

1899-1900

First Division

Darlington	16	12	3	1	42	16	27
Stockton St John's	16	10	3	3	32	17	23
Bishop Auckland	16	9	2	5	41	21	20
Darlington St Augustine's	16	7	4	5	34	27	18
South Bank	16	7	3	6	18	26	17
Crook Town	16	3	7	6	14	24	13
Thornaby Utopians	16	3	6	7	14	25	12
Tow Law	16	3	3	10	23	43	9
Stockton	16	2	1	13	25	44	5

Second Division

Whitby	14	9	3	2	49	23	21
Thornaby	14	8	3	3	29	15	19
Grangetown Athletic	14	7	5	2	36	24	19
Loftus	14	6	2	6	23	24	14
West Hartlepool	14	6	0	8	28	28	12
Scarborough	14	4	3	7	27	34	11
Stockton Vulcan	14	4	2	8	20	36	10
Brotton	14	3	0	11	20	48	6

Dorman, Long & Co. withdrew from the league on 15th November 1899. Shildon United withdrew from the league on 13th January 1900. Both playing records were deleted from the League table.

1900-01

Bishop Auckland	20	12	5	3	61	22	29
Darlington St Augustine's	20	10	5	5	37	25	25
Darlington	20	11	2	7	55	37	24
Stockton	20	8	5	7	34	25	21
Crook Town	20	7	7	6	38	30	21
Scarborough	20	9	3	8	25	28	21
South Bank	20	9	3	8	35	45	21
Thornaby Utopians	20	8	2	10	30	37	18
Stockton St John's	20	7	3	10	23	35	17
West Hartlepool	20	5	5	10	31	37	15
Whitby	20	2	4	14	17	65	8

1901-02

Bishop Auckland	18	12	3	3	48	22	27
Grangetown Athletic	18	9	8	1	34	14	26
Darlington	18	9	4	5	37	22	22
South Bank	18	7	6	5	32	23	20
Darlington St Augustine's	18	7	5	6	31	22	19
Stockton	18	6	7	5	25	25	19
Crook Town	18	5	3	10	29	41	13
West Hartlepool	18	5	3	10	24	48	13
Scarborough	18	5	3	10	20	35	13
Stockton St John's	18	2	4	12	13	41	8

1902-03

Newcastle United 'A'	24	22	0	2	100	14	42
Sunderland 'A'	24	18	4	2	93	22	40
Middlesbrough 'A'	24	13	7	4	66	30	33
Bishop Auckland	24	13	3	8	57	35	29
Stockton	24	9	5	10	35	38	23
Darlington	24	10	3	11	34	50	23
South Bank	24	8	6	10	30	44	22
Crook Town	24	9	4	11	27	41	22
Grangetown Athletic	24	8	4	12	34	47	20
Stockton St John's	24	6	5	13	24	52	15
Scarborough	24	5	4	15	23	69	14
Darlington St Augustine's	24	4	5	15	21	58	13
West Hartlepool	24	3	6	15	27	71	12

Newcastle United 'A' and Stockton St John's had 2 points deducted.

1903-04

Newcastle United 'A'	24	19	1	4	97	23	39
Bishop Auckland 'A'	24	17	2	5	55	27	36
Sunderland 'A'	24	14	6	4	66	32	34
Middlesbrough 'A'	24	12	5	7	56	32	29
Stockton	24	13	2	9	36	34	28
Darlington	24	11	3	10	48	49	25
Grangetown Athletic	24	10	3	11	50	49	23
South Bank	24	9	1	14	42	56	19
Darlington St Augustine's	24	8	2	14	30	58	18
Shildon Athletic	24	8	2	14	28	54	18
Scarborough	24	7	2	15	36	70	16
Crook Town	24	5	4	15	33	62	14
West Hartlepool	24	5	3	16	31	62	13

Stockton St John's withdrew from the league on 8th October 1903. Shildon Athletic were admitted on Stockton St John's resignation and agreed to take over their fixtures. At that stage, Stockton St John's had played three matches (all defeats), which were recorded against Shildon Athletic.

1904-05

Newcastle United 'A'	24	22	0	2	83	12	44
Sunderland 'A'	24	16	3	5	59	29	33
Middlesbrough 'A'	24	13	6	5	69	35	32
Darlington	24	9	6	9	38	38	24
Shildon Athletic	24	8	7	9	48	48	23
South Bank	24	9	5	10	42	44	23
West Hartlepool	24	10	3	11	35	44	23
Bishop Auckland	24	10	2	12	51	49	22
Stockton	24	8	6	10	32	37	22
Darlington St Augustine's	24	9	4	11	34	43	22
Grangetown Athletic	24	8	4	12	36	52	20
Scarborough	24	4	5	15	22	60	13
Crook Town	24	4	1	19	23	81	9

Sunderland 'A' had 2 points deducted

1905-06

Sunderland 'A'	26	21	3	2	90	21	45
Newcastle United 'A'	26	19	4	3	92	14	42
Bishop Auckland	26	15	3	8	45	39	33
Darlington	26	12	7	7	47	47	31
Middlesbrough 'A'	26	12	5	9	59	30	29
South Bank	26	13	2	11	49	35	28
Shildon Athletic	26	11	6	9	40	45	28
Spennymoor United	26	8	6	12	34	34	22
Grangetown Athletic	26	9	2	15	37	43	20
Stockton	26	7	5	14	32	54	19
Crook Town	26	7	5	14	33	57	19
West Hartlepool	26	7	5	14	49	65	17
Scarborough	26	7	2	17	24	93	16
Darlington St Augustine's	26	3	7	16	16	70	13

West Hartlepool had 2 points deducted.

1906-07

Stockton	22	17	2	3	44	16	36
South Bank	22	14	3	5	46	24	31
Crook Town	22	12	1	9	41	33	25
Leadgate Park	22	11	2	9	40	34	24
Bishop Auckland	22	10	3	9	40	33	23
Spennymoor United	22	9	5	8	28	30	23
Darlington	22	9	2	11	30	37	20
Shildon Athletic	22	8	3	11	30	38	19
Grangetown Athletic	22	8	1	13	24	39	17
West Hartlepool	22	7	2	13	33	44	16
Darlington St Augustine's	22	6	3	13	32	44	15
Scarborough	22	7	1	14	34	50	15

1907-08

Stockton	22	13	7	2	49	21	33
South Bank	22	15	3	4	53	26	33
Crook Town	22	12	4	6	40	33	28
West Hartlepool	22	10	4	8	40	32	24
Spennymoor United	22	11	2	9	39	36	24
Bishop Auckland	22	9	4	9	40	36	22
Darlington St Augustine's	22	9	3	10	32	39	21
Saltburn	22	9	2	11	46	47	20
Darlington	22	9	2	11	39	41	20
Leadgate Park	22	6	4	12	33	43	16
Grangetown Athletic	22	3	7	12	21	52	13
Scarborough	22	5	0	17	44	70	10

1908-09

Bishop Auckland	22	14	5	3	67	29	33
South Bank	22	15	3	4	61	34	33
Stockton	22	10	6	6	46	29	26
Crook Town	22	10	6	6	49	40	26
West Hartlepool	22	11	2	9	50	35	24
Grangetown Athletic	22	9	3	10	47	53	21
Darlington St Augustine's	22	8	4	10	48	52	20
Scarborough	22	9	1	12	45	56	19
Saltburn	22	6	6	10	33	42	18
West Auckland	22	6	4	12	32	46	16
York City	22	6	3	13	31	73	15
Leadgate Park	22	6	1	15	30	50	13

1909-10

Bishop Auckland	22	15	3	4	67	37	33
South Bank	22	13	4	5	50	26	30
Stockton	22	13	3	6	68	34	29
Darlington St Augustine's	22	12	2	8	41	35	26
West Auckland	22	9	4	9	35	35	22
Crook Town	22	8	4	10	45	43	20
Scarborough	22	8	4	10	43	49	20
West Hartlepool	22	8	4	10	32	40	20
Knaresborough	22	8	4	10	43	58	20
Saltburn	22	7	4	11	28	46	18
Grangetown Athletic	22	6	2	14	30	44	14
York City	22	4	4	14	36	71	12

1910-11

Eston United	22	15	4	3	56	24	34
South Bank	22	14	4	4	50	23	32
Bishop Auckland	22	13	5	4	67	30	31
Stockton	22	10	6	6	43	27	26
West Auckland	22	10	6	6	39	27	26
Darlington St Augustine's	22	9	4	9	40	41	22
Crook Town	22	8	4	10	40	48	20
Leadgate Park	22	8	3	11	38	43	19
Stanley United	22	6	6	10	29	41	18
Saltburn	22	5	5	12	35	51	15
Grangetown Athletic	22	4	7	11	13	33	15
Knaresborough	22	2	2	18	27	89	6

1911-12

Bishop Auckland	22	14	6	2	60	28	34
South Bank	22	12	5	5	33	18	29
Crook Town	22	13	3	6	37	24	29
Leadgate Park	22	11	3	8	36	32	25
Willington	22	10	3	9	42	36	23
Stockton	22	8	5	9	46	34	21
Darlington St Augustine's	22	8	5	9	44	36	21
Grangetown Athletic	22	7	6	9	25	32	20
Stanley United	22	8	3	11	27	35	19
Eston United	22	7	3	12	33	40	17
West Auckland	22	6	2	14	29	52	14
Saltburn	22	4	4	14	20	65	12

1912-13

Esh Winning Rangers	22	13	6	3	40	22	32
Willington	22	12	4	6	43	26	28
South Bank	22	12	4	6	36	23	28
Crook Town	22	11	5	6	33	23	27
Craghead United	22	11	3	8	51	26	25
Stockton	22	10	4	8	34	27	24
Darlington St Augustine's	22	9	5	8	33	28	23
Eston United	22	9	5	8	44	43	23
Stanley United	22	6	4	12	29	54	16
Bishop Auckland	22	5	5	12	37	52	15
Grangetown Athletic	22	5	2	15	29	57	12
Leadgate Park	22	3	5	14	32	60	11

1913-14

Willington	24	20	2	2	52	17	42
South Bank	24	16	4	4	47	22	36
Crook Town	24	11	5	8	41	27	27
Darlington St Augustine's	24	11	5	8	35	29	27
Craghead United	24	11	3	10	42	36	25
Stockton	24	8	8	8	41	35	24
Bishop Auckland	24	9	4	11	38	35	22
Stanley United	24	7	7	10	33	36	21
Eston United	24	8	5	11	31	38	21
Leadgate Park	24	6	7	11	30	46	19
Esh Winning	24	5	8	11	27	42	18
Grangetown Athletic	24	5	7	12	26	52	17
Redcar	24	4	5	15	30	58	13

1914-15

Crook Town	16	12	1	3	36	10	25
Bishop Auckland	16	10	4	2	42	13	24
Willington	16	8	2	6	37	23	18
Leadgate Park	16	7	4	5	33	22	18
Stanley United	16	7	2	7	31	25	16
Esh Winning	15	6	2	7	25	30	14
Scarborough	16	6	1	9	23	49	13
Darlington St Augustine's	16	3	1	12	22	51	7
Stockton	15	3	1	11	17	43	7

The following three teams withdrew from the league without fulfilling their fixtures: Eston United (12th December 1914), Grangetown Athletic (12th December 1914) and South Bank (29th January 1915). Their playing record was deleted.

1919-20

Bishop Auckland	26	16	6	4	76	23	38
South Bank	26	16	6	4	78	27	38
Crook Town	26	17	4	5	57	24	38
Stanley United	26	13	5	8	52	39	31
Grangetown St Mary's	26	11	9	6	51	41	31
Willington	26	11	7	8	43	36	29
Esh Winning	26	11	4	11	48	34	26
Eston United	26	9	6	11	48	51	24
Darlington Railway Athletic	26	10	4	12	45	58	24
Redcar	26	9	4	13	38	55	22
West Hartlepool St Joseph's	26	7	6	13	34	51	20
Stockton	26	5	5	16	44	70	15
Auckland St Helen's United	26	5	5	16	26	67	15
Scarborough	26	5	3	18	30	94	13

South Bank were declared Champions after a three -way Championship Play-off: – Bishop Auckland beat South Bank 4-2 at Stockton on 4th September 1920. Crook Town beat Bishop Auckland 2-1 at Willington on 11th September 1920. South Bank beat Crook Town 4-0 on 18th September 1920.

1920-21

Bishop Auckland	26	19	5	2	71	24	43
Stockton	26	18	3	5	57	43	39
Crook Town	26	15	4	7	58	39	34
South Bank	26	14	6	6	48	38	34
Willington	26	14	3	9	52	43	31
Darlington Railway Athletic	26	13	2	11	43	39	28
Tow Law Town	26	11	7	8	50	32	27
Langley Park	26	8	7	11	53	48	23
Esh Winning	26	9	5	12	39	39	23
Eston United	26	7	8	11	43	51	22
Stanley United	26	8	3	15	51	56	19
Grangetown St Mary's	26	6	2	18	30	75	14
Redcar	26	5	4	17	22	58	14
Scarborough	26	4	3	19	28	60	11

Tow Law Town had 2 points deducted.

1921-22

South Bank	26	18	6	2	59	23	42
Bishop Auckland	26	15	8	3	53	22	38
Crook Town	26	16	6	4	58	31	38
Stockton	26	13	4	9	59	41	30
Cockfield	26	12	6	8	52	37	30
Tow Law Town	26	13	4	9	52	38	30
Esh Winning	26	12	3	11	39	41	27
Willington	26	9	6	11	55	57	24
Eston United	26	10	3	13	40	52	23
Langley Park	26	8	5	13	34	52	21
Darlington Railway Athletic	26	7	6	13	45	58	20
Scarborough	26	4	8	14	39	71	16
Stanley United	26	5	3	18	36	64	13
Redcar	26	3	6	17	20	53	12

1922-23

Eston United	26	17	3	6	60	41	37
Bishop Auckland	26	16	4	6	54	35	36
Cockfield	26	13	4	9	56	40	30
Crook Town	26	10	8	8	41	43	28
Esh Winning	26	12	3	11	48	47	27
Loftus Albion	26	10	7	9	41	41	27
Stockton	26	11	3	12	49	35	25
Tow Law Town	26	8	8	10	36	39	24
Darlington Railway Athletic	26	10	3	13	35	40	23
Stanley United	26	8	7	11	44	57	23
Langley Park	26	11	0	15	45	60	22
Scarborough	26	10	1	15	51	52	21
Willington	26	9	3	14	37	47	21
South Bank	26	9	2	15	36	56	20

1923-24

Tow Law Town	28	17	6	5	61	34	40
Ferryhill Athletic	28	15	9	4	69	36	39
Bishop Auckland	28	17	3	8	53	33	37
Stockton	28	16	4	8	79	52	36
Crook Town	28	14	8	6	66	50	36
South Bank	28	13	7	8	49	31	33
Cockfield	28	12	5	11	50	43	29
Loftus Albion	28	11	4	13	42	47	26
Eston United	28	9	7	12	56	53	25
Scarborough	28	8	9	11	55	55	25
Stanley United	28	8	7	13	44	65	23
Darlington Railway Athletic	28	8	6	14	45	69	22
Esh Winning	28	6	6	16	36	69	18
Langley Park	28	6	4	18	36	69	16
Willington	28	5	5	18	33	68	15

1924-25

Tow Law Town	28	20	3	5	73	27	43
Crook Town	28	19	4	5	70	29	42
Stockton	28	15	7	6	54	33	37
Bishop Auckland	28	14	4	10	58	37	32
Cockfield	28	10	11	7	50	42	31
Willington	28	12	3	13	67	57	27
Ferryhill Athletic	28	12	3	13	70	60	27
South Bank	28	11	5	12	44	42	27
Loftus Albion	28	12	3	13	50	72	27
Scarborough	28	11	2	15	50	45	24
Stanley United	28	10	4	14	33	60	24
Langley Park	28	9	5	14	31	49	23
Esh Winning	28	8	5	15	42	63	21
Darlington Railway Athletic	28	7	6	15	32	71	20
Eston United	28	6	3	19	32	69	15

1925-26

Willington	26	19	3	4	84	44	41
Stockton	26	17	2	7	79	39	36
Esh Winning	26	17	2	7	76	41	36
Ferryhill Athletic	26	14	4	8	62	42	32
Bishop Auckland	26	13	5	8	64	50	31
Cockfield	26	13	3	10	59	51	29
Tow Law Town	26	11	4	11	58	54	26
Crook Town	26	10	5	11	48	48	25
South Bank	26	10	4	12	37	47	24
Langley Park	26	10	4	12	40	53	24
Scarborough	26	10	2	14	53	72	22
Stanley United	26	5	5	16	49	61	15
Loftus Albion	26	3	7	16	27	87	13
Eston United	26	3	4	19	36	83	10

1926-27

Crook Town	26	18	7	1	79	32	43
South Bank	26	17	4	5	74	43	38
Ferryhill Athletic	26	16	3	7	76	37	35
Tow Law Town	26	15	4	7	74	46	34
Stockton	26	15	3	8	66	42	33
Bishop Auckland	26	14	3	9	68	42	31
Whitby United	26	13	2	11	69	57	28
Willington	26	10	7	9	68	58	27
Cockfield	26	10	4	12	64	55	24
Loftus Albion	26	9	4	13	55	70	22
Langley Park	26	7	2	17	46	84	16
Stanley United	26	3	5	18	40	77	11
Eston United	26	4	3	19	42	106	11
Esh Winning	26	4	3	19	32	104	11

1927-28

Chilton Colliery Recreation Athletic	24	16	5	3	71	35	37
Whitby United	24	14	4	6	63	58	32
Stockton	24	13	4	7	62	42	30
Cockfield	24	10	8	6	50	40	28
Willington	24	11	3	10	78	57	25
Esh Winning	24	10	4	10	58	58	24
South Bank	24	8	7	9	60	63	23
Tow Law Town	24	10	2	12	58	53	22
Ferryhill Athletic	24	7	5	12	52	73	19
Stanley United	24	7	4	13	57	71	18
Loftus Albion	24	7	4	13	48	64	18
Bishop Auckland	24	7	4	13	43	65	18
Langley Park	24	7	4	13	41	62	18

Crook Town were suspended by the Durham F.A. on 7th January 1928 and their playing record was officially deleted from the table on 9th February 1928.

1928-29

Stockton	24	13	8	3	73	46	34
Tow Law Town	24	15	3	6	70	40	33
Whitby United	24	14	4	6	72	47	32
Willington	24	13	4	7	63	49	30
Langley Park	24	9	8	7	50	44	26
Chilton Colliery Recreation Athletic	24	11	3	10	54	55	25
Ferryhill Athletic	24	10	4	10	47	55	24
South Bank	24	6	10	8	44	50	22
Stanley United	24	7	6	11	45	55	20
Bishop Auckland	24	7	6	11	45	58	20
Cockfield	24	6	6	12	41	50	18
Esh Winning	24	7	2	15	40	54	16
Loftus Albion	24	5	2	17	34	75	12

1929-30

Willington	24	16	3	5	71	41	35
Stockton	24	16	1	7	72	36	33
Bishop Auckland	24	11	5	8	58	47	27
Eden Colliery Welfare	24	11	4	9	53	51	26
South Bank	24	9	7	8	60	53	25
Whitby United	24	10	5	9	69	76	25
Ferryhill Athletic	24	11	2	11	53	59	24
Esh Winning	24	11	2	11	56	64	24
Chilton Colliery Recreation Athletic	24	10	2	12	58	54	22
Crook Town	24	9	2	13	40	53	20
Cockfield	24	9	3	12	43	59	19
Tow Law Town	24	6	4	14	49	62	16
Stanley United	24	6	2	16	44	71	14

Cockfield had 2 points deducted.
Langley Park resigned from the League on 11th December 1929 and their playing record was officially deleted from the table.

1930-31

Bishop Auckland	24	17	3	4	75	36	37
Stockton	24	15	5	4	90	35	35
South Bank	24	13	4	7	56	42	30
Tow Law Town	24	12	4	8	43	50	28
Stanley United	24	13	1	10	70	48	27
Cockfield	24	10	7	7	52	65	27
Willington	24	10	5	9	54	47	25
Whitby United	24	8	6	10	56	53	22
Eden Colliery Welfare	24	8	6	10	37	53	22
Trimdon Grange Colliery	24	7	6	11	60	76	20
Esh Winning	24	5	5	14	44	73	15
Chilton Colliery Recreation Athletic	24	5	3	16	44	78	13
Ferryhill Athletic	24	4	3	17	41	66	11

1931-32

Stockton	26	20	2	4	91	32	42
Trimdon Grange Colliery	26	13	5	8	63	48	31
South Bank	26	13	4	9	60	55	30
Bishop Auckland	26	13	3	10	67	49	29
Cockfield	26	10	9	7	69	55	29
Tow Law Town	26	11	6	9	46	45	28
Ferryhill Athletic	26	12	3	11	66	63	27
Whitby United	26	12	3	11	67	66	27
Evenwood Town	26	12	3	11	61	61	27
Chilton Colliery Recreation Athletic	26	11	3	12	59	61	25
Willington	26	10	4	12	55	62	24
Stanley United	26	6	4	16	43	65	16
Harrogate	26	6	3	17	45	79	15
Esh Winning	26	5	4	17	42	93	14

1932-33

Stockton	26	20	1	5	77	34	41
Shildon	26	16	4	6	63	38	36
South Bank	26	14	5	7	59	45	33
Willington	26	14	5	7	68	56	33
Ferryhill Athletic	26	12	4	10	64	51	28
Bishop Auckland	26	11	5	10	67	67	27
Trimdon Grange Colliery	26	11	4	11	62	63	26
Whitby United	26	9	6	11	85	65	24
Cockfield	26	9	5	12	57	64	23
Esh Winning	26	8	7	11	48	57	23
Stanley United	26	8	6	12	53	65	22
Evenwood Town	26	8	5	13	46	60	21
Tow Law Town	26	6	4	16	51	90	16
Chilton Colliery Recreation Athletic	26	4	3	19	42	87	11

1933-34

Shildon	26	16	5	5	81	41	37
Whitby United	26	14	7	5	67	53	35
South Bank	26	12	4	10	48	43	28
Ferryhill Athletic	26	12	4	10	63	61	28
Stockton	26	12	3	11	59	60	27
Willington	26	10	6	10	59	48	26
Cockfield	26	10	6	10	58	49	26
Evenwood Town	26	11	4	11	54	60	26
Trimdon Grange Colliery	26	10	4	12	59	56	24
Bishop Auckland	26	8	8	10	63	61	24
Tow Law Town	26	8	7	11	51	67	23
Chilton Colliery Recreation Athletic	26	9	3	14	47	65	21
Stanley United	26	5	10	11	47	66	20
Esh Winning	26	7	5	14	39	65	19

1934-35

Shildon	26	19	5	2	86	23	43
Stockton	26	17	2	7	88	55	36
Ferryhill Athletic	26	16	3	7	69	43	35
Tow Law Town	26	14	4	8	54	46	32
South Bank	26	14	3	9	49	33	31
Bishop Auckland	26	12	4	10	73	59	28
Willington	26	12	2	12	53	57	26
Cockfield	26	11	3	12	69	73	25
West Auckland Town	26	9	5	12	59	69	23
Trimdon Grange Colliery	26	8	6	12	51	75	22
Whitby United	26	7	5	14	52	65	19
Chilton Colliery Recreation Athletic	26	6	5	15	56	87	17
Stanley United	26	5	5	16	44	80	15
Evenwood Town	26	5	2	19	41	79	12

Esh Winning disbanded on 5th October and West Auckland Town were officially admitted into the League on 18th October 1934.
West Auckland agreed to take over Esh Winning's remaining fixtures including the four matches Esh had played with the following record: –

Esh Winning	4	0	1	3	5	13	1

1935-36

Shildon	26	20	4	2	81	27	44
South Bank	26	19	1	6	86	43	39
Stockton	26	14	5	7	93	64	33
Willington	26	14	5	7	64	47	33
Bishop Auckland	26	10	7	9	66	65	27
Evenwood Town	26	11	5	10	59	63	27
West Auckland Town	26	9	7	10	54	52	25
Ferryhill Athletic	26	9	7	10	65	64	25
Cockfield	26	8	6	12	59	53	22
Chilton Colliery Recreation Athletic	26	8	5	13	62	93	21
Trimdon Grange	26	8	3	15	41	67	19
Whitby United	26	7	4	15	62	83	18
Stanley United	26	6	6	14	53	73	18
Tow Law Town	26	5	3	18	47	98	13

1936-37

Shildon	26	20	6	0	80	25	46
Bishop Auckland	26	19	2	5	70	37	40
South Bank	26	15	4	7	72	49	34
Cockfield	26	15	2	9	67	49	32
Whitby United	26	14	1	11	72	60	29
Stockton	26	12	3	11	77	52	27
West Auckland Town	26	11	5	10	68	58	27
Ferryhill Athletic	26	11	3	12	62	66	25
Evenwood Town	26	10	2	14	58	75	22
Willington	26	10	1	15	63	74	21
Crook Town	26	9	3	14	58	77	21
Chilton Colliery Recreation Athletic	26	7	3	16	53	67	17
Trimdon Grange	26	6	1	19	38	86	13
Tow Law Town	26	4	2	20	39	102	10

1937-38

Ferryhill Athletic	26	21	0	5	81	36	42
Bishop Auckland	26	16	4	6	70	38	36
Shildon	26	16	2	8	72	39	34
Cockfield	26	14	6	6	44	31	34
Stockton	26	14	5	7	69	48	33
Chilton Colliery Recreation Athletic	26	11	6	9	44	45	28
Billingham South	26	11	4	11	59	56	26
Evenwood Town	26	9	4	13	45	55	22
Whitby United	26	8	6	12	47	78	22
South Bank	26	8	4	14	49	56	20
Willington	26	9	2	15	55	66	20
Crook Town	26	9	2	15	41	56	20
West Auckland Town	26	7	3	16	52	68	17
Tow Law Town	26	2	6	18	44	100	10

1938-39

Bishop Auckland	26	21	3	2	94	27	45
Shildon	26	21	2	3	92	27	44
Stockton	26	17	3	6	88	44	37
Billingham	26	15	1	10	76	57	31
Willington	26	13	4	9	75	62	30
Whitby United	26	12	1	13	51	64	25
Cockfield	26	9	6	11	53	55	24
West Auckland Town	26	11	2	13	50	56	24
Ferryhill Athletic	26	9	4	13	62	65	22
Tow Law Town	26	8	3	15	39	81	19
South Bank	26	5	8	13	43	69	18
Evenwood Town	26	7	2	17	43	70	16
Chilton Colliery Recreation Athletic	26	6	3	17	47	95	15
Crook Town	26	4	6	16	52	93	14

1939-40

Shildon	10	9	0	1	47	19	18
Bishop Auckland	10	5	2	3	33	27	12
Crook Town	10	5	1	4	29	24	11
Heaton Stannington	10	3	1	6	26	29	7
South Bank	10	3	1	6	20	34	7
West Auckland Town	10	2	1	7	18	40	5

An Extraordinary General Meeting was held in the Board Room of Bishop Auckland F.C. on Saturday 16th December 1939, owing to the resignations of six clubs because of "War-time difficulties". It was agreed to re-organise the League as from 1st January 1940, and that the "New" League would consist of eight clubs.
After playing seven games between them, Tow Law Town (4) and Willington (3) resigned from the League on the 20 March 1940, thus reducing the League to only six clubs.

1945-46

Stanley United	22	20	0	2	101	29	40
South Bank	22	16	1	5	61	41	33
Billingham Synthonia	22	13	0	9	70	57	26
Shildon	22	12	2	8	57	48	26
Bishop Auckland	22	12	1	9	83	46	25
Evenwood Town	22	9	3	10	45	57	21
Tow Law Town	22	8	4	10	55	59	20
Willington	22	7	5	10	37	52	19
Brandon Welfare	22	7	5	10	42	64	19
Crook Colliery Welfare	22	7	2	13	51	60	16
Ferryhill Athletic	22	5	3	14	44	76	13
West Auckland Town	22	2	2	18	29	89	6

1946-47

Bishop Auckland	26	18	2	6	81	47	38
Crook Colliery Welfare	26	18	2	6	85	50	38
Stanley United	26	15	5	6	81	49	35
Shildon	26	15	5	6	72	45	35
Willington	26	13	5	8	69	53	31
Ferryhill Athletic	26	13	3	10	77	66	29
Evenwood Town	26	10	6	10	65	72	26
Heaton Stannington	26	11	2	13	58	68	24
Billingham Synthonia	26	9	3	14	58	60	21
Tow Law Town	26	9	3	14	59	68	21
West Auckland Town	26	7	5	14	39	62	19
South Bank	26	7	4	15	65	61	18
Whitby Town	26	7	4	15	46	75	18
Brandon Welfare	26	4	3	19	38	117	11

1947-48

Ferryhill Athletic	26	20	4	2	90	40	44
Bishop Auckland	26	17	3	6	90	41	37
South Bank	26	13	7	6	61	40	33
Shildon	26	15	0	11	52	51	30
Evenwood Town	26	12	5	9	53	44	29
Stanley United	26	10	7	9	60	62	27
Tow Law Town	26	12	3	11	58	61	27
Crook Colliery Welfare	26	12	3	11	53	58	27
Willington	26	11	3	12	53	54	25
West Auckland Town	26	8	5	13	57	73	21
East Tanfield Colliery Welfare	26	7	5	14	52	67	19
Whitby Town	26	8	3	15	52	76	19
Heaton Stannington	26	4	7	15	47	66	15
Billingham Synthonia	26	5	1	20	51	96	11

1948-49

Evenwood Town	26	19	4	3	64	33	42
Bishop Auckland	26	19	3	4	79	38	41
Billingham Synthonia	26	16	5	5	69	41	37
Ferryhill Athletic	26	14	3	9	53	49	31
Willington	26	13	4	9	79	55	30
Penrith	26	14	1	11	66	60	29
Crook Colliery Welfare	26	9	7	10	61	66	25
South Bank	26	9	6	11	54	63	24
Shildon	26	9	5	12	59	57	23
West Auckland Town	26	11	1	14	53	63	23
Stanley United	26	7	4	15	47	66	18
Whitby Town	26	7	3	16	39	68	17
Tow Law Town	26	4	5	17	52	79	13
Heaton Stannington	26	3	5	18	41	78	11

1949-50

Bishop Auckland	26	21	1	4	81	28	43
Billingham Synthonia	26	17	3	6	77	46	37
Whitby Town	26	16	3	7	67	42	35
Willington	26	16	1	9	76	46	33
Evenwood Town	26	14	2	10	70	59	30
Tow Law Town	26	12	4	10	63	52	28
Ferryhill Athletic	26	11	5	10	64	67	27
Shildon	26	10	5	11	56	52	25
Crook Town	26	10	3	13	61	58	23
Penrith	26	9	2	15	54	74	20
South Bank	26	8	3	15	46	78	19
West Auckland Town	26	8	2	16	45	89	18
Stanley United	26	5	6	15	46	74	16
Heaton Stannington	26	4	2	20	34	75	10

1950-51

Bishop Auckland	26	20	2	4	101	34	42
Billingham Synthonia	26	17	3	6	70	24	37
Whitby Town	26	15	6	5	75	42	36
Willington	26	14	4	8	81	46	32
Evenwood Town	26	14	3	9	76	58	29
Shildon	26	13	3	10	57	49	29
Crook Town	26	12	2	12	56	66	26
South Bank	26	11	2	13	54	58	24
Stanley United	26	9	4	13	60	64	22
Ferryhill Athletic	26	9	3	14	53	79	21
Penrith	26	7	7	12	43	76	21
Heaton Stannington	26	9	2	15	48	68	20
Tow Law Town	26	4	4	18	41	95	12
West Auckland Town	26	4	3	19	31	87	11

Evenwood Town had 2 points deducted.

1951-52

Bishop Auckland	26	20	5	1	89	26	45
Billingham Synthonia	26	17	3	6	67	35	37
Willington	26	17	2	7	79	49	36
Tow Law Town	26	16	1	9	68	45	33
Whitby Town	26	12	6	8	71	49	30
South Bank	26	12	5	9	64	68	29
Evenwood Town	26	10	7	9	53	47	27
Ferryhill Athletic	26	10	6	10	60	67	26
Crook Town	26	9	6	11	49	59	24
Shildon	26	9	3	14	54	62	21
West Auckland Town	26	7	4	15	43	61	18
Heaton Stannington	26	8	2	16	55	87	18
Stanley United	26	7	1	18	38	81	15
Penrith	26	1	3	22	32	86	5

1952-53

Crook Town	26	19	5	2	106	38	43
Bishop Auckland	26	14	9	3	79	38	37
Whitby Town	26	15	5	6	71	45	35
Shildon	26	12	9	5	60	40	33
Tow Law Town	26	13	5	8	56	54	31
Ferryhill Athletic	26	11	7	8	51	43	29
Billingham Synthonia	26	11	6	9	59	56	28
Willington	26	10	6	10	53	57	26
Penrith	26	9	7	10	58	64	25
Evenwood Town	26	6	8	12	50	56	20
Stanley United	26	8	2	16	49	72	18
Durham City	26	7	4	15	41	69	18
West Auckland Town	26	4	5	17	37	72	13
South Bank	26	2	4	20	37	103	8

1953-54

Bishop Auckland	26	19	4	3	97	34	42
Crook Town	26	19	2	5	95	38	40
Ferryhill Athletic	26	17	5	4	56	27	39
Billingham Synthonia	26	15	2	9	61	44	32
West Auckland Town	26	15	2	9	58	48	32
Durham City	26	15	2	9	62	52	32
Whitby Town	26	9	6	11	58	56	24
Willington	26	11	1	14	48	51	23
Evenwood Town	26	9	3	14	57	65	21
Tow Law Town	26	10	0	16	43	64	20
Penrith	26	8	1	17	39	81	17
Shildon	26	11	2	13	74	68	16
Stanley United	26	3	5	18	33	84	11
South Bank	26	3	1	22	36	105	7

Shildon had 8 points deducted.

1954-55

Bishop Auckland	26	19	3	4	87	44	41
Crook Town	26	16	2	8	93	40	34
Shildon	26	11	8	7	65	47	30
Billingham Synthonia	26	12	6	8	62	49	30
Evenwood Town	26	12	6	8	67	59	30
Stanley United	26	13	4	9	45	64	30
Whitby Town	26	10	7	9	65	58	27
Ferryhill Athletic	26	9	8	9	58	57	26
Willington	26	11	3	12	42	46	25
West Auckland Town	26	8	7	11	58	67	23
Tow Law Town	26	8	5	13	45	72	21
South Bank	26	5	7	14	36	63	17
Penrith	26	5	6	15	38	66	16
Durham City	26	4	6	16	47	79	14

1955-56

Bishop Auckland	26	18	2	6	85	54	38
Crook Town	26	17	3	6	92	44	37
Durham City	26	17	1	8	82	40	35
South Bank	26	12	6	8	51	37	30
Evenwood Town	26	12	5	9	58	49	29
West Auckland Town	26	13	2	11	66	51	28
Billingham Synthonia	26	12	3	11	58	63	27
Shildon	26	10	6	10	70	52	26
Willington	26	10	4	12	58	71	24
Stanley United	26	9	6	11	53	66	24
Ferryhill Athletic	26	8	5	13	42	62	21
Tow Law Town	26	6	7	13	55	80	19
Penrith	26	6	3	17	38	81	15
Whitby Town	26	4	3	19	39	97	11

1956-57

Billingham Synthonia	26	20	2	4	66	37	42
West Auckland Town	26	16	2	8	79	52	34
Bishop Auckland	26	13	7	6	76	48	33
Ferryhill Athletic	26	14	4	8	63	48	32
Willington	26	13	6	7	60	48	32
Crook Town	26	13	5	8	67	62	31
Durham City	26	12	5	9	58	50	29
Shildon	26	11	3	12	60	56	25
Stanley United	26	9	6	11	48	54	24
Evenwood Town	26	8	5	13	58	78	21
Penrith	26	8	3	15	41	65	19
South Bank	26	8	2	16	49	57	18
Whitby Town	26	5	4	17	54	84	14
Tow Law Town	26	3	4	19	37	77	10

1957-58

Ferryhill Athletic	26	20	3	3	90	41	43
Willington	26	16	5	5	66	41	37
Crook Town	26	16	4	6	95	35	36
Bishop Auckland	26	14	6	6	75	49	34
Evenwood Town	26	12	5	9	62	58	29
Durham City	26	11	5	10	57	45	27
Stanley United	26	10	3	13	59	58	23
Tow Law Town	26	10	3	13	57	57	23
West Auckland Town	26	9	5	12	68	72	23
Billingham Synthonia	26	6	10	10	54	61	22
Penrith	26	9	3	14	45	79	21
Whitby Town	26	7	5	14	58	69	19
Shildon	26	7	4	15	51	73	18
South Bank	26	4	1	21	30	129	9

1958-59

Crook Town	28	19	4	5	89	51	42
West Auckland Town	28	16	4	8	80	51	36
Willington	28	15	6	7	65	48	36
Durham City	28	14	5	9	63	52	33
Bishop Auckland	28	13	5	10	76	56	31
Whitby Town	28	13	5	10	70	61	31
Stanley United	28	12	4	12	57	68	28
Evenwood Town	28	13	1	14	54	59	27
Ferryhill Athletic	28	10	5	13	60	72	25
Billingham Synthonia	28	9	6	13	66	70	24
Tow Law Town	28	10	4	14	58	70	24
South Bank	28	7	9	12	48	64	23
Shildon	28	9	4	15	67	83	22
Whitley Bay	28	8	5	15	52	64	21
Penrith	28	7	3	18	43	79	17

1959-60

West Auckland Town	28	19	4	5	63	40	42
Whitley Bay	28	17	6	5	76	37	40
Crook Town	28	18	3	7	84	50	39
Shildon	28	15	4	9	75	50	34
Bishop Auckland	28	15	4	9	55	45	34
Ferryhill Athletic	28	13	4	11	76	46	30
Tow Law Town	28	10	7	11	50	58	27
Stanley United	28	10	6	12	57	69	26
Whitby Town	28	10	5	13	61	62	25
Evenwood Town	28	12	3	13	65	67	25
South Bank	28	11	3	14	55	63	25
Penrith	28	9	5	14	52	66	23
Willington	28	8	6	14	49	64	22
Durham City	28	4	7	17	35	84	15
Billingham Synthonia	28	4	3	21	34	86	11

Evenwood Town had 2 points deducted.

1960-61

West Auckland Town	30	18	8	4	77	36	44
Bishop Auckland	30	19	2	9	85	46	40
Ferryhill Athletic	30	18	4	8	80	56	40
Crook Town	30	15	8	7	79	51	38
Whitley Bay	30	15	8	7	81	57	38
Spennymoor United	30	14	8	8	62	37	36
Stanley United	30	14	7	9	61	56	35
South Bank	30	15	2	13	67	62	32
Penrith	30	11	8	11	53	63	30
Evenwood Town	30	8	9	13	59	59	25
Shildon	30	11	2	17	66	73	24
Billingham Synthonia	30	7	8	15	52	86	22
Willington	30	9	3	18	59	80	21
Tow Law Town	30	8	5	17	54	88	21
Whitby Town	30	7	6	17	52	84	18
Durham City	30	5	4	21	52	105	14

Whitby Town had 2 points deducted.

1961-62

Stanley United	30	22	4	4	91	52	48
Penrith	30	16	8	6	55	31	40
West Auckland Town	30	19	2	9	80	50	40
Whitley Bay	30	18	4	8	95	61	40
Crook Town	30	14	7	9	54	31	35
Spennymoor United	30	15	2	13	71	52	32
Billingham Synthonia	30	13	5	12	83	66	31
Durham City	30	14	3	13	49	49	31
Ferryhill Athletic	30	13	3	14	66	68	29
Bishop Auckland	30	10	7	13	71	69	27
South Bank	30	10	5	15	52	68	25
Shildon	30	10	4	16	58	82	24
Whitby Town	30	9	6	15	61	87	24
Tow Law Town	30	9	3	18	56	82	21
Willington	30	6	7	17	44	90	19
Evenwood Town	30	6	2	22	39	87	14

1962-63

Crook Town	30	21	6	3	82	30	48
Stanley United	30	20	4	6	78	45	44
Penrith	30	17	7	6	60	31	41
Spennymoor United	30	13	12	5	62	45	38
Whitley Bay	30	12	10	8	69	46	34
Billingham Synthonia	30	14	5	11	58	49	33
West Auckland Town	30	13	7	10	66	65	33
Bishop Auckland	30	11	6	13	68	68	28
Tow Law Town	30	12	3	15	62	71	27
Whitby Town	30	12	2	16	62	65	26
Durham City	30	10	6	14	49	55	26
Ferryhill Athletic	30	6	14	10	51	59	26
South Bank	30	9	5	16	46	63	23
Shildon	30	6	9	15	52	87	21
Evenwood Town	30	7	5	18	30	62	19
Willington	30	5	3	22	35	89	13

1963-64

Stanley United	30	18	7	5	94	47	43
Crook Town	30	17	8	5	67	28	42
West Auckland Town	30	15	7	8	67	44	37
Evenwood Town	30	13	7	10	42	38	33
Ferryhill Athletic	30	13	7	10	64	60	33
Penrith	30	14	4	12	69	54	32
Whitley Bay	30	14	4	12	66	52	32
Bishop Auckland	30	13	6	11	62	61	32
Whitby Town	30	13	3	14	57	52	29
Tow Law Town	30	12	5	13	63	60	29
Willington	30	11	7	12	57	73	29
Spennymoor United	30	11	6	13	38	51	28
Billingham Synthonia	30	9	7	14	25	43	25
Shildon	30	10	4	16	55	70	24
South Bank	30	9	6	15	47	78	24
Durham City	30	2	4	24	35	97	6

Durham City had 2 points deducted.

1964-65

Whitley Bay	34	24	5	5	112	45	53
Crook Town	34	22	8	4	86	32	52
North Shields	34	18	8	8	99	60	44
Whitby Town	34	19	4	11	74	52	42
Tow Law Town	34	15	10	9	72	56	40
Willington	34	18	4	12	72	61	40
Spennymoor United	34	16	7	11	53	53	39
Ferryhill Athletic	34	15	7	12	79	62	37
Stanley United	34	16	3	15	86	84	35
West Auckland Town	34	14	6	14	66	54	34
Billingham Synthonia	34	13	6	15	51	79	32
Penrith	34	10	10	14	57	64	30
Bishop Auckland	34	11	6	17	58	73	28
Durham City	34	10	6	18	49	78	26
South Bank	34	9	6	19	67	97	24
Evenwood Town	34	9	5	20	51	80	23
Shildon	34	8	7	19	51	89	23
Blyth Spartans	34	4	2	28	38	105	10

1965-66

Whitley Bay	34	25	2	7	89	46	52
North Shields	34	22	5	7	109	51	49
Bishop Auckland	34	20	8	6	75	33	48
Spennymoor United	34	15	10	9	70	62	40
Tow Law Town	34	14	11	9	66	39	39
Evenwood Town	34	17	5	12	79	56	37
Whitby Town	34	15	6	13	63	57	36
Crook Town	34	14	7	13	82	66	35
Billingham Synthonia	34	14	7	13	59	51	35
Blyth Spartans	34	13	7	14	87	81	33
Ferryhill Athletic	34	13	7	14	57	88	33
Willington	34	12	7	15	64	79	31
Penrith	34	12	5	17	54	62	29
Stanley United	34	13	3	18	78	90	29
West Auckland Town	34	9	9	16	47	66	27
Shildon	34	8	6	20	66	112	22
South Bank	34	8	4	22	56	106	20
Durham City	34	5	5	24	48	104	15

Evenwood Town had 2 points deducted.

1966-67

Bishop Auckland	34	23	8	3	85	34	54
Whitley Bay	34	19	10	5	72	37	48
North Shields	34	20	6	8	90	43	46
Tow Law Town	34	20	4	10	76	42	44
Spennymoor United	34	15	10	9	65	52	40
Crook Town	34	15	9	10	74	62	39
Billingham Synthonia	34	15	8	11	61	46	38
West Auckland Town	34	17	3	14	59	54	37
Blyth Spartans	34	16	4	14	69	63	36
Whitby Town	34	16	4	14	85	75	34
Penrith	34	11	9	14	71	72	31
Stanley United	34	13	5	16	62	70	31
Evenwood Town	34	13	5	16	57	58	27
Ferryhill Athletic	34	10	7	17	56	75	27
Shildon	34	12	3	19	65	88	27
Willington	34	6	8	20	45	77	20
Durham City	34	5	4	25	48	128	14
South Bank	34	4	5	25	44	108	13

Whitby Town had 2 points deducted.
Evenwood Town had 4 points deducted.

1967-68

Spennymoor United	34	28	5	1	99	37	61
Whitby Town	34	24	6	4	107	41	54
Tow Law Town	34	22	5	7	103	57	49
Whitley Bay	34	21	5	8	93	41	47
Crook Town	34	15	8	11	71	67	8
North Shields	34	14	9	11	75	56	37
Durham City	34	15	5	14	83	71	35
Blyth Spartans	34	14	7	13	80	71	35
South Bank	34	12	10	12	58	56	34
Billingham Synthonia	34	13	8	13	63	62	34
Bishop Auckland	34	13	6	15	62	67	32
West Auckland Town	34	12	5	17	57	72	29
Evenwood Town	34	11	7	16	61	86	29
Stanley United	34	10	6	18	53	88	26
Shildon	34	11	2	21	58	81	24
Ferryhill Athletic	34	6	7	21	57	94	19
Penrith	34	4	7	23	47	96	15
Willington	34	4	6	24	45	129	14

1968-69

North Shields	34	26	2	6	106	29	54
Whitley Bay	34	22	9	3	86	37	53
Tow Law Town	34	23	4	7	110	61	50
Evenwood Town	34	22	4	8	81	50	48
Blyth Spartans	34	18	9	7	76	36	45
Whitby Town	34	20	5	9	71	55	45
Spennymoor United	34	15	9	10	73	52	39
Billingham Synthonia	34	16	5	13	76	61	37
South Bank	34	14	9	11	58	51	37
Shildon	34	16	4	14	61	58	36
Crook Town	34	14	7	13	59	59	35
West Auckland Town	34	10	6	18	55	69	26
Durham City	34	9	4	21	49	81	22
Penrith	34	8	6	20	37	68	22
Bishop Auckland	34	8	2	24	43	98	18
Willington	34	6	5	23	33	94	17
Ferryhill Athletic	34	3	9	22	33	83	15
Stanley United	34	5	3	26	50	113	13

1969-70

Evenwood Town	34	26	5	3	83	34	57
Whitley Bay	34	23	6	5	78	26	52
Blyth Spartans	34	23	6	5	92	34	52
Spennymoor United	34	20	5	9	80	48	45
Durham City	34	15	9	10	53	40	39
North Shields	34	18	5	11	71	57	39
South Bank	34	14	7	13	55	51	35
Billingham Synthonia	34	12	10	12	61	62	34
Tow Law Town	34	13	8	13	55	51	32
Whitby Town	34	11	10	13	45	49	32
Shildon	34	10	12	12	53	59	32
Bishop Auckland	34	6	14	14	43	68	26
West Auckland Town	34	7	11	16	37	43	25
Penrith	34	7	11	16	47	72	25
Stanley United	34	10	4	20	37	86	24
Willington	34	8	6	20	45	76	22
Crook Town	34	6	9	19	45	73	21
Ferryhill Athletic	34	5	6	23	32	83	14

North Shields, Tow Law Town and Ferryhill Athletic all had 2 points deducted.

1970-71

Evenwood Town	38	25	7	6	94	36	57
Durham City	38	24	6	8	79	52	54
Ferryhill Athletic	38	22	6	10	75	58	50
Whitby Town	38	19	11	8	82	51	49
Blyth Spartans	38	19	7	12	74	49	45
Whitley Bay	38	18	8	12	65	44	44
North Shields	38	19	6	13	80	64	44
Spennymoor United	38	16	10	12	66	50	42
Tow Law Town	38	18	8	12	58	52	42
South Bank	38	17	7	14	72	63	41
Ashington	38	14	10	14	71	72	38
Shildon	38	13	11	14	76	74	37
Stanley United	38	13	8	17	50	86	34
Consett	38	12	9	17	69	83	33
West Auckland Town	38	9	13	16	41	65	31
Billingham Synthonia	38	9	10	19	45	65	28
Bishop Auckland	38	11	3	24	62	86	25
Crook Town	38	8	9	21	45	66	25
Penrith	38	6	8	24	45	87	20
Willington	38	6	7	25	47	93	19

Tow Law Town had 2 points deducted.

1971-72

Spennymoor United	38	29	6	3	103	26	64
Blyth Spartans	38	24	7	7	85	42	55
Whitley Bay	38	20	10	8	66	29	48
Durham City	38	20	8	10	78	51	48
Consett	38	20	6	12	78	58	46
Shildon	38	18	9	11	98	69	45
Whitby Town	38	18	8	12	75	59	44
Tow Law Town	38	17	10	11	83	72	44
Evenwood Town	38	17	9	12	65	57	43
North Shields	38	14	12	12	61	51	40
Ferryhill Athletic	38	16	8	14	60	58	40
Willington	38	15	8	15	72	59	38
South Bank	38	13	7	18	54	76	33
Penrith	38	13	6	19	52	69	32
Billingham Synthonia	38	11	8	19	55	75	30
Crook Town	38	5	16	17	50	81	26
Bishop Auckland	38	8	9	21	42	72	25
Ashington	38	8	8	22	47	68	24
West Auckland Town	38	6	8	24	45	102	20
Stanley United	38	3	7	28	32	127	11

Whitley Bay and Stanley United both had 2 points deducted.

1972-73

Blyth Spartans	38	28	3	7	102	39	59
Bishop Auckland	38	25	7	6	76	40	57
Willington	38	24	5	9	83	36	53
Billingham Synthonia	38	21	7	10	76	49	49
Spennymoor United	38	20	7	11	70	50	47
Ferryhill Athletic	38	21	4	13	60	56	46
Whitley Bay	38	18	8	12	67	46	42
Shildon	38	17	5	16	72	62	39
Ashington	38	14	10	14	51	45	38
Durham City	38	14	8	16	58	60	36
Consett	38	12	12	14	53	57	36
Evenwood Town	38	15	5	18	52	66	35
Whitby Town	38	13	7	18	58	72	31
Penrith	38	12	7	19	53	80	31
Tow Law Town	38	11	8	19	51	68	30
West Auckland Town	38	12	3	23	39	76	27
Crook Town	38	9	8	21	48	67	26
Stanley United	38	11	4	23	49	88	26
North Shields	38	10	7	21	37	62	25
South Bank	38	9	3	26	49	85	21

Whitley Bay, Whitby Town and North Shields all had 2 points deducted.

1973-74

Blyth Spartans	38	30	4	4	95	32	64
Spennymoor United	38	30	4	4	87	37	64
Willington	38	21	6	11	87	60	48
Bishop Auckland	38	19	9	10	68	43	47
Billingham Synthonia	38	20	7	11	67	50	47
North Shields	38	17	8	13	68	52	42
Tow Law Town	38	18	4	16	62	63	40
Ashington	38	16	6	16	60	56	38
Penrith	38	15	8	15	56	62	38
Durham City	38	16	5	17	74	60	37
Whitley Bay	38	14	8	16	48	48	36
Evenwood Town	38	13	10	15	63	65	36
Consett	38	14	7	17	61	63	35
Ferryhill Athletic	38	14	7	17	47	69	35
Shildon	38	12	9	17	59	62	33
Whitby Town	38	11	9	18	52	76	31
Crook Town	38	9	9	20	44	75	27
South Bank	38	8	7	23	43	77	23
West Auckland Town	38	5	11	22	37	83	21
Stanley United	38	4	10	24	41	86	18

Spennymoor United were declared Champions on 7th May after beating Blyth Spartans 2-1 at Portland Park, Ashington.

1974-75

Blyth Spartans	36	30	6	0	105	38	96
Spennymoor United	36	27	5	4	100	38	86
Bishop Auckland	36	23	5	8	81	33	74
Willington	36	19	12	5	91	53	69
Whitby Town	36	16	8	12	60	53	56
Consett	36	14	11	11	72	72	53
Durham City	36	14	11	11	60	68	53
Tow Law Town	36	14	10	12	59	58	52
Ashington	36	13	11	12	73	61	50
South Bank	36	12	8	16	65	75	44
North Shields	36	9	15	12	58	55	42
Whitley Bay	36	11	8	17	52	65	41
Ferryhill Athletic	36	9	12	15	52	72	39
Billingham Synthonia	36	9	9	18	55	74	36
Evenwood Town	36	9	7	20	40	59	34
Crook Town	36	9	7	20	39	72	34
Penrith	36	9	6	21	47	71	33
Shildon	36	7	9	20	50	79	30
West Auckland	36	4	8	24	29	92	20

1975-76

Blyth Spartans	38	28	4	6	88	36	88
Willington	38	27	6	5	102	43	87
Spennymoor United	38	27	6	5	90	43	87
Bishop Auckland	38	25	8	5	75	32	83
Tow Law Town	38	22	8	8	102	60	74
Whitby Town	38	21	11	6	76	36	72
Ashington	38	18	4	16	60	52	58
North Shields	38	15	7	16	57	49	52
Consett	38	15	6	17	53	56	51
Evenwood Town	38	11	11	16	50	58	44
Horden Colliery Welfare	38	11	10	17	42	62	43
Penrith	38	11	10	17	49	89	43
Durham City	38	10	10	18	36	57	40
Billingham Synthonia	38	10	8	20	39	67	38
Crook Town	38	9	10	19	55	68	37
Shildon	38	9	10	19	43	61	37
Whitley Bay	38	8	11	19	41	74	35
Ferryhill Athletic	38	8	9	21	51	73	33
South Bank	38	7	8	23	41	80	29
West Auckland Town	38	7	5	26	44	98	26

Whitby Town had 2 points deducted.

1976-77

Spennymoor United	38	22	10	6	72	38	76
Consett	38	22	10	6	71	45	76
Whitby Town	38	21	8	9	97	62	71
Crook Town	38	19	11	8	63	40	68
Blyth Spartans	38	19	9	10	80	49	66
North Shields	38	19	8	11	62	51	65
Whitley Bay	38	19	8	11	73	62	65
Bishop Auckland	38	17	9	12	67	47	60
Ashington	38	17	8	13	84	61	57
South Bank	38	15	5	18	53	58	50
Willington	38	13	10	15	66	68	49
Durham City	38	12	11	15	44	53	47
Horden Colliery Welfare	38	12	10	16	59	65	46
Ferryhill Athletic	38	12	10	16	42	58	46
Evenwood Town	38	13	4	21	54	72	43
West Auckland Town	38	12	7	19	45	69	43
Tow Law Town	38	11	8	19	55	73	41
Billingham Synthonia	38	9	6	23	37	64	33
Shildon	38	6	9	23	32	75	27
Penrith	38	4	11	23	49	95	23

Ashington had 2 points deducted.
Spennymoor United were declared Champions on 9th May after beating Consett 3-0 at Hall Lane Ground, Willington.

1977-78

Spennymoor United	38	30	5	3	103	36	95
Blyth Spartans	38	27	8	3	107	37	89
Whitby Town	38	22	7	9	84	61	73
Bishop Auckland	38	22	6	10	82	44	72
Consett	38	19	7	12	78	49	64
Horden Colliery Welfare	38	19	6	13	53	44	63
North Shields	38	16	10	12	55	39	55
Durham City	38	15	9	14	55	51	54
Willington	38	16	6	16	53	62	54
Crook Town	38	12	17	9	56	47	53
West Auckland Town	38	12	15	11	49	51	51
Billingham Synthonia	38	17	8	16	65	64	50
South Bank	38	12	13	13	40	43	49
Whitley Bay	38	13	7	18	46	66	46
Ashington	38	15	7	16	56	54	43
Shildon	38	11	8	19	55	64	41
Tow Law Town	38	9	5	24	59	103	32
Ferryhill Athletic	38	8	8	22	30	69	32
Evenwood Town	38	4	5	29	36	90	17
Penrith	38	3	5	30	25	113	14

North Shields 2 points deducted. Ashington 9 points deducted.

1978-79

Spennymoor United	38	25	6	7	96	43	81
Bishop Auckland	38	25	5	8	96	38	80
Ashington	38	23	7	8	79	47	76
Crook Town	38	21	10	7	63	38	73
Blyth Spartans	38	19	12	7	81	39	69
Consett	38	21	9	8	84	52	69
North Shields	38	21	4	13	76	55	67
South Bank	38	16	11	11	58	47	59
Horden Colliery Welfare	38	17	8	13	64	56	59
Durham City	38	15	9	14	63	62	54
Billingham Synthonia	38	12	12	14	60	55	48
Tow Law Town	38	12	8	18	54	63	44
Shildon	38	11	10	17	52	69	43
Whitby Town	38	11	12	15	55	68	42
Whitley Bay	38	9	9	20	54	77	36
West Auckland Town	38	9	9	20	54	87	36
Ferryhill Athletic	38	10	5	23	43	74	35
Willington	38	7	10	21	41	75	31
Penrith	38	8	7	23	35	82	31
Evenwood Town	38	4	5	29	31	112	14

Consett, Whitby Town and Evenwood Town all had 3 points deducted.

1979-80

Blyth Spartans	38	29	5	4	93	28	92
Spennymoor United	38	26	7	5	83	40	85
Horden Colliery Welfare	38	24	6	8	73	32	78
Ashington	38	21	8	9	88	53	71
Crook Town	38	21	8	9	77	51	71
Bishop Auckland	38	18	9	11	64	54	63
Consett	38	19	4	15	78	59	61
South Bank	38	16	7	15	68	52	55
Shildon	38	16	7	15	70	71	55
West Auckland Town	38	16	6	16	57	52	54
Whitby Town	38	14	10	14	72	62	52
Tow Law Town	38	16	4	18	50	56	52
Evenwood Town	38	14	9	15	49	55	51
Penrith	38	13	5	20	54	72	44
Billingham Synthonia	38	10	12	16	44	72	42
North Shields	38	12	3	23	62	81	39
Ferryhill Athletic	38	9	7	22	38	60	34
Durham City	38	7	9	22	30	63	30
Willington	38	6	5	27	27	105	23
Whitley Bay	38	4	7	27	31	90	16

Whitley Bay had 3 points deducted.

1980-81

Blyth Spartans	38	27	5	6	89	35	86
Spennymoor United	38	26	7	5	82	38	85
Bishop Auckland	38	22	7	9	68	36	73
Tow Law Town	38	18	13	7	83	54	67
Ashington	38	17	12	9	95	66	63
Ferryhill Athletic	38	17	10	11	71	49	61
Shildon	38	17	8	13	56	54	59
South Bank	38	16	9	13	55	44	57
Billingham Synthonia	38	13	15	10	52	51	54
Penrith	38	15	8	15	75	66	53
Whitby Town	38	15	7	16	55	59	52
Horden Colliery Welfare	38	12	9	17	48	65	45
Consett	38	12	6	20	49	54	42
North Shields	38	10	10	18	56	71	40
Evenwood Town	38	10	10	18	41	66	40
West Auckland Town	38	10	10	18	40	67	40
Durham City	38	9	11	18	46	74	38
Crook Town	38	10	8	20	47	79	38
Whitley Bay	38	9	7	22	53	72	34
Willington	38	6	6	26	41	102	24

1981-82

Blyth Spartans	38	25	8	5	77	31	83
Whitby Town	38	23	11	4	64	21	80
South Bank	38	20	7	11	72	44	67
Tow Law Town	38	18	8	12	76	58	62
Spennymoor United	38	16	13	9	59	37	61
Billingham Synthonia	38	17	9	12	57	46	60
Bishop Auckland	38	17	8	13	63	51	59
Durham City	38	17	5	16	75	67	56
Shildon	38	16	8	14	57	53	56
North Shields	38	14	13	11	67	61	55
Ferryhill Athletic	38	16	6	16	57	59	54
Horden Colliery Welfare	38	15	6	17	55	58	51
Crook Town	38	15	6	17	60	69	51
Evenwood Town	38	13	9	16	57	66	48
Penrith	38	13	10	15	63	66	46
Consett	38	10	10	18	46	64	40
West Auckland Town	38	9	10	19	42	67	37
Ashington	38	9	8	21	50	87	35
Whitley Bay	38	8	7	23	47	83	31
Willington	38	3	10	25	46	102	19

Penrith had 3 points deducted.

1982-83

First Division

Blyth Spartans	36	23	11	2	92	31	80
Whitby Town	36	23	9	4	80	34	78
Horden Colliery Welfare	36	21	5	10	65	35	68
Bishop Auckland	36	17	13	6	69	34	64
Spennymoor United	36	17	10	9	70	53	61
Billingham Synthonia	36	16	12	8	71	43	60
North Shields	36	17	7	12	73	46	58
Tow Law Town	36	16	10	10	71	63	58
Consett	36	15	10	11	53	37	55
Crook Town	36	16	7	13	54	47	55
South Bank	36	14	12	10	56	32	54
Ferryhill Athletic	36	14	12	10	53	42	54
Whitley Bay	36	13	8	15	56	50	47
Shildon	36	9	11	16	48	71	38
Evenwood Town	36	9	8	19	49	67	35
Ashington	36	9	6	21	36	73	33
Durham City	36	4	8	24	32	83	20
West Auckland Town	36	5	3	28	37	110	18
Willington	36	2	2	32	26	140	8

Second Division

Peterlee Newtown	30	18	9	3	67	33	63
Gretna	30	18	6	6	63	29	60
Darlington Reserves	30	15	7	8	55	36	52
Hartlepool United Reserves	30	16	4	10	69	46	46
Ryhope Community Association	30	14	6	10	61	55	45
Esh Winning	30	10	7	13	42	60	37
Billingham Town	30	8	11	11	36	47	35
Northallerton Town	30	10	4	16	41	61	34
Norton and Stockton Ancients	30	7	6	17	35	61	27
Bedlington Terriers	30	5	9	16	33	48	24
Alnwick Town	30	5	9	16	31	57	24

Ryhope Community Association had 3 points deducted.
Hartlepool United Reserves had 6 points deducted.

1983-84

First Division

Blyth Spartans	34	23	9	2	74	22	78
North Shields	34	21	6	7	81	51	69
Whitby Town	34	20	7	7	79	33	67
Tow Law Town	34	19	8	7	72	44	65
Bishop Auckland	34	19	7	8	80	39	64
South Bank	34	18	7	9	62	35	61
Billingham Synthonia	34	14	8	12	56	54	50
Gretna	34	15	7	12	65	58	49
Whitley Bay	34	14	5	15	39	60	47
Horden Colliery Welfare	34	12	7	15	48	59	43
Spennymoor United	34	10	9	15	41	57	39
Consett	34	10	8	16	43	58	38
Peterlee Newtown	34	11	5	18	50	78	38
Crook Town	34	9	10	15	38	50	37
Shildon	34	10	6	18	50	66	36
Ferryhill Athletic	34	9	6	19	47	61	33
Ashington	34	7	8	19	39	71	26
Evenwood Town	34	1	5	28	27	95	8

Gretna and Ashington both had 3 points deducted.

Second Division

Chester-le-Street Town	34	25	7	2	84	21	82
Ryhope Community Association	34	23	6	5	66	33	75
Seaham Colliery Welfare Red Star	34	23	5	6	69	30	74
Brandon United	34	20	6	8	67	37	66
Durham City	34	16	11	7	61	38	59
Darlington Cleveland Bridge	34	15	9	10	60	52	54
Hartlepool United Reserves	34	18	5	11	73	52	53
Bedlington Terriers	34	14	7	13	52	41	49
Esh Winning	34	13	10	11	49	55	49
Billingham Town	34	13	6	15	63	51	45
Darlington Reserves	34	12	4	18	47	69	40
Northallerton Town	34	12	6	16	48	52	39
Langley Park Welfare	34	9	8	17	46	76	35
Alnwick Town	34	7	12	15	49	53	33
Shotton Comrades	34	9	5	20	55	76	32
Norton and Stockton Ancients	34	6	10	18	30	55	28
West Auckland Town	34	7	3	24	36	83	24
Willington	34	2	4	28	27	108	10

Northallerton Town had 3 points deducted.
Hartlepool United Reserves had 6 points deducted.

1984-85

First Division

Bishop Auckland	34	26	4	4	92	26	82
Blyth Spartans	34	24	3	7	86	36	75
South Bank	34	19	10	5	62	30	67
Tow Law Town	34	18	10	6	57	45	64
North Shields	34	19	5	10	62	49	62
Gretna	34	17	8	9	56	39	59
Whitby Town	34	17	7	10	61	44	58
Chester-le-Street Town	34	15	6	13	54	44	51
Peterlee Newtown	34	13	7	14	51	44	46
Ryhope Community Association	34	13	6	15	49	55	45
Spennymoor United	34	11	8	15	63	56	41
Billingham Synthonia	34	11	5	18	39	65	38
Whitley Bay	34	8	11	15	51	55	32
Ferryhill Athletic	34	8	8	18	39	70	32
Consett	34	8	3	23	42	95	27
Crook Town	34	6	8	20	32	66	26
Horden Colliery Welfare	34	5	10	19	36	67	25
Shildon	34	5	7	22	41	87	22

Whitley Bay had 3 points deducted.

Second Division

Brandon United	34	27	2	5	102	38	83
Bedlington Terriers	34	25	5	4	77	28	80
Hartlepool United Reserves	34	25	2	7	86	37	77
Billingham Town	34	22	6	6	74	32	72
Durham City	34	21	9	4	73	36	72
Seaham Colliery Welfare Red Star	34	19	7	8	76	41	64
Willington	34	17	5	12	59	57	56
Darlington Cleveland Bridge	34	14	6	14	57	64	48
Langley Park Welfare	34	11	9	14	53	62	42
Ashington	34	11	7	16	59	58	40
Esh Winning	34	12	6	16	46	64	39
Northallerton Town	34	11	5	18	44	71	38
Norton and Stockton Ancients	34	7	7	20	34	69	28
Alnwick Town	34	6	8	20	42	78	26
Evenwood Town	34	7	5	22	41	78	26
Darlington Reserves	34	6	7	21	49	81	25
West Auckland Town	34	7	3	24	47	88	24
Shotton Comrades	34	4	9	21	37	74	21

Esh Winning had 3 points deducted.

1985-86

First Division

Bishop Auckland	38	21	10	7	79	45	73
Bedlington Terriers	38	19	10	9	65	44	67
South Bank	38	18	12	8	66	36	66
Blyth Spartans	38	19	9	10	79	52	66
Tow Law Town	38	18	10	10	72	47	64
Peterlee Newtown	38	19	6	13	66	56	63
Chester-le-Street Town	38	18	7	13	62	53	61
Brandon United	38	16	10	12	72	68	58
Crook Town	38	15	8	15	73	70	53
Hartlepool United Reserves	38	14	10	14	65	69	52
Gretna	38	13	11	14	70	69	50
North Shields	38	14	8	16	65	72	50
Consett	38	13	9	16	44	58	48
Spennymoor United	38	12	11	15	51	54	47
Ryhope Community Association	38	13	7	18	50	69	46
Whitby Town	38	12	9	17	59	74	45
Whitley Bay	38	11	8	19	65	73	41
Ferryhill Athletic	38	11	6	21	62	94	39
Billingham Synthonia	38	8	11	19	47	66	35
Billingham Town	38	6	8	24	46	89	26

Second Division

Blue Star	38	36	1	1	133	15	109
Easington Colliery	38	27	7	4	101	36	88
Guisborough Town	38	25	7	6	88	36	82
Durham City	38	22	9	7	89	48	75
Bishop Auckland Town	38	19	7	12	64	61	64
Seaham Colliery Welfare Red Star	38	17	7	14	63	56	58
Stockton	38	15	9	14	62	56	54
Ashington	38	15	9	14	81	85	54
Norton and Stockton Ancients	38	16	5	17	67	72	53
Alnwick Town	38	13	12	13	62	56	51
Willington	38	15	5	18	53	65	50
Langley Park Welfare	38	11	11	16	43	57	44
Horden Colliery Welfare	38	12	8	18	54	85	44
Shotton Comrades	38	9	12	17	56	82	39
Darlington Reserves	38	9	9	20	45	86	36
Northallerton Town	38	10	5	23	54	83	35
Evenwood Town	38	9	7	22	51	79	34
Darlington Cleveland Bridge	38	10	4	24	55	89	34
Shildon	38	6	15	17	42	66	33
Esh Winning	38	5	9	24	49	99	24

1986-87

First Division

Blyth Spartans	38	29	7	2	87	36	94
Bishop Auckland	38	26	2	10	96	42	80
Spennymoor United	38	20	13	5	89	41	73
Newcastle Blue Star	38	20	11	7	74	34	71
Whitley Bay	38	19	9	10	74	53	66
North Shields	38	18	10	10	65	47	64
Gretna	38	17	10	11	73	57	61
South Bank	38	16	12	10	59	36	60
Tow Law Town	38	15	10	13	50	57	55
Easington Colliery	38	16	5	17	59	59	53
Whitby Town	38	13	13	12	56	63	52
Brandon United	38	12	11	15	55	64	47
Consett	38	14	5	19	46	72	47
Ryhope Community Association	38	11	9	18	47	64	42
Hartlepool United Reserves	38	10	10	18	41	59	40
Chester-le-Street Town	38	7	14	17	37	66	35
Crook Town	38	9	5	24	47	85	22
Ferryhill Athletic	38	7	9	22	42	80	30
Peterlee Newtown	38	7	7	24	31	66	28
Bedlington Terriers	38	6	4	28	40	87	22

Second Division

Billingham Synthonia	36	26	9	1	83	34	87
Guisborough Town	36	24	7	5	87	33	79
Shildon	36	19	8	9	77	47	65
Billingham Town	36	17	9	10	70	43	60
West Auckland Town	36	15	13	8	56	46	58
Alnwick Town	36	15	11	10	45	30	56
Stockton	36	15	11	10	65	51	56
Norton and Stockton Ancients	36	16	6	14	64	47	54
Seaham Colliery Welfare Red Star	36	16	6	14	60	53	54
Ashington	36	14	6	16	67	73	48
Northallerton Town	36	13	6	17	61	74	45
Durham City	36	12	8	16	52	63	44
Willington	36	12	10	14	53	52	43
Shotton Comrades	36	8	16	12	52	64	37
Evenwood Town	36	10	7	19	58	70	37
Darlington Cleveland Bridge	36	8	10	18	45	81	34
Esh Winning	36	8	7	21	44	81	31
Horden Colliery Welfare	36	8	6	22	39	79	30
Langley Park Welfare	36	5	6	25	41	98	21

Willington and Shotton Comrades both had 3 points deducted.

1987-88

First Division

Blyth Spartans	38	28	8	2	106	36	92
Newcastle Blue Star	38	28	3	7	79	33	87
Billingham Synthonia	38	23	8	7	76	41	77
Whitley Bay	38	22	9	7	60	27	75
Guisborough Town	38	18	12	8	63	41	66
Bishop Auckland	38	19	7	12	70	48	64
Gretna	38	17	6	15	69	46	57
Tow Law Town	38	16	6	16	65	72	54
North Shields	38	16	5	17	62	59	53
Brandon United	38	15	7	16	64	61	52
Spennymoor United	38	15	7	16	57	57	52
Shildon	38	14	7	17	61	59	49
Whitby Town	38	12	10	16	57	74	46
Ferryhill Athletic	38	12	7	19	58	75	43
Easington Colliery	38	12	6	20	65	85	42
South Bank	38	10	11	17	34	48	41
Crook Town	38	8	9	21	45	84	33
Chester-le-Street Town	38	7	9	22	38	73	30
Ryhope Community Association	38	5	10	23	40	89	25
Consett	38	5	9	24	44	105	24

Second Division

Stockton	34	21	10	3	78	31	73
Seaham Red Star	34	21	8	5	63	32	71
Durham City	34	19	6	9	55	37	63
Billingham Town	34	14	13	7	60	43	55
Esh Winning	34	14	7	13	47	49	49
Alnwick Town	34	12	9	13	53	47	45
Bedlington Terriers	34	11	11	12	49	46	44
Peterlee Newtown	34	11	11	12	37	34	44
Northallerton Town	34	13	5	16	49	49	44
Norton and Stockton Ancients	34	11	10	13	49	58	43
Horden Colliery Welfare	34	10	13	11	48	65	43
Langley Park Welfare	34	11	9	14	52	57	42
Willington	34	11	7	16	44	53	40
Darlington Cleveland Bridge	34	11	7	16	45	57	40
Ashington	34	10	9	15	45	62	39
Evenwood Town	34	10	8	16	42	56	38
West Auckland Town	34	9	8	17	46	62	35
Shotton Comrades	34	7	9	18	33	57	30

1988-89

First Division

Billingham Synthonia	38	26	6	6	83	34	84
Tow Law Town	38	23	8	7	74	45	77
Gretna	38	22	7	9	80	37	73
Guisborough Town	38	21	9	8	74	37	72
Billingham Town	38	20	4	14	59	47	64
Newcastle Blue Star	38	17	10	11	61	38	61
Brandon United	38	15	8	15	50	60	53
Ferryhill Athletic	38	15	7	16	72	65	52
Blyth Spartans	38	13	13	12	51	50	52
Stockton	38	15	7	16	58	63	52
Spennymoor United	38	14	9	15	47	60	51
Whitby Town	38	13	9	16	56	52	48
Easington Colliery	38	12	11	15	51	57	47
Durham City	38	11	13	14	41	42	46
South Bank	38	12	10	16	46	58	46
Seaham Red Star	38	12	8	18	50	67	44
Shildon	38	9	11	18	50	88	38
North Shields	38	10	6	22	56	77	36
Chester-le-Street Town	38	6	14	18	35	60	32
Crook Town	38	5	8	25	32	89	20

Crook Town had 3 points deducted.

Second Division

Consett	38	30	3	5	89	32	93
Alnwick Town	38	25	9	4	92	36	84
Whickham	38	26	6	6	88	38	84
Prudhoe East End	38	24	6	8	68	32	78
Ashington	38	21	5	12	79	52	68
Peterlee Newtown	38	20	7	11	70	53	67
Bedlington Terriers	38	16	7	15	63	50	55
Horden Colliery Welfare	38	15	10	13	57	58	55
Northallerton Town	38	13	15	10	62	38	51
Ryhope Community Association	38	13	11	14	67	60	50
Murton	38	14	8	16	65	62	50
West Auckland Town	38	12	11	15	66	72	47
Langley Park Welfare	38	13	6	19	58	72	42
Norton and Stockton Ancients	38	11	7	20	52	72	40
Esh Winning	38	10	8	20	42	68	38
Darlington Cleveland Bridge	38	10	8	20	49	83	38
Evenwood Town	38	8	8	22	53	100	32
Washington	38	8	6	24	50	87	30
Willington	38	8	6	24	43	97	30
Shotton Comrades	38	5	9	24	32	83	24

Northallerton Town and Langley Park Welfare both had 3 points deducted.

1989-90

Division One

Bedlington Terriers	40	28	5	7	108	31	89
Dunston Federation Brewery	40	26	7	7	93	49	85
Marske United	40	24	7	9	82	35	79
Durham City	40	24	6	10	95	42	78
Brandon United	40	23	8	9	86	53	77
Peterlee Newtown	40	22	9	9	75	55	75
Tow Law Town	40	20	7	13	90	64	67
Billingham Synthonia	40	18	11	11	81	58	65
Billingham Town	40	19	7	14	74	59	64
Consett	40	17	8	15	63	60	59
Whitley Bay	40	15	10	15	69	61	55
West Auckland Town	40	16	7	17	65	68	55
Jarrow Roofing Boldon Com. Ass.	40	12	12	16	63	71	48
Guisborough Town	40	13	8	19	53	60	47
Chester-le-Street Town	40	13	5	22	61	64	44
Newcastle Blue Star	40	12	8	20	53	83	44
Seaham Red Star	40	14	2	24	59	111	44
Morpeth Town	40	12	6	22	63	78	36
Easington Colliery	40	10	6	24	57	86	36
Hebburn Town	40	5	7	28	33	113	22
Crook Town	40	2	4	34	33	155	10

Morpeth Town had 6 points deducted.

Division Two

Ashington	36	25	5	6	100	41	80
Washington	36	23	10	3	83	35	79
Thornaby	36	23	7	6	85	50	76
Horden Colliery Welfare	36	20	7	9	53	35	67
Esh Winning	36	19	7	10	79	44	64
Northallerton Town	36	16	12	8	75	45	60
Penrith	36	14	12	10	60	52	54
Norton & Stockton Ancients	36	16	9	11	51	51	54
Willington	36	12	12	12	52	46	48
Ryhope Community Association	36	12	10	14	46	53	46
South Shields	36	12	9	15	71	81	45
Prudhoe Town	36	13	5	18	69	66	44
Shildon	36	12	8	16	42	58	44
Alnwick Town	36	9	12	15	53	61	39
Evenwood Town	36	10	5	21	50	97	35
Shotton Comrades	36	8	10	18	49	85	34
Murton	36	9	8	19	53	76	32
Whickham	36	6	11	19	43	68	29
Eppleton Colliery Welfare	36	1	5	30	29	99	8

Norton & Stockton Ancients and Murton both had 3 points deducted.

1990-91

Division One

Gretna	38	30	5	3	86	23	95
Guisborough Town	38	21	12	5	79	43	75
Blyth Spartans	38	20	8	10	80	50	68
Billingham Synthonia	38	20	8	10	72	43	68
Consett	38	19	11	8	67	43	68
Whitby Town	38	16	13	9	66	49	61
Tow Law Town	38	16	10	12	65	64	58
Ferryhill Athletic	38	16	9	13	55	50	54
Northallerton Town	38	14	11	13	50	46	53
Newcastle Blue Star	38	13	13	12	59	48	52
Seaham Red Star	38	12	12	14	44	46	48
South Bank	38	9	16	13	40	43	43
Murton	38	10	11	17	47	59	41
Shildon	38	10	9	19	49	75	39
Whickham	38	10	9	19	44	71	39
Peterlee Newtown	38	7	17	14	57	65	38
Brandon United	38	9	11	18	44	70	38
Stockton	38	10	6	22	40	79	36
Alnwick Town	38	7	10	21	40	78	31
Durham City	38	6	9	23	47	86	27

Ferryhill Athletic had 3 points deducted.

Division Two

West Auckland Town	36	24	7	5	72	39	79
Langley Park Welfare	36	24	4	8	83	40	76
Easington Colliery	36	20	8	8	80	42	68
Hebburn	36	22	5	9	89	56	68
Billingham Town	36	21	5	10	69	39	68
Evenwood Town	36	20	8	8	69	40	65
Esh Winning	36	19	6	11	77	57	63
Prudhoe East End	36	16	10	10	71	46	58
Norton & Stockton Ancients	36	16	3	17	60	67	51
Darlington Cleveland Bridge	36	14	7	15	53	60	49
Bedlington Terriers	36	14	6	16	60	73	48
Ashington	36	14	6	16	47	68	48
Crook Town	36	13	8	15	57	64	47
Ryhope Community Association	36	13	4	19	54	57	43
Shotton Comrades	36	7	9	20	43	73	30
Chester-le-Street Town	36	6	11	19	45	68	29
Washington	36	7	6	23	44	79	27
Willington	36	4	9	23	34	77	21
Horden Colliery Welfare	36	2	10	24	37	99	16

Hebburn and Evenwood Town both had 3 points deducted.

1991-92

Division One

Gretna	38	25	10	3	81	33	85
Murton	38	23	9	6	83	36	78
Whitby Town	38	23	9	6	74	41	78
Guisborough Town	38	22	10	6	81	36	76
Billingham Synthonia	38	21	6	11	70	44	69
Blyth Spartans	38	19	8	11	63	44	65
South Bank	38	18	9	11	68	50	63
Northallerton Town	38	18	8	12	63	53	62
Consett	38	15	5	18	59	59	50
Tow Law Town	38	13	11	14	60	73	50
Seaham Red Star	38	13	9	16	50	57	48
Peterlee Newtown	38	14	3	21	47	70	45
Newcastle Blue Star	38	14	5	19	49	52	44
West Auckland Town	38	11	8	19	45	68	41
Brandon United	38	10	10	18	61	75	40
Ferryhill Athletic	38	10	10	18	45	60	40
Easington Colliery	38	11	7	20	42	61	40
Shildon	38	11	7	20	47	83	40
Langley Park Welfare	38	7	7	24	51	89	28
Whickham	38	4	5	29	38	93	17

Newcastle Blue Star had 3 points deducted.

Division Two

Stockton	38	27	7	4	102	35	88
Durham City	38	26	9	3	82	24	87
Chester-le-Street Town	38	26	8	4	80	36	86
Hebburn	38	27	4	7	101	44	85
Dunston Federation Brewery	38	26	6	6	104	33	84
Prudhoe East End	38	22	4	12	61	36	70
Billingham Town	38	18	7	13	60	47	61
Crook Town	38	16	9	13	54	53	57
Alnwick Town	38	15	12	11	54	60	57
Ryhope Community Association	38	17	5	16	77	59	56
Esh Winning	38	13	9	16	76	74	48
Ashington	38	13	9	16	50	69	48
Norton & Stockton Ancients	38	11	10	17	61	69	43
Shotton Comrades	38	11	6	21	52	66	39
Horden Colliery Welfare	38	10	6	22	52	76	36
Washington	38	8	9	21	36	63	33
Evenwood Town	38	8	7	23	42	105	31
Darlington Cleveland Bridge	38	7	4	27	47	97	25
Bedlington Terriers	38	7	2	29	38	97	20
Willington	38	4	3	31	33	119	15

Bedlington Terriers had 3 points deducted.

1992-93 Division One

Whitby Town	38	26	10	2	104	30	88
Billingham Synthonia	38	25	10	3	98	41	85
Guisborough Town	38	25	9	4	91	35	84
Blyth Spartans	38	26	4	8	83	35	82
Seaham Red Star	38	21	10	7	76	45	73
Durham City	38	21	10	7	73	51	73
Stockton	38	14	15	9	65	59	57
Murton	38	14	12	12	72	65	54
Chester-le-Street Town	38	15	8	15	82	82	53
Consett	38	15	7	16	54	56	52
Northallerton Town	38	13	14	11	54	47	50
West Auckland Town	38	12	9	17	64	76	45
Newcastle Blue Star	38	12	6	20	64	81	42
Tow Law Town	38	11	8	19	65	73	41
Brandon United	38	11	5	22	47	81	38
Hebburn	38	8	11	19	74	94	29
Ferryhill Athletic	38	6	10	22	51	97	28
Easington Colliery	38	6	8	24	51	94	26
Peterlee Newtown	38	3	9	26	40	105	18
South Bank	38	3	11	24	34	95	17

Northallerton Town and South Bank both had 3 points deducted.
Hebburn had 6 points deducted.

Division Two

Dunston Federation Brewery	38	30	5	3	139	34	95
Eppleton Colliery Welfare	38	27	7	4	116	51	88
Shildon	38	25	6	7	93	24	81
Billingham Town	38	24	8	6	89	36	80
Prudhoe East End	38	18	7	13	65	53	61
Evenwood Town	38	18	7	13	75	68	61
Whickham	38	19	3	16	71	62	60
Ashington	38	17	5	16	77	70	56
Alnwick Town	38	16	7	15	51	61	55
Ryhope Community Association	38	16	8	14	67	61	53
Darlington Cleveland Bridge	38	14	11	13	48	53	50
Norton & Stockton Ancients	38	13	5	20	54	79	44
Esh Winning	38	13	4	21	70	82	43
Shotton Comrades	38	11	10	17	53	74	43
Washington	38	10	9	19	54	74	39
Willington	38	12	3	23	61	106	39
Bedlington Terriers	38	11	3	24	64	86	33
Crook Town	38	9	9	20	45	78	33
Horden Colliery Welfare	38	6	8	24	48	99	26
Langley Park Welfare	38	5	7	26	52	141	22

Ryhope Community Association, Darlington Cleveland Bridge, Bedlington Terriers and Crook Town all had 3 points deducted.

1993-94 Division One

Durham City	38	23	11	4	88	39	80
Blyth Spartans	38	22	7	9	81	37	73
Seaham Red Star	38	20	10	8	70	40	70
Whitby Town	38	17	14	7	90	57	65
Guisborough Town	38	17	12	9	71	41	63
Northallerton Town	38	18	7	13	68	39	61
Tow Law Town	38	18	6	14	70	58	60
Murton	38	17	8	13	63	65	59
Shildon	38	17	6	15	59	54	57
Billingham Synthonia	38	15	9	14	57	45	54
Dunston Federation Brewery	38	15	9	14	72	69	54
Consett	38	15	6	17	67	70	48
Ferryhill Athletic	38	11	8	19	61	81	41
Newcastle Blue Star	38	11	8	19	44	65	41
Hebburn	38	12	5	21	55	93	41
Eppleton Colliery Welfare	38	11	7	20	52	76	40
Chester-le-Street Town	38	13	5	20	64	74	38
West Auckland Town	38	10	8	20	49	89	38
Brandon United	38	9	6	23	45	94	33
Stockton	38	9	8	21	46	86	32

Consett had 3 points deducted.
Chester-le-Street Town had 6 points deducted.

Division Two

Bedlington Terriers	36	28	5	3	114	36	89
Peterlee Newtown	36	23	9	4	77	27	78
Prudhoe East End	36	21	9	6	72	36	72
Evenwood Town	36	22	4	10	78	47	70
Easington Colliery	36	20	7	9	77	40	67
Billingham Town	36	21	3	12	88	49	66
Crook Town	36	18	8	10	80	58	62
Norton & Stockton Ancients	36	18	7	11	72	70	61
Darlington Cleveland Social	36	18	2	16	65	68	56
Whickham	36	16	7	13	71	64	52
Washington	36	14	5	17	67	72	47
Esh Winning	36	12	7	17	50	72	43
Langley Park S & S United	36	12	5	19	55	67	41
Shotton Comrades	36	9	9	18	61	84	36
Alnwick Town	36	10	7	19	50	69	34
Willington	36	9	3	24	48	90	30
Ashington	36	8	3	25	46	100	24
Ryhope Community Association	36	7	3	26	37	94	18
Horden Colliery Welfare	36	3	3	30	35	100	12

Whickham, Alnwick Town and Ashington all had 3 points deducted.
Ryhope Community Association had 6 points deducted.

1994-95

Division One

Tow Law Town	38	28	6	4	105	39	90
Billingham Synthonia	38	23	7	8	99	35	76
Whitby Town	38	22	10	6	88	45	76
Bedlington Terriers	38	21	12	5	72	35	75
RTM Newcastle	38	21	9	8	93	42	72
Guisborough Town	38	19	11	8	79	48	68
Durham City	38	17	12	9	75	45	63
Dunston Federation Brewery	38	16	12	10	70	62	60
Consett	38	15	11	12	74	55	56
Shildon	38	12	13	13	57	63	49
Hebburn	38	14	9	15	57	68	48
West Auckland Town	38	13	8	17	47	61	47
Seaham Red Star	38	14	6	18	72	72	45
Peterlee Newtown	38	12	9	17	62	80	45
Murton	38	10	5	23	48	89	35
Chester-le-Street Town	38	8	7	23	57	99	31
Ferryhill Athletic	38	9	6	23	34	80	30
Eppleton Colliery Welfare	38	8	4	26	38	97	28
Northallerton Town	38	9	3	26	35	93	27
Prudhoe Town	38	6	6	26	39	93	24

Hebburn, Seaham Red Star, Ferryhill Athletic and Northallerton Town all had 3 points dedu ted.

Division Two

Whickham	38	26	10	2	103	37	88
Crook Town	38	26	6	6	102	40	84
Stockton	38	26	5	7	116	49	77
Brandon United	38	21	9	8	77	39	72
Billingham Town	38	23	4	11	95	50	70
Hartlepool Town	38	22	9	7	91	50	69
Ashington	38	19	2	17	77	66	59
Evenwood Town	38	17	8	13	72	63	59
Washington	38	17	9	12	74	55	57
Easington Colliery	38	15	10	13	55	51	55
Willington	38	17	3	18	62	61	54
Shotton Comrades	38	15	8	15	86	83	53
Esh Winning	38	15	7	16	78	88	52
Morpeth Town	38	13	6	19	69	67	45
Ryhope Community Association	38	12	9	17	55	62	45
Norton & Stockton Ancients	38	13	4	21	71	83	43
Alnwick Town	38	10	6	22	61	88	33
Darlington Cleveland Social	38	4	5	29	37	140	17
Horden Colliery Welfare	38	3	3	32	42	151	12
Langley Park S & S United	38	3	3	32	40	140	9

Billingham Town, Washington and Alnwick Town all had 3 points deducted. Stockton and Hartlepool Town both had 6 points deducted.

1995-96

Division One

Billingham Synthonia	38	24	8	6	78	34	80
Bedlington Terriers	38	22	12	4	90	37	78
Durham City	38	24	6	8	85	35	78
Tow Law Town	38	23	9	6	82	43	78
Whitby Town	38	21	7	10	100	59	70
Guisborough Town	38	20	8	10	80	54	68
Dunston Federation Brewery	38	20	8	10	75	52	68
West Auckland Town	38	19	5	14	66	57	62
Crook Town	38	17	9	12	59	41	60
Consett	38	17	7	14	76	64	58
Stockton	38	16	8	14	88	71	56
Shildon	38	16	3	19	74	74	51
Seaham Red Star	38	13	11	14	62	66	50
Murton	38	12	11	15	57	53	47
RTM Newcastle	38	13	7	18	68	58	46
Chester-le-Street Town	38	11	9	18	72	78	42
Whickham	38	11	8	19	43	77	41
Peterlee Newtown	38	5	4	29	40	96	19
Eppleton Colliery Welfare	38	2	3	33	26	153	9
Ferryhill Athletic	38	0	5	33	27	146	5

Division Two

Morpeth Town	36	27	5	4	104	40	86
South Shields	36	25	4	7	89	34	79
Easington Colliery	36	23	7	6	86	40	76
Shotton Comrades	36	22	7	7	72	42	73
Northallerton Town	36	18	9	9	70	45	63
Ashington	36	18	9	9	66	48	63
Billingham Town	36	18	6	12	73	51	60
Evenwood Town	36	16	8	12	70	61	56
Prudhoe Town	36	17	4	15	75	69	55
Brandon United	36	16	6	14	59	55	54
Esh Winning	36	13	7	16	80	75	46
Hebburn	36	13	5	18	50	56	44
Washington	36	14	4	18	71	73	43
Horden Colliery Welfare	36	13	3	20	64	74	42
Willington	36	11	8	17	53	75	41
Alnwick Town	36	10	6	20	47	65	36
Ryhope Community Association	36	6	5	25	41	82	23
Norton & Stockton Ancients	36	6	5	25	53	120	17
Darlington Cleveland Social	36	0	4	32	33	151	4

Washington had 3 points deducted.
Norton & Stockton Ancients had 6 points deducted.

1996-97

Division One

Whitby Town	38	32	3	3	131	37	99
Billingham Synthonia	38	28	6	4	109	46	90
Bedlington Terriers	38	28	5	5	113	37	86
Durham City	38	19	11	8	69	50	68
Crook Town	38	19	9	10	88	56	66
Morpeth Town	38	20	6	12	73	56	66
Guisborough Town	38	17	9	12	68	54	60
Tow Law Town	38	14	11	13	76	70	53
South Shields	38	13	11	14	52	63	50
Murton	38	15	5	18	58	80	50
Consett	38	12	11	15	65	59	47
Dunston Federation Brewery	38	12	10	16	64	70	46
Shildon	38	13	7	18	72	86	46
Easington Colliery	38	12	8	18	56	72	44
RTM Newcastle	38	13	3	22	66	87	42
Seaham Red Star	38	7	14	17	50	83	35
Stockton	38	8	10	20	70	105	34
Chester-le-Street Town	38	7	12	19	53	86	33
Whickham	38	5	6	27	38	98	21
West Auckland Town	38	6	3	29	41	117	21

Bedlington Terriers had 3 points deducted.

Division Two

Northallerton Town	36	25	6	5	98	41	81
Billingham Town	36	24	6	6	111	39	75
Jarrow Roofing Boldon CA	36	23	6	7	88	34	75
Ashington	36	22	5	9	71	38	71
Evenwood Town	36	21	4	11	84	46	67
Horden Colliery Welfare	36	20	7	9	67	37	64
Prudhoe Town	36	18	10	8	73	48	64
Shotton Comrades	36	20	6	10	91	43	63
Willington	36	18	7	11	78	54	61
Peterlee Newtown	36	16	8	12	56	56	56
Hebburn	36	16	3	17	66	61	51
Ryhope Community Ass.	36	12	5	19	50	70	41
Norton & Stockton Ancients	36	11	7	18	47	58	37
Brandon United	36	10	7	19	64	76	37
Alnwick Town	36	11	4	21	55	79	34
Eppleton Colliery Welfare	36	6	7	23	44	110	25
Washington	36	6	7	23	43	79	22
Esh Winning	36	7	3	26	44	100	21
Ferryhill Athletic	36	1	2	33	16	177	5

Darlington Cleveland Social left the league – their record was deleted. Billingham Town, Horden Colliery Welfare, Shotton Comrades, Norton & Stockton Ancients, Alnwick Town, Washington and Esh Winning all had 3 points deducted

1997-98

Division One

Bedlington Terriers	38	29	3	6	120	32	90
Billingham Synthonia	38	23	9	6	81	36	78
Guisborough Town	38	23	6	9	84	53	75
Dunston Federation Brewery	38	21	10	7	69	35	73
RTM Newcastle	38	20	5	13	92	70	65
Penrith	38	19	8	11	81	62	65
Morpeth Town	38	16	14	8	75	48	62
South Shields	38	15	19	4	65	38	61
Shildon	38	16	7	15	77	87	55
Billingham Town	38	17	2	19	72	79	53
Tow Law Town	38	16	7	15	78	61	52
Consett	38	13	11	14	60	62	50
Jarrow Roofing Boldon CA	38	11	12	15	64	70	45
Crook Town	38	12	7	19	58	67	43
Seaham Red Star	38	12	7	19	60	83	43
Easington Colliery	38	13	6	19	77	97	42
Stockton	38	10	10	18	54	65	37
Durham City	38	10	7	21	55	67	37
Northallerton Town	38	4	6	28	39	102	18
Murton	38	2	0	36	23	170	3

South Shields, Tow Law Town, Easington Colliery, Stockton and Murton all had 3 points deducted

Division Two

Chester-le-Street Town	36	29	3	4	105	27	90
West Auckland Town	36	24	8	4	85	36	80
Marske United	36	24	5	7	78	30	77
Prudhoe Town	36	20	5	11	87	58	62
Ashington	36	18	7	11	76	52	61
Willington	36	16	6	14	87	65	54
Peterlee Newtown	36	16	7	13	60	55	52
Evenwood Town	36	14	9	13	62	62	51
Alnwick Town	36	15	5	16	68	64	50
Norton & Stockton Ancients	36	14	7	15	58	57	49
Shotton Comrades	36	13	8	15	66	61	47
Hebburn	36	12	10	14	57	43	46
Ryhope Community Ass.	36	12	10	14	60	63	46
Horden Colliery Welfare	36	12	8	16	58	67	44
Whickham	36	14	7	15	51	66	43
Esh Winning	36	11	9	16	58	79	42
Brandon United	36	11	6	19	59	87	39
Eppleton Colliery Welfare	36	4	4	28	29	103	16
Washington	36	1	0	35	24	153	0

Prudhoe Town, Peterlee Newtown and Washington all had 3 points deducted. Whickham had 6 points deducted

1998-99

Division One

Bedlington Terriers	38	33	2	3	128	37	101
Tow Law Town	38	23	6	9	80	49	75
Chester-le-Street Town	38	17	14	7	71	46	65
West Auckland Town	38	19	8	11	65	57	65
Dunston Federation Brewery	38	18	10	10	73	51	64
Guisborough Town	38	18	5	15	68	65	59
Seaham Red Star	38	16	7	15	62	59	55
Consett	38	15	7	16	72	64	52
Morpeth Town	38	15	6	17	54	60	51
Stockton	38	15	6	17	68	76	51
Billingham Synthonia	38	15	7	16	60	56	49
Marske United	38	13	9	16	58	63	48
Crook Town	38	13	7	18	51	60	46
Billingham Town	38	13	9	16	66	81	45
South Shields	38	9	16	13	54	66	43
Jarrow Roofing Boldon Com. Ass.	38	11	10	17	62	85	43
Easington Colliery	38	11	6	21	67	78	39
Newcastle Blue Star	38	12	5	21	59	83	38
Penrith	38	10	8	20	59	82	35
Shildon	38	6	8	24	48	107	26

Billingham Synthonia, Billingham Town, Newcastle Blue Star and Penrith all had 3 points deducted.

Division Two

Durham City	36	29	4	3	101	28	91
Shotton Comrades	36	22	7	7	89	44	73
Peterlee Newtown	36	21	8	7	80	43	71
Northallerton Town	36	20	6	10	73	33	66
Norton & Stockton Ancients	36	20	6	10	73	43	66
Brandon United	36	17	8	11	87	49	59
Hebburn	36	18	4	14	66	54	58
Evenwood Town	36	15	10	11	82	63	55
Whickham	36	15	8	13	51	43	53
Prudhoe Town	36	14	10	12	70	61	52
Ashington	36	14	9	13	64	47	51
Alnwick Town	36	15	5	16	63	66	50
Horden Colliery Welfare	36	13	11	12	53	56	50
Willington	36	13	10	13	58	53	49
Esh Winning	36	9	10	17	59	73	37
Washington	36	10	6	20	55	79	36
Ryhope Community Association	36	5	3	28	29	90	18
Murton	36	4	2	30	33	167	14
Eppleton Colliery Welfare	36	4	1	31	26	120	7

Eppleton Colliery Welfare had 6 points deducted.

1999-2000

Division One

Bedlington Terriers	38	25	8	5	89	26	83
Seaham Red Star	38	23	5	10	64	49	74
Dunston Federation Brewery	38	20	7	11	73	41	67
Marske United	38	19	8	11	67	45	65
West Auckland Town	38	17	14	7	65	43	65
Billingham Synthonia	38	17	6	15	72	64	57
Jarrow Roofing Boldon Com. Ass.	38	15	12	11	64	61	57
Morpeth Town	38	14	15	9	55	56	57
Consett	38	12	18	8	57	43	54
Tow Law Town	38	15	8	15	65	55	53
Billingham Town	38	13	13	12	58	47	52
Guisborough Town	38	15	7	16	57	62	52
Chester-le-Street Town	38	14	9	15	57	67	51
Crook Town	38	13	11	14	55	57	50
Durham City	38	11	13	14	50	61	46
Peterlee Newtown	38	13	7	18	56	76	46
Easington Colliery	38	10	11	17	57	74	41
Thornaby-on-Tees	38	7	12	19	47	68	33
Shotton Comrades	38	4	9	25	37	88	21
South Shields	38	3	7	28	33	95	16

Thornaby-on-Tees were formerly known as Stockton.

Division Two

Brandon United	36	25	9	2	82	24	84
Newcastle Blue Star	36	24	5	7	94	43	77
Hebburn	36	22	4	10	72	35	70
Northallerton Town	36	21	5	10	76	48	68
Shildon	36	20	7	9	62	44	67
Willington	36	21	3	12	81	41	66
Washington	36	19	7	10	95	57	64
Norton & Stockton Ancients	36	18	8	10	70	51	62
Ashington	36	17	10	9	92	36	61
Penrith	36	15	11	10	69	40	56
Alnwick Town	36	16	7	13	78	58	55
Horden Colliery Welfare	36	13	10	13	53	57	49
Prudhoe Town	36	11	9	16	59	74	39
Evenwood Town	36	11	6	19	57	100	39
Esh Winning	36	11	2	23	59	81	35
Kennek Ryhope Com. Association	36	9	7	20	49	70	34
Whickham	36	6	7	23	27	70	25
Murton	36	1	4	31	21	133	7
Eppleton Colliery Welfare	36	0	3	33	22	156	3

Prudhoe Town had 3 points deducted.

2000-2001

Division One

Bedlington Terriers	40	28	5	7	108	31	89
Dunston Federation Brewery	40	26	7	7	93	49	85
Marske United	40	24	7	9	82	35	79
Durham City	40	24	6	10	95	42	78
Brandon United	40	23	8	9	86	53	77
Peterlee Newtown	40	22	9	9	75	55	75
Tow Law Town	40	20	7	13	90	64	67
Billingham Synthonia	40	18	11	11	81	58	65
Billingham Town	40	19	7	14	74	59	64
Consett	40	17	8	15	63	60	59
Whitley Bay	40	15	10	15	69	61	55
West Auckland Town	40	16	7	17	65	68	55
Jarrow Roofing Boldon Com. Ass.	40	12	12	16	63	71	48
Guisborough Town	40	13	8	19	53	60	47
Chester-le-Street Town	40	13	5	22	61	64	44
Newcastle Blue Star	40	12	8	20	53	83	44
Seaham Red Star	40	14	2	24	59	111	44
Morpeth Town	40	12	6	22	63	78	36
Easington Colliery	40	10	6	24	57	86	36
Hebburn Town	40	5	7	28	33	113	22
Crook Town	40	2	4	34	33	155	10

Morpeth Town had 6 points deducted

Division Two

Ashington	36	25	5	6	100	41	80
Washington	36	23	10	3	83	35	79
Thornaby	36	23	7	6	85	50	76
Horden Colliery Welfare	36	20	7	9	53	35	67
Esh Winning	36	19	7	10	79	44	64
Northallerton Town	36	16	12	8	75	45	60
Penrith	36	14	12	10	60	52	54
Norton & Stockton Ancients	36	16	9	11	51	51	54
Willington	36	12	12	12	52	46	48
Kennek Ryhope Com. Association	36	12	10	14	46	53	46
South Shields	36	12	9	15	71	81	45
Prudhoe Town	36	13	5	18	69	66	44
Shildon	36	12	8	16	42	58	44
Alnwick Town	36	9	12	15	53	61	39
Evenwood Town	36	10	5	21	50	97	35
Shotton Comrades	36	8	10	18	49	85	34
Murton	36	9	8	19	53	76	32
Whickham	36	6	11	19	43	68	29
Eppleton Colliery Welfare	36	1	5	30	29	99	8

Thornaby were previous known as Thornaby-on-Tees.
Norton & Stockton Ancients and Murton both had 3 points deducted.

2001-2002

Division One

Bedlington Terriers	40	28	8	4	104	35	92
Tow Law Town	40	26	7	7	90	44	85
Dunston Federation Brewery	40	22	9	9	86	53	75
Marske United	40	21	8	11	56	48	71
Whitley Bay	40	20	8	12	78	49	68
Durham City	40	19	11	10	87	62	68
West Auckland Town	40	19	11	10	80	57	68
Billingham Town	40	16	9	15	67	66	57
Brandon United	40	17	8	15	68	53	56
Billingham Synthonia	40	15	10	15	79	75	55
Guisborough Town	40	16	9	15	68	63	54
Jarrow Roofing Boldon Com. Ass.	40	15	8	17	62	74	53
Peterlee Newtown	40	14	10	16	54	60	52
Chester-le-Street Town	40	14	7	19	63	68	49
Washington	40	13	5	22	54	74	44
Consett	40	11	10	19	60	65	43
Newcastle Blue Star	40	13	6	21	56	80	42
Morpeth Town	40	10	10	20	48	70	40
Ashington	40	11	8	21	62	98	38
Thornaby	40	8	5	27	48	96	29
Seaham Red Star	40	6	5	29	38	118	20

Brandon United, Guisborough Town, Newcastle Blue Star, Ashington and Seaham Red Star all had 3 points deducted.

Division Two

Shildon	38	28	4	6	135	51	88
Prudhoe Town	38	26	7	5	104	32	85
Esh Winning	38	27	4	7	93	39	85
Penrith	38	26	4	8	101	42	82
Easington Colliery	38	24	5	9	87	47	77
Horden Colliery Welfare	38	21	9	8	87	55	72
Washington Nissan	38	23	3	12	95	68	72
South Shields	38	18	8	12	62	41	62
Northallerton Town	38	17	10	11	59	52	61
Kennek Ryhope Com. Association	38	17	8	13	65	47	59
Crook Town	38	16	6	16	53	60	51
Norton & Stockton Ancients	38	14	7	17	66	71	49
Alnwick Town	38	12	12	14	63	74	48
Hebburn Town	38	12	6	20	52	97	42
Evenwood Town	38	8	5	25	46	96	29
Whickham	38	7	5	26	50	90	26
Willington	38	6	6	26	52	114	24
Murton	38	5	7	26	34	108	22
Eppleton Colliery Welfare	38	6	6	26	42	91	18
Shotton Comrades	38	4	4	30	45	116	16

Crook Town had 3 points deducted.
Eppleton Colliery Welfare had 6 points deducted.

Supporters' Guides & Other Titles

This top-selling series has been published annually since 1982 and contains 2001/2002 Season's results and tables; Directions; Ground plans; Photos; Phone numbers; Parking information; Admission details; Disabled information and much more.

The Supporters' Guide to Premier & Football League Clubs 2003

The 19th edition featuring all Premiership and Football League clubs. ***Price £5.99***

The Supporters' Guide to Non-League Football 2003

The 11th edition featuring all Conference, Unibond Premier, Rymans Premier and Dr. Martens Premier clubs. ***Price £5.99***

The Supporters' Guide to Scottish Football 2003

The 11th edition featuring all Scottish League and Highland League clubs. ***Price £5.99***

The Official Football Association of Wales Yearbook & Supporters' Guide 2002-2003

The 3rd edition featuring all League of Wales, Cymru Alliance & Welsh Football League Clubs + results, stats & much more. ***Price £5.99***

Non-League Football League Tables 1889-2002

This book contains every Football Conference, Isthmian League, Southern League, Northern Premier League, Midland League, Northern League, Athenian League and Football Alliance Final Table. ***Price £9.95***

Football League Tables 1888-2002

This book contains every Football League, F.A. Premier League, Scottish League and Scottish Premier League Final Table from 1888-2002 together with Cup Final information. ***Price £8.99***

These books are available UK & Surface post free from –

Soccer Books Limited (Dept. SBL)
72 St. Peter's Avenue
Cleethorpes
N.E. Lincolnshire
DN35 8HU